CHRIST AND THE DECREE

CHRIST AND THE DECREE

CHRISTOLOGY AND PREDESTINATION
IN REFORMED THEOLOGY
FROM CALVIN TO PERKINS

RICHARD A. MULLER

THE LABYRINTH PRESS
Durham, North Carolina

Copyright © 1986 by THE LABYRINTH PRESS

Library of Congress Cataloging in Publication Data

Muller, Richard A. (Richard Alfred), 1948-
    Christ and the decree.

    (Studies in historical theology ; 2)
    Includes index.
    1. Jesus Christ—History of doctrines—16th century.
2. Predestination—History of doctrines—16th century.
3. Reformed Church—Doctrines—History—16th century.
I. Title.   II. Series: Studies in historical theology

(Durham (N.C.)) ; 2.
BT198.M827 1986   230′.42′09031   84-20117
ISBN 0-939464-39-X (lib. bdg. : v. 2)

Printed in the United States of America

For Gloria

Abbreviations

ANF	*The Ante-Nicene Fathers*, ed. Roberts & Donaldson
CC	*Creeds of Christendom*, ed. Philip Schaff
CD	Karl Barth, *Church Dogmatics*, trs. Bromiley, et al.
CO	*Ioannis Calvini Opera*, in *Corpus Reformatorum*
CR	*Corpus Reformatorum*
DNB	*Dictionary of National Biography*, ed. Stephen
DTEL	*Doctrinal Theology of the Evangelical Lutheran Church*, ed. Schmid
Inst.	*Institutio christianae religionis* (1559), cited from OS
NPNF	*A Select Library of Nicene and Post-Nicene Fathers*, ed. Schaff and Wace
PG	*Patrologia cursus completus . . . series graeca*, ed. J. P. Migne
PL	*Patrologiae cursus completus . . . series latina*, ed. J. P. Migne
OS	*Joannis Calvini Opera Selecta*, ed. Barth and Niesel
RD	Heinrich Heppe, *Reformed Dogmatics*, trs. Thomson
RGG	*Religion in Geschichte und Gegenwart*, with superscript, e.g., RGG^{iii} indicating edition
RPTK	*Realencyklopaedie für protestantische Theologie und Kirche*
Sent.	*In quatuor libros sententiarum*—with reference both to Lombard and to various commentators

TABLE OF CONTENTS

PREFACE

The composition of the preface, as authors frequently comment, is surely the most difficult task encountered in the final stages of editing a manuscript. One is tempted to say, with humility, "Go, litel boke," and then say no more. More words concerning a topic about which one has already said so many would be superfluous. All that remains is the expression of the author's gratitude to the many people who have offered support, encouragement, and inspiration during the years of research and throughout the many stages of writing. And this task, no matter how difficult, is undertaken gladly, with deepest appreciation in the hope that the thanks is not inadquate.

My research was made possible by the resources and services of three great American libraries: the Duke University Libraries, the library of Union Theological Seminary, New York, and the Huntington Library in San Marino, California. Special thanks must go to Donn Michael Farris, the librarian of the Duke Divinity School Library, whose help and whose friendship smoothed the way of my research on many occasions. A major post-doctoral grant from the Mellon Foundation gave me the opportunity, for which I am very grateful, to immerse myself in the materials of this study for a year with virtually no other external commitments.

The editorial board of Labyrinth Press also deserves profound thanks. I owe a special debt of gratitude to Professor David C. Steinmetz of Duke University who, as my doctoral advisor, continuing friend, and now general editor of the series in which this volume appears, has been a source of detailed criticism and warm encouragement for more than a decade.

To the staff of the Fuller Seminary word processing office I also extend my thanks, in particular to Margo Houts and Michael Stribling whose talents ironed out many a wrinkle in the production of the manuscript.

Finally, and least adequately, I would offer a word of thanks to my wife, Gloria, who has been my greatest support and encouragement, a continuous source of understanding and inspiration, throughout all the work of researching, writing, and editing.

Richard A. Muller
Fuller Theological Seminary

I

INTRODUCTION

1. PROTESTANT ORTHODOXY: SURVEY OF OPINION

The relationship of the Reformation to subsequent developments in Protestant thought, particularly to the "scholastic" or "orthodox" theology of the late sixteenth and the seventeenth century has, for more than a century, been an object of scrutiny by scholars and theologians in search of their Protestant heritage. In the analyses of Calvin and "Calvinism" especially there has been great interest in the question of continuity or discontinuity between the theology of the master and the doctrine of the successors. Did later writers disrupt the balance of Calvin's thought and produce a distortion of the system developed by the great Reformer of Geneva, or did they simply follow Calvin's lead as they defended and solidified the system of Reformed or Calvinist doctrine? Specifically, did these epigoni construct a system centered upon and controlled by the doctrine of predestination to the detriment of the other focal points of early Reformed thought?

The beginning of modern opinion of the orthodox system as a historical phenomenon occurs with the attempt, following Immanuel Kant's virtual destruction of earlier philosophical and metaphysical perspectives, to create anew the system of Reformed theology.[1] In other words, modern opinion of orthodoxy as a predecessor-system in the Protestant tradition begins with the theological question of the use of the past as posed by followers of the Schleiermacherian and Hegelian attempts to place both theology and philosophy once again on a sound footing. Among the works which raised this question two massive dogmatic studies by Alexander Schweizer, a pupil of Schleiermacher, stand out as setting the tone of investigation for the nineteenth century: *Die Glaubenslehre der evangelisch-reformierten Kirche* and *Die protestantischen Centraldogmen.*[2] According to Schweizer's reading of the older dogmatics, the orthodox Reformed theologians attempted to build a synthetic, deductive, and therefore irrefutable system of theology upon the primary proposition of an absolute divine decree of predestination.[3]

Schweizer focused on the "feeling of absolute dependence" as the central issue in the thought of his teacher and, therefore, on the absolute divine causality, to which according to Schleiermacher "the feeling of absolute dependence points back,"[4] as the central theme and unifying motif in his dogmatic system. In describing predestination, Schleiermacher had argued that "our exposition . . . knows only a single uncondtional decree by which the whole, as an individual system, is what it is in virtue of the divine good pleasure."[5] With these definitions providing the underlying presupposition for his thought, Schweizer could understand predestination as the central dogma of Reformed protestantism in a positive sense: predestination was nothing else than the concept of absolute dependence as defined in terms of the redemptive process. It was to be for his own *Glaubenslehre* the means by which a metaphysic was made possible and, in terms of feeling (as opposed to knowing and doing), the Kantian gap between the rational and the supernatural could be overcome in theology.[6]

Schweizer's method in theology was characterized by an attempt to demonstrate the post-Kantian viability of Reformed dogmatics: in the *Glaubenslehre*, this was accomplished by citation of doctrinal arguments from older Reformed systems under rubrics and propositions established by Schweizer, while in the later *Centraldogmen* the end was achieved through a more historical description of the development of predestinarianism toward its fruition in a post-Kantian metaphysic resting on the feeling of absolute dependence. Schweizer's studies are not works of critical historical scholarship, but are rather descriptions of a theological program which, in turn, draw on the tradition of which he was a part.[7]

Schweizer's view of predestination found an ally in the Hegelian historian of doctrine, Ferdinand Christian Baur, who was able to employ Schweizer's concept of the development of a predestinarian metaphysic as a part of his own theory of the development of doctrine.[8] It was Baur who propounded the then revolutionary hypothesis that the development of doctrine in the early church was the result of an inner dynamic of the basic *kerygma* which led toward the creation of a doctrinal synthesis resolving the tensions implicit in the original message.[9] Baur's analysis of the movement of Protestant theology toward orthodoxy accepts this structure as typical of doctrinal development. Whereas the inner principle of early Christian thought was the interpretation of the person of Christ, the inner principle of Reformed theology was the concept of divine predestination.[10]

One of the important but neglected attempts to study the entire historical development of Protestant theology is Wilhelm Gass' *Geschichte der protestantischen Dogmatik*. Gass represents an opinion similar to that advanced by Schweizer and Baur. Gass, a Hegelian, advanced the view that the form taken by developing Protestantism was the result of a gradual progress toward the realization of an inner principle.[11] This principle functioned to provide a basis within Protestant theology for the adoption of metaphysical structures by the orthodox theologians of the seventeenth century. In order to demonstrate this thesis, Gass reviews the doctrine of the earliest reformers and then proceeds to recount the developments of the seventeenth century in great detail. Gass argues that the metaphysical developments within Protestant thought took place in the seventeenth century under the impact of Suarez' *Disputationes metaphysicae* which had appeared in 1597.[12] Little importance is accorded to Beza, though Gass notes that he introduced a greater precision into the formulation of Calvinist theology. Beza's precise formulation of the doctrine of predestination demonstrated the centrality of the doctrine of election to the Reformed faith. Despite their obvious differences in interpretation, Schweizer, Baur, and Gass represent an analysis of Protestant orthodoxy which saw a positive value in the gradual sophistication of predestinarian structures.[13] As thinkers whose own philosophical position influenced their historical scholarship, they tended to look to internal principles rather than to external pressures for an explanation of the intellectual developments within Protestantism.

Contemporary with the work of Schweizer, Baur, and Gass, an analysis of Protestant orthodoxy which accepted the concept of a developing metaphysic but took a more negative view toward this development was set forth by Heinrich Heppe. Both in his biography of Beza[14] and in his broad analyses of the evolution of Protestant doctrine in the sixteenth and seventeenth centuries,[15] Heppe emphasized the theme of the central dogma. He saw Beza in particular as responsible for placement of the doctrine of predestination in a causally a *priori* position and, therefore, for the clearer formulation of the essential pattern of Calvinism.[16] This is a departure from the position of Schweizer in that it recognizes the theological significance of an alteration of the arrangement of doctrines within the system but, as Jacobs comments, it would show Heppe to be as guilty as Beza of an underestimation of Calvin's intention in placing the doctrine within the soteriological complex.[17] According to Heppe's analysis, Beza's *Tabula praedestinationis* established a metaphysical foundation for subsequent Calvinist or Reformed theology.[18] This thesis, moreover, led Heppe to organize his highly influential synopsis of sixteenth and seventeenth century Reformed theology, *Die Dogmatik der evangelisch-reformierten Kirche*, according to the pattern of the "high orthodox" dogmaticians—Turretin, Pictet, Riissen—placing the doctrine of predestination in relation to the *loci* of God and trinity, above the *locus* of creation.[19] Readers of Heppe's work, as a consequence, have tended to view this particular order as definitive of the theology of sixteenth and seventeenth century Calvinism.

An examination of the sixteenth century systems and, indeed, of the seventeenth century systems written before 1630 reveals a variety of structures and several different placements of the doctrine of predestination. Heppe, unfortunately, adopted an arrangement of doctrine quite atypical of the sixteenth century and not even representative of the theology of Beza: he even cites Calvin on predestination under the doctrine of God and trinity.[20] Several important theologians—Polanus, Trelcatius the younger, Gomarus, Maccovius, Zanchius—did indeed set the decree into the context of the doctrines of God and trinity, and, alone among the writers of his time Maccovius chose to place the decree above the doctrine of the trinity in the *locus* concerned with the divine essence and attributes.[21] Calvin, however, had stated the doctrine of predestination in the context of faith and justification. He was followed in this by Bucanus.[22] A similar soteriological interest is also evidenced by the placement of predestination in the systems of Vermigli, Musculus, and Ames.[23] Others, influenced perhaps by the powerful ecclesiology of Calvin, discussed predestination as part of the doctrine of the church: Ursinus, Danaeus, Perkins.[24] Others still, sensible of the bond between the causality of election and the historical work of Christ, discussed the doctrine of predestination in association with their christological exposition: Keckermann, Walaeus, the "Leiden Synopsis," Downham.[25]

Criticism and use of Heppe's work must also take into consideration his late study, *Geschichte des Pietismus*, in which he traces covenantal themes and the Melanchthonian influence on Reformed dogmatics. Here he manifests a sense of diversity in the Reformed tradition and, via Perkins and Ames, a direct relationship between developing Reformed theology and the rise of pietism.[26] This fact in itself points toward a need to reappraise Heppe's own view of developing orthodoxy and the impact of the doctrine of predestination on the Reformed system.

Yet another view of the problem—a view quite at variance with the prevailing tone of nineteenth century scholarship—is seen in the work of Matthias Schneckenburger.[27] Schneckenburger's major work follows immediately upon the publication of Schweizer's *Glaubenslehre* and of the articles based on Schweizer's thesis published by Baur in the *Theologisches Jahrbuch* for 1847. Schneckenburger argued against both Schweizer and Baur that Calvin and the Calvinists after him followed the order of the Apostles' Creed in their expositions of the doctrine of the trinity and did not deduce their doctrine from a concept of the transcendent God.[28] In contrast to the Lutheran theologians who adhered to the relatively uniform analytic method bestowed upon them by Melanchthon, the Reformed theologians exhibited a considerable diversity of approaches to theology, some following a synthetic deductive method,[29] others tending toward the analytic.[30]

Schneckenburger argues that the Reformed doctrine of predestination cannot be conceived as a consequence of the idea of God and his attributes since the characteristic of Reformed systematics is not the objective determination of the doctrine of predestination but the personal assurance of election by the grace of God. This is a subjective consciousness which is witnessed by Calvin's conception of predestination as part of the *ordo salutis* rather than as part of the doctrine of God. Schneckenburger finds a continuity throughout the Reformed systems of the sixteenth century in this conception of predestination as the result of justification, the subjective or material principle of the Reformation, seeking out its objective ground.[31] The more scholastic form of the doctrine according to which predestination is related to the nature of God is found in the Lutheran as well as in the Reformed systems, even as the arguments against this position are not only Lutheran but Reformed.[32] The primary ground of the doctrine of predestination, of the emphasis on God's absolute and efficient causality in salvation, and of the stress on the doctrine of God and his decree is justification by faith alone.[33] We shall attempt to show in this study that Schneckenburger's conception of Protestant orthodoxy not only deserves attention, but that his view is far more satisfactory than the theory of his opponents.

Both Baur's theory of the realization of an inner principle and Heppe's theory of outside influences are represented in twentieth century scholarship, the former by Hans Emil Weber and the latter by Ernst Bizer. The two schools of thought have, however, grown closer together. Weber does not follow Baur into an overtly Hegelian philosophy of history. Bizer is less involved than Heppe in the work of constructing contemporary Reformed theology.[34] Weber and Bizer have both tended to overlook divergent trends in the development of Protestant orthodoxy. They have become involved instead in the search for a *Zeitgeist*, a vague spirit of the age, which appears only when the manifold detail of history is fitted into a preconceived theoretical shape.

In his *Reformation, Orthodoxie, und Rationalismus* Weber produced a study of Protestant orthodoxy in which the two major branches of the Protestant faith were reduced to their basic principle. According to Weber, Lutheranism is "the system of the doctrine of justification" and Calvinism is "the system of predestinarianism."[35] Weber's study is marred by this broad generalizing search for inner principles which neglects to examine doctrinal interrelationships. The value of Weber's work is also jeopardized by his failure to encounter scholarship which holds an opinion different from his own. Weber does mention Schneckenburger but conflates Schneckenburger's argument with Schweizer's despite the obvious disagreement.[36]

Citing two bitter opponents of Calvinism, the Lutheran polemicist, Hulsemann, and the Arminian theologian, Episcopius, Weber launches his discussion of Reformed orthodoxy as the "predestinarian system."[37] This is the form of "speculative rationalism" taken by seventeenth century scholastic Calvinism as it entered its debate with the "idealistic humanism" of Arminian theology.[38] The Calvinist theme of the justice, lordship, and freedom of God working out redemption in and through the priestly and kingly offices of Christ is set against the Arminian theme of predestination as the working out of Christianity and of salvation:[39] "Die Orthodoxie musste die Bedrohung ihres ganzen Systems spuren"[40]—and not only must it seek out all threats against the system, according to Weber, it must realize all the inner tendencies of its fundamental principle.[41]

Of course, Weber's analysis of the importance of predestination to the Reformed system antedates the work of Jacobs and Locher and therefore stands in the line of nineteenth century scholarship according to which Calvin is viewed as a theologian who had recourse to the doctrine of predestination or, more precisely, election as the "foundation of justification" and who thereby prepared the way for his scholastic successors' emphasis on the decrees.[42] In this, Weber comments with some justice, Calvin with Luther is the heir of the "medieval tradition of the divine will and its sovereign freedom."[43] An underlying theme of Calvin's thought, the doctrine of predestination as representative of the transcendent and suprarational will of God, becomes in a sense the basic rationale or principle of rationality in the system.[44] We may justly question, at this point, whether Weber has pressed too far his own search for a single rational principle in the two main divisions of the Reformation theology.

Weber also represents the Reformed systems as so oriented toward predestination as a systematic principle that the supralapsarian position becomes for him the necessary end result of meditation on the problem of the decrees. He views the tendency of the Reformed system, therefore, as toward a normative supralapsarianism and takes the order of the high orthodox systems— the decrees above creation and fall—as evidence of that tendency.[45] The rigidity of Weber's position is tempered by the fact that he includes in this paradigm, generally, only the Swiss and Dutch Reformed and sets aside the school of Saumur and the German Reformed writers for separate consideration,[46] but there is little attempt on Weber's part to document the actual effect of predestination as a systematic principle on other *loci*.[47] In his analysis of Dort we read that the work of Christ as mediator now points us back, as to a "rational-theological" concept, to the decree, to the work of God's good pleasure, to the divine sovereignty as its ground,[48] while in a rationalistic argument the decree itself is objectively known in its subjective effects—the *syllogismus practicus*.[49]

Bizer, whose arguments are largely in agreement with those of Weber, treats the use of rational method in argumentation, the acceptance of categories of natural theology, the use of historical method of interpretation, and the development of experiential theology in Reformed pietism as a single phenomenon pointing toward seventeenth century rationalism.[50] Yet, the sources demonstrate these to be a series of diverse and often unrelated phenomena. Both Aristotelians and the anti-Aristotelian Ramists advocated strictly logical and rational forms of argumentation.[51] Natural theology did not become characteristic of Protestant orthodoxy but remained a point of contention. Ames denied its validity, while Keckermann labored to separate philosophy as a discipline and as a methodology from theology and theological ethics.[52] The rise of a historical methodology within Protestant orthodoxy, particularly in the Cocceian school, was in part a reaction against rationalistic and speculative thinking.[53] The beginnings of pietism, moreover, represent a profoundly anti-speculative concentration on the faith of the individual. In the works of theologians like Perkins and Ames the attention to "cases of conscience" marks the beginning of a movement opposed to rationalistic and speculative doctrines of God.[54] Perkins' system, *An Exposition of the Symbole*, is characterized by continual application of doctrine to inward piety.[55]

Bizer's *Frühorthodoxie und Rationalismus* is also marred by a failure to examine any individual line of doctrinal development with consistency. The examination of Beza focuses on Christology and predestination. When Bizer turns to Ursinus, he maintains some relation to the earlier focus but emphasizes the problem of "necessity." The section on Danaeus, intended to represent late sixteenth century theology, has lost all connection with the earlier doctrinal themes. It analyzes Danaeus' treatise on the work of creation.[56] In another work, Bizer draws out with more success the relationships and the antagonisms between Reformed orthodoxy in the seventeenth century and Cartesian thought.[57] Here it appears that there was considerably more diversity in Reformed thought and strong anti-rationalistic tendencies than Bizer's study of the earlier period would allow: the form of Protestant orthodoxy represented by Voetius was anti-Cartesian, whereas the relatively anti-scholastic historical-exegetical school of Cocceius was able to produce a hybrid Cartesian-covenantal theology.[58] Indeed, Voetius' insistence on revelation against Cartesian rationalism can be seen as representative of high Calvinist orthodoxy after Dort. But this leaves Bizer with the contradiction that "Bezan" orthodoxy with its incipient Aristotelian rationalism did not necessarily foster rationalism in the seventeenth century.[59] It was the anti-Calvinist, Arminian theology which, in the course of the seventeenth century, became closely allied to Cartesian rationalism.[60] We can detect no unified pattern of rationalism, metaphysics, or natural theology in the theology of early orthodoxy. Protestants remained wary of an independent natural theology.

The problem of scholastic method and its impact on Reformed orthodoxy has been studied by Paul Althaus in his *Die Prinzipien der deutschen reformierten Dogmatik*. Althaus accepts the thesis that the doctrine of predestination provides a speculative ground for Reformed dogmatics and that under the impact of scholastic method this doctrine led the Reformed to develop a rigid system resting on the decrees.[61] On this particular point Althaus gives little attention to sixteenth century theologians after Calvin but moves directly into the seventeenth century, using the theological system of Maccovius as a primary example of the development of doctrine. In view not only of the unique organization of Maccovius' system, in which the decrees appear in the doctrine of the divine essence and attributes prior not only to creation but also to the doctrine of the trinity, but also in view of the warning issued by the Synod of Dort against Maccovius' speculative teaching and resultant *phrases duriores* concerning the decree,[62] Althaus' argument appears in need of some refinement and would be subject to reappraisal if another line of doctrinal development could be traced following Calvin and leading to the early orthodox formulation at the beginning of the seventeenth century.

Avenues of Reappraisal.

If much recent scholarship agrees with the general tone of the nineteenth and early twentieth century approach to orthodoxy, accepting in the main the Schweizer hypothesis of a predestinarian system, there is one major point of difference: now the use of predestination as a central principle is attributed not so much to Zwingli or to Calvin as to Calvin's successors, to Theodore Beza, in particular. In other words, where Schweizer and even Heppe saw the fruition of Calvin's doctrine in a thoroughly formulated structure of the decrees, contemporary scholarship sees a distortion or disruption of Calvin's theology.[63] This altered perspective is possible only following a reappraisal of Zwingli's and of Calvin's thought. In 1919, Paule Wernle could write, reflecting the standard of his day, that Zwingli's theology drew not so much upon scripture or the self-revelation of God in Christ as upon a philosophical view of providential necessity which tended to place even the biblical theism of his more scriptural moments into the context of "einem pantheistischen Gottesbegriff und einer streng deterministischen Auffassung des Verhältnisses von Gott und Welt. . . ."[64] And of Calvin, who far more than Zwingli brought Reformed doctrine into full systematic formulation, Wernle wrote, "Durch ihn wurde die Praedestination tatsächlich das Schibboleth des reformierten Christentums."[65] Since Wernle's time, however, the christocentrism not only of Calvin's but also of Zwingli's theology has been argued principally by Jacobs, Niesel, and Locher.[66]

The reappraisal has not, however, been extended to the Reformed theologians of the latter half of the sixteenth century and, under the terms of Schweizer's and Heppe's arguments, these theologians now appear as the engineers of a one-sided alteration of the Reformed system, away from its originally christocentric pattern toward a predestinarian, indeed, a metaphysically determined structure. Basil Hall, for example, can speak of theologians like Beza and Perkins as distorters of the balance of Calvin's theology: "With Perkins we can see, as with Beza, a more severe, more speculative and less biblical version of the doctrine of grace, lacking Calvin's attempt to give it christocentric emphasis."[67] This scholastic theology "replaced" Calvin's "biblical dynamism by formulae."[68] When Beza "reverted to the medieval scholastic device of placing predestination under the doctrines of God and providence," he "re-opened the road to speculative determinism which Calvin had attempted to close."[69] Similar arguments have been stated by other recent writers—and not only in the examination of Beza's and Perkins' work but also in the analysis of Zanchi's theology.[70]

The shift in Calvin scholarship and its effect upon our view of orthodoxy naturally raises the question of whether or not the orthodox writers themselves had a sense of the need for a systematic balance in their theology and saw in their own way the necessity of maintaining a soteriological as opposed to a theological (in the strict sense of the term) focus in their doctrine of predestination and, therefore, the necessity of maintaining a christological center for all doctrine concerning the salvation of mankind. Moreover, the thesis that the orthodox developed a predestinarian metaphysic as over against a christocentric soteriology cannot be documented—as was the practice in the massive works of Schweizer and Weber—by analysis of the doctrine of predestination in relative isolation from other doctrines and in terms of its potential use as a metaphysical principle. A contextual analysis which explicates the placement and use of the doctrine in the structure of system is what the question demands.

An evaluation of the orthodox writers that points at very least toward a partial reappraisal appears in the lengthy historico-dogmatic analyses found in Karl Barth's *Church Dogmatics*. In these sections, as in his magisterial presentation of nineteenth century German theology, Barth manifests himself well worthy of Harnack's compliment, that he might have been a great historian of doctrine had he not undertaken to become a theologian. Barth is very much aware that Reformed orthodoxy was not a monolithic dogmatic structure but was characterized by a variety of systematic patterns. Beyond this, Barth saw that the several systematic placements of the doctrine of predestination manifest several implications of the doctrine for Reformed theology, not the least of which is the creation of a doctrinal link between the salvation effected in Christ and its application by the Spirit in the soteriology and ecclesiology.[71] Barth also denies, with considerable force, the entire view of Reformed orthodoxy, even in those systems of seventeenth century theologians in which the decrees appear following the doctrines of God and trinity and prior to that of creation, as a predestinarian system with the decree as its central dogma. In this context Barth specifically refers to Beza's *Tabula praedestinationis*, viewing Heppe's perception of it (i.e., as an attempt to deduce the whole of theological system from the decree) as a misinterpretation.[72] More could be said of Barth's historical analysis, but its importance to the argument of this essay favors a subsequent development of Barth's views in connection with a closer examination of the documents.

Taken as a whole, the scholarship raises the basic question of continuity and discontinuity between the Reformation and the post-Reformation theology, in a more restricted sense, between Calvin and the Calvinists. Writers in the nineteenth and the early twentieth century acknowledge a general continuity of doctrine accompanied by a gradual formalization of definition and realization of the systematic implication of fundamental doctrinal principles. According to this perspective, doctrinal continuity could be described in terms of the use and development of predestination as a "central dogma." More recent writers have allowed a christological focus in the theology of Calvin but have maintained a departure from this center of doctrine in the theology of his successors. We now again raise the question of continuity and discontinuity: can we describe a development of system and a process of formalization which alters the method of theology but retains the basic doctrinal insight and the crucial patterns of doctrinal interrelationship evident in the thought of the Reformation and its first codification as noted by writers like Jacobs, Locher, Niesel, and Wendel? Is there, perhaps, on the one hand, a continuity of emphasis on predestination as the guarantee of salvation *sola gratia*—as the older scholarship claimed and perhaps overstated in terms of the "central dogma" concept—and, on the other hand, a continuity in christological emphasis which counterbalances the predestinarian motif within the system?

2. THEOLOGICAL AND METHODOLOGICAL CONSIDERATIONS[73]

Christology, Predestination and the Interrelationship of Doctrinal Loci
    In the early years of the Reformation emphasis on the faith of the individual
and stress on a new found sense of *Christus pro me* placed atonement at the
center of theological concern. Even so, the work of Christ as mediator occupies
the center of Calvin's thought.[74] The following essay will argue in similar terms
that Protestant orthodoxy did not depart from this emphasis, that it developed a
doctrinal structure more formal in definition and more scholastic in method but
nevertheless concerned to maintain a doctrinal continuity with the soteriological
emphasis and christological center of the theology of Calvin and his contemporaries. In this development, orthodoxy completed the transition (already evident in the work of Calvin) from piety and the preaching of reform to the system
of Reformed doctrine. New structures, like the threefold office and the two states
of Christ, were integrated into systems of doctrine as formal principles, indeed,
as new doctrinal contexts elicited from scripture, in terms of which dogmas
received from the tradition—the Chalcedonian christological definition, for example—would be understood and, to a certain extent, reinterpreted. In this
context also, the doctrine of the atonement, because it manifested the gracious
will of God, moved into close relation with the doctrine of election.[75]
    There are, therefore, two primary levels on which the systematic interre-
lationship of predestination and Christology occurs: the level of the eternal intra-
trinitarian relationships of Father, Son, and Spirit, and the level of the temporal
effecting of God's will. Correlation of these two levels of predestinarian and
christological thought is made possible by a series of doctrinal distinctions which
describe the manner in which God's saving will bridges the gap between the
divine and the human. This essay proposes to show, therefore, that one of the
central issues in the positive development of Reformed theology was to demonstrate the continuity of God's saving will with its effects in the temporal order
and the consequent unity of the entire soteriological structure. In this unified
structure, predestination does not oppose Christology nor does it reduce Christology to a mere function of the divine will, a means of effecting an already
decreed salvation.
    In order to argue this point, we will proceed in terms not only of specific
doctrinal definitions and developments but in terms of the underlying assumptions
and dynamics of system, examining the manner in which the several centers of
doctrine within the system interrelate and interpenetrate. We propose two basic
tasks: first, the exposition of the doctrines of predestination and of Christ in their
early orthodox development; and second, the analysis of their relationship one
to the other and to the soteriological structure of the system. This procedure will
reveal, on the one hand, the extent to which not only the decrees but also the
doctrine of Christ was a major focus of doctrinal development in the period of
early orthodoxy, and on the other hand, the relative impact of both of these

doctrinal *foci* on the system as a whole. The method may be characterized briefly as comparative dogmatics.

Toward a Definition of Scholasticism and Orthodoxy

Two terms that appear most frequently in the evaluation of theology after Calvin are "scholasticism" and "orthodoxy." From the first, we need to be clear that these terms are neither laudatory nor perjorative; they are only descriptive of the method and the intention of theologians in the century and a half following the demise of Calvin, Vermigli, and Musculus. In other words, characterization of post-Reformation Protestantism as "scholastic orthodoxy" denotes the historical form of that theology and in no way implies that the theology of the seventeenth century can provide either the right method or the right teaching for the present.

Much American scholarship in the field of Protestant orthodoxy rests upon the definitions given in Brian Armstrong's *Calvinism and the Amyraut Heresy*. In order to analyze the debate between Amyraut and his opponents, Armstrong delineated basic tendencies in seventeenth century orthodoxy which could be identified as "scholastic." He argued that an extensive use of Aristotelian categories in logical, rationally defensible systems was characteristic of the Protestant scholasticism. Reason assumed "at least equal standing with faith in theology." Furthermore, reliance on speculative reason brought about a more philosophically and metaphysically oriented theology grounded on "a speculative formulation of the will of God" than had been seen in earlier Protestantism.[76] Armstrong's arguments are supported by the preference of many seventeenth century Reformed theologians for a synthetic over an analytic order in systematic theology.[77] Against this definition we note that not all of these characteristics can be found in the works of each of the thinkers commonly referred to as "Protestant scholastics." Nor can we pinpoint firmly a time at which Reformed theology as a whole manifested all these tendencies, as it moved from its sixteenth century beginnings toward its seventeenth century completion.[78] Armstrong's definition is not sufficiently broad to characterize the phenomenon as a whole. We are reminded of the difficulties inherent in Maurice Dewulf's protest against those general definitions which included nearly all medieval theologizing within the category of "scholasticism." DeWulf wished to avoid the vague notion of a "theology of the schools" and viewed scholasticism as a normative theology established in the 13th century, having certain definable characteristics.[79] Such limitation fails to do justice to the phenomenon. "Scholasticism" ought simply to indicate the formal theology of the systems and doctrinal compendia developed out of the classroom experience of the academies and universities.

Scholasticism is a methodological approach to theological system which achieves precision of definition through the analysis of doctrinal *loci* in terms of scripture, previous definition (the tradition), and contemporary debate. Even when organized synthetically, such systems tend to concentrate on the analysis

of particulars and for the sake of their educational and polemical goal seek to
establish minute distinctions and precise determinations of doctrine. Beginning
with the era of Melanchthon, Calvin, Bullinger, Vermigli, and Musculus, the
topical approach and the movement toward precision in definition becomes apparent within Protestantism. Succeeding generations of theologians, working to
establish normative definition both in the context of and in opposition to the
systems of preceding centuries, brought this movement to a climax of technical
mastery in the seventeenth century. There is an understandable methodological
continuity between medieval school-theology and the Protestant school-theology:
Protestant scholasticism cannot be defined as an isolated phenomenon of the
seventeenth century.[80]

Orthodoxy and the Form of Post-Reformation Protestantism
    This brings us to the definition of "orthodoxy." Etymologically, the term
indicates "right teaching." As applied to the theologians of the Reformed (and
Lutheran) branches of the Protestant Reformation, specifically in the late sixteenth and the seventeenth century, it indicates several things: first, and perhaps
foremost, it indicates the desire to set forth the true faith as over against the
teaching of the several adversaries confronted in polemic. Right teaching is for
the edification of the church on both the positive and the polemical levels.
Second, "orthodoxy" indicates also a sense of catholicity, of continuity both
with the revelation contained in the scriptural deposit and with the valid teaching
of the church in past centuries. Orthodox theologians of the seventeenth century
felt quite at ease in their use not only of the fathers but also of medieval thinkers.
Third, the term implies a strong relationship between systematic theology and
church confessions, the confessions acting as a subsidiary norm in the development and exposition of doctrinal systems: even at its most rigid and formal
extreme, orthodoxy is theology in and for the church. Fourth, and finally, the
production of an orthodoxy, so-called, relates to the conviction that true doctrine
can be stated fully and finally in a series of strict doctrinal determinations. In
this sense, orthodoxy involves an approach to scripture as the deposit of truth
out of which correct definitions may be drawn. This assumption in itself entailed
the development of a theological method more logical, more rigorous, and more
rationalistic than that of the Reformation, though no less committed to the
principle of *sola scriptura*.
    In the work of this more traditionally "scholastic" group of theologians, the
original Reformation insights into the nature of faith and justification begin to
take a prominent position in a broadly conceived *ordo salutis*, and in turn, the
ordo salutis takes its place within the established structure of dogmatics. Once
this occurs, the relation between the Reformation preaching and the more speculative areas of doctrine—e.g., trinity, predestination, the pre-existence of the
mediator—must be developed. By the same token, the *sola scriptura* of the
Reformation became a series of doctrinal determinations concerning, on one

hand, the character of revelation and revealed theology and, on the other, the limitation of natural theology. The rigidity we encounter in Protestant orthodoxy is the rigidity—perhaps we should say necessary rigidity—of the dogmatic system as contrasted with the dynamic preaching of Reform. This formalization of theology was an inevitable development, tied to the establishment of a church independent of Rome but bound to the catholic tradition. The development of system meant continuity with scholastic dogmatics as Flacius Illyricus argued, with the seven thousand medieval faithful including some eminent theologians who had not bowed the knee to the Roman Baal.[81] Continuity with the preaching of Reform would be guaranteed first, by the maintenance within the systematic structure of the insights of the Reformers and second, by the formal adaptation of the system under the impact of those insights.[82] We need to be aware from the outset, therefore, that the question of continuity or discontinuity of Protestant scholastic theology with the western theological tradition is highly complex and not at all to be reduced to the relationship of the doctrine of predestination developed by Beza or Zanchi to that of Calvin. Rather the question must be raised in terms of the influence of Calvin and his contemporaries upon a developing Augustinian theology the roots of which extend into the middle ages, indeed, back to Augustine; in terms also of methodological continuities and discontinuities both with the Reformers and with the medieval doctors; and finally in terms of the changes that occur in theological ideas as they develop systematically, recognizing that continuity is found in developing traditions rather than in a static reproduction of ideas from one generation to the next. This broad question of continuity and discontinuity must be answered, of course, with attention to a broad spectrum of doctrinal and philosophical issues, many beyond the scope of a single study. We focus here on predestination and Christology and the problem of central dogmas or doctrinal *foci* as an approach to one aspect of the broader question.

PART I

REFORMED THEOLOGY
IN ITS FIRST CODIFICATION

The Systems of Calvin, Bullinger, Musculus and Vermigli

II

PREDESTINATION AND CHRISTOLOGY
IN THE THOUGHT OF CALVIN

1. FUNDAMENTAL DISTINCTIONS IN CALVIN'S THEOLOGY

Underlying much of the scholarship in which an attempt is made to distinguish between the theology of Calvin and that of his successors is the assumption that Calvin's own thinking, if it rests upon any principle, rests on a scriptural principle, whereas that of his successors, in its search for consistency, rests upon certain specific doctrinal principles as, for example, the so-called "central dogma" of predestination. Several observations must be made. In the first place, the fully developed scholastic systems of the early orthodox period—e.g., Polanus' *Syntagma theologiae christianae*—elaborate at great length upon Scripture as the *principium cognoscendi*, the cognitive ground, of theology. Calvin's successors may have formalized the *sola scriptura* of the Reformation into a *locus de scriptura*, but they maintained the scriptural principle as the basis of their theological enterprise. In the second place, if Calvin did attempt to draw his theology directly from Scripture as the sole norm and authority for Christian doctrine, he also most certainly found in Scripture certain doctrines and certain perspectives on doctrine which provided his theology with its basic motifs: scholars have variously denoted the sovereignty of God, predestination, and Christology as the center of Calvin's thought.

Beyond this, the demands of order and coherence which led Calvin to move from the simple catechetical structure of the early editions of the *Institutes* to the more formal, more systematic presentation of doctrines found in the 1559 edition cannot ultimately be separated from the development of system in the sixteenth century. The question that needs to be asked is not whether Calvin is a scriptural theologian and the Reformed scholastics unscriptural rationalists, but whether the doctrinal motifs drawn by Calvin from scripture are echoed, elaborated, developed, or neglected and set aside by the systems of the "orthodox" or "scholastic" thinkers of subsequent generations.

In delineating fundamental principles and distinctions in Calvin's theology we do not, therefore, refer to the underlying recognition of the self-revelation of God as the sole source of the doctrines relating to man's salvation but to a series of subsidiary motifs or principles derived from the scriptural revelation, which govern the shape and interests of Calvin's doctrinal system. As Paul Jacobs has cogently argued, a trinitarian ground of doctrine serves to unite the predestinarian and christological motifs and to manifest the ultimately soteriological rather than metaphysical or speculative interest of Calvin's predestinarian formulations.[1] Indeed, once the trinitarian ground is recognized, the seemingly variant views of Calvin's thought as focused on the sovereignty of God, on predestination, on Christology, or on the work of salvation performed by Christ and the Spirit, all begin to impinge upon a common interest and appear as related epicenters in the trinitarian structure of the *Institutes*.

In turning to the specific problem of the interrelation of predestination and Christology we observe that the trinitarian principle functions as a regulator of doctrines, while the christological principle, itself focused on the fact that Christ is God manifest in the flesh, *Deus manifestatus in carne*, serves as the center in the light of which all aspects of the *ordo salutis* must be understood. The predestinarian principle establishes causally the center of the system as the work of God in Christ.[2] This means that there can be no *Deus nudus absconditus*, no God abstractly considered apart from his work, in Calvin's system: we remember that all references to God "without particularization" refer to the entire Trinity. Faith itself must be defined in relation to the entire Trinity and all saving knowledge of God recognized as mediated by Christ.[3] In short, Calvin will not allow reference to a God who decrees salvation eternally apart from a sense of the trinitarian economy and the effecting of the salvation in the work of the Son of God incarnate. Built into Calvin's system is an interrelation and interpenetration of predestination and Christology: in Emmen's words, "even as there is a christological element in Calvin's doctrine of predestination, so is there a predestinarian element in his Christology."[4]

Even as Calvin's fundamental theological principles are the doctrines of the trinity, of Christ as *deus manifestatus in carne*, and of the causality of salvation focused on Christ, so are his primary doctrinal distinctions the means by which he overcomes the infinite separation of the divine nature from the flesh it seeks to redeem. Calvin's primary doctrinal distinctions deal with the problems of temporality and eternality, finitude and infinitude, humanity and divinity. The separation is overcome in Christ, the mediator, in whose person the temporal, the finite, the human is reconciled with the eternal, the infinite, the divine.

Both the revelation of God and the work of salvation are accommodated to the forms of human perception or reception. Theology must focus on Christ since, "In this ruin of mankind no one now experiences God as Author of salvation in any way, until Christ the mediator comes forward to reconcile him to us."[5] Faith takes Christ as its proper foundation and is grounded in his weakness and humiliation.[6] Even so, the "order of faith," unlike the order of *loci* which normally obtains in theological systems, begins with the incarnate one.[7] There must, therefore, always be a tension between those doctrines concerning God in himself and those doctrines concerning God as he comes into relation with man, just as there will be a tension between natural knowledge of God and saving knowledge revealed in Christ.

Herein we detect the reason for Calvin's ultimate separation of the doctrines of predestination and providence. In the order of *loci* of the scholastic systems, both of these doctrines were conceived as decrees of God similar in form but distinct in purpose, the former special, the latter general. The decree of providential care does not have a primarily soteriological function, while the decree of predestination has as its intention the salvation of the elect. Under the impact of his reassessment of the problem of saving knowledge, Calvin altered the structure of doctrine in the last edition of his *Institutes* leaving predestination in substantially the same place it had occupied in 1539 and 1541 but returning providence to a more traditional placement in the doctrine of God.[8]

Barth comments on this placement of predestination as indicative of the fact that for Calvin this doctrine was the "consummation" of the doctrine of reconciliation and then remarks, significantly, on the arrangement of book III,

> In the third book, *De modo percipiendae Christi gratiae*, we are led from the work of the Holy Ghost actualized in faith to repentance and the Christian life, the latter being seen from the standpoint both of its outlook on eternity and also of its conditioning in time.[9]

Indeed, the concept of predestination or of divine decrees can only be properly understood as it is seen to represent one aspect, the causal aspect, of an eternal solution to the temporal predicament: it is the vertical line of the saving will that intersects, at a particular temporal moment, the history of salvation and the life of the individual in that history.

The mediated character of saving knowledge provides the foundation for a series of crucial distinctions in Calvin's thought. Calvin makes a primary distinction between the truth known to God and the accommodated nature of revealed truth. The form of saving knowledge, like our salvation itself, conforms to man's need.[10] The person of Christ, the *Deus manifestatus in carne*, God manifest in flesh, provides the middle term, both *medius* and *mediator*, the midpoint and the go-between in which and by which this primary distinction is resolved.[11]

> He is the way because he leads us to the Father. He is the truth and the life because in Him we apprehend the Father. Therefore all theology separated from Christ is not only empty but also mad, deceiving, and counterfeit.[12]

Parallel distinctions, resolved in Christ, must be made between the eternal, infinite, omnipresent Word of God and the Word incarnate in Jesus Christ, and between God's eternal decree and its execution in time. Both in the thought of Calvin and in the thought of later Reformed theologians these distinctions underline the profound interpenetration of Christology and predestination.

The christological distinction maintains that the divine nature of the Son cannot be enclosed by or imprisoned within a human nature. In its union with the flesh the Word does not become finite even though it is wholly given for the sake of man.[13] Because of its prominence in Calvin's thought, this doctrine has been called the *extra calvinisticum*. It appears frequently, however, in the works of the church fathers and was a prominent motif in the Augustinian Christology.[14]

Calvin states the principle at a crucial point in his Christology, as he moves from his doctrine of the birth of Christ to the doctrine of the two natures:

> For even if the Word in his immeasurable essence united with the nature of man into one person, we do not imagine that he was confined therein. Here is something marvellous: the Son of God descended from heaven in such a way that, without leaving heaven, he willed to be borne in the virgin's womb, to go about earth, and to hang upon the cross; yet he continuously filled the world even as he had done from the beginning.[15]

The transcendence of the divine nature provides Calvin with the conceptual background for his doctrine of the union of the divine with human nature in Christ. The absolute transcendence of Christ's divinity represents on one hand Calvin's ever present concern for maintaining the sovereignty of God while on the other it demonstrates his effort to underscore the reality of Christ's human nature and its identity with the nature of all men.[16] The *extra calvinisticum* preserves the integrity of both natures and the mystery of the union.

A final element in our description of the *extra calvinisticum* is the dictum *finitum non capax infiniti* used by later exponents of Reformed doctrine. It does not appear to have been used by Calvin himself.[17] Several modern scholars have argued that the phrase is not even a proper description of Calvin's doctrine.[18] Nevertheless *finitum non capax infiniti* provides a key to our understanding of the *extra calvinisticum* and of Calvin's views on *kenosis* and *communicatio idiomatum* as well. The word *capax* can be translated as "bear" or "contain." In this sense of the word the old dictum might well indicate a philosophical argument, which as Willis comments, "reflects crudely naive spatial categories" and a "quantitative" conception of God and man.[19] Yet we should be wary against leveling such a criticism when *capax* also indicates "ability to grasp" or "fitness" for a given purpose. The phrase *finitum non capax infiniti* is better rendered "the finite is unable to grasp the infinite." As Oberman argued of Calvin, the inverse, *infinitum capax finiti* reveals the positive implication of the doctrine.[20] The infinite God grasps finite human nature *sola gratia*.[21]

Calvin never tires of arguing that man is incapable of reaching, grasping, comprehending the divine.[22] He disallows speculation concerning the nature of God or of God's decree. Christians must look at Christ and know God in him rather than "wander through . . . speculation and seek above the clouds."[23] We do not comprehend the divinity of the Son but only its revelation in the flesh. We do not see the full glory of God, but rather acknowledge its presence, hidden and lowly, in the incarnation by the grace of the Holy Spirit.[24] Like the other distinctions we have noted, the distinction between the eternal decree of predestination and its execution in time plays an important part in Calvin's soteriology. We must take issue with Bray who has argued that this distinction was first stated by Theodore Beza and was one of the characteristics by which later Calvinism may be distinguished from the thought of Calvin.[25] Calvin refers to the concept frequently in his commentaries:

> The decree (decretum) was eternal and ever-fixed, but it must be enacted in Christ, because in him it was purposed.[26]

> We must bear in mind the distinction between the secret will of God and his will revealed in Scripture.[27]

> The secret purpose of God . . . is manifested in His own time by the calling.[28]

> And if God's will is that those whom He has elected shall be saved by faith, and He confirms and executes (exsequitur) His eternal decree (aeternum suum decretum) in this way, whosoever is not satisfied with Christ but enquires curiously about eternal predestination desires, as far as lies in him, to be saved contrary to God's purpose. The election of God in itself is hidden and secret. The Lord manifests it by the calling with which he honors us.[29]

The distinction serves to designate the part of predestination that remains hidden and manifests the part of predestination that may be explained.[30] In a famous passage of the *Institutes* Calvin notes that man's curiosity seeks "forbidden bypaths" when it attempts to penetrate to the secret will of God:

> For it is not right for men unrestrainedly to search out things that the Lord has willed to be hid in himself, and to unfold from eternity itself the sublimest wisdom, which he would have us revere but not understand, that through this also he should fill us with wonder. He has set forth by his Word the secrets of his will that he decided to reveal to us. These he decided to reveal insofar as he foresaw that they would concern us and benefit us.[31]

Calvin avoids undue speculation but also discusses predestination in terms of his distinction between God's truth and the accommodated nature of revealed truth and the distinction between the eternal decree and its execution in time. We know of election in Christ, since he provides, as the incarnate mediator, the middle term, the resolution of the distinction, by which the decree is effected in the elect. Christology and predestination can no longer be viewed in isolation one from the other.

The presence of these distinctions in Calvin's theology manifests an element of continuity between Calvin's theology and the fundamental motifs of Scotist and late medieval Augustinian theology.[32] Beyond this, as Reuter saw, the discovery of continuity between Calvin's theology and the late medieval understanding of God and his transcendence not only explains the theocentricity of Calvin's system but also highlights the profound departure from medieval theology embodied in Calvin's codification of the Reform. For the objective and ontic grounding of doctrine in a generally Scotist perception of God pressed Calvin, on the one hand, toward a far more powerful emphasis on the divine self-revelation in Scripture as the ultimate ground of doctrine than had been contemplated in the late medieval theology, and on the other hand, toward a powerful emphasis on the subjective and noetic resolution of the problem of transcendence in Christ and in the believer's perception of Christ as the ground of the godly life. Calvin adds to the governing concept of divine transcendence a sense of the immediacy of the divine for those who belong to God in Christ.[33]

2. CALVIN'S DOCTRINE OF PREDESTINATION

John Calvin was part of a long line of thinkers who based their doctrine of predestination on the Augustinian interpretation of St. Paul.[34] Rather than call predestination the central dogma of Calvin's system, we recognize its importance within a larger complex of soteriological motifs. Within that complex it functioned as the keystone of a doctrinal arch,[35] having a unitive significance within the structure of Calvin's thought.[36] The concept of an eternal predestination of the elect functions as a corollary of Calvin's emphasis on God's free and sovereign grace in salvation: the problems of human inability and man's reliance for salvation upon the sovereign grace of God as mediated by Christ are the two grounds of Calvin's predestinarian conceptuality.[37]

The central definition of the double decree around which subsequent discussion revolves is as follows:

> We call predestination God's eternal decree (*aeternum Dei decretum*), by which he compacted with himself what he willed to become of each man. For all are not created in equal condition, rather, eternal life is foreordained for some, eternal damnation for others. Therefore, as any man has been created to one or the other of these ends, we speak of him as predestined to life or to death.[38]

And at somewhat greater length,

> As Scripture, then, clearly shows, we say that God once established by his eternal and unchangeable counsel (*immutabile consilio*) those whom he had determined once for all to receive into salvation, and those whom, on the other hand, he would devote to destruction. We assert that, with respect to the elect, this counsel was founded upon his freely given mercy, without regard to human worth; but by his just and irreprehensible but incomprehensible judgement he has barred the door of life to those whom he has given over to damnation. Now among the elect we regard the call as a testimony of election. Then we hold justification another sign of its manifestation, until they come into the glory in which the fulfillment of election lies. But as the Lord seals his elect by call and justification, so, by shutting off the reprobate from knowledge of his name or from the sanctification of his Spirit, he, as it were, reveals by these marks what sort of judgment awaits them.[39]

Predestination, Providence, and the Divine Will

Apart from the tentative ecclesiological location of predestination in the 1536 *Institutio* and in the catechism of 1542 (which was not without its influence on writers like Ursinus, Danaeus, Perkins and perhaps even Melanchthon in the final edition of his *Loci communes*), Calvin gravitated toward an understanding of predestination as the focal point of soteriology. This, according to Barth, was the result of Calvin's need for a "more comprehensive consideration of the question" of the systematic significance of the decree and, in a sense, the ground for the "more radical turn" given to the issue of predestination by later Reformed writers.[40] The order that Calvin adopted made "the doctrine of election in some degree the consummation of that of reconciliation, introducing it not in the middle or at the beginning, but as the ultimate and decisive word which sheds additional light upon all that has gone before."[41]

Barth's argument serves to underline the point that the 1559 *Institutes* does not represent a movement of predestination out of the doctrine of God but a clarification of the place given to predestination already in 1539 and 1554, effected chiefly by the removal of providence to the doctrine of God. Despite the logical association of predestination with assertions regarding the character of the divine will, Calvin chose against any systematic attempt to "deduce" other doctrine from that of the decrees.[42] The solidification of this placement of doctrine in 1559 and the similarity of placement in the catechism of 1537 and the *Confessio Gallicana* may be seen as a centralization of predestination in a physical sense so that, like the doctrines of God and providence in Book I and the doctrine of Christ in Book II of the *Institutes*, it can provide an explanation in terms of the divine sovereignty and grace for all that precedes and follows it.[43]

When Calvin wrote of providence and predestination, he did not adopt the scholastic determination of predestination as a special category of providence. Both in his 1539 edition of the *Institutes* and in the treatise, *De aeterna praedestinatione dei* (1552), Calvin set providence below predestination in his order of discussion, implying that the work of providence lies under and serves predestination. Predestination occupies much the same position in Book III of the *Institutes* (1559) that providence occupies in Book I. Even as providence represents the power of God maintaining and nourishing the world so does predestination show forth God's gracious will in calling and preserving the body of the church.[44] But the salvation of man is the great purpose of the entirety of God's work: "God has destined all things for our good and salvation."[45] Predestination attains a logical priority over providence since predestination more than providence tends toward this end.

The result of this particular implication for the systematic relationship of predestination to providence—and perhaps to all other doctrine—is to create a tension within the structure of the *Institutes* itself. The traditional relation of the doctrines seems to be denied as well as omitted, leaving room for a variety of formulations in the thought of Calvin's followers. Wendel suggests that this conditioning or determining of providence by the eternal decrees of predestination might lead one to expect that Calvin would have "put predestination immediately after the exposition on providence—even, indeed, before the chapters on creation. . . ."[46] Wendel does not, however, carry his argument to its logical conclusion. If predestination does indeed become determinative of providence in the logic of Calvin's system, might not the positions of predestination and providence be reversed? Predestination, as Otten hypothesized, can be set first as the general principle followed by providence, the means of execution.[47]

Calvin's use of the language of necessity and of fourfold causality in discussing these doctrines relates his thought not only to the formulation of Augustine but also to the tradition of medieval Augustinianism.[48] We note the relationship particularly in the Aristotelian causal structure utilized by Calvin in his interpretation of Ephesians 1:5-8: predestination described according to its first, formal, material, and final causes. This passage and its exegesis, moreover, are crucial to Calvin's doctrine insofar as they stress the relationship of Christ as mediator to the decree.[49] Calvin comes to terms with the scholastic Augustinianism of primary and secondary causes and of the necessary ordering of events and things at the level of primary causality without a disruption at the level of secondary or inferior causality of the contingent character of things or of the responsibility of human beings for all acts of will.[50] "Here," comments Mozley, "is the doctrine of the schools. . . ."[51] Here also is Calvin's defense against the charge of Bolsec that he had followed Lorenzo Valla in the development of an utterly deterministic system: this is not a thoroughgoing necessitarianism insofar as it respects contingency and real possibility at the level of secondary causes. Calvin could state categorically that God had not "necessitated the sin of men."[52]

Election, Reprobation, and the Causal Order

The epistemological order of the 1559 *Institutes* does not represent a categorical rejection of other orderings of *loci*. Although he placed faith prior to predestination in the *Institutes*, Calvin never ceased to emphasize the causal priority of God's elective decree. "Election . . . is the mother of faith."[53] Faith leads the Christian reverently to examine the decree: "we must climb higher, lest the effect overwhelm the cause."[54] In order to understand the merit of Christ, a Christian needs "go back to God's ordinance, which is the first cause" (*quae prima causa est*).[55] While Calvin preferred to follow the inductive order of faith in search of assurance, he made full use of the language of Aristotelian causality to demonstrate the synthetic and *a priori* structure of the *ordo salutis*. We have already noted Calvin's commentary on the first chapter of Ephesians. A similar interest in the causal order appears in Calvin's commentary on Romans 8:28: "It is certain that Paul notes the order, so that we may know that the fact that everything happens to the saints for their salvation depends on the free adoption of God as the first cause" (*prima causa*).[56]

In Calvin's formulation both election and reprobation rest on the sovereign will of God and are to be equally considered as results of a single divine counsel.[57] Unlike many of his contemporaries and successors, Calvin did not shrink from the conclusion that permission and volition are one in the mind of an eternal and utterly sovereign God: reprobation could not be viewed simply as a passive act of God.[58] This teaching represents the more fully deterministic side of Calvin's doctrine—a point at which the early orthodox would modify formulae and seek other models. Nevertheless, in view of Calvin's emphasis on knowledge of God, reprobation does not appear the exact coordinate of election. It occurs apart from Christ and therefore apart from any mediated knowledge of God.[59] If those men who remain in the mass of perdition inquire into themselves they can only know their own sin and infer its penalty of damnation. They cannot know of the decree of reprobation as a cause of their condition.[60] As Jacobs comments, reprobation is set in stark isolation from other doctrine.[61]

There is no particular attempt to emphasize the trinitarian aspect of the doctrine at this stage of the exposition. Nevertheless Calvin does not project here an image of the Father as *deus nudus absconditus*.[62] Calvin insists that the Son is more than a means to the end set forth by the Father. Christ elects in common with the Father and may be considered as the "author" of the decree.[63] This formulation points toward a distinction between the second person of the trinity considered as God and the person of the Son in his mediatorial office, in union with the flesh: ". . . although Christ interposes himself as mediator, he claims for himself, in common with the Father, the *jus eligendi*, the right to choose."[64] The certainty of Christ's mediation and the certainty of his promise are grounded in his divinity, since the promise he conveys in his incarnation *sub forma servi* is the same promise which he decreed in his eternal divinity.[65]

Election is preeminently a demonstration of God's gracious will in Christ shown forth in calling, justification, and sanctification. It is a doctrine that naturally comes into relation with the doctrines of faith and church, of word and sacrament and, in view of Calvin's placement of the doctrinal topics in the last edition of the *Institutes*, with the doctrine of the last things as well.[66] It provides a causal focus for soteriology and, as such, is a doctrine of central importance— but only in relation to its temporal anchor, the work of Christ. We know of our election as it is manifested and confirmed in Christ. Election is not to be inferred from works.[67] Assurance ultimately rests on Christ who is the "mirror" of election.[68]

Assurance of Salvation: The Problem of the "Practical Syllogism"

Wilhelm Niesel has emphatically denied that Calvin's thought includes the so-called *syllogismus practicus* of later Calvinism which, in its consideration of signs of election apart from Christ, seems to depart from the *sola gratia* that characterized early Reformed theology.[69] Yet Calvin does point to an assurance that comes not directly from Christ and the Gospel but from the effects of the application of Christ's work and from the effects of the hearing of the Gospel.[70] Calvin offers not a denial of the *syllogismus practicus* but a warning against its misuse and misinterpretation.[71] Christ is the foundation of election and assurance, but there is an assurance also to be gained from the spiritual benefits conferred upon the elect by God.

In presenting his arguments on effectual calling,[72] Calvin notes that whereas the preaching of the Gospel finds its source in the election of God (*Evangelii praedicatio ex fonte electionis scaturit*), preaching itself cannot be a ground of assurance, since preaching addresses both the elect and the reprobate.[73] The effectiveness of the divine call, then, is not immediately obvious from the fact of Christian preaching. This problem, in turn, raises the problem of assurance: for there is truly a call and the call does rest upon the free election of God. "If indeed we ask whom he calls, and according to what reason: he answers, those whom he has elected."[74] The call of the Gospel makes God's eternal election manifest: thus it is faith that confirms election, verifies it, seals it upon the heart.[75] Assurance begins with this result, with faith, not with the decree itself. The theological principle operative here is, of course, the distinction between the decree and its execution: assurance derives from faith, "since if we try to penetrate to the eternal ordination of God, that profound abyss shall swallow us."[76] The doctrine of election, as it is preached, derives, however, from revelation in which the ordination of God is made plain.[77]

This remaining separation of the objective declaration of God's electing will from the subjective apprehension of election by faith leads Calvin to approach the formulation of the *syllogismus practicus*.

> Therefore, as it is wrong to make the force of election contingent upon faith in the gospel, by which we feel that it appertains to us, so we shall be following the best order if, in seeking the certitude of our election, we cling to those latter signs which are sure attestations of it.[78]

Faith recognizes that the objective preaching of election in the Word of God has its subjective reference, but final confirmation of personal salvation derives from the "latter signs," the *signa posteriora*, of election. Calvin fully recognizes the danger in this thought and strives to avoid reducing the quest for assurance to empiricism: there can be no movement from personal righteousness upward to the eternal counsel apart from the Word in Scripture or apart from Christ in whom we are adopted.[79] "Still," and here Calvin introduces briefly the confirmatory latter signs, "this does not prevent believers from feeling that the benefits they receive daily from God's hand are derived from that secret adoption."[80]

If Niesel overstates his case in claiming "Nowhere does Calvin teach the *Syllogismus practicus*," he is nevertheless quite correct in separating Calvin from all teaching which infers election from outward activity and from any formal, logical solution to the problem of assurance. In addition, Niesel has a very clear sense of the relationship of an empirical *syllogismus practicus* to the problem of predestination as a "central dogma."

> The position which Calvin thus takes up makes it clear that his theology is something very different from a predestination system of thought concerning the relation of God and man, in which the *Syllogismus practicus* is assigned an important place. It becomes clear that Calvin is strictly concerned with the theology of revelation and that his teaching is wholly centered on Jesus Christ.[81]

If the system of doctrine is to remain christocentric, Christ and the Word of God which calls man to Christ must remain the center and focus of assurance. Any other focus—particularly an empirical focus upon outward signs of election—creates an alternative structure of assurance, indeed an alternative structure of redemption according to which Christ's objective satisfaction for sin hardly touches the life of the believer and the whole of piety looks to the decree, to the promulgation of the *deus nudus absconditus*. This possible function of a highly developed, empirical form of the *syllogismus practicus* makes the problem of assurance and its formal solution an index of the relation of predestination and Christology within the Reformed system, for it is here in particular that the decree, the vertical causal axis of the soteriological structure can begin to overshadow or exclude the horizontal or temporal axis of salvation denoted by the work of Christ and its application by the Spirit.

3. PATTERNS IN CALVIN'S CHRISTOLOGY

The Economy of Salvation and the Divine Transcendence

Most scholars have recognized the orthodoxy of Calvin's Christology. Emile Doumergue spoke of the doctrine of the *Institutes* as "an energetic return to the Council of Chalcedon, to the fundamental western Christology, that of Augustine, of Tertullian, of Irenaeus."[82] Yet Doumergue also perceives that Calvin's agreement with the Fathers rests much more on a similarity of concern for "the two terms of the problem, the divinity and the humanity," than upon the use of traditionally Chalcedonian language.[83] In fact, the way in which Calvin conceived these "two terms of the problem" provided one of the grounds for his vision of the interrelationship of predestination and Christology. What is more significant than either his agreement with or reliance upon the Fathers is Calvin's selective use of particular forms of patristic Christology and soteriology: pre-Chalcedonian motifs and the specifically western perspective as established by Hilary, Ambrose, and Augustine.[84] This western Christology, as different from the divinization paradigm of the East, stressed the distinction of natures in the *mediator Dei et hominum* and, in its historical emphasis, held a strong relation to the Augustinian soteriology of grace and election. Grillmeier comments in particular on the "historical approach" of Hilary and on the dynamic soteriological relation into which Augustine drew his Christology.[85] Calvin would intensify this soteriological relation by emphasizing the historical form of Christology and the place of Christology in the temporal economy of salvation.

Calvin begins his Christology not with the doctrine of the union of two natures in Christ's person but with the essentially Anselmic argument concerning the necessity of the mediator, the God-man. Here again Calvin has not only examined scripture as a source of doctrine but has drawn upon the tradition critically in his search for structures conducive to the codification of the Ref-

ormation insight. Whereas the medieval scholastics used the Anselmic argument
as an objective counterpoise in the Sentence commentaries and Summas to the
Abelardian theory of atonement, they only infrequently utilized it structurally
and, therefore, unlike Calvin did not find in it a basis for generating new patterns
and definitions in the Christology as a whole. As a structural (as opposed to a
purely doctrinal) element of system the argument for the necessity of the God-
man does, however, bind Calvin's Christology firmly to the Augustinian tradition, looking back, as it does, to pivotal arguments and structural elements in
the Christology of Augustine's *Enchiridion*[86] and also to the *Breviloquium* of
Bonaventure.[87]

Calvin's restructuring of doctrine has a twofold effect. First, the traditional
person-work paradigm is superseded by a doctrinal model in which the function
of mediation becomes determinative and the person of Christ must be considered
in and through his office.[88] And second, the structure of argument makes us
aware, from the very first moment of the christological exposition, of the causal
ground of the plan of salvation.[89] Christology and predestination are bound
intimately together. The necessity of Christ's mediation, says Calvin, was not
an "absolute necessity" but "stemmed from a heavenly decree on which man's
salvation depended": the person of the mediator is necessary to our salvation,
but the sending of the mediator rests entirely on the sovereign freedom of God
in his grace.[90] We encounter here, again, the Scotist underpinnings of much of
Calvin's thought; for the Anselmic argument becomes useful to Calvin by way
of the Scotist assault upon it. Once we have seen that Anselm's argument imposes
no necessity upon God and that God alone decrees the patterns of the work of
salvation, then the demolished rationalism of the *Cur deus homo* functions structurally within the faith rather than rationally as demonstrative of faith.[91]

Having established the principle of mediation as the proper ground of Christology, Calvin passes on to an examination of the true humanity assumed by
Christ, the *Deus manifestatus in carne*.[92] Calvin understands the work of Christ
as necessarily predicated upon the union of divinity with a real human nature,
differing from the rest of mankind only in its sinlessness. He rejects any explanation of sinlessness as a result of the virgin birth: the central issue for Calvin
is that Christ is a true man, "in the likeness of sinful flesh," but sanctified by
the Holy Spirit. In the interest of establishing the integrity of this sanctified
humanity as human, Calvin stresses the bestowing of "gifts" upon Christ by the
Spirit as distinct from the issue of the *communicatio idiomatum* within the person
of the incarnate one.[93]

Although the title of this section of Calvin's christology indicates stress on
the true humanity of Christ (Christ's divinity received treatment in connection
with the exposition of the trinity[94]), the underlying theme of the chapter, in
contrast to the historical and economical stress of the chapter preceding, is the
distinction between finite man and infinite God and the mystery of incarnation
as the resolution or reconciliation of this opposition in the person of the mediator.

Even as Calvin stresses the integrity of the human nature so does he also press the transcendence of the divine: this chapter is the primary *locus* for his development of the *extra calvinisticum*.[95]

Calvin's Doctrine of the Two Natures

Only after two initial chapters (II.xii and II.xiii) in which the historical and economical context for the divine work of incarnation is established and the relation of infinite God to the finite creature in Christ is described, does Calvin turn to the traditional problem of the two natures in the person of Christ. Having already announced the historical person of the mediator in terms of the soteriological task set before the person, his interest is not in the metaphysical problem of how such a union of natures is possible but the reality of the historical person of the mediator and the necessity of seeking the person of Christ not in the eternal person of the Son but in the incarnate mediator.[96] Calvin willingly adopts the traditional language of one person in whom two natures are conjoined—even as elsewhere he can distinguish between "the person of the mediator" and the "human flesh which he has put on."[97] It is nevertheless only in union with human nature that we recognize the person of the mediator.[98] In other words, Calvin's Christology and, I believe, much of the Reformed Christology after him is neither a traditional "Christology from above" nor a modern "Christology from below" but a Christology developed out of the historical line of the covenant-promise which points, as by a soteriological necessity, to the concrete, historical person of the God-man. Like the traditional "Christology from above," Calvin's Christology recognizes from the outset the divinity of Christ; but like the "Christology from below" Calvin's thought focuses on the concrete Christ in history and on the integrity of the human nature, the *forma servi* encountered by faith in the temporal dispensation of salvation. This insistence on the integrity of the human nature has often led to the association of Calvin's Christology with the ancient Antiochene position: the reality of Christ's divinity could never be stressed to the abolition of true humanity. Emphasis is placed on the historical revelation of the Son: "that our faith may arrive at the eternal divinity of Christ, we must start off from that knowledge which is nearer and easier."[99]

Calvin does, in fact, speak of the "person of the mediator" prior to the incarnation, in reference to the Old Testament witness.[100] His statements have, however, a different purpose and systematic implication than the Chalcedonian emphasis on the eternal person of the Son. Calvin's interest is still in the work of mediation between God and man and on the identification of Christ as mediator. The eternal Son is designated as mediator prior to the incarnation and performs his office in the communication of God's Word to man.[101] Furthermore, Calvin's doctrinal determination of the Son as God emphasizes the full Godhead of the Son rather than the eternal generation of his person as stressed by Chalcedon and by the later Greek theology.[102] As person the Son subsists in relation to the Father by generation, but as God—considered according to his divinity—he

contains in and of himself the full essence of the Godhead.[103] Here we encounter
the concept of the *aseity* of Christ's divinity so crucial for the later Reformed
treatment of predestination as a function of soteriology or, more precisely, of
the larger trinitarian-christological structure of doctrine; and also we here come
to the other pole of Calvin's Christology, the emphasis on the transcendent
divinity of the Son which is revealed in the person of the mediator, the God-
man.

    This particular set of issues and the manner in which they are developed
by Calvin and by the Reformed tradition in general point to the Augustinian
basis not only of the Reformed doctrine of predestination but also of the Reformed
Christology. The underlying reason for Calvin's perspective both on election
and on the christological center of theological meditation and also on the way
in which the issues of the divine sovereignty, the temporal economy of salvation,
and the entrance of God into the temporal economy in Christ, is the context of
Augustinian theology in which his doctrine takes form. As with Augustine's
theology, Calvin's thought seeks the ultimate resolution of these issues—the
character of the divine willing and the mode of entry in the person of the mediator
of the divine into the temporal economy—in the doctrine of the trinity.

    These formulations do not occur in their entirety, however, within the formal
bounds of Calvin's Christology, since the Christology properly deals only with
the person of the incarnate mediator while the doctrine of the Trinity relates
Calvin's understanding of the divine persons. Under the head, therefore, of the
trinity Calvin speaks of the relation of the Son to the Father. He understands
the generation or origination of the Son from the Father neither in terms of time
nor in terms of being.[104] There is a subordination in order described by the
generation of the Son and by the procession of the Spirit but no subordination
relating to divinity or essence.[105] Calvin states his opinion most emphatically in
an angry response to the criticisms to which his doctrine had been subjected by
two pastors of Neuchatel, Chaponneau and Courtois. They had denied the self-
existence of the Son as had Caroli before them.[106]

    Against Chaponneau and Courtois Calvin set the words of St. Paul, "in
Him dwelleth the fulness of the Godhead."[107] This implied, argued Calvin, the
self-existence or aseity of Christ's divinity:

> Truly this is where these donkeys are deceived: since they do not consider that the
> name of the Son is spoken of the person, and therefore is included in the predicament
> of relation, which relation has no place where we are speaking simply (*simpliciter*)
> of the divinity of Christ.[108]

Clearly, when Calvin spoke of the divinity or essence of Christ his primary
concern was not the Chalcedonian question of relation.[109] The doctrinal issue
was little changed in 1558 when Calvin responded to the anti-trinitarian heresies
of Blandrata and Gentilis. According to Gentilis, "The Father is a unique essence
. . . the Father is the only true God; it is he who gives his essence to the other

persons of the Divinity."[110] In response Calvin again affirmed the Son's aseity: "as to his essence, the Son is *absque principio*, while considered as to his person, he finds his *principium* in the Father."[111]

As Wendel notes, the carefully enunciated concept of the aseity of each of the persons of the trinity provides a strong guide and influence in the formulation of Calvin's Christology. The position argued against Chaponneau, Courtois, Caroli, Blandrata, and Gentilis, though nominally a trinitarian, and thoroughly metaphysical, problem, reflects certain soteriological issues. It underlies the christologically determined structure of the doctrines of salvation into which the doctrine of predestination was ultimately placed by Calvin's early orthodox successors. Calvin teaches a high conception of Christ's divinity at the same time that he emphasizes Christ's full humanity.[112] This dual focus of doctrine frames the problem of mediation so essential to Calvin's thought. And in the resolution of this problem of mediation, the relationship between predestination and Christology is established definitively and its character determined by an overarching concern with the manner in which the transcendent and triune God effects the economy of revelation and salvation.[113]

Christ's Threefold Office

Calvin's doctrine of the *munus Christi* is also of basic importance to his conception of mediation, to the development of a christologically determined structure relating to the decree and its execution, and to the general development of Reformed Christology. In Calvin's thought, moreover, the doctrine of the *munus triplex* becomes for the first time in the history of dogma a strict doctrinal category and a formula determinative of the shape of Christology.[114] By means of the *munus triplex* the unity of Christ's person is bound to the unity of Christ's work; for in the historical-scriptural pattern of Calvin's Christology, the doctrine of the threefold office confirms the fundamental testimony to the God revealed in the flesh for the work of mediation and redemption. His doctrine of the office of Christ is descriptive of Christ's work as a whole and demonstrative of the manner in which his work is applied to believers.

The concept of "office" as it appears in dogmatics refers to the calling and anointing of the incarnate one to the task of redemption and finds its scriptural basis in the names "Christ" and "Messiah" which may be translated as "anointed one."[115] The Son of God, therefore, is not properly called Christ apart from his office, for it is there, in his official capacity, that he manifests as the true fulfillment of the offices of the Old Testament his threefold work as prophet, priest, and king. The historical and soteriological dynamic which led Calvin to the conception of the *persona mediatoris* here brings about an equally historical view of the Christ—an emphasis upon the name "Christ" as the preeminent representation of the divine saving purpose within the temporal economy of promise and fulfillment. The person of the mediator is, moreover, anointed to a unified work of obedience and redemption in which the two natures conjoin, neither the divine nature nor the human nature alone constituting the *mediatoris persona* or the *mediatoris officium* for only the one who occupies a middle position between God and man (*medium gradum statuit inter Deum et nos*) can fulfill the divine-human work of salvation: in the *mediatoris officio* God and man come together in harmony.[116] In the eternal plan of God, the mediator appears as the one ordained by the divine will to effect a salvation otherwise impossible. Calvin explicitly predicates the historical person of the God-man and the office of mediation on the decree (*manavit ex caelesti decreto*).[117]

Calvin's conception of the anointing of the person of the mediator is not the twofold anointing described by Ursinus, Perkins, and Polanus. It does, however, contain the germ of the later conception. The whole person is anointed according to his human nature: the gifts of the Spirit are bestowed on the humanity for the sake of the office and belong to the entire person by reason of the *communicatio idiomatum*.[118] Calvin parallels this theme with another formulation in his Christology. The Son of God is "appointed . . . to be the overseer of our salvation." Calvin seems to imply that the Son, like the humanity he assumes, is designated.[119] Neither in his divinity nor in his humanity does Christ mediate by nature.[120] The office is "suprapersonal," since the office is instituted by a call to service from beyond the person.[120] It is but a step from these motifs and the conception of Christ as mediator according to both natures to the later doctrine of a twofold anointing.

The three aspects or functions of Christ's office, then, represent the three offices of ancient Israel to which men were anointed as servants of God and continue, following the discussion of the two natures of the person of the mediator (II.xiv), the historical line established in the initial discussion of the necessity of the mediator (II.xii).[122] Whereas the *persona mediatoris* appeared earlier as the fulfillment of the promise in the line of the covenant, the *mediatoris officium* or *munus triplex* appears now as the fulfillment of the life of God's people in the historical line of the community. The prophet, the king, and the priest are united in Christ, are perfected, and are thereby fulfilled and brought to a conclusion in the one who is both king and priest forever after the order of Melchizedek. In each of these aspects of his office Christ is a servant of the will of God like the anointed officers of Israel but, unlike them, finally and fully servant, in perfect obedience. This service does not end with the conclusion of Christ's earthly ministry but continues after the resurrection for the sake of the church, and is therefore the means by which the temporal and eternal, reconciled in the person of the mediator, are also reconciled in and for believers when the temporal line finally meets its end in the judgment of God.[123] The office of Christ, thus, belongs to the person of the mediator not only in his taking the form of a servant but also in his exaltation to the right hand of the Father. Although Calvin does not use the states of humiliation and exaltation as a specific doctrinal determination in the argument of the *Institutes*, his conception of the office of Christ points toward the relationship established between these two doctrines by his successors. The office of Christ like the movement from humiliation to exaltation describes the whole work of Christ and thereby serves again to direct attention structurally and functionally to the historical and economical perspective of Calvin's Christology.[124] In describing the work of Christ as a threefold office, Calvin presses upon us the historical continuity of the covenants, the historical dynamic of salvation from promise to fulfillment, and the historical nexus of the divine saving causality toward which the entire economy of salvation points.[125]

The question of how Christ accomplishes this office of mediator, according to his humanity or according to his divinity, raises a significant contrast between the generally a-historical and metaphysically conditioned Christologies of Chalcedon and of the medieval scholastics and the pronouncedly historical and functionally oriented Christology of Calvin and the Reformed tradition. When the Christology proceeds from the formulae concerning the eternal person of the Son who assumes flesh to the relation of natures in the union, then to the question of how Christ is mediator, and only subsequently to the discussion of the historical, atoning work—the classic "Christology from above"—the question is quite naturally answered "ideo verissime dicitur mediator secundum quod homo"[126] because the work of mediation focuses upon the flesh which is assumed and not upon the eternal person who assumes it. Quite to the contrary, the functional and historical Christology of Calvin tends to refer the work of mediation not to the nature assumed but to the person who performs the work. Whereas the medieval scholastics who asked the question affirmed Christ as mediator according to his humanity in order to state that the eternal divine person, apart from the hypostatic union, does not mediate, and to focus the act of mediation on the work of satisfaction as performed by the human nature of Christ within the personal union,[127] Calvin and those who followed his arrangement of doctrine strove to manifest the unity of the person in the unity of the work. Here the focus of the act of mediation is the divine-human person rather than the flesh assumed by the divine person.[128]

Christ's Intercession as the Limiting Factor in Soteriology

This doctrine of Christ's high priestly intercession not only extends Christ's atoning work toward its application but also defines the limits of atonement. Unlike the value of Christ's death in payment for sin, the intercession that he offers to the Father on behalf of mankind is strictly limited.[129] From this contrast of sacrificial with intercessory work, apart from any limiting factor external to Christology, Calvin was able to distinguish between the universal and particular aspects of Christ's work. Brian Armstrong has argued rather unconvincingly from Calvin's exegesis of the universalist passages of Scripture that Calvin did not hold a concept of "limited atonement."[130] Armstrong assumes that the infinite value of Christ's death, the payment made for all sin, and the universal call of the Gospel weigh against the concept of an atonement intended only for some.

Yet Calvin could comment, as in his exegesis of I John 2:2, that he did in fact accept the Lombardian distinction between the "sufficiency" of Christ's work for all sin and its "efficiency" for the elect alone.[131]

Much of the dispute over the doctrine of "limited atonement" in Calvin's thought can be laid to rest, moreover, by an examination of Calvin's own language. In a strict sense, "atonement" is not Calvin's word: Calvin uses *expiatio*, *satisfactio*, and *reconciliatio* as well as the more general term *redemptio* (particularly in *Institutes*, II.xvi.4-6). The two former terms refer to the work of Christ as it relates to the problem of sin and guilt, *expiatio* indicating specifically the propitiation or propitiatory sacrifice (i.e., the "atonement") and *satisfactio* indicating the reparation or amends made for the wrong against divine justice. Here Calvin insists on the fulness of Christ's work, the complete expiation or satisfaction for sin—which is to say an unlimited "atonement." On the other hand, the benefits of Christ's death, the *reconciliatio* or actual *redemptio*, the restoration and purchase of individuals, is restricted to the elect, to those upon whom Christ bestows his benefits; and, thus, if the term "atonement" is loosely construed to mean "reconciliation" or "redemption," Calvin arguably teaches "limited atonement." In fact, Calvin's usage of an unlimited *expiatio* or *satisfactio* and a limited *reconciliatio*, *redemptio*, or as we shall see *intercessio*, follows closely the old distinction between sufficiency and efficiency and well fits what is loosely called "limited atonement" not only in Calvin's thought but also in later Reformed theology.

Calvin's distinction between the universal and the particular aspects of the work of Christ is closely related to his discussion of Christ's intercession and the application of Christ's benefits. This discussion contains a very graphic passage to the effect that Christ "turns the Father's eyes to his own righteousness to avert his gaze from our sins."[132] The intervention of the mediator between the Father's wrath and the fortunate sinner, reflects and parallels Calvin's christological formulation of election: only the work of the mediator can reconcile man to God and make effective the saving will of God. "Both repentance and forgiveness of sins . . . are conferred on us by Christ, and both are attained by us through faith."[133] Redemption or reconciliation is limited in the final analysis not by a predestinarian structure as Armstrong assumes, but by the bestowal of the benefits of Christ's death upon only those who are engrafted into Christ and regenerated according to his image. Christ is the *electionis authorem* who with the Father exercises his right to choose those who are to be his.[134] Election and the work of expiation and reconciliation are conjoined because both are founded in Christ:

> And surely, the inheritance of heaven belongs to none other than the Children of God. Indeed, it is unfitting that those not engrafted into the body of the only-begotten Son be considered to have the place and rank of children.[135]

The focus of Calvin's discussion of the office of intercession is the efficacy of Christ's work for men: "Thus we see that we must begin from the death of Christ in order that the efficacy and benefit of his priesthood may reach us. It follows that he is an everlasting intercessor."[136] It is superfluous to speak of a hypothetical extent of the efficacy of Christ's work beyond its actual application. As shown in the doctrine of election, salvation is not bestowed generally but on individuals. The Gospel appeal is universal but Christ's intercession, like the divine election, is personal, individual, particular.[137]

4. CHRIST AND ELECTION
THE INTERRELATIONSHIP OF TWO FOCAL POINTS
IN CALVIN'S THEOLOGY

In the course of our discussion of Calvin's Christology, we have observed the development of a doctrine of Christ that is primarily "functional"[138] or historical and economical in its intimate relationship to the soteriological structure and that, in and through its functionality, is tied to the doctrine of predestination. On the one hand predestination, viewed as the doctrine of the decree and its execution in time, represents the causal ground of salvation, the eternal saving will touching and redeeming temporal humankind. On the other hand Christology, viewed as the doctrine of God manifest in the flesh, represents the historical focus of the saving work, the eternal and infinite God grasping and drawing to himself finite and fallen human nature. Elements in Calvin's Christology and in his doctrine of predestination point, therefore, toward a systematic relationship between Christ and the decree that lies at the heart of Calvin's theology and that draws on the fundamental distinctions with which Calvin wrestled in his attempt to codify the Reformation insight.

The precise relationship of Christ to the decree takes on, as Reid pointed out, considerable importance to the whole of theology, and the question of whether Christ can be subordinate to the decree as a means to an end or whether Christ, in his relation to the decree, stands somehow prior, becomes crucial to an understanding of Calvin's thought and its place in the Reformed tradition. We have already noted three points in the doctrine of predestination where christological concerns have an impact: the definition of election as "in Christ," the assertion that predestination is known only in Christ, and the statement that Christ himself is the "author of election" together with God the Father. The third of these points illustrates well what Jacobs calls "*die trinitätstheologische Verankerung*" of Calvin's teaching on election[139]—and it presses definitively beyond the purely functional level of doctrine. Against two writers who viewed predestination as the governing concept in Calvin's thought, Jacobs could argue,

> The opinion of Kampschulte and O. Ritschl, that Christ has a merely formal significance for Calvin's doctrine of predestination, utterly misunderstands the fact that Christ and election belong to one another inextricably—as inseparable as water and a fountain; Christ correctly understood, is the "index": Christ is election itself.[140]

In the work of reappraisal, the hyperbole of Jacobs' last phrase was justified, and it serves to carry the day not only against the older scholarship, but also against Reid's contention that Calvin failed to press his christological concerns to their proper conclusion in the doctrine of election.[141]

There is, however, a need to go beyond Jacobs' argument and to ask, in the light of the trinitarian ground of Calvin's doctrine, how Christ is not only "election itself" but also more than election, how Christ not only appears within the *ordo salutis* but also provides the *ordo salutis* with its proper foundation. In one sense, the *ordo salutis* precedes and defines the mediator and his work just as the historical sweep of the covenant provides its temporal context. The foundation of man's salvation, the Christ, is revealed as being both divine and human and, consequently, as the only one fitted to the task of mediating the wholly divine offer of salvation to the wholly human recipients of God's redemption.[142] Christ stands, as mediator, between God and man but also between the decree and its execution and must somehow be subordinate to the decree:

> In discerning Christ's merit, we do not consider the beginning of merit to be in him, but we go back to God's ordinance as the first cause. For God solely of his own good pleasure appointed him mediator to obtain salvation for us.[143]

The mediator himself is elect for the purpose of redemption. The perfection of his humanity rests upon God's gracious will alone.

In this crucial link between his Christology and the larger soteriological exposition Calvin does not rest on his own exegesis for authority. The central points of his argument are given not in his own words but in those of Augustine.[144] The passage Calvin chooses sheds an important light on his doctrine of predestination and its importance for the entire system. Augustine states that not only predestination but grace is manifested most clearly in the man Jesus. Christ is elect through grace and "through no preceding merits of works or of faith."[145] The humanity of Christ is the highest example of the resounding *sola gratia* of divine election. For this reason the active obedience of Christ is for the sake of man's salvation, rather than for the sake of Jesus' worthiness. Christ's merits are certainly not intended to make his human nature worthy of exaltation to the right hand of the Father![146] The entire work of the mediator is for man. Following Augustine, Calvin argues that Christ is predestinated to be our head even as we are predestinated to be his members; he is revealed as the source of the grace that flows through those who are his.[147]

The doctrinal question of the predestination of Christ traditionally rested on the exegesis of Romans 1:3-4, where Christ is designated as the descendant of David according to the flesh and designated as the Son of God according to the Spirit. Augustine understood the Vulgate's use of *praedestinatus* as an indication of the eternal will and ordination of God.[148] This interpretation seems to have been accepted with some modification by the Council of Toledo (675) and by medieval theologians such as Peter Lombard and Thomas Aquinas.[149]

The man Jesus or, more precisely, his human nature was predestined to be the Son of God in incarnation. According to this formulation, it is not the person of the mediator that is predestined but only the abstraction of the human nature which has no subsistence independent of the person. The soteriological ground of this predestination is the intention of God that men be conformed to the image of Christ and partake of his merits. The predestination of Christ according to his human nature establishes the form of man's redemption.[150]

Calvin attempts to move beyond this doctrine to a conception involving the whole person of Christ, the concrete, historical *mediatoris persona*. He also chooses not to rest his doctrine entirely on the traditionally employed passage.[151] Rather he founds the doctrine on passages which speak of the sending of the Son, which "demonstrate . . . that . . . God appointed Christ as a means of reconciling us to himself."[152] The eternal determination of Christ as Redeemer manifests God to be the "author of our salvation" who "does not go outside himself" for the source of the blessings of salvation:[153] the triune God, indeed, seeks within his triunity and freely determines the person of the Son. Here lies the eternal pole of Calvin's Christology. Yet, Calvin speaks of the person of Christ as *Deus manifestatus in carne*. There is no speculative consideration of the natures apart from their union in the person. Calvin must depart from a doctrine which examines the predestination of an abstract humanity which does not exist apart from the person of Christ. A similar redefinition of the predestination of Christ is seen in the theology of Bonaventure—who will apply the divine determination neither to the Word, since the divine Word disposes all things, nor to the human nature abstractly, but to the God-man as the foundation of the predestination of mankind to salvation. Calvin, I believe, goes farther still than this, but the underlying theological motivation is similar and the precedent, which places Calvin once again in continuity with Franciscan and ultimately Scotist rather than Thomist thought, is significant.[154]

Since Christ is mediator, according to both natures,[155] the election of his humanity correlates with the designation or self-designation of his divinity for the work of redemption. This correlation appears in the broader context of Calvin's Christology where the *kenosis* is considered as part of the *status humiliationis* and the *status humiliationis* is applied to the divine as well as to the human nature.[156] Several passages in the commentaries, moreover, may indicate that, according to Calvin, the eternal Word, the second person of the Trinity, is designated in the saving will of the Godhead for the work of salvation.[157] In a similar vein, Calvin could speak of the mediator as electing God and as designated go-between. The mediator reveals the truth of God because he himself is God. Christ witnesses faithfully to the election of all believers eternally in God since he himself is one with the Father who has chosen the elect in eternity.[158] Yet as mediator he is designated to the work.[159] As mediator Christ is subordinate to the decree while as Son of God he is one with the Father and in no way subordinate.[160] The Son as God stands behind the decree while the Son as mediator is the executor of the decree. The relationship between the distinction concerning the decree and its execution and the *extra calvinisticum* now becomes clear. In the execution of the decree or work of salvation, the Son of God is wholly given, in subordination to the eternal plan, as mediator. But the Son as God *a se ipso* cannot be wholly contained in the flesh or in any way subsumed under the execution of the decree.

The predestinarian structure (the decree and its execution) and the christological structure (the Son and his manifestation in the flesh) together provide a basis for the parallel development and mutual interpenetration of the doctrines of predestination and the person of Christ. More than that, these two structures bear witness to Calvin's concern to state, without diminution of the ontological problem the two poles of the theological problem—eternity and temporality, transcendence and finitude. Viewed from the human side, from the point of view of temporality and finitude, the working out of God's plan in believers and the person of the mediator are inseparable. In Jacobs' words, "Christ is election itself." The concrete person of the mediator, the God-man, toward whom the covenant history points and in whom the historical dispensation of salvation is fulfilled, manifests in time and history the eternal will of God to save. And just as his person, the agency, the center, and ultimately the content of revelation, points back from the historical to the eternal trinitarian identity of God, so does his office as mediator, itself the fulfillment of the threefold mediation of the Old Covenant, point back from itself as *medius*, as midpoint, to the saving decree which he effects in the elect.

From the divine side to which Calvin, in his desire to avoid speculation, only points indirectly, from the vantage of eternity and transcendence, the decree and the Christ, considered as God, are inseparable. For Christ is one with the Father, is author of salvation, and claims with the Father the right to choose. Christ is more than "election itself" and more than the "index" or "mirror" of election. In the depth of the triune God, to whom both the person of the mediator and the work of salvation point, Christ is the electing God. In terms of the trinitarian ground of theology, Christ can never be reduced to a mere means. Where Reid stands correct in his appraisal of Calvin is that Calvin never sought to develop this more speculative side of his doctrine, never meditated in detail upon the trinitarian ground of theology as the point at which the lines of christological and predestinarian doctrine converge.

III

THE SYSTEMS OF CALVIN'S CONTEMPORARIES

Unlike the theology of the Lutheran Church, the theology of the Reformed Churches does not derive from a single source. Calvin's influence was great but not exclusive. The systematic writings of Heinrich Bullinger, Wolfgang Musculus, Pierre Viret, Andreas Gerardus Hyperius, Benedict Aretius, and Peter Martyr Vermigli present perspectives different from that of Calvin. In this chapter, which is of necessity selective, I have restricted my analysis to Bullinger, Musculus, and Vermigli, the more influential thinkers of the above-mentioned group in the development of the Reformed soteriological structure.

1. PREDESTINATION AND CHRISTOLOGY
IN THE THOUGHT OF HEINRICH BULLINGER

Heinrich Bullinger (1504-1575), Zwingli's successor in Zurich, produced three major works which cover the entire ground of Christian theology. The first of these systematic efforts is the series of doctrinal sermons known as the *Decades*, published in four volumes between 1549 and 1552.[1] In 1556, Bullinger published the ten books of his *Compendium christianae religionis*, a brief system, as its title indicates.[2] Then, in 1562, during a period of personal illness, Bullinger wrote a final testament to his faith. This document appeared in 1566 as the *Confessio helvetica posterior*.[3] The following discussion of Bullinger's thought focuses on the two latter documents and their structure with some reference to the doctrinal content of the *Decades*.

Bullinger's Compendium Christianae Religionis[4]

The *Compendium* begins by presenting the concept of sola scriptura as a prolegomenon to theology.[5] Scripture and its use are the subject of the entire first book of the *Compendium*. Book Two treats the articles of God and his works. Following this, Bullinger concerns himself with the doctrines of man, sin, and the first promises of God in covenant with fallen humanity. Then follows a treatment of grace, justification, and faith framed by expositions of Law and Gospel. Bullinger concludes with discussions of prayer, the sacraments, good works, death, and the last judgment. The *Compendium*, considered as a system of theology, presents perhaps the least polemic, most irenic compend of doctrine produced during the Reformation.[6]

Bullinger begins his doctrine of God with a statement concerning the divine self-revelation in Scripture as the basis for his teaching on God and the divine attributes. The link is therefore forged with the preceding chapter and the transition made from what early orthodoxy would call the *principium cognoscendi* to the *principium essendi theologiae*. Scripture teaches what God is, his nature and power, and also his relation to his creatures.[7] These preparatory sections lead to a lengthy affirmation of the trinity and spirituality of God: "Deum unum esse substantia, trinum personis: spiritum immensum."[8] This revelation of the triune God in Scripture relates, moreover, directly to Christ in whom God truly reveals himself to his servants, for it is by reason of Christ that the Word teaches the pure truth of God. Thus we know the truth of the doctrine of the Trinity, which otherwise lies beyond the capability of our minds.[9]

What follows next is a discussion of the attributes of God which reflects the scriptural names and descriptions of the deity without explicit reference to metaphysical or philosophical categories.[10] There is, moreover, no mention here of a divine decree: Bullinger's conception of God's providential care implies no rigid causal structure but rather a sense of the power and life of God undergirding and sustaining all things. In Bullinger's concept, *divina providentia sunt atque moventur*, we encounter a hint, perhaps, of the scholastic sense of God as first mover, but the intention is hardly to propose a series of philosophical distinctions: instead Bullinger gives a brief glimpse of the unstated Aristotelian presuppositions of sixteenth century thought and perhaps of the traditional discipline behind his thought.[11] Similarly, the treatment of sin and fall relates more to the problem of creation in the image of God and re-creation or regeneration in Christ than to problems of God's will and permission.[12]

Rather than immediately presenting election as the cause of man's salvation, Bullinger stresses the covenant of grace. In Book Two of his *Compendium* he comments on the protevangelion of Genesis 3 as the beginning of the covenant.[13] From the moment of man's fall God has willed to redeem him from "the guilt and punishment of sin, from the curse and eternal damnation." These fruits of sin are to be "imputed" to Christ, the "blessed seed," that those who believe in him might obtain "righteousness and life everlasting."[14] Having provided man with this means of escaping the penalties of the fall, God requires him to be obedient and to renounce the devil. The formal beginning of covenant, defined as a two-sided or duopleuric agreement, is, however, with Noah:

> And this is that covenant which in the sacred scriptures God is said to have inaugurated with mankind, which was initiated with Noah, and then renewed with Abraham, set into writing by Moses, and then established and confirmed by Christ. This covenant God has enjoined upon humanity by his laws, as the God who is the God of mankind, who supplies its needs, and who through Christ perfects it and

communicates to it all heavenly blessings: and in turn men must acknowledge this God alone and beyond him none other, must trust, call upon, and adore him alone, must persevere in this faith and in their life observe all his laws.[15]

Whereas Bullinger, more than Calvin, seems to stress the mutual character of covenant and the necessity for obedience in covenant, this stress is not an indication of widely divergent patterns in Reformed theology.[16] Bullinger nowhere intends to disrupt the basic monergism of the Reformed system. Later Reformed writers were able to utilize both the monopleuric and the duopleuric definition within a single system as representative of the two poles of Christian life, salvation by grace and human responsibility.[17] Duopleuric language describes not man's entrance into covenant but his life under the covenant, as implied in the *usus legis normativus*. At this point, distinctions between "Calvinist" and "federal" schools of Reformed thought reduce to structural as opposed to doctrinal divergences: the larger systematic context of Bullinger's *Compendium* makes clear that his view of covenant does not conflict with the *sola gratia* of the decree. Synergism is definitively rejected when Bullinger defines justification as given *gratis* by the grace of Christ to faith and then defines faith, the condition of justification and the source from which all good works flow, as the gift of God.[18]

The center of Bullinger's soteriology is the work done for us in Christ and the prevenient grace in regeneration, which joins us to Christ— Christ, the mediator of the covenant, the one in whom the eternal and the temporal, the divine and the human causality are reconciled by grace alone. Like Calvin, Bullinger resists the impulse to found his Christology formally on the Chalcedonian symbol. The historical effecting of the covenant promise in Christ and the disjunction of dispensations in the one covenant as pointing to Christ provide the shape of the doctrinal exposition. "Men are not justified and saved by the law of Moses, but by the grace of God in Christ."[19] By justification man is "absolved and acquitted in the judgment of God, from the accusation of the law" that his sins might not be imputed to him. In the place of sin, "the righteousness of Christ [is] imputed" to the faithful.[20] The whole of our salvation rests on the love of God which precedes the sending of his Son as the "propitiation for our sins."[21] Bullinger here draws together the themes of covenant and of the imputation of righteousness noted earlier in the discussion of the protevangelion: here we see the promise of God grounded in the propitiatory work of Christ and applied to believers by the forensic imputation of Christ's righteousness and, as demonstrated later in the lengthy discussion of Christ's satisfaction (Liber V, cap. v-vii), the profound historical, indeed *heilsgeschichtlich* thrust of Bullinger's presentation. His concern is with the historical manifestation of God's saving will.

Bullinger sets forth predestination as the bridge between justification by grace alone and Christ, the mediator. Predestination stands, here, in the midst of emphasis on the historical-temporal line of salvation, as the vertical-causal axis of doctrine uniting the infinite and the finite in Christ: it is the immediate corollary of incarnation which stands, in turn, as the nexus of the divine and human, the point of reconciliation eternally designated in the will of God. Bullinger also seems to move in the same direction as Calvin toward a doctrine of the eternal determination of the Son to be the mediator, a development beyond the medieval teaching concerning the predestination of Christ and a development which stresses the Trinity as the ground of doctrinal formulation.[22] The formulation is infralapsarian: God determined from eternity to exercise his grace and to exhibit it to his world through Christ, which is to say that God in eternity foresaw the fall of his creature and therefore also eternally prepared a remedy according to which he ordained his Son to be sent into the world to assume human nature and to restore fallen man.[23]

In Christ, then, is found the means by which salvation becomes possible, the medicine by which the lost world is healed (*medicina qua perditus mundus reparandus erat*), for Christ the Lord was effectively and perfectly (*potenter et perfecte*) instructed in obedience and redemption to the end that nothing requisite to his redeeming work—reparation, reconciliation, redemption, purgation, renovation, and the bestowing of righteousness to life eternal—was lacking.[24] In Christ, which is to say in the Son of the living God and of the Virgin Mary, the fulness of grace and of all heavenly blessings are bestowed on mankind: for he is our mediator, redeemer, king, priest, reconciler and liberator, and, above all, he is the "fulness of our perfection" who "satisfies the divine law" and by reason of his righteousness pleads our cause.[25]

The theme of Christ's satisfaction now becomes, for Bullinger, the dominant soteriological issue, the subject matter for three chapters as he moves from grace and justification, via Christ and the decree, to faith.[26] Without presenting the formal, Anselmic structure characteristic of the Christology of the *Institutes* and several of the later systems, Bullinger has manifested the doctrine of Christ's satisfaction as the historical goal of the covenant promises and as the causal focus of the divine will to save, making Christology hinge on functional concerns and, as with Calvin, modifying the pattern of doctrinal definition away from a purely Chalcedonian Christology "from above." For Christology now serves not only to define the once-for-all entrance of the divine into the human condition but also to anchor the historical dynamic of the system and bind it to the divine saving causality. Bullinger's stress on the satisfaction theory of atonement and the doctrine of the imputation of Christ's righteousness is, of course, a point of continuity with Calvin and Musculus, but his presentation of the concepts in the *Compendium* witnesses to a more rigorous doctrine. Here Bullinger provides a clearer model for later orthodoxy than any of his contemporaries.

Bullinger also adumbrates later theology in his transition from the statement of Christ's work to the doctrines concerning its application. Faith, he argues, is the medium by which fallen humanity receives Christ.[27] All implication of synergism is excluded by Bullinger's initial statements: "faith is not of men, but is the mere gift of God, by the Holy Ghost, which lightens men's minds with his grace and word."[28] Faith is both knowledge and a strong confidence in the saving character of that knowledge: by grace, the heart and mind trust in the promises of God.[29] God is the source, the foundation, and the object of faith. Faith, in turn, can never be human opinion. It is a feeling of God's grace gained through meditation on the articles of belief as conveyed in the Apostle's Creed.[30] Bullinger here demonstrates an ability to draw on scholastic definition while maintaining the mood of an instruction in piety.

Under the *locus* of faith Bullinger approaches the exposition of the Apostles' Creed, a procedure followed by early editions of Calvin's *Institutes* and by the Heidelberg Catechism. Here he states a traditional Nicean doctrine of the person of Christ but under the impact of the historical emphasis on the line of the covenant-promise, presents the view of Christ as mediator according to both natures. Soteriological and covenantal themes enunciated earlier reappear briefly and provide a context for the christological discussion: transition from the credal article concerning creation to the articles dealing with Christ presupposes the history of the promise and the eternal counsel of God.[31] When we confess faith in Christ, we acknowledge him not only as Son of God, Lord, Messiah, redeemer and liberator but also the ground of our hope in and faithful apprehension of promises of God.[32] Christ is the one eternally appointed to redeem fallen creation. He is the divine Son of God who dwells among us, having been made flesh, the "one inseparable person" in whom we confess two natures. Like Calvin, Bullinger argues that the whole Christ, true God and man, is our only mediator and savior.[33]

Although one scholar has gone so far as to develop an analysis of predestination or foreordination as the central theme of Bullinger's theology, it is surely not a prominent feature of the *Compendium*.[34] What we encounter in the *Compendium* is an emphasis on God's eternal gracious purpose in creation, in covenant, in Christ. Covenant, Christology, and therefore the whole soteriological structure are founded on an eternally gracious will.[35] What Bullinger stresses in his doctrinal exposition, however, is not the decree but its execution in time.[36] This distinction he seems to have held in common with his contemporaries as a barrier to speculation concerning the inner life of the Godhead.

The doctrinal structure which stands out as most original in Bullinger's *Compendium* is the definitive establishment of the gracious covenant of God as the ground for our understanding of Christology and soteriology.[37] Bullinger accords to the covenant a position in relation to his doctrine of God much like the position of an infralapsarian doctrine of predestination. Conceived in terms of the salvation of fallen man, of man *creatus et lapsus*, the covenant gives doctrinal structure to the divine preservation and redemption of man in the historic promises of God from the protevangelium of Genesis 3:15, to the promises given to Noah and Abraham, to the promise fulfilled in Christ.[38] The eternal purpose of God is manifest in the covenant promise much in the way that the eternal decree, in later Reformed systems, is manifest in its execution in time. Nevertheless, the covenant is not the sole ground or the central structure of Bullinger's theology. It points to and is fulfilled in the work of Christ.[39]

The Second Helvetic Confession
In turning from Bullinger's *Compendium* to the *Confessio Helvetica posterior*, we move to his final view on the order and structure of Christian doctrine and to a confessional work that eventually attained a normative status among the Swiss Reformed and that, in its patterns and definitions of doctrine, had considerable impact on the ultimate structure of Reformed theology. The *Confessio* adumbrates the order of later systems in its preliminary focus on scripture as the norm of doctrine, the problem of the interpretation of scripture, and the doctrine of God's unity and trinity (chapters I-III). Following two chapters dealing with right worship (IV and V), Bullinger sets forth the series of providence, creation, the fall and sin, free will, predestination, Christ, law, gospel, repentance and conversion, justification, faith and good works (VI-XVI, inclusively).

The interrelationship of predestination and Christology in Bullinger's *Confessio* develops out of a more pronounced christocentrism and a stronger emphasis on the causality of individual salvation than is found in the *Compendium*. Here the doctrine of predestination appears as a distinct *locus* set into immediate relation to the *loci* concerned with man's sinful condition and to those concerned with the person and work of Christ.[40] Indeed, predestination as formulated in an infralapsarian form becomes the gracious nexus between man's sinful inability and the salvation wrought in Christ. In Barth's classification the *Confessio* belongs to the same general category as Calvin's argument in the 1537 catechism and despite the obvious differences, the 1559 *Institutes* and also the Vermigli-Massonius *Loci communes* of 1576. All these systems "seek to present predestination as the principle and key to the whole doctrine of reconciliation, or soteriology."[41] Here the doctrine of the decree follows immediately upon the doctrine of sin, having been given "precedence over Christology as well as soteriology."[42] Juxtaposition of predestination with sin and the problem of will represents a powerful affirmation of soteriological monergism: human inability answered directly by the electing will of God.

Bullinger's definition is strongly soteriological in its orientation and manifests not only a christological emphasis but also a causal and an epistemological relation to the Christology. This definition is also stated as a doctrine of single predestination which utterly refuses to analyze causally the problem of reprobation. In this Bullinger is distinct from Calvin, Vermigli, and Musculus:

God has from eternity, freely and of his mere grace, without respect to men, predestined or elected the saints, whom he wills to save in Christ. Therefore not without a means, though not according to any merit of ours, but in Christ and according to Christ, has God elected us; those who are engrafted in Christ by faith, these has He elected; those truly are reprobate who are outside of Christ.[43]

Were this passage interpreted as an expression of causal ordering, it might be taken to indicate an election on ground of faith, so intent is Bullinger on stating the identity of the elect with the faithful, of the predestinate with those who are in Christ.[44] Bullinger elsewhere demonstrates his reliance on the principle of salvation by grace alone by defining the repentance that precedes faith as "a mere gift of God and not a work of our strength"[45] and then stating that "faith is a mere gift of God, which God alone of his grace gives to his elect according to his measure, when, to whom, and to the degree he wills."[46] When Bullinger does state the causal order, election appears at the foundation of regeneration, conversion, faith, and justification so that it is all the more striking that he deemphasizes the causal order in his *Confessio* for the sake of manifesting more clearly the christological grounding of election and the universality of God's promises. The sense of causal grounding in God and Christ alone appears in the phrases, *nullo hominum respectu* and *non propter ullum meritum nostrum*, but it can hardly be called emphatic; and the identification of the reprobate as *extra Christum* avoids even the traditional infralapsarian distinction between a positive willing to elect and a negative passing over in reprobation. What Bullinger presses on us is the fact that election relates directly to Christ, whereas reprobation, whatever the causal explanation, is outside of Christ.[47]

Much like Calvin, Bullinger viewed predestination as a hopeful doctrine, a teaching which underscored the sovereign ability of God to effect his saving will. But more than Calvin and like Musculus, Bullinger strove to show the pastoral and positive side of the doctrine in its universal application:

> . . . although God knows who are his, and in places mention is made of the small number of the elect, it is good, however, to hope for all, and not rashly judge any man to be reprobate. Paul says to the Philippians, 'I thank my God for you all' (indeed he speaks to the whole Philippian Church). . . . [48]

The Lord himself, comments Bullinger, set aside rash inquiry into matters of election and exhorted all to seek the kingdom. The doctrine of the decree ought neither to bring about despair nor to conduce to carelessness of the law. As Augustine taught, election and predestination ought to be preached together with admonitions and doctrines concerning salvation.[49]

The christological epistemology sketched out by Bullinger rules out the *syllogismus practicus* and a causal-empirical direction in soteriology: we must, comments Bullinger, "work out our salvation in fear and trembling" (Phil. 2:12), refer to our baptism and engrafting into Christ and attend to the universal promises of God to the faithful (*promissiones Dei . . . universales fidelibus*).[50]

We therefore condemn those who, outside of Christ, inquire whether they are elect and what God has ordained for them from all eternity. For indeed the preaching must be heard and believed: if you believe and if you are in Christ, without a doubt you may consider yourself elect. For the Father has made manifest in Christ his eternal intention of predestination, as the Apostle has declared (II Tim. 1). Therefore the magnitude of the Father's love toward us as revealed in Christ ought to be taught and examined before all things. . . . For Christ is the mirror in whom we may contemplate our predestination.[51]

For Bullinger, as for Calvin, Christ is the mirror, the *speculum* in which we see reflected our own election. The concept of Christ as *speculum praedestinationis nostrae* in the chapter on predestination finds its christological analogue in the very first phrases of Bullinger's discussion of the Savior:

Even so we believe and we teach that the Son of God, our Lord Jesus Christ, was from eternity predestined or foreordained by the Father to be the savior of the world; and we believe him to be begotten not only when he assumed flesh of the virgin Mary, nor only before the foundations of the world, but before all eternity, and that, ineffably, of the Father.[52]

The predestination of Christ here assumes formal prominence. So crucial is it to Bullinger's point that it is placed on a par, structurally, with the eternal generation of the Son. And the juxtaposition occurs in such a way as to imply the designation of Christ as savior according to both natures.

The theme of the predestination of Christ, moreover, serves to place the very traditional person/work Christology that follows into the context of the economy of salvation.[53] This being said, however, it must be emphasized that the Christology of the *Confessio helvetica posterior* is formulated almost entirely in terms of the patristic norms of doctrine. Bullinger defines the fulness of Christ's divinity against Arius, the fulness of his humanity against Apollinaris, and the union of natures in one person without confusion against Nestorius and Eutyches. "Therefore we hardly teach that the divine nature in Christ suffered, or that Christ is still in this world according to his human nature, by way of being ubiquitous."[54] This distinction of natures, according to Koch, is the "essential issue" (*Kernproblem*) of Bullinger's Christology, which Bullinger maintained not only here and in the *Compendium* but also in an explicit polemic against the Lutheran, Brenz: for Bullinger the redemptive work of Christ and the continuing unity with the church, his body, was grounded in the reality of Christ's humanity and the eternal union of Christ's human nature, in its integrity, with his divine nature.[55]

Much like the order we will find in Musculus' *Loci communes*, the message of scripture as completed in the Gospel of Christ provides the point of transition between the objective ground of salvation accomplished by Christ and the application of that salvation in repentance, conversion, and justification.[56] This structure stands in contrast to the pattern of Calvin's *Institutes* where the trinitarian, credal structure of doctrine places the doctrine of the Holy Spirit prior to the explication of the *ordo salutis*. Whereas in Calvin's system and in those systems that follow its pattern (as, for example, Bucanus' *Institutiones*), the order of salvation has a pneumatological as well as a christological and causal foundation, in Bullinger's system the role of the Spirit carries less emphasis. The causal relation established by the decree between the temporal economy of revelation and redemption centered upon Christ and the individual's place in the redemptive process becomes the primary systematic interest.

2. MUSCULUS' LOCI COMMUNES[57]

Wolfgang Musculus (1497-1563) was a highly reputed exegete and theologian nearing the end of his career when in 1560 he compiled and published his *Loci*. Musculus intended to write not a system of piety but a scripturally sound guide to the various theological topics ranging from the doctrine of God to the doctrines of man and the church. Scholastic influences are more easily detected here than in the work of Calvin or of Bullinger,[58] though Musculus frequently modifies or rejects the older theology. He views as useless such topics as the character of God's will toward men of no religion or the logical problem of approaching the divine will.[59] Nevertheless, he pays careful attention not only to problems of divine causality explained in traditionally Aristotelian fashion, but also to the argumentation of the scholastics, Occam in particular. Elsewhere, Musculus cites Scotus, Lombard, and Biel.[60]

In addition, Musculus' exegetical method, akin to Bucer's rather than to Calvin's, manifests a link between the dogmatic side of medieval exegesis and the *locus* method frequently adopted by the Protestant scholastics. While Musculus was concerned with the meaning of the text, he was also interested in eliciting from the text the substance of doctrinal determinations or in clearing away, by means of the interaction of logic with textual problems, seeming contradictions in Christian doctrine. He therefore frequently elaborates lengthy dogmatic excurses, as in the massive commentaries on Isaiah and Matthew.[61] Indeed, Musculus, more than his immediate contemporaries in the Swiss Reform, manifests a certain consciousness of system-building. More than they, he will state his organizational principles, give the reason he formulates doctrine in a particular way, the rationale for his placement of a *locus* within his system.

The series of *loci* that provide the content for Musculus' doctrine of predestination and of Christ is significant for its order and organization: covenant, grace, redemption, incarnation, the Gospel of Christ, scripture, ministry, faith, election, repentance, justification, good works, forgiveness. As with Bullinger the doctrine of covenant serves as the transition point from the historical order of man's sin to the historical order of divine grace breaking in upon and redeeming man's sin. It provides, therefore, the context of divine grace in which the historical work of salvation in Christ and also the historical application of that work in the individual will occur. The other pivotal points in this series are Christology and predestination or, in Musculus' historico-soteriological perspective, incarnation and election. We note also that Musculus' pronounced interest in the doctrine of the divine attributes and specifically in the attributes of power and will did not lead to any deemphasis of the soteriological relation of the doctrine of election: it is noted at many places in these *loci* and elaborated only in the exposition of the *ordo salutis*.

Redemption, Incarnation and the Eternal Counsel

Musculus' Christology, like that of Calvin and Bullinger, develops out of a discussion of the testaments, of the covenant, and of the grace of God.[62] It is contained in two heads, the redemption of mankind and the incarnation of the Word. Musculus first distinguishes between the general and special covenant. The former pertains to God's care of the whole earth.[63] The latter is God's agreement with "the elect and believing," which is first manifest in the promise to Abraham and to his descendants in faith.[64] The special covenant is eternal in God, eternal in its victory over death, and eternal in the power according to which it is set forth.[65] It may be argued against this view that there are, in addition to the covenant made with Abraham, the covenant of law made with Moses and the new covenant or testament made in Christ. These three covenants represent the times or seasons of world history.[66] But this temporal dispensation of covenant in no way represents a disruption of the eternal saving will: the underlying dynamic of Musculus' theology identifies the oneness of God's gracious will throughout its several dispensations in terms drawn from the classic Pauline text, Ephesians 4:3-6, ". . . one body and one Spirit . . . one Lord, one faith, one baptism, one God and Father of all . . . ," as a volitional unity resting upon the triunity of God and the union of the elect with God in Christ.

> There are three principal times which embrace the whole world: the first which was before the law, the second under the law, the third after the law. Then also there are three designated persons, the leaders of the separate times, Abraham, Moses, Christ. And each time had its own dispensation of religion, which is called in scripture *berith*, i.e., *pactum* or *foedus*. It does not follow, however, that there are three substantially distinct covenants (*foedera*) as far as the salvation of mankind is concerned. There is one God and Father of all, who is above all and through all and in all. There is one Lord, savior and redeemer of all, Christ Jesus; one Holy Spirit; one kingdom of the elect and blessed prepared since the beginning of the world; one grace of heavenly calling; one faith; one hope of life eternal; there is one body, one people, and one universal church of the elect properly so-called, which from the beginning of the world to its end embraces all the elect and the faithful: and (thus) there is a single and perpetual covenant of God with the elect in all things firm and sure, and there is one ongoing worship (*pietas*) and justification of believers. Truly, the dispensation of this one covenant, grace, faith, church,

religion and worship is not one and perpetual: rather it has been instituted in several ways and according to the quality of the times by the counsel of the divine wisdom.[67]

The covenant in both the Old and the New Testaments, Musculus asserts, springs from the free and eternal grace of God. Thus, in the examination of God's grace, thought turns to "the purpose of the eternal covenant" and ultimately to the graciousness of the divine nature.[68] Following a critical analysis of late medieval scholastic teaching on grace, Musculus comes to his own definition: grace is the ground of redemption, "the purpose of the will of God, from which the whole dispensation of our redemption flows forth (*profluxit*)."[69] This definition stands as the source of correct distinctions concerning divine grace: grace is either "proponing" or "operating"—"gratiam hanc Dei dividendam esse in proponentem & operantem," the former referring to God's eternal decree to send his Son as savior into the world and the latter to the creation of man in the image of God, the plan of salvation in Christ, the establishment of the covenants with man, and the private working of grace in the hearts of the elect; the former to the will which was in God before the constitution of the world, the latter to the working-out of that will in all dispensations of the covenant.[70]

Intentionally, then, Musculus strips away scholastic distinctions between the prevenient grace that creates free choice, the habit of grace that follows as the condition for divine acceptation, and the cooperating grace that works sanctification—intentionally, because in the gap created by his excision of the scholastic categories, he inserts his own distinction between proponing and operating grace.[71] The larger categories proposed by Musculus stand in a positive relation to the nominalist distinction between *potentia dei absoluta* and *potentia dei ordinata*, whereas the categories rejected are precisely those proposed by Biel as belonging to the *potentia ordinata* and representing the synergistic pole of the doctrine of grace.[72] Musculus retains the nominalist perspective but affirms, within that perspective, not only the sovereignty of God *de potentia absoluta* but also the sovereignty of divine grace *de potentia ordinata*, a soteriological monergism. The structure is of considerable interest because of its affinity both with Bullinger's systematic emphasis on covenant and grace and with Calvin's use of the distinction between the eternal decree and its execution in time.

In treating next of the redemption of mankind, Musculus makes explicit the crucial distinction between decree and execution, eternal ground and temporal work of salvation. The language here is an exact reflection, a mirror image, of the language employed by Musculus at the beginning of the *locus* on grace: there we move from the temporal dispensation of covenant to its ground in the eternal grace of God "ut post rivum ad ipsum fontem accedentes"; now in moving from grace to redemption, we proceed from eternal foundation to execution, "a fonte salutis nostrae progredi ad illius rivum, hoc est, a consilio divinae gratiae ad opus illud ab aeterno praedestinatum"—"from the fountain of our salvation proceeding to its river, that is, from the counsel of divine grace to its eternally predestined work."[73] Musculus thus uses the distinction between eternal and temporal, the ontological, epistemological and soteriological *non capax* addressed to finite and fallen man as the pivotal issue in the description of redemption in Christ. Christ, as the fulfillment in time of the eternal gracious covenant, represents to us the resolution of the distinction, the merciful *capax* of God assuming flesh in order to perform in the office of the mediator.

Musculus moves from his discussion of grace to his analysis of the work and person of Christ: *De redemptione generis humani* (cap. 17) and *De incarnatione verbi Dei* (cap. 18). Christ's work precedes the traditional description of incarnation as *assumptio carnis* in Musculus' order of discussion. As in Calvin's system we here encounter the person of the mediator, in the historical line of the covenant, as the God-man who alone can perform the work of redemption that has been ordained from eternity.[74]

Incarnation, as the temporal focus of the work of redemption, provides for Musculus' system the necessary nexus between the vertical axis of divine causality, the electing will of God, and the historical axis of human history, the life of mankind in covenant and under grace. Christ's coming in the flesh and his historical work, accomplished according to the eternal plan of God, provide both the fulfillment of the historical course of the covenant and, as fulfillment, the sum of the scriptural message, the Gospel.

This interpretation of the order of Musculus' *Loci* as focused on the christological exposition is confirmed by Musculus' comments on the genealogy of Matthew, chapter one. On one level, the confession of belief in Jesus as the Christ stands in contrast to the generations of Abraham, Isaac, and Jacob as a religion greater than that of the Jews and not simply a continuation of the line and faith of ancient Israel: now is revealed a promise of redemption to all mankind given in Christ, *servator noster*. As our *servator* Christ is sent by the Father, anointed by the Spirit and has, by the reconciliation accomplished in his blood, prepared the way for us to our eternal heavenly country (*coelestia nos & perpetua patriae nostrae*).[75] Juxtaposition of the historical series of past generations with the hope of the future life in Christ leads Musculus to seek the foundation of the historical dispensation in the eternal counsel of God. The high counsel of God has been accomplished in the promise given to Adam in paradise and then subsequently to Abraham and then to David to the end that Christ's coming also be recognized by us as belonging to the *consilium Dei*.[76]

Musculus, like Calvin, poses the question of the necessity of Christ's redemptive work. He sees a real danger in saying that Christ *must* perform this work since such an answer implies that redemption is somehow man's due— such an answer negates the grace of God.[77] Christ's work must rather be seen to flow freely from the eternally given grace of God, from the eternal counsel of God.[78] Nevertheless, just as the eternal counsel provided the ground for the historical economy of the covenant, so does it here provide the foundation for the historical work of the mediator in the line and as the fulfillment of covenant. So emphatic is Musculus' stress on the historical line of the effecting of God's salvation as a determinant for his soteriological structure that the doctrine of the atonement now receives full development prior to formal examination of the person of Christ. In the work of redemption, he argues, the incarnate Word pays a ransom to God the Father and breaks the power of sin and Satan. This ransom is the self-offering of the mediator as a sacrifice for man's sin, according to his priesthood. Atonement by sacrifice makes possible the union of man with God in and through Christ. Following the Anselmic argument closely, Musculus states that the destruction of the power of Satan in no way involves payment to Satan, who is ever beneath the power of God, but must be a payment made to God himself that he might be reconciled with mankind and in the reconciliation destroy the hold of evil.[79]

Musculus'doctrine of Christ's person appears next, viewed from the perspective of Christ's work. The economy of salvation clearly controls the order of the *loci*; we have moved from covenant, to the eternal gracious intention of God, to the "redemption of the human race" (cap. 17) in which the theory of atonement is outlined and then, via the work of Christ to the "incarnation of the Word of God" (cap. 18). But, equally significantly, the economy is defined by the vertical axis of gracious willing, manifest in the Word assuming flesh.[80] Musculus introduces here an Augustinian question he shares with Vermigli that resolves in terms of the underlying dynamic of his system the consistency of the divine will and intention with its execution in time. Scripture, notes Musculus, does not say "Et Deus caro factus est" but "Et verbum caro factum est." The term *Deus* would indicate the whole Godhead, but the text of Scripture specifically refers to the person of the Word and, therefore, raises the question of why the Word or Son and not the Father or the Spirit was incarnate. The question arises in an Augustinian context where the language of trinity tends away from subordination of the Son toward an emphasis on essential equality and essential unity.

By way of answer, Musculus states a series of standard arguments: the restoration of the world was to be accomplished by wisdom (and the Word is the divine wisdom); the Son who "is from another" was more fittingly incarnate than the unoriginate Father; the one who was Son in his divinity became also son in his humanity—an act more fitting (*conveniens*) than one becoming son in his humanity who was something other in his divinity. These answers, even if correct, do not satisfy Musculus, who compares the problem, as stated, to the problem of three girls sharing the same dress. The answer must press more deeply into the nature of redemption as the reason for incarnation, into the relation of the eternal word to the temporal person of the mediator and of the eternal will of God to its execution in time:

> . . . the three persons of the holy triad effect this work of incarnation, but only one truly puts on the flesh. . . . It appears to me that neither the Father nor the Spirit but the word must be incarnate, not only because he is Son in his divinity or because the world was formed by him: but for this most telling reason, that the Word is the

counsel of God itself, the decree coeternal with the Father concerning the salvation of mankind, in whom our redemption was eternally predestined, in whom we are elect unto adoption as sons of God, as stated in Ephesians chapter one. Wherefore the whole work of our redemption could not be accomplished but by this Word: which neither can nor will diverge from the eternal predestination of the will of God.[81]

Musculus, like Calvin, has a sense of the eternal determination within the life of the Godhead of the Son or Word for the work of redemption. The work of redemption cannot diverge from God's eternal predestination precisely because the work of redemption is grounded in the intra-trinitarian relations of the persons who, as one God, decree salvation eternally both in its ends and its means. This trinitarian argumentation also implies a conception of limited atonement which rests on the divinity of Christ; for Christ, as true God, must be of the same intention in the work of salvation as is the Godhead in its eternal plan.

Musculus also dealt with the election of Christ, the other pole of the interrelationship of the doctrines of Christ and the decree. The Greek of Matthew 12:18 Musculus renders, "Ecce puer meus quem elegi in quo sibi bene complacuit anima mea," generating the dogmatic problem of the election of the Son. He notes that the Hebrew original of Matthew's citation would produce "servus meus" (Is. 42:1). This point in fact leads Musculus to the crucial doctrinal issue: how can the Son of God be viewed as subordinate not only as elect of God but also as servant of God? "It is not improper that Christ is called by the prophet servant of God, since this is said not of his divine nature and majesty, but of the human dispensation, as not of the form of God but of the form of a servant which he has assumed, as Paul testifies (margin: Phil. 2)."[82] He is the servant of God not as if he ministers to God but insofar as he ministers to others, having been called as Apostle (Heb. 3:2) and *nuncius magni consilii.*[83]

The election of Christ, therefore, "is referred not to his sonship but to the dispensation of our salvation."[84]

> Thus, as he is son of God, he is not elect, but as servant, emissary, and Apostle of God, sent into this world for our redemption. And it is not improper for the Father to refer to the Son as elect for the sake of obedience to a unique office. In this manner the prophets call Christ elect of God. . . . And I Peter 2 (v. 4) calls him the stone elect by God.[85]

The election of Christ, then, refers both to his assumption of humanity, the form of a servant, and to his office in redemption for the accomplishment of which his servant condition was requisite. Christ is truly the head of the elect, the *caput electorum.*[86]

Musculus' doctrine of election

In almost scholastic fashion, Musculus sets forth the order of the questions within his chapter on election: "Quid sit esse electum, Sitne electio Dei, quotuplex sit, quando, quo respectu, in quo: quos, quales, et ad quid elegerit: et postremo, an aliquos reprobarit."[87] Scripture, comments Musculus, contains two separate usages: first, the connotation of a choice of one thing or person out of a group of others and second, the distinction of someone or something as excellent. The second meaning of election does not apply to the doctrine, but only the first: "Thus, by the elect of God we mean those who are chosen by him out of all the multitude of mortals, according to his special counsel."[88] The next topic simply clarifies the first: election is truly of God. Scripture has testified in many places not only that God can but that he does choose some men for himself and that his choice, as the choice of the creator and disposer of all things, is utterly just.[89]

Musculus next recognizes three distinct elective wills of God: the election of men to salvation, the election of the nation of Israel, and the election of ministers. The issue before him in this particular *locus* is, however, the first of the series only, election to salvation.[90] The fourth of the questions concentrates on election to salvation and the time of election:

> The Apostle readily expressed this particle (i.e., quando), saying, Who chose us before the foundation of the world (Eph.1). And yet, before the world was made, no mortal man existed. He chose us therefore as not yet existing: and that only so that the elect might have no occasion to boast.[91]

Thus, election is the appointment of men to salvation prior to their earthly existence, prior to birth—and is, consequently, a doctrine of great assurance to God's people: God surely will not cast us off, now that we exist, if beforehand he has so graciously chosen us.[92] Even so, the last of the elect to be born into the world is no less graciously chosen than the first, and the body of the elect, the church, like the individual elect of God, rests firm and unassailable because of God's election.[93] The fall, moreover, does not appear to be included in Musculus' conception of the eternal counsel of God.[94]

Musculus next raises the issue of foreknowledge and predestination. There is a danger to right understanding if the terms are not carefully distinguished: God not only foreknows the elect, he also predestines them. All things predestinated by God are also foreknown, but, clearly, there are things within the foreknowledge of God that God does not predestinate. We may thus understand that God foreknows evil and yet is not its cause.[95] Musculus, then, allows place for the divine permission and formulates his doctrine with less causal rigor than does Calvin.

In what respect has God chosen those who are his? Musculus begins by noting the multitude of reasons for human choice—beauty, profit, quality—and by distinguishing human from divine choice. For God elects us as not yet existent. Beyond this, the foreknowledge God has of us as individuals manifests us all as children of wrath and unworthy of his choice.[96] The argument, significantly, despite the stress on the eternity of the divine counsel, is infralapsarian. Nor can we claim, continues Musculus, that God chose us because of a foreknowledge of godliness and obedience: all the good that resides in us results from his grace as the fruit of election. Lombard rightly argues that the choice is of God's free mercy and that grace is not given on account of faithfulness but for the production of faithfulness.[97]

Since we are elect in respect of no quality in ourselves, we must seek out the reason for our election in God alone. As scripture states, we are chosen according to the divine good pleasure (*beneplacitum*): it would therefore be improper to seek out the cause more fully. We cannot penetrate to a "cause of the causes" (*causarum istarum causae*).

> Therefore we must consider the certainty of our election and salvation, in that it is grounded on his good pleasure, will and purpose, whose will is most free, interest and right most high over all things, truth immutable, pleasure steadfast forever, purpose most effectual, and power subject to no impediment. In addition, this agrees with the nature of the divine goodness, the proper nature of which is to have mercy and to do good to men. . . . Wherefore it is impossible that our election, accomplished according to his pleasure, will and purpose, could change or be set aside.[98]

In the sixth section of his *locus*, Musculus comes to the question, "in whom are we elect?" and therefore to the christological focus of his doctrine. We are obviously not elect in and of ourselves, for we deserve no such mercy; the choice resides in the will and purpose of God (*voluntatis ac propositi Dei*) and rests temporally on the *medium* in which we were constituted as the elect prior to the foundation of the world.[99] Musculus now raises pointedly, in a contrast between election and reprobation, the issue of mediation: election is not merely a positive choice but a communion, reprobation not merely a negative choice but an exclusion from communion. Thus election requires a mediator between God and man who assures the communion of elect man and electing God.[100] Reprobation, by contrast, stands as immediate or unmediated, finding its remote cause in the divine non-election but its immediate cause in the sinful inability of humankind. These considerations lead Musculus to argue, much as he did in his Christology, indeed, in a nearly identical construct, that the eternal creative Word is also the mediator of election.[101] Election, therefore, can be defined as God's choice in Christ and on account of Christ of some men to salvation and, by extension, God's eternal appointment of Christ to be the mediator and head of the elect.[102]

> Wherefore we must consider this mystery of our election, not by halves or piecemeal, but as a whole, but with its components joined fully together, and with a full and firm faith, with devotion, honor, and gratitude in Christ our mediator, head and savior: and for the confirmation and certitude of our salvation consider in our hearts, how our election, with the mystery of Christ, rests and subsists upon the eternity and the counsel of God.[103]

These final words of assurance lead Musculus to a lengthy disquisition on the subjects "whom God has chosen" and "what sort of persons God elects." He is careful to note that human perception cannot distinguish the elect from the reprobate nor can the elect know one another. Rather than pursue the question, we ought to assume all the faithful to be elect.[104] And when we would seek out our own election, we must follow the same guide: we know our election by our faith in Christ, by Christ in us, and by the inward testimony of the Spirit. "I ask," says Musculus, "what more certain testimony could there be of the grace of election and adoption, than the Spirit of God himself?"[105] The faithful Christian recognizes the Spirit within him in the grace of adoption and from this infers redemption and eternal salvation. This great consolation in the doctrine of election and assurance gives the lie to all who would not preach this doctrine to the church.[106] Even so, recognition that the elect are distinguished only by their justification in Christ sets aside all glorying in the flesh and points believers to the grace of God in Christ the mediator: the elect, like all men, are born in sin and under condemnation. The doctrine of election, therefore, defines for us a salvation by grace alone.[107]

The purpose of God's election relates, for Musculus, to our creation *ad imaginem ac similitudinem Dei*, for in the very creation of man, the creature was destined for the blessedness accomplished in the elect through Christ.[108] Here, as with Calvin, we may see a remnant of the Scotist sense of the priority of incarnation over sin; we also see both here and in the view of the elect as *nondum existentes*, a supralapsarian tendency linked to christological and soteriological concepts. The divine purpose must be considered in two ways: relative to God and relative to man. God elects us for the sake of manifesting the glory of his grace and for the sake of our eternal felicity. In short, we are chosen to become the children of God and partakers of a heavenly inheritance by reason only of the incomprehensible grace of God.[109]

In the final section of his discussion Musculus comes to the doctrine of reprobation. This topic ought not to shroud the grace of election in darkness. It is best to follow the pattern of the Apostle in praising God's election and speaking but little of reprobation.[110] Nevertheless, the very fact of God's election manifests the fact of reprobation: there are elect and non-elect. On this point Musculus turns to Lombard for definition:

> He predestinated those whom he elected, the rest he truly reprobated. Thus, he reprobated whom he would, not because of future merits, but for a most righteous truth far removed from our comprehension. We do not call those reprobate who are reprobate for an inward evil of their nature, or who are apart from the true and good . . . but those whom God rejects or reprobates when he elects those whom he will.[111]

The reprobate are simply those who do not obtain the grace of election. All, considered in themselves, are sinful and deserving of reprobation.[112] Like Calvin, Musculus refers the universalist passages of Scripture to all classes of men rather than to the whole of mankind: the only alternative to this interpretation is the assumption that God's will is ineffective or void.[113]

This definition accords also with the Augustinian definition of free will set forth by Musculus in an earlier *locus*.[114] Man, the servant of sin, cannot stand firmly in godliness unless his will and faculties are regenerated by God.[115] The utter graciousness of this deliverance demonstrates the need to distinguish between man before the fall and man after the fall, the children of the world and the children of the kingdom of God, the faithful and the unfaithful, the corrupt and the regenerate, the elect and the reprobate.[116] Regeneration and the freedom to do good are properly the work of Christ.[117] The problem of free will is resolved only in "the analogy of faith and the simplicity of the Holy Scriptures."

> Faithful men do not dispute of the secret counsels of God . . . , of the necessity of the prescience and providence of God, of destiny and chance occurrence: whose labyrinth let him that is wise diligently eschew in this matter . . . but they look unto only this sign in this case, that they may know the corruption of mankind in Adam, and the restoration which is by Christ, to their profit and to the glory of the grace of God.[118]

Much like Calvin, therefore, Musculus can assert that examination of the labyrinth of the decree or counsel of God, when severed from faith and scripture, can only darken the truth and trouble the conscience.

Musculus' meditation on the problem of human will serves to locate one element of the systematic or doctrinal foundation of election in the human predicament—what Mozley described as the basic Augustinian motive toward formulation. Nevertheless Musculus also reflects, without disturbing this pattern, the scholastic analysis of predestination according to its causal ground, the will of God. He appears more consistently supralapsarian than Calvin but no less christocentric. What strikes us is Musculus' readiness to discuss will as an attribute of God but, coincident with this, his ability to forestall any attempt to relate the divine willing as such directly to individual salvation: the *voluntas Dei* understood in the primary sense as divine good pleasure or benevolence toward us (*beneplacitum vel benevolentia Dei erga nos*) is manifest as mediated in Christ. It is the will of God that those who believe his Son will have life eternal.[119]

The *benevolentia Dei erga nos* as "exhibited" in Christ appears, moreover, as universal in its reference. Musculus interprets the text of Ephesians 1:4-5 as a gracious support of weak consciences. When conferred with other texts concerning the work of salvation (John 3:16; 6:40 and Romans 8:31ff.) the declaration of God's predestining will, "this divine benevolence toward us in Christ is manifest as universal."[120] Not for perturbation then, but for consolation of the pious spirit, are these revelations of election, for we are elect in Christ and Christ himself is the moving cause of election (*Christum faciens electionis causam*).[121] Similarly, in his comments on I Timothy 2:5-6, Musculus stresses the sufficiency of redemption for all without pressing the issue of efficiency for the elect only.[122]

Musculus' central interest, throughout his several meditations on the divine will, has been to emphasize the gracious revelation of that will in Christ. This means that the metaphysical or causal side of the doctrine deriving from the scholastic formulation in no way detracts from the christological center of Musculus' teaching. Indeed, Christ is manifest at the center of both the horizontal or economical and the vertical or causal patterns in the redemptive process. If any one doctrinal concern can be cited as the basis for this balance it must be Musculus' concern for the relation of Christ's divinity to the question of Christ's election in particular and of the elective will of God in general, insofar as this concern seeks out a higher ground for predestination than the divine will, the only ground which could be higher, the being of God as trinity.

3. VERMIGLI'S LOCI COMMUNES[123]

Despite their late date the *Loci communes* of Peter Martyr Vermigli (1500-1562) belong more to the systematic ground of Reformed theology than to the beginnings of orthodoxy. Vermigli's earliest published work dates from the time of his lectureship at Oxford (1547-1553). His mature work belongs to the period of Calvin's, Bullinger's, and Musculus' productivity. The collection of commonplaces or *loci communes* out of Vermigli's lectures, treatises, and disputations was posthumous (1576). The compiler and editor of the *Loci*, Robert Masson, used Calvin's *Institutes* of 1559 as his model.[124] Masson himself added new material in a second edition (1583) and the translator of the English edition (also 1583) noted that he had "placed some certaine things in a more exquisite order" and had "heaped more matter of Commonplace out of Master Vermigli's Commentaries than did Massonius."[125]

Following Massonius' organization, the second book of the *Loci communes* presents Christ the Redeemer first as he "appeared to the fathers" under the Law and then as he is given in the Gospel.[126] All mankind is corrupt in Adam. From the very beginning of the human race grace is mediated. An essential unity of promise binds the testaments together, though the promise is given clearly and fully only in Christ. The third book analyzes the "causes and general means" by which we receive the grace of Christ. The fourth and final book deals with the outward means of grace, the church and the work of the Holy Spirit in Word and Sacrament.[127]

Although the topics of Vermigli's third book are congruent with those of Book III of Calvin's *Institutes*, Massonius' order represents a somewhat rationalized structure. In moving from predestination to calling, faith, hope, adoption, justification, Christian liberty, patience in affliction, prayer, and eternal life the *Loci communes* follow the causal pattern of the *ordo salutis*. The effect of Massonius' order here is to emphasize the relationship already present in Vermigli's thought between Christology and election and to manifest as entirely gracious the relationship of believers to Christ. The divine counsel here provides, in Barth's words,

> the climax of that activity which begins with the gracious God and is completed in sinful man. In it we look backwards from God's electing and man's election to Christ Himself, the basis of the salvation which God has wrought. And in it we

look forward to the status of the Christian and to the church where this salvation is applied to and avails for us.[128]

Among later systems not only the *De oeconomia foederum* (1693) of Hermann Witsius (which Barth notes) but also the *Medulla s.s. theologiae* (1623) of William Ames follow this pattern.

This arrangement of doctrine and, specifically, the relation established between Christology and predestination, though clearly not Vermigli's, cannot be said to misrepresent his doctrine. Vermigli's own view of predestination has been characterized, together with that of his contemporaries, as "both Scriptural and Christological in its essential pattern, despite the other emphases that developed in the rationale of the sixteenth century polemic."[129] This reading of the situation by J. C. McClelland has been recently confirmed by J. P. Donnelly who adds to his appraisal the accurate and pointed comment, referring to Walter Kickel's analysis of Beza, "Martyr's treatment suggests that Aristotelianism and a christocentric theology are not quite so antithetical as Kickel imagines."[130]

Christology in the Vermigli-Massonius Loci Communes

The initial argument of this chapter was culled by Massonius from a doctrinal *locus* on II Samuel 7:18—on the problem of God coming among men. God comes to us, comments Vermigli, in many ways, but he comes *proprie tamen & singulariter* as the Son of God in human nature for the salvation of mankind. This temporal presence of one of the persons of the indivisible Trinity generates the problem of the relation of God as Trinity to the incarnation:

> For if indeed God is everywhere, we nevertheless say he came, for he took human nature: and thus we say that he came to us and presented himself to us, the Father, the Son, and the Holy Spirit. For if indeed the works of the trinity which are inward are also singular—such as to generate, to spirate, and to proceed—these indeed are done by the divine power which is common to the three persons; however those (works) which pertain to externals, are indivisible. How then, you ask, is the Son alone said to be incarnate?[131]

In approaching an answer, Vermigli divides the question in good scholastic fashion into two categories, *actio* and *opus*, for clarification. Scripture describes the *actio*, the action, of the sending of the Son as belonging to the Father and the Spirit: "efficiens enim causa & actio, ad tres personas pertinuit." For not only the Father and the Spirit, but the Son also was the cause of his coming: although the thought is difficult, adds Vermigli, the Son is both the cause and the effect.[132] Nevertheless, the *opus*, the work of incarnation, pertains to the Son alone, because the Son alone assumed human nature and human nature is conjoined only with the hypostasis of the Son (*coniuncta est cum sola hypostasi filii*). When Scripture refers to the incarnation, death, and resurrection, it shows Christ as both cause and effect, and the work performed as pertaining solely to the Son as incarnate.[133]

As in Calvin's Christology we begin to see here a structure in which the Son considered as God is equal but as mediator is subordinate to the Father. Vermigli's distinction, like Calvin's, rests on a trinitarian structure and looks to Augustinian teaching on the Trinity and Christ as its source.[134] As Hagenbach pointed out, the concern for divine unity which must view all works of God *ad extra* as works of the entire Trinity, to the point of emphasizing the triune character of Old Testament theophanies and of the incarnation itself, is a characteristic of the Augustinian trinitarian-christological paradigm.[135] In addition, this Augustinian view of the Godhead and its manner of working exerts a systematic pressure toward formulation of a trinitarian ground of all doctrine and specifically toward description of the intra-trinitarian relationship which grounds the triunity of all *ad extra* relations of the divine persons as they enact the economy of salvation.

The composite nature of the *Loci communes* becomes all too apparent as Massonius extracts a doctrine of the two natures from Vermigli's commentary on Romans 9:3-5. The section consists in a massive concatenation of verses proving the humanity and divinity of Christ and hardly can be utilized as a guide to a definitive Vermiglian Christology, but the language of the initial argument is remarkably like Calvin's in its concentration on the historical God-man: "Paul in Romans 9, presents an excellent commendation of Christ, where he confesses two natures conjoined in the same person, so that Christ is constituted out of both."[136]

A fuller exposition of the hypostatic union is found in Vermigli's dialogue on the two natures of Christ and in his exposition of the Creed, the latter alone being included in the several editions of the *Loci communes*. "We are constrained," argues Vermigli, "to confess (as faith itself testifies to us), that this Christ is none other than one person in whom the divine and human nature are indissolubly united."[137] This definition, which presents Christ as the historical God-man, rather than follow the strict pattern of Christology "from above," carries over into Vermigli's comments on John 1:14 that follow immediately as the basic christological text: "By the terms Word and Flesh, he (the Evangelist) means nothing other than that these two natures, namely God and man, are perpetually associated in the person of Christ."[138] "Flesh," Vermigli adds, indicates the whole of human nature: and scripture testifies in a multitude of places not only to the verity of Christ's humanity but also to the truth of his divinity. Vermigli's Christology here also follows a Reformed rather than a Thomist pattern, refusing to separate the concepts of person and work and considering the person of Christ only in connection with his historical manifestation.[139] The central issue addressed is the work of salvation performed by the God-man: in Sturm's words, "What Christ does and suffers is but a representation of that which he is; and that he is both God and man both grounds and effects our redemption."[140] The typical Reformed pattern also appears in a lengthy epistle written by Vermigli from Strassburg in February of 1556 to the church in Poland:

that Christ did not suffer according to his divinity, that he is mediator according to both natures, and that Christ is both Son of God and Son of Man.[141]

Vermigli's discussion of the titles of Christ, like the arguments in his letter to the Polish church, manifests as his central concern the inseparability of the christological topics of person and work. Vermigli begins by defining the name "Jesus" as "savior" and identifying "Christ" as a translation of the Hebrew "*Meschiah*," the one "anointed" like the kings, prophets, and priests of the Old Testament.[142] Even as the unction of men of old to their offices was not an external or symbolic anointing but an inward spiritual gift, so do Christ's anointing and his title as anointed one refer to the fulness of spiritual gifts given to him.[143] In Vermigli's exposition of the Creed, the "double name" of Jesus Christ follows immediately upon the discussion of Christ's two natures: the identification of the God-man provides the meaning of his name. The name "Jesus" indicates the one who "frees the sons of God from their sins and therefore from all evil" whereas "Christ"

> signifies the anointed of God and the sanctified King: which well describes him who by the spirit and the word directs and leads the sons of God to life eternal. Therefore, by reason of the two natures whereof he consists and because of these two names it is easily perceived that the title by which we praise him, Lord, applies to him most perfectly.[144]

A *locus* extracted from the commentary on I Corinthians 15:3 covers the same issues as the next division of the Creed, suffering, crucifixion, death, burial, and resurrection.[145] The death and resurrection of Christ stand as the "two principal and main points" of Christian religion, to which all other issues refer. This statement in itself argues the central emphasis of Reformed theology in the sixteenth century to be soteriological. Vermigli writes,

> Let no one tell me that God might have redeemed the world in another way or that it was not entirely necessary for the salvation of man that the Son of God was affixed to a cross. For once we determine that God is the most wise and just considerer of things, we will acknowledge that his election of the means of salvation most vehemently opposed the nature of sin when he decreed to give over His Son to a most ignominious death, that he might rid his elect of sin.[146]

Two important issues appear immediately: first the question of the necessity of Christ's death, and second the interrelationship of Christology and predestination. Vermigli will have more to say concerning the problem of necessity; here he simply refers to the decree and seems to speak of the mode of salvation as a necessity of the consequence.

Christ's death and resurrection, even as they are the ground of our union with God and belong to us as we are conjoined to Christ, so also do they belong to all those joined to Christ throughout history. Vermigli here argues the centrality of Christ in the history of salvation as manifest in the suffering and deliverance of the people of God. In them in past ages Christ also suffered: indeed, the passion and resurrection of Christ began *a primis usque temporibus* and were manifest in time in Christ himself. Thus the apostles confirm Christ's resurrection with words concerning the deliverance of the Davidic kingdom.[147] This temporal relationship does not in any way deny the uniqueness of Christ's death: the death of the Son of God is the greatest sign of God's love toward us.[148] The specific argument contrasts with the Christologies of Calvin, Bullinger, and Musculus, but in its general systematic implication stands very close to the historical focus they each expressed; for here Christ stands as the nexus in time of the eternal saving will of God and the way of human salvation. Indeed, this argument is consistent with the Reformed view of a complete salvation offered to faith under the old covenant.

It was fitting, argues Vermigli, that something be offered to God which would placate him in proportion to his displeasure over sin either equally or more abundantly (*aut aeque, aut etiam magis placere posset*). Nevertheless, when the question is raised why the death of Christ, as such, was pleasing to God, the answer must be only the greatness of God's love because God might have been contented with any other thing: "Potuisset quidem Deus alia quapiam re contentus esse."[149] Surely God did not derive pleasure from the suffering of his Son, nor was this the only means by which God could declare his mercy; for God is not compelled to do anything.

> If you ask, whether it was necessary that the Son of God die, I answer, there can be no necessity of coaction considered here: nothing indeed is in God by violence. Neither was there a necessity of nature. For although there are many things in the divine nature by necessity: which is to say, that it is one, or three, or that it generates the Son, and similar things, yet it would be wicked to assume that any external effect impose a natural necessity: for that which God does he does freely, and that which he does not do, he freely does not do. Nor do we suppose a necessity according to the proposed end: for man's salvation might have been effected by many other ways and means. But it was necessary that Christ die according to the purpose of the divine providence and counsel: for God decreed it should be so. This indeed he did chiefly to declare his infinite love.[150]

What is significant here is that Vermigli, for all his basic Thomist inclination and training, has, like Calvin, followed a Scotist mode of argument by denying any necessity placed upon God: the work of the mediator, as for Calvin, rests upon the decree, the eternal counsel alone.

In fairly strong contrast to his less-than-Thomist approach to the problem of the necessity of Christ's death, Vermigli took a position on the doctrine of Christ's merit reflective of the Thomist analysis. Whereas Calvin had argued the merit of Christ to be infinite on the ground of the decree, Vermigli pointed to Christ's divine person as the basis for Christ's all-sufficient satisfaction. Here, he even undercuts the argument of Scotists to the effect that God might have acted in another way but chose to follow this particular pattern.[151] The divergence of argument can only be reconciled by referring the former argument strictly to the reason for Christ's death and the latter equally strictly to the value of Christ's satisfaction: that this is the case may be argued from Vermigli's comment in the former passage that Christ's death was either equal to or greater than the divine displeasure, which seems to harmonize with the Thomistic pattern of the latter passage.

Vermigli does not pose as precisely as his contemporaries the problem of the *satisfactio Christi*, but he does state that the sufferings laid upon Christ were "according to the manner and measure of the sin."[152] God might, Vermigli again comments, have reconciled himself to mankind by other means, but this was the only way in which the justice of God might be satisfied.[153] As Isaiah says (53:5), Christ suffered his wounds and afflictions for our sake. We ought also to recognize in Christ just how severely God punishes sin and therefore avoid sin in ourselves: here Vermigli again asserts an exemplar theory of atonement as the lesson to be drawn by his readers.[154] All in all, he contributes little to the development of a strict satisfaction theory. Nor do we find in the Christology of the *Loci communes* a formulation relating to the problem of limited atonement, though in conjunction with Vermigli's doctrine of predestination and its effects, a limited efficiency or application of Christ's work can easily be inferred, particularly in the light of comment cited earlier that God decreed the death of his Son "that he might rid his elect of sin."

Predestination in the Vermigli-Massonius Loci Communes

The work of Vermigli that Massonius selected as the *locus de praedestinatione* serves admirably: it is a systematic treatise written out complete by Vermigli as the dogmatic result of his exegesis of Romans 8:28-9:33 and placed between chapters nine and ten of his commentary on Romans (1558).[155] Vermigli thus had developed his doctrine prior to the publication of Calvin's definitive treatment of predestination in the 1559 *Institutes*. Examination of Vermigli's statement confirms his independence from Calvin. As Donnelly has argued, the more important positive influences upon Vermigli are Aquinas and Scotus among the scholastics with some intensification of the doctrine deriving from Gregory of Rimini and from Martin Bucer among the Reformers.[156] Having ruled out Calvin as a direct influence, we must not forget the substantial doctrinal agreement between Vermigli and Calvin, perhaps because of the influence upon both Calvin and Vermigli of Scotus and Bucer and because of their equally strong rootage in Scripture and in the Augustinian tradition.

Vermigli's treatise on predestination divides into four sections: an exegetically grounded definition of predestination, a discussion of the causes and then of the effects of predestination, and finally, an examination of the decree in terms of its power and force, particularly insofar as it had been attacked as a doctrine of "necessity," subversive of free will and responsibility.[157] In addition to this basic structure of exposition, Vermigli notes two prior problems. First is the idea of an eternal predestination suitable for teaching and preaching—a problem that he discusses in terms of patristic debate, noting particularly the fifth century debate in southern Gaul. Second, if the idea is teachable, the question still must be raised as to whether or not there is a divine predestination. This latter, comments Vermigli, is the "logicians' question"; here we see a hint of the scholastic mentality, the recognition that the topic itself must be established as a valid topic prior to discussion.[158] First, the doctrine of predestination is of great profit, for it teaches godly men to put their trust in God alone.

> For we cannot acknowledge the gifts of God, unless we acknowledge the source that bestows them. The source, indeed, is the free purpose and mercy of God which he has revealed to those elected before the foundation of the world. . . . This doctrine leads men to glory not in themselves but in God.[159]

The doctrine of predestination is obscure and unprofitable to any who would seek out the divine reason for the election of one man and the rejection of another. Nor should anyone refer to the doctrine of predestination when inquiring concerning the propriety of an act. Rather, we ought to seek out God's will as revealed in scripture: predestination is not at all obscure as it is stated in scripture.[160] The anti-speculative thrust of early Reformed doctrine in no way militates against detailed discussion of predestination, election, and reprobation. All should recognize that their being in Christ rests not on their ability but upon God, that they are predestinated to be like the Son of God and ought to live godly lives, and that in knowing this will of God they gain profound assurance of salvation.[161]

Vermigli can now develop the more philosophical side of the objections leveled against predestination: that it is a doctrine of "fatal necessity" (*necessitatem quidem fatalem*) which brings men to desperation.[162] There are two possible constructions that can be placed on the word "fate." The first is pagan and unacceptable to Christians: it indicates an ineluctable influence from the stars which bends both God and man. The other meaning may be held by Christians: that is, here fate refers to the "ordinem causarum, qui Dei voluntate gubernetur."[163] Yet in this latter sense, the heathen term "fate" is improper because this predestination of God that orders all things in no way alters their nature as it relates to necessity and contingency.[164]

The word "predestination" in Greek, *proorismon*, comes from the verb "to determine and appoint before," which itself relates to the noun *oros* or *terminus*. Even so, the elect are said to be divided from the non-elect: "Disterminantur igitur electi a non electis."[165] Just as *destinare* indicates the firm and constant determination of a thing, so does *praedestinare* indicate a firm decree, but in two ways: predestination may refer both to the eternal determination of God "ante iacta mundi fundamenta" or to the present execution (*executionem*) of the decree. Vermigli here restricts his analysis to consideration of the eternal decree or counsel, insofar as the execution is merely the "declaration" of an eternal predestination.[166] In this ultimate and fundamental sense, predestination refers to the divine counsel (*consilium*) which destines or appoints all things so that nothing occurs by chance or fortune: whatever God creates or does implies both a use and an appointed end of that thing.[167]

Although Vermigli would not define election and reprobation as coordinate halves of a double decree and would tend toward a formulation of doctrine much like later infralapsarian formulations, his sense of an overarching divine sovereignty is unquestionable, and he clearly would have repudiated any doctrinal structure in which God was denied utter and complete sovereignty over all things: "neither the wicked, nor the devil himself, nor sins can be excluded from predestination: indeed all of these things are used by God according to the manner that he wills."[168] Even so, the Apostle (Rom. 9:22) calls the wicked "vessels of God, in whom he reveals his wrath" (*vasa Dei, quibus iram patefacit*) and Solomon (Prov. 16:4) states that God has made the wicked for an evil day. Referring to the above argument, he comments,

If then this construction is placed upon predestination, it refers to all things in common. The word would signify nothing other than God's eternal disposition of his creatures to his use. But the sacred scriptures do not frequently use the word except with reference to the elect: though in the fourth chapter of Acts we read (v. 28) 'They gathered to do whatsoever thy hand and counsel had predestined to be done': which words, if they are referred to the death of Christ and the redemption of humanity, do not refer to anything beyond salvation by election. But if they also refer to those who had gathered against the Lord, they comprehend also the reprobate. Now let us judge according to the most frequent usage of scripture. After all, the theologians, the scholastics, speak of the elect alone and not the reprobate as predestinate. And we shall, for the present, follow this opinion—not for the reason which the scholastics adduce, for it is quite weak, as we shall argue further on, but because this is the general usage of scripture. Therefore in this treatise the saints only will be comprehended under the name predestination. For that reason, I judge, Augustine titled his book, *De praedestinatione sanctorum*, which signifies the decree of God by which the saints are appointed to the communion of salvation: reprobation is set as an antithesis to predestination.[169]

Having thus restricted the positive predestinating will of God to the elect and defined reprobation as an antithesis set over against this positive saving will, Vermigli approaches the problem of foreknowledge and predestination. In Romans 8:28, Paul explicitly connects foreknowledge with predestination: in God these things are ultimately the same, comments Vermigli, but we distinguish them for the sake of our understanding. The argument into which Vermigli now moves breathes the air of scholastic distinctions. God's knowledge (*notitia*) extends further than his prescience (*praescientia*), for his knowledge extends not only to past, present, and future but to things which are not and shall not be (*quae nunquam futura sint*), their possibility or impossibility.[170] Prescience or foreknowledge relates only to those things which shall come to pass (*quae futura sint*). Prescience, therefore, requires a will which precedes it, for nothing comes into existence unless God wills it. Nevertheless, not all that God foresees is predestined by him, for he foreknows the reprobate who shall be damned.[171] Vermigli's full definition of predestination goes beyond Calvin and points toward the full-scale description of the *ordo salutis* that we find in early orthodox writers like Ursinus. Vermigli, nevertheless, is not formulating a predestinarian system, but simply manifesting the doctrinal relationships into which the doctrine of predestination moves as exegesis builds into theological *locus* and *locus* points toward system.

> Predestination is the most wise counsel (*propositum*) of God by which he has decreed firmly from before all eternity to call those whom he has loved in Christ to the adoption of sons, to justify by faith; and subsequently to glory through good works, who shall be conformed to the image of God, that in them the glory and mercy of the Creator might be declared.[172]

This definition presses both toward a purely soteriological and essentially infra-lapsarian definition of predestination and toward a discussion of the counsel or purpose of God behind the elective decree, the *propositum Dei*. *Propositum* refers both to predestination and to its antithesis, reprobation. The emphasis of Vermigli's argument, however, falls upon election: Paul in Ephesians declares "nos esse praedestinatos iuxta propositum Dei," and defines the divine purpose as God's "good pleasure" or *beneplacitum*. This good pleasure or purpose stands behind the will of God by which God works that which he has determined in his counsel,[173] yet the primary thrust of the doctrine is with reference to a gracious drawing of the elect out of their misery, the infralapsarian pattern of man con-sidered *creatus et lapsus*:

> Indeed we must remember that the love, election and predestination of God are ordered among themselves and follow on one another for a certain reason. First, all men in their unhappy estate are presented to the knowledge of God, as needy and miserable, then those whom God of his pure and simple mercy loves and for whom he wills the good are distinguished from those he passes over, who are not comprehended within his benevolence: by this discretion they are said to be elect; the elect, truly, are appointed toward their end.[174]

A similar infralapsarian tendency appears in the definition of reprobation. For though sin cannot be considered the cause of reprobation, since reprobation, unlike damnation, is from eternity, nevertheless the reprobate are passed over as fallen and sinful, as sinners unloved by God and sent to a just damnation. Reprobation belongs to the eternal *propositum Dei*, but it refers to the creature as fallen in sin and by nature miserable.[175]

After a lengthy analysis of the concept of necessity in the thought of the "schoolmen," Martyr distinguishes between absolute necessity (*necessitas con-sequentis*) and a necessity of consequence (*necessitas consequentiae*). The will of man, under the will of God and operating within the bounds of man's nature, is subject to a "necessity of consequence" but not of "coaction."[176] Vermigli

here makes a careful distinction between a certainty in the mind of God concerning our bondage in sin coupled with the conjunction of God's predestination
with our unimpeded willing, and an absolute necessity of coaction by which
God does violence, in an external sense, to our wills. He affirms the former but
denies the latter. Man sins freely of his own will. He sins necessarily as a
consequence of the fall, but not by present compulsion.[177] The doctrine set forth
by Martyr follows the basically Augustinian model of Reformed doctrine.

In the saving choice of God, love is prior to election and election prior to
predestination. Those men set apart by the love of God from the mass of mankind
are said to be elect. God's predestination, according to Martyr, is the purpose
of God under which God has decreed to call those whom he has loved in Christ
to adoption as sons, to justification by faith, and to glory.[178] Similarly, Calvin
conceived of no election apart from Christ and also set the love of God prior to
the sending of the Son.[179] The primary difference between Calvin and Vermigli
is in the use of the term "predestination," which Martyr would apply only to the
active will and proper work of God in the salvation of the elect and not to God's
passing over of the reprobate. This distinction is based upon Martyr's acceptance
of the concept of a permission or passive willing in God, a concept which Calvin
rejected. Vermigli appears to have followed Thomas Aquinas closely in his
formulation of this portion of his doctrine. He defines predestination not as the
prior decree but as the act of God's will by which he determines the eternal
destiny of those he has chosen out of love.[180]

Reprobation is God's decree in eternity "not to have mercy on those whom
he has not loved." These are passed over and left in their sins. They are justly
condemned that God might declare his wrath against sin and manifest his glory
in righteousness.[181] Vermigli, therefore, is more distinctly infralapsarian than
Calvin or Musculus. Reprobation remains a negative will, a decision to withhold
mediation and to leave some men to a fate of their own making.[182] Clearly, the
scholastic foundation of Vermigli's argument is not the cause of a more rigid
formulation of predestination but of a less overtly deterministic conception of
the decrees. Vermigli's studied Thomism allows him to posit the free action of
secondary causes and his analysis of God's positive willing creates a distinction
between will and permission in the Godhead,[183] which relates directly to the
more infralapsarian construction placed on the concept of reprobation.

Though this is certainly not the full double predestination of some of the
seventeenth century thinkers and though it presses less in that direction than
Calvin's doctrine or Musculus', we must nevertheless take exception to Mc-
Clelland's statement, ". . . in the sixteenth century the question of 'double'
predestination was not at issue, but rather the subtler problem of the relation of
predestination to *foreknowledge* in God."[184] These are two distinct issues, equally
subtle, and both present in Vermigli's thought. The very fact that Vermigli so
carefully defines reprobation as a passing over but nevertheless allows a repro-
bating will in God manifests the problem posed by theories of "double" and

"single" predestination. It manifests also a scholastic subtlety which sees the problem as more complex than a simple distinction between "single" and "double" predestination: there is only one will in God and it wills only the good. Yet this will is expressed as election of those God loves and the rejection of those God does not love. The difference between election and reprobation, as Vermigli defines it, is that God in election appoints the means, Christ and his work, as well as the end of salvation, whereas in reprobation God appoints only the end and not the means, sin.[185] Nevertheless, even though God is not the efficient cause of sin, sin is within the bounds of the divine willing. This is an issue of causality, not a rationalization of foreknowledge and foreordination. Indeed, Vermigli, like Calvin and like the later orthodox, makes a distinction between reprobation and damnation: the reprobate are damned for their sins, but the cause of their reprobation resides in the will of God alone and derives from the divine purpose.

More important to the present inquiry is the series of causal arguments by which Vermigli relates the incarnation and the death of Christ to his doctrine of predestination.[186] Neither the incarnation nor the death of Christ are causes of the divine counsel; rather, they depend upon it. Vermigli views Christ's incarnation and death as foremost effects of predestination, indeed, as the ground and foundation of subsequent effects of predestination. Election is in Christ and the gracious benefits given by God to the elect are given through Christ. Our utterly free and gracious election is mirrored in the utterly free and voluntary assumption of the flesh by the Son of God so that Christ is the foundation (*principium*) of all the good things given to us according to the divine purpose, though not the cause of predestination properly so called.[187] The effect of this argument is to imply a christocentric structure for the whole of doctrine: the divine causality guarantees the central position of the mediator in the soteriological structure.

EPILOGUE: CHRIST AND THE DECREE
IN THE FIRST CODIFICATION OF REFORMED THEOLOGY

In denominating the work of Calvin, Bullinger, Musculus, and Vermigli as "the first codification of Reformed theology," we point toward an initial stage in the codification of Reformed doctrine in which fundamental tendencies and basic structures were delineated, underlying relationships between doctrines established, crucial definitions of doctrine set, and the foundation for subsequent development of doctrine laid down. We are not to understand this formulation, even in the magnificent conception of Calvin's 1559 *Institutes*, as a completed edifice. For all the attractiveness of the early Protestant systems—their strength of piety, their proximity to the preaching of reform, their profound biblicism and, indeed, their repudiation of a scholasticism which seemed to have wandered far from the biblical deposit of revelation—they represent no more of a terminal point in the history of Christian thought than the systems of other periods. We can no more ask Reformed theology to conclude its development in the 1559 *Institutes* or in the *Second Helvetic Confession* than we can halt the movement of modern theology with Schleiermacher or Ritschl, who stand among its founders and codifiers. But we can ask the important questions of the central themes set forth by Calvin and his contemporaries, of the manner in which they set the stage for doctrinal development, and of the continuity and discontinuity in form and in content between their theology and the theology of their successors.

In each of the three systems we have reviewed in this chapter, we have encountered a doctrinal structure significantly different from that of the *Institutes* and, in addition, points of emphasis that contributed to the development of orthodoxy in ways which Calvin's thought did not. Nevertheless, we have also found a common ground of doctrinal agreement: predestination and Christology both serve to focus and to ground the soteriological structure and themselves both develop out of the context of an overarching concern to delineate the pattern of divine working in the economy of salvation. Musculus and Calvin accept the Anselmic argument on the necessity of the God-man as the starting point of Christology, drawing together the central issues of the temporal execution of God's plan and mediation between God and man as the form taken by the execution. All four of the thinkers examined set forth Christology as the fulfillment of divine grace manifest in history and around this theme, in what Melanchthon termed *historica series*,[188] unite the themes of creation, fall, sin, covenant, and the ordering of man's salvation. Melanchthon's analysis of *historica series* in the 1559 edition of his *Loci communes* provided early sixteenth century theology with an explicit organizing principle already acknowledged in practice by the early systematizers of the Reformation. This *historica series* concept merges easily with expositions of the temporal results of the eternal decree and thereby exemplifies the continuity in structure, apart from distinctions over the synthetic or analytic placement of the doctrine of predestination, between the early Reformed systems and the beginnings of orthodoxy. Vermigli shows some sympathy with this point of view in his exposition of the Creed while Massonius' ordering of Books I and II relies upon it extensively. Musculus and Bullinger emphasize the historical covenant from Abraham to Christ and the unity of the promise in its several dispensations. Bullinger is perhaps even more thoroughgoing than Musculus in tracing the origins of covenant to the protevangelion and the story of Noah.

Regeneration by grace alone provides the point of contact between the concepts of a sovereign predestination and a *foedus dipleuron*. Bullinger contributed to the development of the Reformed doctrine of predestination and also, with Musculus, to the process culminating in the thought of Perkins, Polanus, Rollock, Ames and Wollebius by which the predestinarian and federalist themes were united in one cohesive system. Nor should we neglect Calvin's place in this development. As has been shown conclusively by Hoekema, Calvin did not propose a one-sided testament in Christ to the exclusion of a two-sided covenant agreement between God and man.[189] Of the early Reformed theologians, Musculus comes the closest to a formulation in which the relationship between the covenant and the decrees appears clearly drawn.

Predestination in its Doctrinal Context and Systematic Relationships
     In the four systems examined, we have seen the deliberate development of the doctrine of predestination in a primarily soteriological context—either as the bridge between the humanly insurmountable problem of sin and the order of salvation founded on Christ (Bullinger), or as the bridge between the christological *locus* and the *ordo salutis*, the explicit divine causal ground for the individual application of Christ's work (Vermigli-Massonius), or as the point of contact between the preaching of the Gospel concerning Christ and its effective reception in the individual, the divine ground of the faith by which we are justified (Musculus), or, finally, the culmination and explication of the saving process reaching from Christ and his work, to the work of the Spirit, to the order of faith, regeneration, Christian life, and the justification that is by faith (Calvin).
     In each of these systematic structures, though standing in slightly different relationships with the basic soteriological schema, the doctrine of predestination appears as the preeminent expression of the sovereign grace of God. Of the four thinkers examined, Bullinger demonstrates the least willingness to develop a speculative doctrine of the decrees, and he did object to the double predestinarian emphasis of Calvin's doctrine and to the inclusion of the fall in the counsel of God.[190] On a more speculative level, Vermigli's doctrine reinforced the proto-infralapsarian tendency of Bullinger's formulation. Yet there was no disagreement over the necessity of grounding the concept of salvation by grace alone in the eternal and unalterable will of God. Bullinger, Musculus, Vermigli, and Calvin, despite differences in formulation, postulate virtually the same order of salvation. Furthermore, if the predestinarian structures set forth by Calvin and Vermigli seem to be more rigid and more oriented toward problems of causality than those of Bullinger and Musculus, there was no intention on the part of either of undercutting the christological focus of Reformed doctrine. As Reformed thought moved from piety to system, these more detailed and fully defined structures proved necessary to the work of explication and defense. Even so, Vermigli's sophisticated discussions of causality and distinctions between the positive will and the permission or passive will of God would prove more influential than Calvin's formulations as would his more infralapsarian definition of the decrees and his more "scholastic" method. None of the four juxtapose predestination with the doctrine of God.
     It is nevertheless true that in all of these systems, the doctrine of predestination has the double reference, a relation both to the soteriological and to the strictly theological issues. Drawing on Mozley's paradigm, we can only conclude

that the emphasis on divine causality given to Augustinian doctrine by the medieval scholastics has not been overlooked by Calvin and his contemporaries and that their own Augustinian perspective includes the interpretation of Augustine's doctrine—not to mention the doctrine of Paul—though the perspective of a highly developed systematic tradition in which the relation of the decrees both to their original Augustinian referent, the soteriological problem, and also to their scholastic referent, the divine power and will can and must be elaborated. In fact, the several different placements of predestination witnessed in this first codification of Reformed theology all serve to manifest the decree as a ground of salvation supportive of and, to a certain degree coordinated with, the Christology. And even as the doctrine of the incarnate mediator points back to the personal relations at the heart of the Godhead, so does the christologically and soteriologically oriented doctrine of predestination point back to the eternal saving intention of the one three-personed God.

Whereas placement of the doctrine enables a theologian to point out more clearly certain of the relationships between doctrinal *loci*, it is to the definition of doctrine rather than to the placement that we must look when asking questions concerning the causal rigor of the system. When Calvin illustrates the soteriological issues at the heart of his doctrine of predestination and undergirds the *sola gratia* of justification by his a *posteriori* placement, he in no way "softens" the impact of the doctrine. Indeed, insofar as he removes predestination from its scholastic location as one of the presuppositional issues in the elaboration of the system and interjects it into the soteriological portion of the treatise, he may be seen to give greater causal rigor, a more pronounced causal focus, to his soteriology. The same conclusion must be argued from Vermigli's *Loci communes*: Massonius' soteriological placement of predestination makes very clear the relationships with Christology and with the application of Christ's benefits already present in the treatise, but this placement in no way blunts the point of the treatise that the divine causality is utterly sovereign and undergirds all things, even the sins of the wicked. We will encounter in early orthodoxy no analysis of causality more rigorous than those of Calvin and Vermigli and no presentation of the language of necessity more aware of scholastic distinctions than that of Vermigli.

If we will give Calvin the palm for producing the most perspicuous Christology of his generation, we must divide the laurels between Calvin and Vermigli in judging the influence of their respective doctrines of predestination. Whereas Calvin's basic structure and definition, which designates election and reprobation as almost coordinate halves of the decree, had more impact than Vermigli's fairly medieval distinction between *praedestinati* and *praesciti*, between a predestination of the elect and a reprobation not strictly characterized as a "predestination," the infralapsarian definition of election and reprobation together with the finely-tooled scholastic analysis of the freedom of secondary causality presented by Vermigli would eventually be enunciated as the confessional norm of Reformed theology. Vermigli also, more clearly than Calvin, both grounds reprobation in the eternal purpose and, at the same time, manifests it as an unmediated will which does *not* stand as first cause in relation to the secondary causality of sinning.

Some mention must be made here also of Bullinger and Musculus. For if these writers did not produce definitions as clear as those found in Calvin and Vermigli, they did confirm the general tendency of Reformed doctrine and give greater prominence to the historical line of saving causality than either Calvin or Vermigli. Bullinger contributed important structural insights into the relation of covenant with Christ and decree, and Musculus more than any of his contemporaries pressed into soteriological service the distinction between decree and temporal execution. Musculus, in particular, by means of this distinction was able to show the function of the decree in determining the christocentric shape of the work of salvation and, in so doing, manifest the underlying unity of perspective above and beyond the various possible locations of the *locus de praedestinatione* within the system.

The early placements of the doctrine of predestination, therefore, both underscored the soteriological purpose of the doctrine and left room for development of alternative patterns among later thinkers. For if the relation of the decrees to the doctrine of God was not spelled out in detail, the language of Aristotelian causality employed by Calvin and Vermigli and the tendency toward scholastic usages found in Musculus demanded that the relationship be acknowledged. Similarly, the experiential emphasis of Calvin's placement and exposition of predestination, no more than the economical and christological implications of Musculus' treatment, hardly rule out but in fact demand recognition of the ontic and metaphysical implications of the doctrine: for we must experience in life and in history a valid representation of God's will if theology is to have any meaning. In all four of these early Reformed writers, the eternal will of God, together with the work of Christ, becomes a ground of the entirety of Christian existence. Thus the discussion of the decree by later thinkers occurs in four basic locations: in an *a priori* position in relation to the doctrine of God as the *principium essendi* (Zanchius, Polanus, Scharpius and Trelcatius); in a christologically determined location (Beza, Keckermann, Walaeus, Downame); in the soteriological structure placed *a priori* (Ames) or *a posteriori* (Bucanus); and in the ecclesiology (Danaeus, Ursinus, Perkins).

The Christological Focus of Reformed Theology
If the early Reformed theology expended much effort in describing the ground and the historical-causal pattern of man's redemption, it also attended closely to the description of the epistemological and causal nexus in and through which the eternal will of God received its temporal expression. The decree of predestination and its execution in time are incomprehensible apart from Christ. For Calvin in particular, Augustine provided the answer to the christological

problem with his emphasis on Christ's mediation, his conception of the *aseity* of the Son, and his use of the Philippian hymn as a guide to understanding the dynamic of the economy of salvation presented in the Apostles' Creed. The reappraisal of Christology undertaken by Reformed theologians in this period also drew upon the theoretical constructs of Anselm to underscore the necessity of the work of Christ to the entire redemptive schema. Just as the decree provided an eternal or metaphysical ground of salvation, so did the death of Christ offer a temporal basis; for if election was the presupposition on which human regeneration from a state of total inability was made possible, then atonement was the presupposition for the putative justification of the unworthy creature.

In Calvin's thought we see the clear delineation of Christ's threefold office, the powerful emphasis on Christ as God manifest in the flesh, the doctrine of the election of the mediator, the well-constructed trinitarian ground, and the concept which came to be known as the *extra calvinisticum*. None of the other systems presents a structure which unites all these concepts in so coherent and paradigmatic a manner, drawing them into relation with the covenantal history of the Old Testament on the one hand and on the other with the covenanted and regenerate life of humanity under the New Testament.[191] Just as the distinction between the eternal decree and its execution is resolved in and through the person of the mediator, so also does the person of the mediator become in Calvin's system and also, though perhaps not so clearly, in the systems of Bullinger and Musculus, the nexus of the temporal and the eternal, the one in whom the historical dispensation of God's salvation conjoins with and rests upon the eternal purpose.

Calvin's christological structure, therefore, presents itself as a more carefully integrated whole than any of the others. Musculus' system treats of incarnation after atonement in a chapter separate from the rest of the Christology. In his separation of the covenant and the *loci* related to it from the credal exposition Bullinger presents two christological structures within one system. The Vermigli-Massonius *Loci communes* manifest a similar problem though obviously for a different reason. The importance of Bullinger's *Compendium* and Musculus' *Loci* for Reformed theology rests on their highly unified conceptions of the economy of salvation. They demonstrate the centrality of the doctrine of the covenant of grace to Reformed theology and its role in the creation of an anti-speculative soteriology emphasizing not the decrees but the dispensation. The final edition of the *Institutes* had gone a step further than Bullinger's *Compendium* by conflating the credal exposition of earlier editions with the main exposition of doctrine. Where Bullinger and Musculus go further than Calvin is in the extent to which they allow concepts like covenant, grace, predestination, and Christ's work of mediation to interpenetrate one another.

Although the structure of Vermigli's *Loci communes* was not without influence, the chief importance of his systematic essays was their Thomist method and their more complex "scholastic" treatment of certain doctrinal issues. Like

Musculus' more nominalist or Scotist formulations, Vermigli's Thomist usages demonstrate the capacity of Reformed theology even in its early stages for formal development. Not only was Vermigli a Thomist, he was also an infralapsarian who followed the pattern of traditional Augustinianism. Together with Bullinger he set the tone of the Zurich theology and exerted a strong influence on the Heidelberg theologians and the Reformed confessions. Similarly, Vermigli's more strict determination of the twofold designation of Christ as mediator moved beyond the ground broken by Calvin and prepared the way for the formulations of Ursinus, Perkins, and Polanus. Taken together, the systems of Bullinger, Vermigli, and Musculus exert an influence on later Reformed thought parallel and supplementary to Calvin's emphases on the economy of salvation and the work of mediation, though with less attention to the problem of knowledge and a greater emphasis on historical, causal, and even ontological issues.

In all of these systems of the first codification, we encounter the formal or structural impact, the systematic realization of the initial polemic of the Reformation, against the medieval penitential system and its tendency to make the work of Christ peripheral, in a practical sense, to the application of grace. While recognizing the danger of such a generalization, it needs to be pointed out that the structure of the medieval system was christocentric only in a formal sense: Christ merits the grace bestowed by God upon his body in the sacraments. But the work of grace itself represents the infusion, by God as *primum movens*, of a gracious *habitus* into the believer via the sacraments. As is manifest by the very order of Thomas' *Summa theologiae*, the sacraments must follow Christology immediately because the issue is not so much the application of Christ's benefits as the dispensation of grace within the church and through the church's proper work, *ex opere operato*.[192] On the Protestant side, this systematic pattern was demolished by Luther's interpretation of Paul. The early Reformed systems invariably argue, in their very structures, the direct appropriation of Christ by faith unto justification. As if to manifest this new systematic form all the more clearly, predestination enters as effective in and through Christ. The Godhead remains first cause, but the system no longer has recourse to God as *primum movens* who works via the sacraments. The causality of salvation now appears as mediated by Christ: we seek not the first mover's activity in the sacramental system but the grace of God directly accessible in Christ, the *medius* and *mediator*.

As we noted at the beginning of this chapter, Calvin's theology was more than a simple meditation on biblical themes, a scriptural theology organized around certain central distinctions and motifs. We conclude also that several of these fundamental motifs represent the beginning, in Reformed theology, of a search for doctrinal system and synthesis in which dialogue with the tradition occurs and, in addition, modification and development of traditional themes. By way of example: the doctrine of predestination at this point of its development in the Reformed systems, was hardly a central dogma. Rather it was for Calvin and his contemporaries the doctrinal expression of, or as Barth commented, "the ultimate and decisive word," concerning the Reformation insight into salvation by grace alone. Yet the doctrine as expressed by these thinkers was more than simply a scriptural doctrine: it was also an Augustinian doctrine, argued as Augustine had argued it, as the divine resolution of the problem of original sin and human inability; and, likewise, it was a doctrine drawn perhaps grudgingly from the schoolmen, argued in the language of the scholastics, as a doctrinal issue hedged by definitions of necessity and contingency, primary and secondary causality.

Similarly, the issues addressed by and the forms produced in the Christology of these early codifiers draw not only on scripture but also, via scripture and therefore critically and productively, on the tradition. In particular, the refined argument on the necessity of the mediator as a divinehuman person—the great "*cur Deus homo?*" argument of Anselm—appears with emphasis both in Calvin's and in Musculus' Christology but adapted to the historical and economical concerns drawn by the Reformers from Scripture rather than to the cosmological interests of Anselm's day. A more radical development occurs when Calvin meditates upon the theme of the *munus* or *officium Christi* and presses the old twofold structure described by the scholastics toward his concept of the *munus triplex*, the threefold office. Or again, as a corollary both of the argument for the necessity of the God-man and of the renewed attention to the *munus Christi*, Calvin and his contemporaries were led to meditate on and to modify the traditional view of Christ as mediator according to his human nature: for the early Reformed codifiers, Christ is mediator as he is the God-man, which is to say, according to both natures.

The development of positive doctrine in the sixteenth century would be an elaboration of the positions and a resolution of the problems and tensions posed by Calvin and his contemporaries, accomplished in the context of the church's tradition and under the scriptural mandate of the Reformers. As we move away from this historical grounding of the Reformed system toward a more explicit and detailed statement of the doctrines of the Reformation, we need to be conscious of the establishment in ever more precise terms and ever more formal doctrinal determinations, of the underlying patterns, the objective theological foundations of the system. As we have seen in several places in these early Reformed systems: in the Augustinian or generally Western motifs expressed in the Christology and in the related stress on the historical economy of salvation, in the sense of the unity of the work of the Godhead *ad extra* as the common work of the three persons of the Trinity, in the distinction between the eternal decree and its execution, and in the general sense of a distinction between and a soteriological resolution of the infinite and the finite, the eternal and the temporal, the divine and the human, there is an underlying dynamic of theology at work, pressing Reformed thought as system, toward the enunciation of the consistency of God's intention and will to save with the temporal enactment of that will in the work of Christ and in the *ordo salutis* and, consequently, toward the definition of the fundamental trinitarian principle of all theology.

The work of Calvin, Bullinger, Musculus, and Vermigli, seen from this vantage point, seems not as a finished system but as the initial, as yet incomplete, reconstruction of the theological edifice criticized, disrupted, and radically transformed by the Reformation assault upon elements in late medieval scholasticism and upon the abuses of Rome. The christological focus of the doctrines of salvation and the predestinarian guarantee of the *sola gratia* of justification were in the thought of these early Reformed systematizers and would be in the thought of their successors the primary *loci* around which this reconstruction would take place. In addition, the underlying continuity of these early systems with late medieval scholastic meditations on problems such as the divine transcendence and the relation of the divine will to finite humanity, unstated because of the polemical context, would provide a basis for the more explicitly scholastic approach to theology developed by the successors of the Reformers during the formation of Protestant orthodoxy.

PART II

THE FORMULATION
OF ORTHODOX SYSTEM

Reformed Theology in its Second Codification

Division 1
The Movement Toward Orthodoxy

IV

PREDESTINATION AND CHRISTOLOGY IN THE THOUGHT OF THEODORE BEZA

Theodore Beza (1519-1605) was Calvin's chosen successor. He was a powerful force in the defense and development of Reformed theology in the latter half of the sixteenth century.[1] Nevertheless analysis of Beza's place in the development of Protestant orthodoxy must take into consideration the fact that Beza wrote no system of doctrine comparable to those of later orthodox thinkers. Historians who wrote prior to the current reappraisal of Calvin did not accord Beza a great deal of influence in the formation of orthodox doctrine.[2] Following reappraisal of the theology of Calvin by Jacobs, Bauke, and others, the weight of the allegation of predestinarianism has fallen on the so-called *epigoni* and in particular on Theodore Beza. According to Ernst Bizer, Beza's theology represents the entrance of a rationalistic spirit into Protestantism.[3] This rationalism was supplemented by natural theology, historical demonstration, and a pietistic theology of experience to the point that the credibility of revelation was "founded upon the demonstrable facts of the case and upon its rational, conceptual necessity."[4]

In this chapter I intend to examine several of Beza's treatises, emphasizing his *Tabula praedestinationis* (1555) and his *Confessio christianae fidei* (1558). The former work has been viewed as Beza's point of entrance into the realm of metaphysical speculation, and the latter has received attention from Bizer in his analysis of Beza as a founder of orthodoxy. Beza's Confessio must also rank as his most important essay in systematic structure. Because of the early date of these works—both previous to the final edition of Calvin's *Institutes* and well within the period of the first codification of Reformed theology—it will also be necessary to examine later works of Beza. Throughout the analysis my interest will be in arriving at a balanced picture of Beza's role in the movement toward orthodoxy and in the development of doctrine during the period of his greatest influence (ca. 1560 - ca. 1585).

1. THE TABULA PRAEDESTINATIONIS (1555)

Recent studies of Beza and of early orthodoxy have regarded the *Tabula praedestinationis* as the basis of a necessitarian metaphysic and as a major influence in the movement toward formal solidification of Calvinism into a predestinarian system.[5] Beza is said to have moved the doctrine of predestination out of the soteriology where Calvin had located it and into the doctrine of God.[6] Quite surprisingly, therefore, the first chapter of the *Tabula* contains not a systematic pronouncement but a lengthy justification of the homiletical and pastoral use of the doctrine of predestination. Beza's comments are drawn in large part from Augustine. Beza advocates the preaching of predestination in order that those who have ears may hear and be assured of God's eternal gracious purpose.[7] From the outset Beza emphasizes not the development of a predestinarian system of theology but the application of election to the life of piety. His purpose in preaching and teaching election, even in preaching the doctrine of the double decree, is the assurance of the elect. Like election, reprobation must be taught and not hidden away. It should be preached that the elect might learn humility.[8]

Assurance of election, however, as distinct from preaching, is inward. Since the number and identity of the elect and the reprobate belong to the decree of God, assurance must be personal rather than corporate. Nor can we discern the election or the reprobation of others: all we know is the testimony of scripture that those who have been predestinated from eternity to be adopted as sons in Christ will, in time, be effectually called and then through faith in Christ justified, sanctified, glorified. Personal assurance results from the inner testimony of the Spirit of adoption, who cries "Abba, Father" in our hearts and whose power and efficacy perform their work in us.[9] Beza, clearly, had no concern to press toward the *syllogismus practicus* in 1555. Our knowledge of reprobation, however, can only be general, and our efforts ought only to be directed toward the invitation of all to salvation.[10] Beza's homiletical and soteriological concern is apparent.[11]

Beza's second and third chapters bring into clearer perspective the grounds for the usual interpretation of the *Tabula*: the implications of the argument are supralapsarian and indicate a tendency toward a schematization of the relationship between God's decrees of election and reprobation and his decrees to create man and to allow the fall.[12] This, too, is the implication of the famous diagram or *Tabula* for which the treatise is best known. Beza does not, however, set forth an explicit conception of the "order of the decree." Indeed, he expresses a like concern with Calvin in denominating Christ as the source of ultimate assurance; for though we have the testimony of secondary causes like faith and its fruits, we must seek out Christ, our head, to know the truth of the eternal decree—in Christ we are eternally adopted.[13] Beza can also, in the diagram, point to the unmediated character of reprobation and therefore to the inexact correlation of the two sides of decree.[14] Therefore, in understanding election we can look upward to Christ as the mediator of salvation within the temporal order, but in understanding reprobation, where there is no mediator, our temporally bound glance can seek no further than our own sins.

Beza's doctrine, then, is not the sophisticated supralapsarianism of seventeenth-century controversy. The problem addressed by the seventeenth century was whether or not God, in his promulgation of the eternal decrees, considered man as a being to be created and liable to fall (*creabilis et labilis*) or as a being already created and fallen (*creatus et lapsus*). The issue is much more refined than Beza's statement of the eternal indifference of the decree. It is even more refined than the problem of the "ordering" of the decrees concerning election, reprobation, creation, and fall. The issue faced by later controversy is that of the manner of the divine apprehension of man's as yet uncreated nature.[15] The *Tabula* contrasts the eternal mystery of the decrees with the temporal reality of man's sin. The sense of logical priority in the ordering of the decrees derives from a recognition of the temporal reality of sin and fall. Beza is not concerned with the logical separation of a decree to permit the fall from the human event of fall.[16] He refrains from prolonged discussion of God's eternal purpose and concentrates on salvation and damnation as present, temporal, and individual concerns.

Even so, Beza's *Tabula praedestinationis* disappoints those who would seek a strong association of the doctrine of predestination with a speculative doctrine of God and of God's absolute will. Beza comes closest to discussing the doctrine of God in his second chapter where he elaborates on the theme of God's will in election. But he manifests, like Calvin, an anti-speculative stress on the execution of the decree in time: God's will to elect some men to salvation is made manifest to us through temporal effects and scriptural revelations.[17] Discussion emphasizes neither the immutability of God's will nor the contents of the eternal will of God respecting election and reprobation: these things are known only to God himself, though their existence is revealed to us in scripture. Beza examines not the decree but its effects, not the absolute will of God but the working-out of election in the world. The theology here differs from Calvin's not so much in doctrine as in clarity of pronouncement.[18] Similarly, Beza makes a careful distinction between the ordinance and the working-out of reprobation: from man's view the reprobate are justly damned for their own sins and lack of faith, but scripture tells of the "first cause of their damnation," God's decree. Beza maintains a doctrine of full double predestination while nevertheless insisting that reprobation justly refers to man's own wickedness and obstinate refusal to apply the blessings of Christ to himself.[19]

These distinctions between the eternal will of God and the economy of revelation and salvation serve as a logical transition from Beza's statement of the doctrine of predestination and his exposition of the manner in which God has eternally determined to execute his decrees. God's decree of election and reprobation rendered it necessary that he enfold man in sin and disobedience for the sake of the justice and the utter mercy of the decree.[20] In this doctrine of a necessary fall and a necessary imputation of sin, we encounter the clearest note of determinism in the *Tabula*.[21] Yet Beza falls short of the extreme conclusion of this logic: he states explicitly that God is not the author of sin and that while man sinned by necessity, he did not sin by compulsion. Certain things are not allowed by God but nevertheless occur by his will since God ordains all things and extends his providence even to secondary causes.[22] A less deterministic even proto-infralapsarian view can perhaps be detected in Beza's presentation of the origin of sin as, in Otto Ritschl's words, "the psychological moment in which the human soul freely and of itself turns toward evil."[23]

The distinction between the eternal decree and its execution in time raises the issue of mediation and leads Beza here, like Calvin, to derive the doctrine of the two natures of Christ from the necessity of mediation and from the Anselmic concept of the divine-human person of the mediator who alone is capable of performing the work of salvation.[24] Apart from the doctrine of predestination itself, which is the stated subject of the treatise, that of the person of the mediator is the only other doctrine fully analyzed in the *Tabula*: the causality of predestination focuses upon the causality of mediation. This christological focus provides an important indication of Beza's primary soteriological emphasis. In addition, Beza's insistence that Christ, according to his divinity, is "the very same substance" as the Father "and God eternal with him," like the similar formulations we have found in the work of Calvin and Musculus, limits the subordination of Christ to the decree to his work as mediator of salvation.[25] Kickel is therefore incorrect in his claim that Beza replaced Christ with a causal structure at the center of his theology and denied Christ "his place as the cornerstone and criterion of knowledge for theology."[26] Not only has Beza argued that Christ, as the one in whom we are adopted, is the ultimate proof of the gracious electing will of God (cap.ii.4), but he has also, here, made Christ the center and focus of his causal structure. More than Calvin, Beza argues the relationship of Christ and the decree in terms of a formula of limited redemption. The work of the mediator not only manifests the mercy of God but also makes clear the justice of God against sin to the end that the single sacrifice of Christ might result in the sanctification of the elect.[22]

Similarly, at Montbéliard Beza demonstrated his ability to argue in terms of a larger christological structure which was capable of containing and guiding the doctrine of predestination. Beza denied the charge that by speaking of Christ as the executor of election he lost sight of Christ as the foundation of the decree. Beza resolved the issue of making a distinction between Christ as mediator and Christ considered according to his divinity as eternal God:

> On the one hand, therefore, Christ is considered as the efficient cause of predestination with the Father and the Holy Spirit: on the other as being the first effect of the predestination itself, on account of the servants mercifully elect in him.[28]

In 1586, therefore, Beza was able to draw together into a carefully formulated doctrinal determination the metaphysical primacy of Christology over predestination implied in the *Tabula* and shadowed forth in the work of Calvin and Musculus.

In the sixth chapter of the *Tabula* Beza turns to the subject of the final execution of God's counsel in salvation and damnation. A just condemnation lies upon the unrighteous. Only those who have been engrafted into Christ and have been "made one with his body," the Reformed doctrine of the *unio mystica*, are counted righteous, being justified in Christ and sanctified unto righteousness and holiness.[29] These elect cannot be recognized by men since their new life is "hidden in Christ" (*ipsorum vita prorsus in Christo est abscondita*): their election and reward appears only on the last day when they receive the eternal life merited for them by Christ.[30] God damns those who remain in the sin of Adam, even those who died before the coming of Christ.[31] Here too Beza presses toward a concept of limited engrafting more explicit than Calvin's formulations and more illustrative of the tendencies of early orthodoxy. Yet Beza's formulation appears to be as much a result of the problem of unbelief and the question whether or not Christ definitely "purchased repentance, faith, or obedience for those for whom he died"[32] as a rational deduction from the decrees.

Following this exposition Beza returns to his initial theme, the value of the doctrine of predestination. He cautions against misuse of the doctrine and against the "vain and curious speculation" which attempts to make the hidden counsel of God conform to human reason. Beza repudiates that speculative separation of foreknowledge (*praescientia*) from the eternal counsel (*propositum*) which would postulate an unconcerned foreknowledge to God or which would divide up the decree. Those who argue in this fashion will become lost in a "labyrinth" from which they can never be extricated.[33] The doctrine must not be preached in a fashion which leads hearers to apply it to individuals. Instead, the eternal counsel should be taught so as to demonstrate its close relation, by way of the gracious divine causality, to the doctrine of faith and, thereby, manifest "free justification by faith" as grounded in eternity.[34]

Beza's *Tabula praedestinationis* or *summa totius christianismi* is hardly a system of theology. It is simply a description of the decree and its execution in time, in short a treatise on the order of causes in predestination. It is remarkable for its strong christological focus, and it hardly points toward a structure of system in which the decree is lodged in or in juxtaposition with the doctrine of God because it does not present the doctrine of God as a point of entry into the problem of the decree.

2. BEZA'S CONTRIBUTION TO THE SYSTEMATIC STRUCTURE OF REFORMED THEOLOGY

Among Beza's many systematic treatises the *Confessio christianae fidei* (1558) and the *Quaestionum et responsionum christianarum libellus* (1570) stand out as the most compendious efforts in the creation of theological structure. In the remainder of this chapter I propose to use these two works as guides to Beza's thought. The basic structure of the *Confessio* is determined by seven heads of doctrine: the unity and trinity of God, the Father, the Son, the Holy Spirit, the church, the last judgment, and the difference between "the doctrine of the papists and these of the holy catholic church."[35] It appears to be the triune God and his work *ad extra* that provided Beza with the shape of his system rather than a causally rigid conception of the decrees. The order of the *Quaestionum* also fails to show Beza as a rigid predestinarian: God, scripture, the Trinity, Christ, the application of Christ's benefits to sinful man, faith, justification and sanctification, providence, predestination. In the second part of the *Quaestionum* (1576), Beza wrote of the Spirit, the church, sacraments, prayer and hope. The order here, apart from the placement of providence, reflects the *a posteriori* "order of faith" of Calvin's *Institutes* of 1559.

The Causal Order and the Practical Syllogism

In his *Confessio*, Beza subjoins to his doctrine of the Trinity a brief, introductory comment concerning "the eternal providence of God." Nothing, declares Beza, happens accidentally or apart from the most just decree of God although God himself is neither the author of sin nor a participant in the act of sinning. Rather the power and goodness of God is such that God works his good, just, and holy ends incomprehensibly and despite the opposition of Satan and of sinful mankind.[36] Prior, then, to any elaboration of the doctrine of the Trinity into a discussion of the persons and prior also to all discussion of the divine work *ad extra*, Beza proposes, as it were, the ground rule for all theological meditation on God and his works: the created order stands totally under the divine decree, conceived as providence. The divine causality stands, therefore, at the forefront of Beza's thought even in 1558, but it must not be conceived in such a way as to make God the author of sin or, as Beza would subsequently assert, so as to impede or overthrow secondary causality.[37]

Providence again appears under the doctrine of God the Father, who is creator of the world by his Son and sustainer of all creation by his providence. In this latter context Beza defines providence as the power of God in the Holy Spirit who proceeds from the Father and the Son.[38] Not once does Beza mention predestination under these heads. He does allude to it tangentially in his doctrine of angels where he speaks of the angelic host "messengers for the preservation of the elect," the devils having fallen from the body of angels by their own free will.[39] As if to make clear beyond all doubt the trinitarian ground of theology enunciated in the doctrine of providence, Beza devotes a separate section to the doctrine that "the works of the trinity are inseparable."[40] Similarly, the *Quaestionum* establishes its trinitarian ground before proceeding to the main body of theology. The order here—God, scripture, Trinity—reflects that of the *Confessio Gallicana* and the *Confessio Belgica*.[41]

The juxtaposition of providence and predestination in Beza's *Quaestionum* suggests a fairly rigid causal structure—no more rigid, perhaps, than the similar juxtaposition in the 1539 edition of Calvin's *Institutes*, but nevertheless worthy of examination. Significantly, Beza draws no connection between these doctrines and his *locus de deo*. Nor does he explicitly define predestination as *pars providentiae*.[42] Like the *Institutes* Beza's *Quaestionum* represents the doctrine of the decrees as the revelation of God's will to save sinful man. Predestination, as the concept of an all-inclusive divine causality in salvation, demonstrates the possibility of the seemingly impossible *ordo salutis* outlined prior to the doctrine of the decree. Beza does manifest an interest in precise and traditionally "scholastic" distinctions, like that between necessity and compulsion or between primary and secondary causality.[43] But the difference between Beza's theology in 1570 and earlier Reformed doctrine is more of degree than of substance. In his *Quaestionum* Beza also shows a tendency toward the adoption of an analytic method in discussing predestination, a more speculative, *a posteriori*, argument than witnessed by his earlier thought[44] leading within five years to the *syllogismus practicus* of the *Catechismus compendarius*.[45]

The *syllogismus practicus* appears in Beza's thought as, at most, a partial solution to the problem of assurance. Beza frequently spoke of the inner witness of the Spirit as a ground of assurance, particularly in the context of justification and sanctification.[46] This accords, on the one hand, with Beza's forensic definition of justification and, on the other, with his recognition that sanctification could not be equated with progress toward a sinless life; in neither case could the empirical *syllogismus* enter the picture as sole ground of assurance. But when Beza asks the question of the Christian life that results from faith, justification, and sanctification, proceeding, that is, from the divine cause to its human effects, he more pointedly even than Calvin, demands that good work follow.[47] Throughout Beza's works there is a tension between the spiritual and the empirical grounds of assurance: there is, in the relatively late study on Ecclesiastes, a denial of any use of material riches as a sign of justification or election[48]—but in the isolated statement of the *Catechismus compendarius*, the syllogism rears its head in unabated form.

As Bray remarks, we encounter in Beza hardly a trace of Calvin's teaching concerning Christ as the ground of assurance.[49] There is a strong christological center in all of Beza's attempts at systematic formulation and we sense everywhere the connection between Christ and the decree, but on the problem of assurance, which must always relate causally to the decree, there is little christological discussion. In a sense, then, Beza allows more of a separation to occur between the *munus Christi* and the *ordo salutis* than does Calvin, to the end that the causal-empirical and pneumatological interests of the *ordo* predominate. It is here, though only here, that Niesel's warning concerning the relationship of the *syllogismus practicus* to a predestinarian system counts against Beza. Walter Kickel has called attention to this analytic-empirical tendency in Beza's *De praedestinationis doctrina* (1582).[50] Yet Kickel, like Bizer, presses his argument too far. His contention that Beza abstracts from the Pauline problem of the rejection of Israel a rational doctrine of double predestination and from the Pauline attempt to "found certainty of salvation in the wonderful word of promise" a rational and *a posteriori* conclusion concerning the passive stance of man before the will of God neglects the non-empirical, internal, but nevertheless *a posteriori* character of the Apostle's argument and neglects also the implications for individual salvation by grace alone, which most exegetes from Augustine onwards have found in the text of Romans chapters 8 and 9.[51]

The Exegetical Foundation: Romans and Ephesians

Beza's exegesis of the key *loci*, Romans 8:28-9:23 and Ephesians 1:1-6, stands as an attempt to clarify the language of predestination and to advance Reformed interpretation toward a scholastic consistency. The doctrinal tendency is toward a guarded supralapsarian formulation resting principally on Beza's reluctance to place anything outside of the divine foreknowledge or to allow an opposition between the divine will and permission: the God of Scripture is not a *Deus otiosus*.[52] Despite this formulation and its tendency toward rigid causal schematization, Beza chooses to depart from Calvin in acknowledging in God a category of permission, following Augustine's terminology, a "willing permission," in order to make more understandable the existence of sin and evil under the divine decree.[53] Beza can thus avoid viewing God as the author of sin and, at the same time, speak of the determinate knowledge God has not only of the elect and the means of election but also of the causes of the damnation of the reprobate,[54] for nothing falls outside of the divine willing, even when certain events are clearly contrary to God's will.

Beza's analysis of the "lump" or *massa* of Romans 9:21 moves more toward the supralapsarian reading than Calvin's: it is not satisfactory, comments Beza, to identify the *massa* as the human race already fallen and corrupt, for Paul here seeks out prior causes and fastens on the mercy and justice of God and the manifestation of divine glory in a just decree. The issue is that God decrees by his right and according to his will alone (*pro suo jure & mera voluntate*). How great an injury it would be to God if we were to conceive of his decree as resting on the result of human activity, or to hypothesize a second divine decree, a reactive decree, subsequent to the corruption of the creature![55]

Beza's exegesis of Ephesians 1:1-8, however, mirrors Calvin's almost exactly: the "blessed God and Father of our Lord Jesus Christ" (v. 3) is identified in the initial brief analysis as the "*causa efficiens nostrae salutis*." Beza here adds the qualification, which he, together with Zanchi, Perkins and Polanus, will seek to clarify, that the efficient cause is not "God universally and confusedly considered" but the "Father." The "material cause" is Christ who bestows upon us "one spiritual and salvific blessing" while the proximate end of election (*causa finalis proxima*) is our salvation.[56] Significantly, when Beza turns to his extended exegesis of the fifth verse, he recognizes the need to declare that the electing

God is not the Father apart from Christ and the Spirit, not the *deus nudus absconditus*: considered as God and therefore as *homoousios* with the Father and the Spirit, Christ must be said also to elect us. The divine essence is not subject to division. Our election in Christ, which implies some subordination of Christ to the eternal counsel of God, refers to Christ as he is mediator and *Deus manifestatus in carne.*[57] This argument relates directly to the extended analysis of the problem of subordination to be encountered later in Beza's explanation of Christ as *medius* and *mediator* and stands as a corollary in the doctrine of predestination to the Reformed view of Christ as mediator according to both natures.

Predestination in Systematic Context: Christology and Soteriology
The third section of Beza's *Confessio* contains a close analysis of the doctrines of sin and redemption and therefore draws into close association the doctrines of Christ and predestination. In contrast to the *Tabula* where predestination provides the context for christological discussion, Beza here develops the doctrines of predestination, creation, and fall under the larger category of Christology, thereby relating these doctrines primarily to the soteriological issues at the core of his exposition. Beza initially affirms the divinity of the Son and then states in brief the concept of the Son's ordination or designation from all eternity to the work of mediation. This ordination was the decree of God to unite the Son to a human nature for the sake of the salvation of the elect.[58] Beza thus juxtaposes a concept of the aseity of Christ's divinity with a concept of his designation to the work of mediation. This juxtaposition, moreover, provides the basis for Beza's statement of the doctrine of election: since election is in Christ, the essentially christological issue of the eternal designation of the mediator provides a foundation on which the doctrine of election rests.

Since God is perfectly just and merciful, all he does regarding man is an expression of grace. Since God is eternal and immutable, all he does regarding man is ordained from eternity according to the general principles of the doctrine of providence.[59] Although all things, even secondary causes, are decreed by God, "there is no fault or sin in the eternal counsel of God."[60] Some men, continues Beza, are justly condemned while others are mercifully saved according to the ordination of God. Creation and fall, therefore, both belong to God's demonstration of his justice and mercy.[61] God created man in a state of goodness and purity,[62] but deemed it necessary for the sake of his purpose that man fall from original righteousness.[63] According to the decree of God man sins necessarily but by his own fault to the end that God might reveal his mercy and justice in salvation and damnation.[64] As in the *Tabula* but more pronouncedly here Beza moves toward a necessitarian pattern in his discussion of the causes of the fall. He seems to draw on Calvin's more rigid causal language and, here, to augment it with the argument that the fall was necessary for the sake of the justice of the decree.[65] If we juxtapose these formulations with the emphasis on the freedom of secondary causes noted earlier, the verdict must be not a thoroughgoing determinism but an occasionally enunciated necessitarian tendency in tension with other elements in the system.

Beza's predestinarianism, therefore, balances the two foundational issues, the divine will and the problem of original sin, found in the medieval scholastic paradigm but moves toward integration or resolution of these themes more on the side of the divine will and the problem of necessity than did Calvin, which is to say, with a stronger reliance on the scholastic paradigm than on its original, Augustinian model. This ability to achieve a balance of elements such as necessity, freedom and contingency, overarching divine causality and the view of predestination as gracious remedy, rests largely on Beza's ability to move toward the more complex argumentation of scholasticism where the very method of theological discourse is designed to resolve distinctions into an organic whole. Viewed from a methodological perspective, Beza's scholasticism is an essentially conservative phenomenon, a meditation on the tradition and its tools which intends not to distort but to sustain the Reformation insight. Like the logic of Ursinus and Zanchius to be examined in the next chapter, Beza's logic tends toward the appropriation of traditional paradigms. In this case, the tendency is to reexamine the older analyses of the *voluntas Dei* for the sake of clarifying and grounding the *ordo salutis*.

A supralapsarian tendency based on the same argumentation as found in the commentary on Romans is evident in the *Quaestionum et responsionum*. According to an immutable decree prior to all other causes, God constitutes some in Christ out of mere grace and others in Adam according to his justice, vessels elect to glory and reprobate to wrath.[66] The federal implication is strong here, as it was in the Adam/Christ argumentation of the *Tabula*, pointing perhaps to the eternal will of God as a will to enter covenant. Once having made the supralapsarian statement, Beza distinguishes between the primary causality of God, which includes all things, and mediate causality, for God may, prior to all things, ordain some to salvation, others to reprobation, and nevertheless not be the direct and immediate cause of the sins which merit damnation: no one is damned unless he has in himself the reasons for his damnation.[67] As for the seeming universalist language of I Timothy 2:4, *non sit universalis, sed indefinita enuntiatio*:[68] thus the call and the promise are not universal, not even in the sense that all men are called to salvation on condition of belief, since faith itself rests on the decree.[69] Nevertheless, subsequent to such rigidly causal argumentation Beza can, much like Calvin, argue that reprobation can never be completely coordinate with election. The decree to save the elect and the decree to damn the reprobate are manifestly distinct in their execution: the former rests upon the faithful apprehension of Christ while the latter rests upon the sin of the reprobate and its fruits. Thus, the one decree of God is known in the elect as most merciful and in the reprobate as most just.[70]

The somewhat extended analysis of the will of God, a feature we will note also in Zanchi's thought, cannot be called speculative in the sense of a major addition of new material to the body of Christian doctrine. If we seek an explanation of its presence in the *Quaestionum et responsionum*, we must look on the one hand to the emphasis on divine sovereignty present in Calvin's thought and perhaps to the massive treatment of the divine will in Musculus' *Loci Communes*, and on the other hand to the generally Scotist and nominalist underpinnings of the Reformed theology mediated by Calvin and Musculus. The systematic antecedents of Beza's theology are structures in which the *voluntas Dei* rather than the *bonitas or iustitia Dei* is the prior category.[71] Indeed, Beza's interest in the divine will is not speculative in a strict, metaphysical interpretation of the term: he manifests no desire to rise above the order of causes to contemplation of the naked attribute. Rather, he seeks to explain how the existence of sin can be explained in a world where all things are ultimately constituted by divine decree.[72] God moves even evil wills, but in respect to the principal mover, the thing or act is good and evil only in respect to the secondary causality: Beza allows a divine permission which is ultimately in accord with the divine will.[73] Beza also wants to argue (much as Calvin had) that necessity, as decreed by God, does not impede the contingency or freedom of secondary causes.[74]

So too, in his claim that the sin of the first man causes a necessary corruption to descend to all his progeny, Beza produces a more rigidly causal determination than his predecessors without effecting a great distortion in the larger soteriological perspective of his *Confessio*.[75] This, after all, is the christological section of the *Confessio*, and despite the supralapsarian implications of these formulae, they are governed not by the *loci* of the Godhead, the divine attributes, or the divine works *ad intra* but by the loci concerned with mediation. Later Reformed theologians did not, moreover, uniformly follow Beza in this aspect of his thought but frequently considered the transmission of sin in a federal sense because of the implication of all men in Adam's sin or because of the fact of generation.[76] Beza's analysis of the problem of sin accords more with an infralapsarian than with a supralapsarian conception of the decree: here the decree manifests its remedial and Christology its functional character. Had the creation of man and the fall been the extent of God's plan, all mankind would merit destruction. But God is not only most just; he is also most merciful and has decreed from eternity the manner according to which all the evil resulting from the sin of man might be directed to the fuller declaration of the glory of his name. Therefore, some are ordained from eternity to be the recipients of divine graciousness while others are left to be justly condemned under the power and wrath of God.[77]

Christology as the Historical Nexus of Divine Saving Will and Temporally Given Promise

To the end of this gracious redemption, God promised and constituted Christ Jesus to be the one mediator between God and man. The manner (*modus*) of this redemption, moreover, was to be the incarnation of the Son of God as promised in the revelation gradually and progressively given from Adam to John the Baptist, announced by prophets and patriarchs, and adumbrated by figures under the Law.[78] Despite differences between the two covenants or testaments, the continuity of the promise in the historical line of God's people points to the one covenant between God and man which is Jesus Christ himself. The difference between the covenants is but the difference between shadow (*umbra*) and fulfillment (*adventus*).[79] Beza here confirms Calvin's view of one covenant mediated by Christ under several dispensations and points again to his interest in covenant-theology as the development of the Adam/Christ motif and as the expression of the historical axis of the divine saving causality.

This historical order by which Beza moves from the fall to his doctrine of Christ is more judicious than that of Bullinger's *Compendium* of 1556. Indeed it parallels the pressure toward more perspicuous codification evident in the last two editions of Calvin's *Institutes* and in the works produced by Reformed theologians of the late sixteenth century. The ordering of this chapter may be viewed as an advance over the order of Calvin's 1543 *Institutes* and as a step toward the final recension of 1559: we need to be open to the possible influence of Beza upon Calvin. Though, of course, the crucial structure utilized by early orthodoxy to describe the mediator in his work, the *munus triplex*, derives from Calvin specifically and does not appear at all in Beza's christological *loci*. Already in 1558 Beza focused on the historical line of the economy of salvation as it points toward the person of the mediator and therefore placed his comparison of the Old and New Testaments (*Conf*.iii.18) immediately prior to his extensive analysis of Christ as mediator and God-man (*Conf*.iii.19), a structuring of doctrine accomplished only in the 1559 edition of the *Institutes*. Several differences between the theology of Beza and that of Calvin are also apparent in 1558. Beza's thought shows a greater tendency toward rational and propositional argumentation. Beza's version of the Anselmic "*cur Deus homo?*" argument is at once more traditional in its logic, less intimately related to the text of scripture, and more strict in its form than the argument of *Institutes* II.xii.1. Some of the difference, of course, derives from the condensed, confessional form, but the fact remains that Beza's confession and particularly the argument for the divine-human person of the mediator is more logical and propositional in character than other confessional and catechetical works of the day.

Beza's covenant doctrine leads him toward the argument, typical of Reformed theology after Calvin, on the necessity of the God-man: the mediator of this covenant, in order to fulfill his work, must be true God and true man. "It was necessary," Beza begins, "that the mediator of this covenant or reconciliation be true man, but without either original sin or the stain of the fall."[80] This fact appears both from the justice of God and from the corrupt condition of humanity under God's wrath: a true man needs to exist who can approach God in a work of reconciliation—it being fitting that the work be accomplished from man's side by one who fulfills the requisite righteousness and thereby makes satisfaction to God for the sins of mankind. Since such a work cannot be accomplished by a sinful man, the mediator must not only be true man in body and soul but also a man not tainted by the fall, a man whose human nature remains in its integrity.[81]

In the following section Beza turns to the other side of the argument: "Why it was necessary for Christ to be true God." Beza's formulation, insofar as it reduces the argument to propositional form and defines its basic divisions, points directly from the Anselmic argument to the doctrine of Christ, the mediator, according to both natures. "This same mediator," Beza argues, "must be not only man but also true God."[82] For if he were not God, he would not be a savior capable of performing the work of salvation. Next Beza proposes a clarification of his point that even more closely reflects the Anselmic logic: under the perfect justice of God the penalty for sin must be proportionate to the sin itself, but a sin which offends against the infinite majesty of God must be infinite and therefore merit an infinite penalty; thus for the penalty to be paid, the one who pays it, though a man, must be at the same time infinite and therefore true God.[83] The mystery of the God-man was fulfilled when the eternal Son of God "took on himself the form of a servant," a whole human nature with all its infirmities, and was incarnate by the Holy Ghost of the Virgin Mary.[84] This formulation is significant in view of the shape of Polanus' system at the end of the century since it leads Beza to state his concept of the *exinanitio* as, by implication, a part of the *humiliatio Christi* before he states formally the doctrine of the personal union. The historical or economical motif predominates.

Christ as Mediator and "Mean" or "Mid-point": The Official Subordination of Christ

Although Beza's argumentation in the 1558 *Confessio* pointed directly toward its corollary in Reformed doctrine, the view of Christ as mediator according to both natures, the God-man in the historical line of the covenant-promise, Beza saw no need in the *Confessio* to argue the latter point at length—Calvin's mounting controversy with Stancarus stated the argument well enough for the time. But after Calvin's death, Beza found himself drawn to emphasize the point and to elaborate it at length: indeed, the Reformed position, as a new departure reflecting a new set of systematic problems[85] would have to be defended with all the ammunition at hand, biblical and traditional. In a sense, the maintenance of ground gained in encounter with tradition and with increased polemic was to be the agenda of Beza's subsequent Christological argumentation. Again, scholastic method appears primarily as a tool intended to support the theology of the Reformation.

The Christology of Beza's *Quaestionum et responsionum* contrasts strongly with that of the *Confessio*: whereas the earlier document reflects in all probability the developing structures of the *Institutes*, the later work reflects, without entirely setting aside the historical and economical emphasis first taken by Beza, the increased interest in the traditional patristic question of the hypostatic union. We

now see in Beza's Christology a blending of the orthodox Chalcedonian formulation with the economical, historical view, inherited from Calvin, of Christ
as mediator according to both natures—a juxtaposition of the traditional language
of the eternal person assuming flesh and the language of the *mediatoris persona*
encountered in the historical economy of redemption. The pressure of the traditional formula leads Beza to argue at length both in the *Quaestionum et responsionum* and in the elaborate *Epistolarum theologicarum* from the same period
that the view of Christ as mediator according to both natures, i.e., as *mediator*
in his condition as *medius*, is a valid development of christological orthodoxy.[86]

Beza distinguishes between the terms *medius* and *mediator*, showing their
relationship within his christological structure: *medius* indicates either a thing
"between two extremes" or a "quality" or "condition" of a person, while *mediator*
signifies a "conciliator" and not necessarily a person placed in a middle condition
or state.[87] Christ is, therefore, both a *medius* and a *mediator*. We might even
draw the conclusion, not explicitly made by Beza, that *medius* applies to the
crucial concept of the *status duplex* even as *mediator* reflects the *munus triplex*.
The Logos or Word, therefore, is never less than the Father when considered in
himself as God, not even in the *intercessionis officium*, for the Logos is *medius*
not as Logos but "by reason of the union of natures" (*unionis naturam respectu*)
and is *mediator* not as Logos but "by reason of the disposition of his work or
office" (*ratione officii habita*).[88] Thus, if the essence alone is considered, the
Father and Son are one and are one God, for in Christ there are two things or
natures in their integrity, but there is only one person of the mediator not two,
and the person of the mediator, as such, stands in a middle place between God
and man.[89] This argument performs two functions in Beza's thought. First, it
provides the problem of the reconciliation of unreconcilables, the infinite divine
and the finite human, with a proper solution: it describes the manner of entry
of the divine Son into the temporal economy of salvation in terms reflective of
the basically Augustinian teaching on Christ's *aseity* and its corollary, the so-
called *extra calvinisticum*. Second, it supplies the christological analogue of the
initial trinitarian statement concerning the designation of the Son to the work of
mediation. In other words, the voluntary self-subordination of Christ to his office
reflects the concept of an eternal election or designation of the Son and, as such,
stands prior to the temporal execution of the decree, just as the Son, as eternally
willing to be mediator, stands prior to the eternal decree. In both instances the
logic is trinitarian and christological rather than purely causal.

The terms *medius* and *mediator*, then, are understood of the incarnate one
without implying any subordination of the Son to the Father. Singly, neither of
the natures could be a mean. Of itself the divine nature in Christ is equal to the
Father, while the human nature is fully of the substance of mankind.[90] Christ
cannot be considered as *medius* by nature between God and man since he is
medius and a *mediator* only as he is one person in two natures, both God and
man, subordinate to the Father in his divinity only by reason of "the form of a

servant which he has assumed," and superior to man in his humanity only by reason of union with the divinity of the Son.[91] This formula represents a defense of the doctrine of the *Institutes* and of Calvin's letters against Stancarus, but again Beza has moved toward a clearer determination of doctrine though losing, perhaps, some of the paradox and mystery of Calvin's doctrine. He also has brought the specifically Western analysis of the problem of subordination to bear upon the christological formulae in a more rationalized form than that found in the *Institutes*, manifesting in the christological *locus* the underlying trinitarian pattern adumbrated by Calvin. The crucial issue for Beza, as for Calvin and his contemporaries, is that the work of reconciliation belongs to the "whole person" of the mediator and not restrictedly to one nature or the other.[92]

At the outset of his theological epistle, Beza states that Christ in his *hypostasis*, considered according to his person, was made mediator in his incarnation—mediator, in a general sense, for all mankind but specifically mediator for the faithful, since the term *"mediator"* includes the idea of reconciliation.[93] This assertion brings Beza to the point that he must encounter the claim of the tradition (on the basis of I Tim. 2:5) that Christ was mediator according to his human nature only. Here, the character of the movement toward orthodoxy and scholastic formulation is manifest in Beza's writing as a striving for precision and clarity of doctrine by means of a careful division and definition of subject. The patristic argumentation utilized by Calvin against Stancarus is broadened, the formidable name of Aquinas is mentioned, and the continuity of the Reformed view with the dogmatic intention of the tradition affirmed.

The fathers, quite correctly, comments Beza, refused to view the natures separately as mediators:

> Indeed the term mediator describes nothing other than the office and work of reconciliation, which would not be possible unless this one was at once both God and man. For if he had been only man, human nature would have remained ever separate from divinity: and if, similarly, he was only God, God could not have been conjoined with man: and thus Christ would not have been mediator, that is, would not have reconciled God and man, which Augustine intended by his statement, "Divinity without humanity does not mediate, and humanity without divinity does not mediate . . ." that is, Christ is not mediator or reconciler, as God alone or as man alone, but as the man-God and God-man, in one and the same person.[94]

The fathers distinguished between this middle condition of Christ and his reconciling work or office: they distinguished, argues Beza, between Christ as *mesos* or *medius* and Christ as *mesites* or *mediator*. As he is God and man and thus between God and humanity, Christ is *medius*; he is not *mediator* properly so called unless he is viewed as performing the work of reconciliation between God and the faithful. The patristic doctrine that Christ is mediator according to his human nature may be interpreted as a statement of the inability of the divine nature, apart from its union with the human, to stand as *medius* between God and man.[95] Beza finds the most important objection to this argument in medieval scholastic Christology. He cites Thomas Aquinas, who argued that "the divinity or Word relinquishes nothing in its work of mediation" since the divine nature and ordination can never be "between extremes" but is instead the "highest extreme," nor is the divine nature merely a "proximate cause" but the "first cause" of the conjunction of natures. In short, he is the "author of mediation" and not the mediator.[96]

Beza's response to the issue posed by Thomas is significant not just for its positive statement of a Reformed response but also for its relative incompleteness: it manifests the need (which Beza himself does not completely satisfy) for a full examination of the relation of the trinitarian ground of theology to the problems posed for Christology and for the economy of salvation by the historical and causal emphases of the Reformed system. Beza comments,

> I answer that we do not here consider the divine nature absolutely, but in its relations, that is, in the hypostasis of the Word, which alone (not, indeed, the Father and the Holy Spirit) assumed human nature. Thus the Word, coequal with the Father, in respect of its essence (in which, doubtless, one and complete, he subsists, in manner like the Father, distinct according to his properties) is in no way impeded from being subordinate to the Father according to his office of reconciling the human race, not according to nature, I say, or according to essence, which is unitary, but according to the office of mediation or reconciliation. And so the Word is thus the eminent cause and the author of mediation, in respect of the human nature assumed (from which it cannot be separated, though however distinguished), nonetheless in respect of the Father and by his will, has received to himself this mediatorial function, and sustains the means, indeed, the motive causes [i.e., of reconciliation].[97]

The argument comes directly out of the line of thought we encountered in Calvin and it is more explicit, more scholastic, in its precise division of the argument, but it still leaves unanswered the basic trinitarian question of the will of the Father and the Son, as one, and the relation of this one saving will to the persons in the Godhead. We see here, in Beza, pressure toward a more explicit formulation of trinitarian theology, toward a formula concerning Christ and the economy of salvation, somewhat like the *pactum salutis* motif of the seventeenth century federal theologians, but addressing not so much covenant as the problem of the divine willing. Here, in the christological analogue to the logic of his comment on Ephesians 1:5, Beza manifests the trinitarian ground of Christology and the relation of the will of the Son to the work of mediation.

If Beza's Christology reflects Calvin's concern for the manifestation of the mediator in the economy of revelation, it also draws the Reformed determination of the person of the mediator into a specifically Chalcedonian context.[98] In the theology of Beza, therefore, we encounter the tension between the historical emphasis and an a-historical "Christology from above." At the Montbéliard Colloquy, Beza and Andreae agreed on the Chalcedonian formula as the basis of orthodox Christology and then debated the *communicatio idiomatum* largely from the Greek fathers, thus obscuring on the Reformed side the distinctively historical patterning of the Christology as formulated by Calvin, Bullinger, and Musculus.[99] Indeed, we see in Beza, as we will see in Ursinus and Zanchius, comparatively less attention given to the positive development in system of distinctive Reformed structures like the threefold office than to the definition of the minutiae of Reformed doctrine within the context of traditional orthodoxy.

We have seen, already, a concern in Beza's thought to draw Christology and predestination together as interrelated doctrines of central significance to his systematic formulation. We now look to his doctrine of the atonement, strictly speaking, of the *satisfactio Christi*, as a gauge of the impact of the doctrine of the decree. The *Confessio* manifests little interest in the relation between Christ's work and the execution of the decree concerning the elect: Christ, says Beza, bore our sins from the moment of his conception to the time of the resurrection, fulfilling thereby all righteousness—as, indeed, our unrighteousness demanded. He revealed the will and the words of the Father and by his death "satisfied most fully for our sins."[100] We encounter here no sense of limitation other than the emphasis on *pro nobis* though, as we have seen in the analysis of Calvin's position, the fullness of Christ's satisfaction for sin was never questioned but only the application of his work limited. And that is precisely the formulation offered by Beza at Montbéliard where he expressed reluctance to adopt, without alteration, the distinction between sufficiency and efficiency.[101]

In neither of his major systematic efforts did Beza attempt to set forth a predestinarian system. He surely did not adopt the structure of his *Tabula prae-destinationis* as a model for either his *Confessio* or his "epitome" of doctrine, the *Quaestionum et responsionum*. Both of these works have strongly stated doctrines of predestination, but neither work allows the necessitarian aspects of this doctrine to exert influence on other *loci*. Raitt has argued well that the decrees effect no alteration of Beza's doctrine of the Lord's Supper, and Maruyama has shown that there is surprisingly little influence of the doctrine of predestination to be detected in Beza's ecclesiology.[102] Beza's predestinarianism really serves only to clarify and to ground his conception of the *ordo salutis*. Moreover, the necessitarian structure of election, both in the *Tabula* and in the *Confessio*, is taken up into the larger structure of God's saving will and its mediation in and through Christ. And this structure of mediation in turn rests upon the trinitarian ground of all doctrine, here made explicit not only by determinations within the *loci* but also by the triune structure of the *Confessio* itself. Although I am aware of no dogmatician of early orthodoxy who chose either the *Quaestionum* or the *Confessio* as an exclusive model for a system of doctrine, Beza's conception of the *ordo salutis* and of the relationship of predestination to Christology did exert an influence on the formulation of Reformed orthodoxy particularly in terms of the careful doctrinal determinations produced by Beza in his systematic essays. Beza's *Confessio* did have an influence on Reformed confessional theology: the *Confessio Hungarica* relied heavily on

Beza's work.[103] One system of the seventeenth century, John Downame's *The Summe of Sacred Divinitie* (1630?), follows Beza in subsuming predestination under Christology.[104]

In conclusion, Bizer, Kickel, and Dantine have overstated their case greatly. Fully developed Reformed orthodoxy does not appear in Beza's theology nor does a thoroughly rationalistic and necessitarian perspective on theology. The more cautious judgment of Beza found in the monographs of Bray, Raitt, and Maruyama appears to be more fruitful. Beza was a transition figure. He moved beyond Calvin in his use of scholastic terminology and in the precision of his doctrinal statements. But his "scholasticism" was moderate even by sixteenth-century standards as set by Vermigli, Zanchi, Ursinus, and Polanus, to name only a few. The analytic-empirical method adopted by Beza in his last discussions of predestination represents his most serious departure from the spirit of early Reformed theology, but like the *syllogismus practicus* it produced, it did not become normative for later Reformed statements of the doctrine of predestination. This analytic-empirical tendency is, moreover, balanced out by Beza's christological emphases, particularly the development of the concept of Christ's mediation, and by a consistent stress on the economy of salvation. This stress upon temporal economy is manifest in the ever-present distinction between the decree and its execution, in the strong covenant-motif of the *Confessio*, and in the use of the doctrine of predestination primarily as a ground for the *ordo salutis* in his major systematic structures. It would be a mistake to say that there were no deterministic tendencies in Beza's thought, but these tendencies existed in tension with a christocentric piety and a very real sense of the danger of determinism.[105] Beza did not produce a predestinarian or necessitarian system nor did he ineluctably draw Reformed theology toward formulation of a causal metaphysic. Nor did he develop one *locus* to the neglect, exclusion, or deemphasis of others. Beza's role in the development of Reformed system may better be described as a generally successful attempt to clarify and to render more precise the doctrinal definitions he had inherited from Calvin and the other Reformers of the first era of theological codification.

V

REFORMED THEOLOGY IN HEIDELBERG:
ZACHARIAS URSINUS AND JEROME ZANCHI

1. URSINUS ON CHRIST AND THE DECREE

In 1561 elector Friedrich III of the Palatinate commissioned two young theologians, Zacharias Ursinus (1534-1583) and Caspar Olevianus (1536-1587), to prepare a catechism for use in his dominions.[1] The catechism they produced, an epochal work in itself, became the basis for Ursinus' highly influential *Doctrinae christianae compendium*.[2] More than any other Reformed system—with the possible exception of Bullinger's *Compendium christianae religionis*—the *Heidelberg Catechism* and Ursinus' *Doctrinae christianae compendium* stress the economy of salvation. In this economy God's electing will and his saving work in Christ must conjoin.[3]

Like Calvin, Ursinus introduces his doctrine of the mediator with Anselm's argument on the necessity of mediation. "A mediator is required who is both God and man,"[4] who as man must be like us in all respects but for sin and as God must be so united with human nature as to sustain his humanity in its bearing of the infinite punishment of sin.[5] This doctrine of the mediator has as broad structural implication for Ursinus' system as it had for Calvin's *Institutes*. Ursinus placed prior to it only the doctrine of man, his Fall, and his sinful estate. The doctrine of the mediator precedes and governs the doctrine of the covenant and the Gospel, the doctrine of faith, and the credal exposition. Indeed, Ursinus treats of the questions concerning God, creation, and providence between his introduction of the concept of mediation and the Christology proper. All the credal articles belong to the faith "by which we are made partakers of the mediator."[6]

The mediator, Jesus Christ, is the Son of God. The Son mediates since the Father works not through himself but through another. The Father "is sent by no one, but himself sends the mediator." Neither can the Holy Ghost be mediator since he is "sent by the mediator into the hearts of the elect." The Son is therefore uniquely the mediator.[7] He is our comfort since he is the one sacrifice sufficient for the expiation of sin, the true revealer in that sacrifice of the justice of God, the one who gives assurance of eternal life. "The doctrine of the mediator is the foundation, and substance, of the doctrine of the church."[8] Christ is both *mediator* and *medius* because he reconciles God and man and, as the God-man, stands between and joins the two extremes,[9] reconciling the eternal and the temporal, the infinite and the finite.

Christ accomplishes his work by means of a covenant, "inasmuch as every mediator is the mediator of some covenant, and the reconciler of two parties."[10] The covenant as described by Ursinus, relates in one formulation the concepts of *foedus dipleuron* and *foedus monopleuron*:

> [the covenant] is thus a mutual pact between God and men, in which God confirms to men that he will be merciful to them, remit their sins, give unto them a new righteousness, the Holy Spirit, and life eternal, through and on account of the Son, the Mediator: in turn men obligate themselves to God for faith and repentance, that is, for the receiving of this great benefit of faith and for the offering to God of true obedience.[11]

God has revealed this covenant as one reconciling agreement in two dispensations, the Old and the New Testament, the former being temporal and physical, the latter eternal and spiritual, the fulfillment of God's salvation. In the New Testament, continues Ursinus, the word *diatheke* takes the place of the Hebrew *berith* and brings with it the dual connotation of covenant and testament. *Diatheke* refers therefore both to the mutual covenant between God and man and the testament made in Christ and given graciously to man. Quite clearly, in this latter sense, the covenant or testament was not capable of fulfillment on the part of man and became the work of the mediator.[12] We have already seen, in the discussion of Bullinger, that the concept of a *foedus dipleuron* when related to the doctrine of regeneration and an Augustinian view of the nature of man, was hardly incompatible with the concept of God's sovereign election. Here the synthesis becomes apparent.

Christ in His Person and Office

The discussion of "God the Son" forms the first *locus* of Ursinus' Christology. It is an expansion of the catechetical question, "Why is the Son of God called Jesus, that is, a Savior?"[13] The doctrine of the mediator divides into two parts, the one having to do with "the person of the mediator," the other with his office. The doctrine of the office or work of Christ itself divides into two parts, the humiliation and the glorification of Christ. Instead of following the person-work paradigm, Ursinus moves toward a more integral, economic, and soteriologically oriented model. He begins by analyzing the names or titles of Christ, developing the soteriological implications of "Jesus" and then coming to the title "Christ," prior to the exposition of "only-begotten Son" and the conception of Jesus by the Holy Ghost of the Virgin Mary. The strict person-work model breaks down and an emphasis on mediator and office appears prior to the doctrine of the two natures:

> Jesus is the proper name of the mediator: Christ is, as it were, an additional appellation; for he is Jesus in such a manner that he is also the Christ, the promised

savior and Messiah. Both titles designate his office, yet not with the same clearness; for whilst the name Jesus denotes the office in a general way, that of Christ expresses it more fully and distinctly; for the name Christ expresses the three parts of his office, viz.: prophetical, sacerdotal, and regal. The name Christ signifies the anointed.[14]

Anointing not only indicates the gifts of the Spirit to the humanity of Christ, but also the ordination of Christ to his office. This anointing refers, therefore, to both natures.[15] Ursinus develops here one implication of Calvin's thought, the expansion of the concept of anointing toward conformity with the doctrine of Christ as mediator according to both natures. Whereas the humanity of Christ is anointed by the gifts of the Holy Spirit, the divinity of Christ is said to be anointed insofar as it is designated to the office. This formulation, like those we will subsequently outline in Polanus and Perkins, manifests the Reformed interest in seeking, in the depth of the triune God, the ground and foundation of soteriology. A similar motive appears in the work of Ursinus' contemporary, Olevian, in his pressing of the covenant doctrine toward acknowledgment of an intratrinitarian covenanting activity.[16]

The office, then, like the person of the mediator, is a unity in which the names and acts of the mediator refer to his whole person *in concreto* while each nature participates in the work in a manner proper to it.[17] The names or titles under which the office is considered and which are referred to both natures of the God-man are prophet, priest, and king: this conception of the threefold office appears as an outgrowth of the structure of Calvin's Christology even as does the primary concern for the "person of the mediator." Christ is always mediator, even prior to the incarnation when it was Christ in and through whom God had fellowship with men. The prophetic office of Christ, therefore, refers as much to the Son *incarnandus* as to the Son *incarnatus*. Christ was sent "immediately" by the Father to "reveal the will of God to the human race" and to gather the people of God. He is called "Word" not only in reference to his relation to the Father "but also in respect to us, because he is the person that spake to the fathers, and brought forth the living word, or gospel, from the bosom of the Father."[18] In his discussion of Christ as priest, Ursinus restricts the topic carefully, analyzing the relation of Christ's priesthood to the sacrificial office in the Old Testament but reserving the doctrine of Christ's satisfaction for the credal articles of the passion and crucifixion. The presentation of the kingly office, Christ's rule over the church and his defense of the church from the attacks of "external and internal" enemies, is also quite brief and designed to provide a bridge to the question, "But why are you called a Christian?" (q. 32). There Ursinus discusses the Christian life as an office, prophetic, priestly and kingly, communicated by Christ to believers.[19] The emphasis throughout is on the economy of salvation.

The development and change of christological models is also evident in Ursinus' recourse both to the Augustinian paradigm of aseity and to a late Greek paradigm of enhypostatic union. "The divine essence," he writes, "is communicated from the Father to Christ wholly, according to his divinity."[20] Since he is fully God and of the same essence as the Father, the Son has all of the divine attributes, one of which is self-existence. "The Father has, therefore, communicated to him the life by which he lives by himself, and by which he quickens all creatures, which life is that one and eternal Deity."[21] As God, Christ is eternal, and in his eternity, he is a person prior to the "flesh which he assumed."[22] This eternal person of Christ is equal to the Father and the Spirit both in essence and operation.[23] Ursinus here moves toward a more traditional and a more speculative christological determination than Calvin, and he strikes a more even balance than Calvin between the Western and Eastern christological models. At the very least, a certain tension must now be noted between the historical interest so manifest in the overall structure of Ursinus' system and the non-historical perspective of the late Greek patristic conception, the anhypostasis of Christ's humanity and the enhypostatic union, as they impinge upon one another in these formulations. In addition, the presence here of trinitarian principles like aseity is also a departure in organization from the *Institutes*. The resemblance between this and Perkins' analysis, again, will be quite striking with Perkins pressing the economic still more to the fore.

    The problem of aseity, of the relationship of the three persons of the Trinity in and to the unity of divine essence and the bearing of these issues upon the divine economy occupied Ursinus also in the lengthy *De tribus personis in una deitate* found in his fragmentary *Loci theologici* and in his *Defensio adminitionis Neostadiensis*. In the former document, Ursinus states as a major objection to the doctrine of the Trinity the argument that the mediator between God and Israel, as necessarily inferior to God, cannot himself be God. The subordination of the mediator, counters Ursinus, is real but it refers to his office and not to his nature. Again, the one sent by God is not God himself but an inferior. This subordination relates not to essence but to person since the Son, as sent, is distinct from the Father personally but not essentially.[24] Nor is the sending of the Son or, for that matter, the *missio spiritus sancti* the sole work of the Father but rather the work of the three persons. For "the Son, however, and the Holy Spirit assent constantly to the will of the Father, and themselves will to do what the Father wills by them to do."[25] In the order of divine persons, the will of the Son follows the will of the Father, but with respect to the divine nature, it is not incorrect to say that the Son is sent by himself.[26] We find the distinction, in a less elaborate form in Ursinus' catechetical meditation on the divinity of the Son: subordination "is true of the office: it is false concerning [his] nature . . . inequality of office does not remove the equality of nature or of persons."[27]

    As did Calvin, Ursinus makes the distinction between essence and person, arguing the aseity of the Son considered as to his essence but not as to his person. For it is not as if a divine essence is generated or a person is begotten out of the divine essence. The Son is begotten of the Father, and, as begotten, receives the divine essence by communication without disturbing the integrity of the essence so that at one and the same time the Son has the essence and the Father both has and retains it.[28] Thus, properly speaking, "the essence, thus, of the three persons, because it is one and the same, exists of itself: even so the person of the Father is not from another nor proceeding, but from itself: but the persons of the Son and the Holy Spirit are not from themselves: the Son, indeed, is from the Father, the Holy Spirit from the Father and from the Son, the essence of the Father being communicated to them."[29]

At the beginning of his *locus de natura Dei* Ursinus adumbrated these themes and sketched out in brief summary the relation of the essence and persons of God to the economy of creation, revelation, and salvation:

> God is essence, spiritual, intelligent, eternal, of a nature other than that of all creatures, incomprehensible, perfect in himself, immeasurable, of immense power, wisdom, goodness, just, true, pure, merciful, kind, free, wrathful against sin: which [essence] is the Father eternal, who from eternity begets his image, the Son; and the Son, the image coeternal with the Father; and the Holy Spirit proceeding from the Father and the Son: even so divinity is revealed by the undoubted word, transmitted by prophets, apostles, and divine testimonies, that the Father with the Son and the Holy Spirit created the heaven and the earth and all creatures in them; and is present to all creatures, even as he conserves and rules them by his providence and works all good in all things: and that in the human race, conformed to his image, he elects or gathers to himself the eternal church on account of his Son, and by him, as from him, this one and true divinity, in connection with the inspired transmission of the word, is known and worshipped; who is praised in life eternal; and who is the judge of the just and the unjust.[30]

Ursinus here allows the priority of the Father in order to be manifest without sacrificing the essential equality of the three persons. In addition, his emphasis on the unity of essence and the unity of operation thereby implied, provides a foundation for the definition of the decree as an essential act of God; that is, as the common work of the three persons. The essentialist aspect of theology which so powerfully enters the Reformed tradition in the generation after Calvin, rather than representing the incursion of a metaphysical impulse, appears here as part of the establishment of a trinitarian ground of theology, according to which the work of Father, Son, and Spirit is manifest as a unity and the relations of the persons *ad intra* correlate consistently with the revealed economy of the persons and with the revealed economy of salvation as effected in the common work of the persons *ad extra*.

In his exposition of questions thirty-five and thirty-six of the catechism Ursinus moves beyond the topics suggested by the questions, the conception and birth of Christ and the benefits we receive from them, and inserts a formal discussion of the doctrine of the two natures.[31] Ursinus divides his presentation of the doctrine of the two natures into four sections, each section addressing one of the following questions:

> I. Are there two natures in the mediator?
> II. Are these natures one or two persons?
> III. If but one person, what is the nature of this union?
> V. Why was it necessary that the hypostatic union should be constituted?[32]

Again the scholastic *quaestio* emerges from the catechetical question. Several issues arise immediately from the questions themselves: in the first place, Ursinus sets his doctrine of the two natures into the context of the teaching concerning the historical mediator, addressing the person as constituted in two natures. He has developed the doctrine of the divinity of Christ at length and has discussed the virgin birth; now he treats the two natures under the topic, "What profit do you receive by Christ's holy conception and nativity?" Similarly, the final question of the four, following the presentation of the two natures doctrine, returns the argument to the economical and historical focus of the earlier Anselmic argument on the necessity of the God-man. In the second and third questions, particularly in the phrasing of the second, we note a resemblance to the title of Calvin's chapter (II.xiv) on the two natures: the argument stresses the Reformed rejection of Nestorianism.

As previously in the doctrine of the mediator and his office Ursinus now argues the reality of Christ's humanity from the task Christ was sent to fulfill:

> The office of mediator demanded in Christ, our deliverer, a true human nature taken from ours, which had sinned, and which was to be redeemed through him, etc., as above. It was necessary that the same nature suffer which had sinned. But our nature sinned. Therefore Christ had to take this on himself, and not a nature created out of nothing, or brought down from heaven, etc. Nor merely did it behoove our mediator to take upon him our nature, but it was further necessary that he should retain and keep it forever; because the Father receives us into his favor only on the condition that we remain engrafted into his Son. This consolation, too, that Christ is our brother, that he bears our nature, is necessary for us, even in eternity. We are flesh of his flesh and bone of his bone (Eph. 5.30). This consolation we would lose, if Christ had not truly assumed and retained our nature: since without it he would not be our brother.[33]

There are two distinct natures in Christ, but only one person: Christ's humanity, though full and complete, does not subsist of itself apart from its union with the Word, and insofar as it does subsist, in part of another, that is of the mediator.[34] In thus moving to formulate his doctrine of Christ's person in terms of post-Chalcedonian Greek Christology, Ursinus recognizes the possible "dangers and abuses" of the language. Perhaps he even senses that his Christology as a whole follows another paradigm. With the intention of maintaining the integrity of the person of the mediator despite his use of the language of anhypostasis and enhypostasis, Ursinus argues, "thus the *Logos* is not the whole person of the mediator, although he is, of himself, a whole and complete person according to his divinity."[35] As a final note in his exposition, Ursinus draws the nonhistorical Chalcedonian doctrine into the sphere of the historical economy:

Above are given the reasons why the mediator was, of necessity, at once a true and perfectly righteous man and also true God, which it is not necessary to repeat here. For the same reasons there needed to be a hypostatic union of natures in the mediator: in order that he be at once true man and true God, who setting aside his righteousness and life, might be able to merit and restore ours.[36]

Christ in Humiliation and Exaltation

The concluding note of his exposition of the person brings Ursinus next to consider the work of Christ, considered in terms of the concept of the two states. In the *historia* of his life as recounted by the evangelists, Christ is shown to be the Messiah not only through his fulfillment of the prophecies of the Old Testament but also in "consideration of the humiliation and obedience which he rendered unto his Father."[37] The concept of *historica series* found in Melanchthon may be an influence here. As Berkhof comments, the doctrine of the states of Christ "was first developed among the Lutherans when they sought to bring their doctrine of the *communicatio idiomatum* in harmony with the humiliation of Christ as it is pictured in the Gospels."[38] Ursinus refers both the humiliation and the passion to the entirety of Christ's life:

> By the term passion we understand the whole humiliation, or the obedience of the whole humiliation, all the miseries, infirmities, griefs, torments, ignominies, which Christ, from the moment of his birth to the hour of his death, suffered for our sake, both in soul and in body.[39]

Perhaps following the originally Lutheran paradigm, Ursinus does not consider the *humiliatio* according to both natures nor does he connect it with the *kenosis* and the incarnation as later Calvinists would.[40]

Nevertheless, Ursinus does employ the *locus classicus* of the doctrine of the two states, Philippians 2:6-7, to explain the way in which the Son, equal to the Father, subordinated himself in his work, an argument typical of the developing Reformed theology. For although all works *ad extra* are the common work of the three persons, it is only the Son who is incarnate; thus, such texts as John 14:28, "the Father is greater than I," refer to the voluntary self-humiliation of the Son and his obedience even unto death.[41] The terms *forma Dei* and *forma servi* indicate primarily for Ursinus the essential equality and the mediatorial "inferiority" of the Son, while the alteration of the state or condition of the Son can be described either as *humiliatio* or *exinanitio*.[42] The burden of these formulations, moreover, is to explain according to Scripture the way in which the infinite God reaches out and grasps the finite creature. Indeed, much of Ursinus' argument in his discussion of the nature and trinity of God is designed as a ground of his system and specifically of the work of God in Christ.

The Reformed adaptation of the doctrine is strongly manifest in Ursinus' interpretation of Christ's descent into hell: against the Lutheran reading of the creed and following the model of Calvin's *Institutes*, Ursinus includes the descent in the *status humiliationis*.[43] He attacks explicitly the "papist" idea of a "*limbus patrum*" and in a veiled polemic confronts the Lutheran interpretation. Christ's body, dead and in the grave, descended nowhere. The "descent" cannot apply to Christ's omnipresent divinity. The verb, therefore, must be interpreted figuratively.[44] Since the Scriptures do not indicate that Christ ever made himself present in hell for the purpose of manifesting his victory,[45] the credal passage surely intends to depict no actual descent but to contrast the deepest humiliation of Christ with his highest glorification; it describes the torments he suffered not only in body but also in soul for our sake.[46]

It is also at this point that Ursinus presents his doctrine of the atonement, the *satisfactio Christi*. Perhaps the most obvious characteristic of his formulation is its Anselmic foundation. Christ "suffered in such a manner, according to his humanity, that by his passion and death, he satisfied for the infinite sins of men."[47] Because of the union of the natures, it may be maintained "that the person which is God and man, redeemed the church with his blood, which he shed in respect to his humanity."[48] The Aristotelian categories guiding Ursinus' thought now come to the fore: the "impelling cause" (*causa impulsiva*) of the passion is threefold. The impelling or moving cause is God's love of mankind, manifested in the gift of his Son, in his compassion toward fallen man, in his purpose to "repair the injury of the devil, who turned us from the Most High, and spoiled his image in us."[49] The final causes of the passion teach of the same love of God but "in a different respect":

> The principal and final causes of the passion of Christ, are the revelation and manifestation of the love, mercy, and justice of God, in that he did not spare his Son for us; and that his passion might be sufficient ransom for our sins, or for our redemption. There are, therefore, two chief final causes, the glory of God and our salvation.[50]

The formulation is more precise both in terms of the distinction of the properties of the natures within the person and in terms of the causal analysis of the work of salvation than in Calvin's formulation in the *Institutes*. Indeed, this argument as set forth by Ursinus is more precise and "scholastic" in its form than anything we have yet encountered in the systems of Reformed theologians.

Limited redemption appears primarily as a christological and soteriological rather than a predestinarian principle parallel to but not governed by the concept of election:

> Christ satisfied for all, as it respects the sufficiency of the satisfaction which he made, but not as it respects the application thereof; for he fulfilled the law in a twofold respect. First, by his own righteousness; and secondly by making satisfaction for our sins, each of which is most perfect. But the satisfaction is made for ours by an application, which is also twofold; the former of which is made by God, when he justifies us on account of the merit of his Son, and brings it to pass that we cease from sin; the latter is accomplished by us through faith. For we apply to ourselves the merit of Christ, when by a true faith, we are fully persuaded that God,

for the sake of the satisfaction of his Son, remits unto us our sins. Without this application, the satisfaction of Christ is of no benefit to us.[51]

Ursinus' definition makes no specific reference to election. There is even the possibility of interpreting the passage synergistically, when no account is taken of Ursinus' affirmation elsewhere that faith depends on the decree.[52] What appears prominently is the scholastic distinction between the sufficiency and efficiency or application of Christ's work. Significantly, Ursinus does not explicitly associate the efficient application of Christ's work with the electing will of God at this point. The connection is made in the doctrines of faith and predestination, but the doctrine of the decree does not here become the central doctrine around which the system crystallizes and by which other *loci* are determined. More importantly, the root issue both of the Reformed view of predestination and of the concept of "limited atonement" begins to appear here, at least by implication: the root issue is not election *per se* but the delimitation and determination of God behind his saving work, the divine intention in sending Christ to be mediator and redeemer. In this root issue of the divine intention, moreover, Christology and predestination are inextricably intertwined.

Ursinus draws the concept of election into consideration when he begins to discuss the application of Christ's benefits and Christ's intercessory office. Like Calvin he argues that the work of Christ does not apply universally in its efficacy because Christ intercedes only for the elect and thereby extends to them only the benefits of his death.[53] Those benefits are "justification and remission of sins" and "regeneration or the renewing of our nature by the Holy Spirit" both in body and soul signified by Christ's death, burial, and descent into hell.[54] These benefits also appear as part of the *ordo salutis* proper, demonstrating the interpenetration of christological and predestinarian structures in Ursinus' system.[55] Similarly, the resurrection of Christ, which marks the beginning of his glorification, represents to us the continuing "efficacy and power of Christ, in preserving the blessings which flow from his humiliation. . . ."[56] The office of mediation continues in eternity as perfect intercession grounded in the work completed.

As the conclusion of his christological exposition Ursinus deals with the credal articles of the *status exaltationis*: the resurrection, the ascent into heaven, the *sessio Christi*, and the coming in judgment, following throughout the Reformed interpretation. Ursinus here develops the *extra calvinisticum*: Christ's "human nature, which is finite, is in but one place; but his infinite nature, to be sure, divine, is in his human nature and without it, and for this reason everywhere."[57] In connection with this specifically Reformed conception of the relation of Christ's divinity to his humanity, Ursinus also develops his conception of the aseity of Christ's divinity: the *sessio* manifests Christ as equal in power to the Father and as the one through whom the Father governs all things immediately. In the ascension and *sessio* Christ's human nature receives the perfection of glory while his divine nature reveals itself, laying aside its humiliation.[58] In this new state Christ maintains the office of mediator for the church, and even as the infirmities of his human nature were laid aside, so will the earthly infirmities of the church, when it is united with its Lord in the heavenly kingdom.[59] Here again the distinction made between the infinitude of God and the finitude of the creature becomes the ground for a doctrinal determination in which the infinite accomplishes that of which the finite is incapable: in the person of the mediator infinite God grasps finite humanity immediately, by grace alone.

Ursinus on Predestination: Freedom, Necessity, and Contingency under the Divine Will

In addition to the discussion found in *Doctrinae christianae compendium*, Ursinus wrote a treatise on predestination in which scholastic tendencies are more evident and in which his exposition relies more heavily on Aristotelian categories. Here also he cites with great respect the treatises of Theodore Beza and Peter Martyr on predestination.[60] There is no reference to Calvin. Ursinus argues first that detailed explication ought not to be necessary. Scripture is sufficiently clear and quite opposed to vain speculation.[61] Following this scriptural principle frees Ursinus from strict adherence to any previous formulation: the very fact that he shows no preference between the doctrines of Beza and Vermigli, the former tending toward supralapsarianism, the latter decidedly infralapsarian, demonstrates a certain freedom in formulation.

As in the *Doctrinae christianae compendium*, Ursinus begins his exposition by distinguishing between providence and predestination. The distinction is "between the whole and the part":

> For Providence is the eternal, immutable and most excellent counsel or decree of God, whereby all things tend to the glory of the creator, and the salvation of the elect. Predestination is the eternal counsel of God, of beginning and perfecting the salvation of the elect, & desertion or utter casting out of the reprobate to punishment: wherefore it is comprised of Election and Reprobation as its parts.[62]

Ursinus' balance of election and reprobation as coordinate halves of the decree resembles the doctrine of Calvin and Beza, as does his subordination of providence to the *ordo salutis*. The initial definition, however, which distinguished between "the whole and the part" follows the Thomistic definition of providence as *pars providentiae*.[63] In this he agrees with Vermigli.

Ursinus distinguishes between God's active providence by which God is the "efficient cause and author of things" and God's passive providence according to which he permits the evil caused by finite agents. Evil occurs according to the decree of providence but not by it since in his passive willing or permission God simply refrains from hindering the sinful acts of fallen man.[64] Blame for sin, therefore, falls upon the agent freely committing the act while whatever goodness exists in this life belongs positively to the working of God. Even so, all creation depends on God's will to bestow being on contingent things. God's justice requires that all things exist to his glory even to the extent that "all creatures of the world should perish" rather "than his glory . . . be left unsatisfied."[65] God may permit injustice and sin to exist but only that their destruction might redound to his glory.[66]

Having learned well from both Melanchthon and Vermigli, Ursinus chose to bind together the issues of predestination and philosophical necessity in his discussion of the problem of man's free will.[67] Since God is the "first cause and author of all good things" creatures enter the scheme of causality only at the instrumental level where they are used by God in his "excellent and most free will."[68] The creature, as a mutable and secondary agent, works uncertainly when left to its own instincts and devices. The freedom of an uncertain and contingent nature can be used or "altered by God" without disruption of the causal structure of the world.[69]

> God alone is simply and absolutely free, that is, of himself moving all things, in himself moved by and depending on none, having in himself the reason, and cause of his purposes, with greatest power and authority disposing all things; and from eternity, if so he had been pleased, imposing necessity and contingency upon all things, himself not bound by anything.[70]

Calvin had often argued in terms of the Aristotelian categories of causality, but here in addition to the concepts of primary and instrumental causality, we encounter the concept of God as the unmoved mover. This is one of the more fully developed uses of Aristotelian-Thomistic conceptuality in the Reformed theology of the sixteenth century.

Once these categories of causality have been stated, Ursinus returns to his distinction between the freedom of God and the freedom of the creature:

> . . . the liberty of reasonable creatures is not absolute, that is, depending on no other; for although they move themselves by some internal cause, their understanding offering some object, and the will of its own accord without constraint (*coactione*) choosing or refusing it, yet they are ruled over by another agent, who both offers objects of what nature and quality, however and to whomsoever it pleases him, and also by them and through them affects, moves, inclines, and bows the wills of whomsoever or whatsoever he will. . . . He does not, accordingly, remove but rather conserves and increases the freedom of will, by the general and special divine providence and operation.[71]

Contingent liberty, then, is increased by providence. God acts to cause goodness or refrains from hindering evil, thereby allowing men to move beyond their abilities toward God's goodness. The end of this providence is the highest liberty of man's will, which by means of God's moving of the will toward the good, shall ultimately be able to will only the good, in perfect freedom and conformable to the will of God.[72] This Augustinian conception of freedom provides the context in which the problem of causality must be viewed in Reformed thought, with the paradox of the electing will of God granting freedom by determining the salvation of the elect as its logical result.

Ursinus proceeds to define effects according to the same Aristotelian categories that he used to define causes; and again the basically Reformed, Augustinian conceptuality is given a framework that shows a growing tendency toward the use of a more traditionally "scholastic" mode of expression. A good cause produces good effects, an evil cause evil effects; even so a contingent and mutable cause produces contingent and mutable effects. A necessary and immutable cause must have like effects: even as God is necessarily and immutably good, so are his will and his activity necessarily good.[73] All things, therefore, are good insofar as they exist and evil only insofar as they fall from the path for which they were intended by God.[74] All things, in respect of the liberty and freedom that is theirs, act contingently, uncertainly, and with dependence on secondary causes as well as on their own wills; yet these same things are necessary in respect of God's immutable decree.[75] As with Vermigli, the issue here addressed is not so much the extent of the divine causality (which is assumed all-pervasive) as the freedom of secondary causes under the divine will and the ordained place of these causes in the plan of God.

Predestination in Ursinus' System: the Ordo Salutis and its Ground

Ursinus refrained from including these particular issues and problems in the *locus* on predestination in his system of doctrine. He related predestination to providence as part to whole[76] but defined the decrees more as part of his soteriology than as the ground of a causal metaphysic. In the *Doctrinae christianae compendium* the doctrine develops out of the *locus de ecclesia* as the transition to and ground of the *communio sanctorum*. Predestination is

> the eternal, most righteous, and immutable counsel of God concerning the creation of man, the permission of man to fall into sin and eternal death, the sending of his Son in the flesh that he might be a sacrifice, and the salvation of some by true faith and conversion through the Holy Spirit and the word for the sake of the mediator, by and on account of whom they are justified, raised to glory, and given eternal life; whilst the rest are left in sin and death, raised to judgment, and cast into everlasting punishment.[77]

Ursinus places himself in direct line with the earlier Reformed theologians. Yet unlike Calvin, Beza, Vermigli, Musculus, or Bullinger, Ursinus formulates an entire soteriology in miniature. Ursinus makes explicit his soteriological emphasis by allowing the christocentric *ordo salutis* to give form to the locus of predestination. He places the decree above creation and fall and includes God's permission to allow the fall in the decree but in an infralapsarian manner conceives the electing will of God as drawing men out of a condemned mass, leaving the rest to their merited destruction.

Ursinus' description of the *ordo salutis* develops with precision the vertical and causal axis of Reformed theology and establishes a more strict *ordo* than that given in the systems of Calvin and his contemporaries. But he does not exclude or undercut the economical or historical axis on which the catechetical system as a whole is based. We see here a brief drawing together of themes, much like the description of the all-encompassing work of the triune God given at the beginning of the *Loci theologici*, in which Ursinus imparts his sense of the interrelationships of doctrine under an overarching conception of the consistency of the divine saving will as it enters and effects the temporal economy of salvation.

Scholastic method appears both in Ursinus' use of syllogism as a means of exposition and in his emphasis on the causal structure of election and reprobation. While the efficient cause of election and reprobation is the good pleasure of God and the final cause his glory, a free and contingent causality explains the damnation of unbelievers: "The cause of damnation which is sin, is wholly in man."[78] The decree itself, however, rests not on foreknowledge of good or evil acts but on the good pleasure of God. Even "the merit of Christ applied to us by faith" must be considered a result not a cause of election. "The effect of election is the entire work of salvation and all the stages of our redemption."[79] These effects include "the establishment and gathering of the church," the gift of Christ as mediator, effectual calling, conversion, faith, justification, regeneration, good works, perseverance, resurrection to glory, and eternal life.[80] We recognize here the full *ordo* embodied in Beza's *Tabula* and soon to be set forth in Perkins' *A Golden Chaine*. Like Beza and Perkins, Ursinus can also list the causes of reprobation.[81] In addition, Ursinus has established here a definite relationship between predestination and Christology which respects the requirements of the Reformed trinitarian structure: he argues subordination of the "work, . . . gift, and mission of Christ"[82] to the decree, a subordination which reflects that of the Son to the Father in the execution of his office as mediator.

This strong sense of the causal structure of salvation does not detract from the christological content of the doctrine of assurance. Ursinus asks, "To what extent may we know the predestination of God; and can we, and ought we to be certain of it?"[83] The answer, though highly scholastic in its distinctions and argumentation, explicitly rules out any causal-empirical solution.

> Election and reprobation are known in general, as there are some elect and some reprobate: but not in particular, as, that this one or that one is chosen. But of our own election in particular, we not only may, but ought to be certain, the knowledge of which is obtained, *a posteriori*, that is, from our conversion to God, or from true faith and repentance. For we believe and know ourselves with certainty to be elect to life eternal insofar as we hold fast to belief in Christ and belief in life eternal.[84]

The causal order is so defined in terms of Christ and faith that there can be no external determination of assurance.

Ursinus' agreement with Calvin, Beza, and Perkins in the general structure of the *ordo salutis* demonstrates that his placement of the doctrine of predestination in the context of the ecclesiology does not in and of itself indicate a less strict form of the doctrine. In the words of Hermann Bavinck,

> Whether predestination is made a part of the doctrine of God (the *a priori* order) or is treated at the beginning or in the middle of the doctrine of salvation (the *a posteriori* order) does not necessarily imply an essential difference in principle.[85]

The *a priori* placement indicates a theological, while the *a posteriori* indicates a soteriological, or in the Arminian systems, an anthropological emphasis.[86] Ursinus' *a posteriori* placement of the doctrine does not obviate the central theological consideration intended by the *a priori* position. The chief end of predestination is God's glory, not man's benefit, just as it is the chief end of man to glorify God and not to profit himself.[87]

The conclusion of Ursinus' doctrine of predestination manifests a fundamental concern of Reformed theologians in the formulation of the doctrine of the decrees: the failure of the visible church to conform to the membership of the invisible church of the saved in eternity. "The elect are not always members of the church, but it is however necessary that they be drawn to the church. . . . So the reprobate are sometimes members of the visible church and are not always estranged from the church."[88] The elect can fall, though "never wholly and finally." The reprobate may temporarily have or seem to have "the gifts accorded to the faithful in the church."[89] We obtain our assurance not from these visible things but by the knowledge that our salvation is wholly from God.

2. CHRISTOLOGY AND PREDESTINATION IN THE THEOLOGY OF ZANCHI

When Ursinus' tenure as professor in the *Collegium Sapientiae* in Heidelberg was cut short in 1568 due to ill health, the Heidelberg theology passed into a second stage. Ursinus continued to lecture on the catechism and, presumably, to expand and clarify the formulations contained within his program of lectures. His successor in the university was of a similar scholastic frame of mind: Jerome Zanchi (1516-1590), an Augustinian canon who fled his position in Lucca, had been trained in Thomist scholasticism at Lucca and drawn to the Reform by the theology of Peter Martyr Vermigli. He was a considerably older man than his associates in Heidelberg and must be regarded as an important link between the Reformed faith and its medieval background, as the representative of a type of scholasticism which was never entirely absent from the Reformation.[90]

Both in his *De praedestinatione sanctorum* and his *De natura Dei seu de divinis attributis*, Zanchi sets forth the attributes prior to his discussion of the decrees.[91] As Donnelly suggests, the primary model for the latter treatise may well be the first book of Thomas Aquinas' *Summa theologica*, but there are also other models and influences impinging on Zanchi's thought. The system of thought imbibed by Zanchi in Italy was a modified Thomism which had been accommodated to doctrinal and philosophical developments in the late Middle Ages, and Zanchi himself was deeply influenced by the teachings of the Reformers, whose works he had read extensively. In addition, unlike both his medieval scholastic predecessors and his Reformed scholastic successors, Zanchi chose to set the doctrine of the Trinity prior to the doctrine of the divine nature and attributes in a massive first tome of his projected Protestant 'Summa'. For this paradigm we must look back beyond Aquinas to the Sententiae of Peter Lombard and the Breviloquium of Bonaventura. Finally, as Donnelly himself notes, the order of loci in Zanchi's De natura Dei is somewhat different from that of Thomas' Summa.[92] For all his Thomistic training, Zanchi elaborates the doctrine of the divine will at length as a major focus of his doctrine of God and, more significantly, does so above the loci dealing with the goodness and justice of God, just as he sets the omnipotentia Dei above the sapientia Dei, indicating, it would seem, a strong voluntaristic as opposed to an intellectualistic, an Augustian, perhaps Scotist rather than a Thomist leaning.[93]

Zanchi was hardly an imitator of Calvin.[94] When he manifests definite ties to the thought of other theologians, as in his De praedestinatione sanctorum, he goes to the roots of the Reformation theology, to Augustine's anti-Pelagian treatises, to Luther's De servo arbitrio, and to Bucer's commentary on Romans for confirmation of his views.[95] Zanchi presents the picture of a Reformer of the era just following that of Calvin, Vermigli, and Musculus, whose views had much the same foundation as theirs, but who, because of his immersion in the systems, techniques, and philosophy of late medieval scholasticism, was able to add another dimension to Reformed theology in the sixteenth century—the dimension of detail and of clear continuity with the medieval theological tradition.[96]

Predestination and the Divine Will

Zanchi's theses on the will of God in the De praedestinatione sanctorum manifest this blending of influences and the service to which a training such as Zanchi's might be put in arguing the Reformed view of the unity of God's plan of salvation.[97] Translated into the terms of soteriology, the immutability of God's will demonstrates the sovereignty and consistency of the divine will to save. Since God's will can never be contrary to itself, a distinction must be made between the sufficiency of Christ's satisfaction for all sin and its efficiency only for those who belong to Christ and for whom he intercedes.[98] Even so, when he moves from the discussion of the attributes to the formulation of his doctrine of predestination, Zanchi focuses first on the love and the hate of God. God's love is the eternal benevolent will of God to have mercy on his servants. Though all mankind partakes of the benefits of God's providence, his love is bestowed on the elect only in the gift of eternal life.[99] The sole cause of this love is in God. God's hatred is eternally and justly directed against iniquity. The love of

God, therefore, leads him to elect some to eternal communion with him in Christ while punishing justly the sins of others.[100] This is precisely the Thomist formulation we encountered earlier in the thought of Vermigli. It can hardly be considered more rigid or rationalistic than Calvin's doctrine since it leads naturally to an infralapsarian conception of the decree.[101]

Election, according to Zanchi's *De praedestinatione sanctorum*, is the special predestination of God: it is God's "eternal, most wise, and immutable decree, constituted by him in eternity, by which certain men in the trap of deepest sin and death, and one with all the fallen are, according to his merciful will, rescued graciously through Christ."[102] Like Vermigli, Zanchi follows an Augustinian definition rather than the pattern of the *Summa theologica*.[103] Thus, the argument from the attributes does not produce the logical exactitude of the supralapsarian position. This strictly infralapsarian theme resounds still more clearly in Zanchi's *De natura Dei*, for here he sets predestination in the context of God's larger work of creation, salvation, and judgment. By meditating on the effects of the decree, writes Zanchi, we can see that God created man according to his own image and likeness, giving him will and knowledge and permitting him to fall into sin, to bring death upon himself and upon all mankind. Then God ordained to redeem some from sin and death rather than relinquish all humanity; thus in Christ he has mercifully liberated them from sin into righteousness, death into life eternal. The others he has justly left in their sins and under the power of death.[104]

Personal knowledge and assurance of predestination to life, as an issue quite apart from our intellectual understanding of the decree as a revealed doctrine, cannot be based upon any apprehension of the decree itself. According to Zanchi, we can know of our election and obtain certainty of predestination only from the effects of the decree: "*Quo melius mysterium hoc intelligatur, res a posteriori, hoc est, ab effectis.*"[105] The Christian man infers his election from his consciousness of faith, from his personal perception of justification being worked in him, and from the inner and immediate testimony of the Spirit.[106] Thus neither the placement of the decree above creation nor the consideration of the decree among the attributes, the *a priori* placement, lead Zanchi to deviate from the epistemological emphasis of his predecessors, from the *a posteriori* apprehension of the decree in the *ordo cognoscendi*, the order, as Calvin would say, of faith. This is certainly not the *syllogismus practicus* of Beza. Zanchi makes no mention of inference from works, though he does go further than most Reformed theologians in his belief that the elect can be recognized among our fellow men— not, however, with such precision that the reprobate can be identified.[107]

It is Zanchi, then, and not Beza, who was the first of the successor-theologians to place the doctrine of predestination definitively into relation with the doctrine of God in the order and arrangement of system, but Zanchi, more than Beza, tends toward infralapsarian definition of doctrine and the underlying Augustinian sense not of a metaphysical determinism but of an irresistible divine answer to the bondage of man in sin. This infralapsarian perspective contrasts with what might be termed a supralapsarian placement of the doctrine. Zanchi's definition and his sophisticated approach to the minutiae of system is scholastic in terms of its method and approach to theology and insofar as it recognizes and acknowledges roots in the theology of the late middle ages, Thomist and Scotist, but it in no way presses toward a deterministic theory either of the divine authorship of sin, or of the negation of human responsibility, or of the utterly empirical induction of assurance from the effects of the decree. Zanchi defines the decree in relation to man *creatus et lapsus* and views election as remedy to the end that his doctrine will be soteriologically and christologically oriented, all of the divine work reflecting the purpose of the triune God to save mankind in Christ through the application of Christ's work by the Spirit.

The Decree and the Trinitarian Ground
These definitions of predestination still leave unanswered the questions we have already seen raised in the thought of Calvin and his contemporaries: how does the work of Christ relate to the decree. Is Christ merely the means to an end and is the decree ultimately formulated apart from Christ in the profound and eternal depths of the Godhead? In the vast detail of his *de tribus Elohim* and *De natura Dei*, some of the Augustinian determinations on Trinity and Christ, particularly the concept of the Son as *autotheos* considered according to his essence, come together to propose a solution. We are not surprised to find references to the divinity of the Son and to the Son's place in the economy of salvation in *De tribus Elohim*[108]—but the references also occur, quite frequently, in *De natura Dei*.[109] Zanchi is concerned, even in the latter work, with the manner in which the attributes are reflected in the doctrine of the Son's divinity and in the doctrine of Christ's earthly work. In addition, following the usage of Calvin, Zanchi frequently refers to the pre-incarnate Son as "Christ."[110] These interests lead him to make specific determinations on the relation of the Father and the Son in the work of salvation and in its eternal ground, the decree.

Like Calvin, but with more precision, Zanchi defines the Son as essentially equal to the Father, as *autotheos*, thereby making the important systematic distinctions between the Son in his essential Godhead, the Son as person in relation to the other persons of the Trinity, and the Son in his office as mediator.

> The Father alone is *autotheon*, in this sense: since he alone is from himself, and has nothing from another: the Son, however, both in what he is and in what he has, has all from the Father, and is God of God: because of which all things that he receives he bears to the Father: all this we easily allow. But in turn this too is confessed, Christ also is *autotheon* in another sense: for surely insofar as he is God according to essence (which may be said for the sake of explanation), which essence although it is communicated, is entirely without antecedent principle: and so in the Son it is from itself (*seipsa*), just as it is in the Father. [111]

Even though the Son receives all from the Father insofar as he is generated or begotten, this sonship implies no subordination: the Son is not a dependent essence. The communication of essence from the Father to the Son does not make the Father the source of the essence and the Son in some way the dependent recipient.

> So also of life. Insofar as the Son has life, he has it from the Father, John 5:29. But that life which is one and the same with the life of the Father, is not from another but from itself. And thus Christ is himself life (*autozoon*) and has life of himself (*autozoe*), and thus also the Father. I indicate the same concerning essence. And for this reason the Son also, as I have explained, is in this sense *autotheos*, and as a consequence, by reason of this essence, which is utterly the same in the Father and the Son, the Father and the Son are one only God.[112]

This stress on the Son's aseity must lead, when the implications of the position are developed, to a strong sense of the equality of the Son with the Father in the essential, as opposed to the personal and economical acts of the Godhead: the persons of the Trinity, Father, Son, and Spirit must be one in will as well as one in essence without any sense of subordination in the internal and essential counsel and acts where issues of personal relation and the *oeconomia* or *dispensatio* of the divine will do not obtain. The essential oneness and equality of the persons in the work of salvation appears from Christ's words concerning the elect, "all mine are thine and all thine are mine" (John 17:10). Taken as a general proposition, these words point toward the unity of Christ with the Father: "*Essentia igitur, & Deitas Patris, est etiam essentia & Deitas Filii.*"[113] Christ, indeed, by his very act of praying to the Father establishes the distinction of persons. He does not say 'You are I and I am you' so that when he speaks of oneness, he speaks things essential (*de rebus essentialibus*) and not of personal properties (*non de proprietatibus*).[114]

Having drawn out with such emphasis the essential equality of the Father and the Son, Zanchi must make a distinction concerning Christ's role, as God, in the ordaining of the elect to life and his role, as mediator, in the execution of the decree, for in the latter capacity, a certain subordination is evident. Zanchi therefore juxtaposes two propositions: "God predestinates us in himself" and "in Christ we are elect, this truly in himself." The proposition that God predestinates us in himself in no way excludes or opposes the teaching that we are predestinated in Christ: for as Christ, the Son of God, no less than the Spirit, is one with the Father and himself God, he together with the Father elects us. This, comments Zanchi, is the meaning of John 13:18 where Jesus said he knows whom he shall choose.[115] Yet the distinction between the Father who predestines and Christ through whom we are predestinated also obtains since Christ is the mediator sent from God, our mediator before God. As such, Christ is the one in whom we ought to inquire after the fact of our predestination; we find ourselves in Christ by faith and thereby attain certainty of the election which is accomplished in him.[116] "And thus when the Apostle says we have been elected in Christ, Christ is set forth for consideration not as purely God and not simply as man, but as at once God and man, in the eternal office of the mediator."[117] We note in passing Barth's suggestion that this variety of doctrinal distinction, which places the focus of God's elective work in Christ but which also sets Christ in his divinity prior to the decree, given the dynamic of the orthodox system, might have overcome the problem of the concept of predestination, the *deus nudus absconditus*.

Zanchi's Confession as Systematic Model

Zanchi did not live to complete his *Summa* and to examine the impact of these formulae on a fully developed soteriological structure, but he did publish, toward the end of his life, an extended confession of faith, the *De religione Christiana fides*, setting forth the thought of the German Reformed churches in the decade before the codification of early orthodoxy in the theologies of Polanus and Perkins.[118] The work remains important for an understanding of Zanchi's thought since, unlike the previously mentioned treatises, it manifests the systematic context of Zanchi's conception of God's sovereign will and predestination.

The confession proceeds in a manner which would become typical of Reformed orthodoxy, setting forth first a doctrine of Holy Scripture as the Word of God revealed to man. Zanchi meditates briefly on the prologue to John. God himself is inaccessible and unknowable. He is made known to us in Christ.[119] Zanchi follows Augustine in seeing the church as the authoritative agency for the transmission of the Gospel, and follows the Protestant interpretation of Augustine in denying the priority of church over Scripture.[120] The tradition of the church, therefore, can be of assistance in the interpretation of Scripture but can never become a rule of doctrine.[121] Christians accept, however, the earliest of writings of the church, the Apostles' Creed, as a valid statement of "the chief principles of faith,"[122] indeed, as a paradigm for system.

Zanchi follows a credal model in the remainder of his system, teaching first of God and his trinity in unity as the doctrinal ground of his system. When we confess three persons distinct in their personal subsistence but one in essence, we teach of an eternal, immeasurably good, omnipotent, living, and most perfect deity.[123] The Son and Spirit, as *homoousios* with the Father, are no less omnipotent than he: essential properties cannot be separated from the divine essence, and the essence belongs in common to the persons. Father, Son, and Spirit are omnipotent, yet there is one omnipotence, not three, for there is one God. Significantly, Zanchi does not here separate the topics of divine triunity and divine attributes. His title for this second chapter reads, "De Deo, divinisque personis et proprietatibus" and the exposition consistently argues the equal predication of attributes of all the persons in the essence, confirming what we argued earlier concerning the priority of the Trinity in Zanchi's projected *summa*. The doctrine of trinity in unity provides the ground for understanding the exposition "De praescientia et praedestinatione Dei" in the following chapter. This triune

God not only foreknows but also decrees all things in his eternal counsel whether they deal with "the creation and government" of the world or with "the selection . . . of the church out of the uncleanness" of mankind. Nevertheless, there remains place for free and contingent activity on the part of the creature since, according to Zanchi's view, the divine foreknowledge is a broader category than the positive, decretive will of God, including also the divine permission.[124] The corporate aspect of the decree of salvation is elaborated at greater length and with more emphasis on union with Christ in Zanchi's *De ecclesia*.[125] The church is the *Regnum Christi*, the *Civitas Dei*. It is the mountain which destroys the kingdoms of the world and which is brought to a fullness and exaltation through succeeding stages of election, calling, justification, and glorification:

> insofar as all of us be from this earth as a mass, lost in Adam, subject to death; nevertheless, from this mass he elects for himself and exalts us in that highest level of dignity, that we might be the bride of Christ, of the Son of God, heirs of eternal life, and of the whole world: further that we might be holy, immaculate, made one flesh with Christ, and his body, that with him in eternity we might reign in heaven, and all creatures be represented in us, and all blessings, which through Christ accrue to us, and grace follow us, by means of his mercy and gracious purpose.[126]

Zanchi clearly does not view predestination as an isolated metaphysical presupposition but as a vital part of soteriology. As with Ursinus, it is not only christological; it is also ecclesiological, deriving from an Augustinian conception of the human situation and of the end of man. The decree stands as the eternal ground of divine saving causality which operates in the world through ordained means without disrupting the freedom and contingency of secondary causes.

Zanchi views man as *creatus et lapsus* under the decree.[127] Indeed, the passing reference to Romans 9:22, *vasa irae ad interitum*, stands diametrically opposed to Beza's supralapsarian exegesis of the passage: for Zanchi, God's wrath addresses children of Adam fallen in and through their ancestor who because of their fallenness are justly condemned and because of God's eternal purpose passed over in the gift of grace necessary to salvation. His personal confession, therefore, reflects the confessional norms of Reformed theology, and like the definitions found in his larger systematic works, emphasizes God's foreknowing of the fall as voluntarily produced by man within the divine permission; in other words— quite contrary to Gründler's findings—the infralapsarian position. Placement of the doctrine above the *locus de creatione* does not correspond to supralapsarianism. The concept of reprobation takes a minor role, stated briefly and then set aside in the exposition of the free gift of calling and justification in Christ.[128] We are predestinated in Christ not only to the end of "eternal life and glory" but also to the means, to faith and to our engrafting into Christ.[129]

Scripture tells us to seek assurance from Christ himself. Assurance is gained in faith, in the inward perception of our reliance on Christ, and in our sincere love of God and neighbor.[130] Again Zanchi avoids the *syllogismus practicus* in its Bezan form. He can argue that the doctrine of predestination is given to us in the Scriptures not that we might neglect Christ and "grow insolent," and surely not to breed despair, but rather that we recognize salvation in Christ alone.[131] The doctrine is no use to anyone outside of Christ (*extra Christum servari posse neminem*). By this doctrine we recognize that "the foundation of our whole salvation was laid in him before the world was made."[132] We are led to look to Christ for assurance and certitude in times of temptation, to study, broaden, and expand the bounds of our faith in Christ, to bestir ourselves to strive for holiness and good works, to give up all pride in ourselves and "glory in the Lord."[133]

Following this exposition Zanchi moves on to treat of the omnipotence of God's will and of the creation of the world, of man's first estate, and of God's providential care.[134] The divine omnipotence appears as a separate *locus* in Zanchi's confession, as the transition between the eternal counsel and the work of God in creation. God wills omnipotently all that he makes. His omnipotence extends to things he does not will and to mere possibility: "Credimus, Deum ita esse omnipotentem, ut non solum quae cunque voluit ac vult, fecerit & faciat: verum etiam infinita, quae non vult, & velle & facere possit. . . ."[135] This omnipotence, as previously defined by Zanchi, pertains to all persons of the Trinity.[136] Yet, much like Vermigli, Zanchi emphasizes the freedom of secondary causes: "Respectu Dei, omnia necessario, respectu nostri multa contingenter evenire." Thus Christ died freely according to the free will of Herod and Pilate, even though all occurred necessarily *respectu Dei*.[137]

The christological focus and infralapsarian schema of Zanchi's thought are apparent in his doctrines of the fall and redemption. He does not, like Beza, speak of the necessary imputation of Adam's sin to his posterity for the sake of the decree. Zanchi specifically states the permissive will of God in the fall and places the blame for the fall fully upon man, "the devil tempting him, and God in no way impeding, but according to his counsel letting Adam fall from his hand, by spontaneous disobedience and of truly free will, he fell." The reason for the fall lies, therefore, neither in God, nor in the nature created by God, nor was it lodged in things, but in man alone, in his will.[138] The first sin results in the loss of divine gifts and of the "integrity of nature." Adam sinned not only for himself but for all humanity which "was then in his loins." The exposition is related to the early covenantal emphasis on Adam as the federal and natural head of humanity.[139] Zanchi's exposition follows the form of the Pauline doctrine of recapitulation, linking the disobedience of Adam to the obedience of Christ, to the end that the divine purpose in Christ becomes the focus of the entire system.[140]

From the earliest times God promised salvation in Christ. Adam was not "a private person" (*privatus persona*) but the parent, original, and head of all humanity who ought to have transmitted to us the original righteousness in which he was created. God has provided a second head (*aliud caput*) for the human race through whose obedience "a true and heavenly righteousness, holiness and life might be given to all the members."[141] This promise followed on the first transgression. As many men as have believed in the promise of Christ since the beginning of the world "were engrafted unto him by this faith" and "made partakers of his . . . obedience, passion, death, and resurrection. . . ."[142] Like Bullinger, Calvin, Musculus, and Ursinus, Zanchi postulates the oneness of the covenant of grace in all time.[143]

Zanchi's lengthy christological exposition follows immediately upon his exposition of the law and takes its departure from the earlier themes of covenant and redemptive history. In the fullness of time, "the promise of redemption, made unto the first man . . . was accomplished by the second."[144] This second Adam is the eternal Son of God born of woman, truly God and man, like us in every way but without sin. He made himself subject to the law for the sake of its fulfillment, and he was obedient even unto death. By his sacrifice and effectual ransom, he redeems men from sin and renews the image of God.

Here, perhaps, we see the Thomist influence: Zanchi, much like Vermigli and in contrast to the Scotist position of Calvin, predicates the infinite value of Christ's work on the hypostatic union and the *communicatio idiomatum*: "morte & sanguinis effusione, hoc est, infinitae virtutis (erat enim sanguinis Dei) sacrificio, efficacissimoque. . . ."[145] Several issues emerge from this opening paragraph of Zanchi's Christology. First, Zanchi does maintain the historical and federal pattern both by enunciating a theme of promise and fulfillment and by reiterating the theme of the first and second Adam. Second, the prominent use of this Pauline theme of recapitulation, which we have also seen in the other Reformed Thomist of the sixteenth century, Peter Martyr Vermigli, emphasizes both the christological focus and the infralapsarian character of the divine saving will as it is revealed in history. Third, we find evidence of the incompleteness of the movement toward orthodoxy insofar as the initial historical patterning of system does not penetrate far into Zanchi's christological locus and result in the development of the distinctive Reformed structures of threefold office and the *mediatoris persona* as defined by Calvin. We encounter instead a typical Christology "from above" and the traditional person-work paradigm. *De religione Christiana fides* contains a fully-developed Chalcedonian statement of the doctrine of the two natures in which Zanchi declares the consubstantiality of the divine nature of Christ with the Father and the consubstantiality of the human nature with mankind.[146] In this context Zanchi, like Ursinus, affirmed the anhypostasis of Christ's human nature. The point appears as a definitive response to the charge of Nestorianism so frequently leveled in the polemic with Lutherans.[147] Since the impersonality of Christ's human nature received its first major development in Western thought in the theology of Aquinas, Zanchi's use of the concept may also be regarded as evidence of his Thomist training.[148]

The traditional, Chalcedonian, person-work paradigm of the *De religione christiana fides* stands, however, in marked contrast to the economic model of

Zanchi's *De incarnatione*. In the *De incarnatione* the *exinanitio Christi* and the *status humiliationis* provide the basic Christological paradigm. Whereas Zanchi does not deal with the concept of the determination of the Son from all eternity to be the mediator in the *De religione Christiana fides*, this concept does appear in his *De incarnatione filii Dei*.[149] The Son makes himself less than the Father in his determination to assume the flesh, though in his divinity he is equal to the Father.[150] The contrast of the ontic, metaphysical issues associated with Chalcedonian doctrine with the economical motifs generated by the conceptions of the designation of the mediator and his self-evacuation manifests a certain tension between paradigms within Zanchi's Christology: the assumption of flesh does not alter the nature of the Son, but, as Zanchi argues in his treatise on the incarnation, it does alter the state of his person.[151]

Zanchi also affirms the unity of the person of the mediator in terms of the unity of his work. The work is one, each nature performing what is proper to it and acting in total harmony with the other, within the common work of the person.[152] There is no communication of properties between the natures so that the predication of human qualities of the person detracts nothing from the divinity and the presence of divine attributes in the person implies no change in the humanity.[153] There is, rather, a gracious communication of gifts to the human nature as a result of the union in order that it might perform the work of redemption.[154] Whereas the impersonality doctrine stands as the final and successful attempt of Alexandrian Word-flesh Christology to make the unity of two ontological disparates seem possible, the *communicatio idiomatum in concreto* militates against the reduction of Christology to an ontological puzzle. *Communicatio idiomatum in concreto* merges well with a Christology formulated in the historical line of the covenant-promise: the concept of the impersonality of the human nature is the natural result of an a-historical Christology from above. The presence of both concepts with such emphasis in Zanchi's Christology manifests the tension of the two perspectives in the one system, a tension which Reformed orthodoxy would not entirely overcome.

What separates this Christology as a whole from the Greek Christology is the absence from Zanchi's and from Reformed doctrine in general of a genuine ontic and metaphysical problem concerning the union of the natures. The need to make the hypostatic union comprehensible or at least definable within the bounds of a given ontology so evident in the teaching of the Greek fathers does not appear to have concerned Zanchi. The personal union is accepted as historical fact resting on the divine initiative in *exananitio*, and definition of the union, as of the impersonality of the human nature, now occurs within the historical frame of an accomplished incarnation, the human nature being defined as within the divine-human person of the mediator. This paradigm, even more than the affirmation of impersonality, lifts the Reformed doctrine entirely out of the sphere of Nestorian and Eutychian problems, the determining factor in the definition of the person of Christ being no longer the ontological problem but the economy of salvation and, as with Calvin, the relation of finite to infinite in the work of salvation.

Zanchi draws no broad, traditional theory of atonement and develops no concept of the threefold character of Christ's office, though he was surely aware of both concepts and did hold to the concept of atonement as expiation for sin in a substitutionary sense, much like the doctrine propounded by Calvin, though here too the Anselmic dimension is lacking. Zanchi prefers language of *expiatio* to language of *satisfactio*, emphasizing the sacrificial and the priestly as opposed to the transactional aspect of Christ's substitutionary work. As he moves to the doctrine of the application of Christ's benefits he restates the concept of recapitulation, of participation in Christ as the Second Adam.

The Christology of Zanchi's confession argues, in a negative way, the point we have made concerning the interrelation of Christology and predestination. There is a strong christological element in Zanchi's doctrine of predestination and a powerful christocentrism witnessed by the covenant and recapitulation motifs in his *loci* on creation, fall, and redemption. Yet none of these issues appear prominently in the Christology proper. If in other writers we have seen a restructuring of Christology caused by the questions of predestination and the relation of eternal God to the temporal economy, we see here precisely the opposite. In the one Reformed Christology of the period where none of the basic restructuring around themes of mediation, threefold office and two states has taken place, there also we encounter little or no sense of the relation between Christology and predestination: the question is not one of central dogma (for this has been argued of Zanchi with as little hard evidence as it was once argued of Calvin) but of the pressure of system to manifest the interrelationship of its several doctrinal focal points. In Zanchi's *De religione christiana fides*, quite distinct from his *De tribus Elohim*, *De natura Dei* and *De incarnatione*, that question has not been fully worked out, as evidenced by the Chalcedonian person-work Christology formulated as a traditional Christology "from above."

Significantly the economic, covenantal themes together with the doctrine of election, the horizontal and vertical motifs that give shape to Zanchi's confession, reappear when Zanchi moves from his Christology to his soteriology, from the doctrine of Christ's work to his doctrine of the application of Christ's benefits. After his restatement of the covenant theme and the concept of Christ as second Adam, Zanchi raises the point, related to his insistence on the infinite value of Christ's work, that the "grace of redemption and salvation" are seriously offered to all but are in fact communicated only to "the elect who are made one with Christ."[155] Whereas the grace of redemption and salvation to life eternal are truly offered by God to all, "these things are not communicated except to those who from eternity are elected and predestined in Christ the head of all the elect and as his members are made participants in his salvation; these are ultimately in their own time called by the Gospel, given faith by the Holy Spirit, and made one with all those who are united to Christ."[156]

The interplay of scholasticism and Reformed theology in Zanchi's thought does not produce a predestinarian system in which the decrees dominate as the central dogma. Predestination demonstrates that salvation is given entirely graciously and in Christ alone. Christology and Christ-centered piety pervade his system of doctrine. We ought in no way to diminish the importance of predestination to Zanchi's thought, no more than we can diminish the importance of the doctrines of the Trinity, of the divine essence and attributes, of Christ and his word, or of the church, but the doctrine appears as one focus among others which relates to and is interpreted in terms of other *foci*.

EPILOGUE: THE MOVEMENT TOWARD ORTHODOXY

Looking back briefly over the ground we have covered in this examination of "the movement toward orthodoxy" we note a definite change in the style of theology. Formal elements that had already been present in the beginnings of Reformed theology now show themselves more obviously. Aristotelian categories of causality are employed without hesitation. But what differences we detect are nevertheless a matter of degree and not of substance. When the systematic works of Beza, Ursinus, and Zanchi are compared to those of Bullinger, methodological differences appear quite strongly, yet Ursinus' and Zanchi's conception of covenant and its overarching relevance for the entire economy of salvation compares favorably with Bullinger's doctrine. When comparison is made with Calvin, the differences still exist but in a less pronounced form. Calvin's doctrines of providence and predestination relied heavily on Aristotelian categories of causality even though Calvin made less attempt at "scholastic" accuracy in his pronouncements. Philosophical content in the *Loci* of Vermigli and Musculus places them very close in emphasis to Ursinus, Zanchi, and the later works of Beza. We have experienced, in other words, no sudden shift but a series of gradations.

If we turn to the method of presentation, perhaps the greatest change is evidenced. Beza, Ursinus, and Zanchi have moved to establish and develop a school-theology.[157] The forms of the *quaestio*, the *locus*, and the disputation clearly dominate the field, having taken the place of a less-formal style of presentation while overall structure has not yet been fully determined. Beza's theology manifested both analytic and synthetic method, although with a general preference for synthetic as witnessed by the theses debated under Beza and Faius in the academy toward the end of the century.[158] In Heidelberg we encounter both tendencies: Ursinus standing for the analytic approach, Zanchi following a more Thomistic format and establishing a correlation between the divine attributes and the divine work *ad extra*, a synthetic pattern. In none of these thinkers, however, does the more exacting "scholastic" method result in a loss of the scriptural and christological norms of doctrine.

Use of the divine attributes in doctrinal exposition is a case in point. Both

Ursinus and Zanchi have recourse to the attributes in explications of the work *ad extra*: Ursinus in his discussions of providence and the last judgment, Zanchi in his analysis of predestination. Ursinus attempts to show the way in which God's existence, power, wisdom, and justice imply his providential care; the supposition of a God who does not govern is tantamount to a denial of the nature of God. Just as the attributes of God determine the character of his relation to created things, so do they determine his relation to sinful mankind at the judgment; the justice and mercy of God will be satisfied. Similarly, Zanchi utilizes concepts of the wisdom and foreknowledge of God, the freedom of his will, his immutability, his omnipotence, justice, mercy, and love to elucidate the character of the decrees. In neither case is there an attempt to derive a doctrine by strict *a priori* deduction from the divine attributes. Providence, the final judgment, and predestination have all been revealed in Scripture. The issue addressed by these rather strict and scholastic pieces of argumentation is the consistency of God's relationship to the world order.

Of the three transitional theologians examined, moreover, only Zanchi definitively drew the doctrine of predestination into relation with the doctrine of the divine essence and attributes. In his *De natura Dei* Zanchi asks not whether the attributes demand a doctrine of predestination but whether predestination, like other qualities and acts predicated of God, can indeed be properly attributed to the deity. Beza provided no single model for the placement of the doctrine and only in the late *Theses theologicae* written not by Beza but by his students in the Academy, do we encounter the decree in relation to an extended treatment of the attributes and providence. But even here we see only the decision to organize the system synthetically, not the decision to deduce all doctrine from a single principle. Beza himself produced no extended systematic treatment of the essence and attributes of God. The lengthy treatment of the divine will in the *Quaestionum et responsionum* does not stand in relation to the briefly stated doctrine of God but after the christological exposition and prior to the discussion of providence, predestination and the order of salvation. It is not an abstract statement of principle but is directed toward the explanation of God's works.[159]

Ursinus' *loci theologici* do treat the doctrines of God's trinity and unity in a more scholastic fashion, but there is no attempt to draw out a metaphysical structure of the decrees at that point. Zanchi therefore stands as the only one of the transition figures who developed a synthetic paradigm like that of high orthodoxy in which essence, attributes, and decrees stand together: but Zanchi framed his entire system with the doctrine of the Trinity at the forefront, and his treatment of the divine essence and attributes frequently presupposes both trinitarian and christological issues. His doctrine of predestination, moreover, tended to be infralapsarian and did not represent an attempt to create a purely metaphysical, speculative structure out of touch with the tradition of Augustinian definition or overly influenced by philosophical categories of essence.

The doctrine of predestination, then, has altered little in detail and implication and it has not become the dominant force in reformulation of other *loci*. On the other hand, the frequently neglected subject of Reformed Christology has proven a fruitful area of investigation. There we encounter a considerable development of doctrinal structures, each emphasizing the way in which the divine will manifests itself in the economy of salvation or the manner in which the divine person of the mediator is revealed to us in the work of Christ. Concomitant with this development we have seen the almost dialectical return of the Chalcedonian formulation of the dogma of the two natures of Christ to the Reformed system. Because of the polemical need for a standard of orthodoxy in discussion of the person of Christ, the Chalcedonian formula so obviously neglected at an earlier stage of Reformed theology now reappears as a boundary or guidepost for Christology, but it must now take its place in a system the primary emphasis of which is the temporal dispensation of God's eternal will to save both in covenant and in the more predestinarian *ordo salutis*.

The economic, historical pressure upon the Christology results in greater interest in themes like *kenosis* and humiliation as in Zanchi's *De incarnatione*; in the doctrine of Christ as mediator according to both natures as in Beza's various systematic essays and in Ursinus' *Doctrinae christianae compendium*; in the Anselmic structure of a necessary mediation as required by the economy of salvation, again, as found in the thought of Beza and Ursinus; and finally in the tendency toward a formal restructuring of the Christology around themes of *munus triplex* and *status duplex*, seen primarily in Ursinus' theology. These alterations of christological pattern, all of which tend toward making Christology appear as the doctrinal focus of the divine saving will as it enters the temporal order, are characteristic of the movement toward orthodoxy—though in no thinker examined, Beza, Ursinus, Zanchi, is the christological reformulation along these lines complete. What Calvin, Bullinger, and Musculus began would be completed not by these immediate successors but by the generation of Polanus and Perkins.

The attempt to define further the relationship of Christology and predestination seen in Zanchi's *De Tribus Elohim* appears both as a positive impulse within the system, the result of a movement already discernible in the first codification of Reformed theology to make Christ the true center of the soteriology not merely formally but also effectively; and it appears also as the continuation of a drive against the medieval system where the transition from the formal availability of salvation on the basis of Christ's work to the effective application of grace, as merited by Christ for his body, occurs in the sacraments. Whereas in the Thomist system grace came from God, as first mover, through the sacramental instruments, with no great stress on faith in Christ as the ground of justification, here the effective work of the decree is focused on Christ as author, mediator, and object of faith. Election is not only in Christ but also of Christ and by Christ. Although these formulations stand in the context of the developing scholastic system, they point toward a continuing concern for the

Christ-centered piety of the Reformation. Indeed, the more speculative and perhaps rigid formulations of transition-figures like Zanchi must be understood both as results of a new systematizing drive in the third generation of the Reformation and as the attempt to define ever more thoroughly the ground gained by the original reform. The christocentric focus remains; the doctrine of predestination has seen a metaphysical or theological placement foreign to Calvin's generation, but it is no more deterministic for all its further elaboration. The doctrine of the divine attributes, if quite in contrast to Calvin's theological style, has at least the precedent of Musculus' *Loci communes* and appears in no way to undercut the soteriological and christological exposition set below it in the order of system.

In the years between 1563 and 1577 Ursinus and Zanchi gave to Reformed theology a formal structure and a detailed analysis of individual *loci* which, for its comprehensiveness and uniformly high level of argument, was not equalled in the Geneva of Beza. They produced a synthesis of Reformed theology with the established scholastic method, related in its central motifs not only to the thought of Calvin but also to the theology of Bullinger, Vermigli, Musculus, and to that of Luther, Melanchthon, and Bucer. If, however, Ursinus and Zanchi more than Beza provide the transitional theology between the Swiss Reformed systems of the mid-century and the international Reformed theology of the early orthodox codification, they nevertheless stand with Beza as theologians working within the doctrinal structures established by their predecessors, not seeking so much to alter as to develop implications. Beza's great work, which neither Ursinus nor Zanchi could rival, was the establishment of Reformed New Testament exegesis on a firm textual ground: his *Annotationes* are without peer in the sixteenth century.

As Wendel commented in his analysis of the *Institutes*, the underlying definitions and perspectives have been set by Calvin, and, we add, by his contemporaries. Beza, Ursinus and Zanchi built upon that basic set of definitions: the movement toward "orthodoxy" witnessed in the writings of Beza, Ursinus, and Zanchi continued in scholastic form and with more attention to minutiae the theological and systematic development already discernible in the first codification of Reformed theology. The scholastic form or forms adopted by these thinkers ought to be viewed not as a deviation but as the attempt to define and establish more firmly the doctrine of thinkers like Calvin, Bullinger, Musculus, and Vermigli within the bounds of extant system. The theological system of the late middle ages, replete with definitions, distinctions, and fine nuances of doctrine, in which Calvin and his contemporaries had been trained is now, in the movement toward orthodoxy, put to the service of the Reformation. This movement, moreover, bespeaks a twofold continuity, despite the alteration of theological method: first, there is the continuity in doctrine which appears not so much in the simple restatement of Calvin's or Bullinger's or Musculus' or Vermigli's position, but in the careful systematic development of their doctrinal emphases; second there is the continuity between the scholastic discipline according to which the early Reformers were trained and the scholastic method used by their successors in the writing of theology. The discontinuity here, the specific use of a method which was not employed by earlier Protestants, may be explained in terms of a desire to preserve both the message and the underlying theological discipline of Calvin and his contemporaries (not to mention that of the scholastically trained Luther and Bucer at the outset of the Reformation), for the message could hardly have been preserved and surely not defended had the basic discipline been lost. It is also true that neither Beza, nor Ursinus, nor even the compendious Zanchi has completed in his own elaboration of doctrine the development of Reformed theology into scholastic orthodoxy. We move on to Polanus and Perkins with a sense of incomplete, of partially formulated system.

PART II

THE FORMULATION
OF ORTHODOX SYSTEM

Division 2
The Early Orthodox Codification

VI

CALVINISM AT THE CLOSE OF THE SIXTEENTH CENTURY: POLANUS AND PERKINS

1. PREDESTINATION IN THE DOCTRINAL STRUCTURE OF EARLY ORTHODOXY

As we have seen throughout our study of the formation of Reformed orthodoxy in the mid-sixteenth century, there was considerable variation in doctrinal structure, though little change in fundamental doctrinal emphases. Where formulations changed, particularly in the area of Christology, this occurred as a result of structural alteration and a relative freedom in relation to earlier, even to historically definitive conciliar statements of doctrine. The doctrine of predestination itself remained the palladium of a theocentric conception of causality and of the Reformed insistence on the sovereignty of God in all things, especially in the work of salvation. Here, more than in the christological *locus*, the problem of causal priorities becomes explicit and the temporally enacted *ordo salutis* finds itself mirrored in a metaphysical *ordo rerum decretarum*, a statement of the logical priorities within the eternal purpose of God. The question that must be asked of this *ordo rerum decretarum* is the why and wherefore of the more speculative approach and the effect of such speculation upon the soteriological connections which earlier theologians have established for the doctrine of predestination. Two thinkers instrumental in the development of this approach were Amandus Polanus von Polansdorf (1561-1610) and William Perkins (1558-1602).

Several methodological and structural precedents for the dogmatic forms of early orthodoxy appeared in the works we have already examined. Much formalization of doctrinal structure had taken place in the works of Calvin and his contemporaries, and still more in the works of Beza, Ursinus, and Zanchius, men whose thought was characteristic of the years following 1560. In addition, the confessional literature of the Reformed Church, far more than that of the Lutheran, had produced paradigmatic structures for the systematician. Neither prior to nor within the period of early orthodoxy, however, did the doctrine of predestination come to reside definitively in the group of *loci* deriving from consideration of the Godhead. And while the logical and causal structure of Aristotelianism had come to provide the basic physical and metaphysical outlook, by the time of Polanus and Perkins the logical formulations of Peter Ramus offered a partial alternative which most obviously affected the form and the method of argument.[1] The variety witnessed in earlier systems of Reformed doctrine persisted into the era of codification.

A Lutheran in early life, Amandus Polanus von Polansdorf turned to Reformed theology after 1580. He visited Basel and Geneva in 1583, served a Moravian community as pastor and teacher, and in 1596 accepted the professorship of Old Testament at Basel. Polanus is remembered as an exegete, as translator of the New Testament into German, and as a theologian of considerable stature who, with J. J. Grynaeus, saw to the establishment of Calvinist orthodoxy in Basel. In 1590 Polanus published a compendium of doctrine, the *Partitiones theologicae*, which he organized according to the Ramist method of bifurcation, and in which the typically Ramist division between faith and obedience is observed as an organizing principle. His *Syntagma theologiae christianae* (1609) follows the pattern of the *Partitiones* but in considerably greater detail. In both systems Polanus first considers Scripture as the source of all edifying doctrine. The Word of God, given to the church in the writings of the prophets and the apostles, contains a perfect delineation of the "way to eternal life."[2] This word may be divided into two parts, the doctrines of faith and the doctrines concerning good works.[3]

From Polanus' second division we learn that the doctrines of faith teach either of God or of the church, and those of God either of his essence or his works. The doctrine of God's works, therefore, springs directly from consideration of his essence. No one, argues Polanus, can understand the activity of God *ad extra* without first understanding the nature and existence of God as a trinity of persons, one in essence and intention.[4] Polanus, like Ursinus and Zanchius, does not so much derive God's work from consideration of his essence and attributes as attempt to show the direct and necessary correlation between the existence and sovereign will of God and the created order, the patterns of revealed knowledge and the economy of salvation.[5] Despite this causal structuring of system and the relation of predestination to providence, Polanus does not use the decrees as a basis for altering the contents of other *loci*: the *a priori* structure implies no greater determinism than that present in Calvin's *Institutes*. Polanus has only clarified, and perhaps rationalized, the causal and historical series of doctrine and manifested more obviously their conjunction.[6] All in all, the soteriological emphasis remains unchallenged, the doctrine of predestination simply affirming the invincibility of divine grace in the *ordo salutis*. As Barth commented of the orthodox systems, "There was no question of making the . . . doctrine a derivative principle for all the rest."[7] The decree is no more than the unwavering and inalterable purpose of God prior to creation and providence.[8]

And even in the *Westminster Confession* and the theologians mentioned [i.e., Polanus, Wendelin, Burmann, Turettin, van Mastricht, among others], it was not a matter of deducing all dogmatics from the doctrine of predestination. They did bring the doctrine into direct relationship with the doctrine of God. They placed it at the head of all other doctrines. And this meant, of course, but meant only, that in it they found the first and decisive word which we have to receive and proclaim in respect of the will of God in relation to creation; the word of which we have always to take account in everything that follows. If we read their expositions connectedly we are more likely to get the impression that from the standpoint of its systematic range and importance they gave the doctrine too little consideration rather than too much.[9]

Barth's statement flies off in complete contradiction to the general tendency of modern scholarship on this point. Barth admires the restraint of an entire group of systematicians who are generally accused of the greatest extremes in predestinarian speculation. Indeed, Barth comments that election, as it stands under the general doctrine of the decrees, "was never regarded or treated as an integral part of the doctrine of God" by the Reformed orthodox.[10] We note Maccovius' *Loci communes* as the proverbial "exception that proves the rule."

The crucial point at which this formulation moves beyond Calvin is in its examination of causal priorities in the mind of God: the *opera Dei ad intra* and the *ordo* within the decree undergirding the external *ordo salutis*. Clearly, this is a theological step that Calvin and his contemporaries did not take, a step which belongs to the process of argumentation, division of subject, speculative elaboration of the original doctrinal ground (i.e., the first codification of Reformed Theology and the confessional position), and rationalization of dogmatic stance characteristic of the age. A similar, if doctrinally antagonistic, development is evident both in Arminius' division of the decree into four component parts descriptive of logical and causal priorities in the divine mind and in Molina's development of a *scientia media* between the divine *scientia necessaria* and *scientia visionis*. What we contend here is that this rationalizing process did not ignore the relation of the decree as *operum Dei ad intra* to the trinitarian life of God and to the christological center of the *ordo salutis*. In short, this speculative development of the doctrine of predestination arose in the context of scholastic theology and of the adaptation of scholastic method by Reformed theologians, but it arose for the specific purpose of carrying on in new language and via a more strict theological method the basic christological and soteriological insights of the Reformers.

William Perkins (1558-1602) was perhaps the most eminent English Reformed theologian of the late sixteenth century, everywhere recognized, along with Peter Martyr Vermigli, Theodore Beza, Lambert Daneau, and William Ames, as a major exponent of Reformed theology.[11] Heinrich Heppe viewed Perkins as a "father of pietism" and characterized that most causal of Perkins' treatises, *A Golden Chaine*, as a study of the ground of piety and of holy living. According to Heppe, the focus of Perkin's theology was the mystical union of the believer with Christ. A similar position was taken by August Lang, and more recently, Christopher Hill has spoken of justification by faith as the overriding concern of Perkins' theology.[12] In his excellent two-volume study of pietism, Stoeffler confirms these appraisals of Perkins' theology speaking of *A Golden Chaine* as the earliest work representative of the pietistic spirit of Puritanism. Stoeffler finds the work "Calvinistic" to the core as witnessed by its "hard doctrine of predestination," but the difference between Perkins' and Calvin's perspective appears not as a hardening of the doctrine of predestination but instead as a greater emphasis on Christian life and practice.[13]

Nevertheless, scholars have not agreed on either the character of Perkins' thought or his place in the development of Reformed theology. In the view of Basil Hall, Perkins contributed greatly to the distortion of Calvinism into the form of a predestinarian metaphysic.[14] A similar analysis comes from the work of Ian Breward who views Perkins' doctrine of predestination as following Beza and Zanchi toward a "more speculative doctrine of predestination"[15] in which the christocentric approach of Calvin is lost. In reference to *A Golden Chaine*, Breward comments:

> Not only does he begin with an account of God's being which showed how God's action was inseparable from his essence, he also discussed predestination in connection with the doctrine of God. The work of Christ was discussed within the context of predestination rather than providing the key to the decrees of God.[16]

Similar arguments, reflecting both Hall's and Breward's reading of *A Golden Chaine* and their argument that Perkins' predestinarianism represents a distortion of Calvin's teaching, appear in Kendall's analysis of the development of Calvinism in England.[17] All three of these authors accept the reappraisal of Calvin's theology as christocentric but, as noted in general in the introductory chapter, retain Schweizer's theory of the predestinarian system as descriptive of orthodoxy. Neither Hall, nor Breward, nor Kendall seems sufficiently cognizant of the relationship between Perkins' theology and pietism, nor are they sufficiently aware of the christological and trinitarian developments in the thought of Perkins and his contemporaries.

This diversity of opinion can be attributed directly to the impression made by Perkins' *A Golden Chaine* upon Hall, Breward, and Kendall. They view the work as a system of doctrine and conclude that Perkins was the formulator of a metaphysical structure according to which all doctrine was interpreted. Lang, however, disputes the thesis that Reformed theology developed into a rigid predestinarianism and refuses to view Perkins' treatise as a system of doctrine.[18] This interpretation proves to be the more fruitful, particularly in view of the striking omissions of doctrines from the plan of *A Golden Chaine*.[19] In addition, the "*armilla aurea*" or "golden chaine" is the name traditionally given to the *ordo salutis* of Romans 8:29-30. The piece, like Beza's *Tabula*, is no more than an elaboration of the order of causes contributing to salvation and damnation.[20]

2. THE DEVELOPMENT OF CHRISTOLOGICAL STRUCTURES
IN EARLY REFORMED ORTHODOXY

Preliminary definitions in Polanus' Christology

Polanus' contribution to the development of Reformed Christology draws profoundly on the basic distinctions between infinite God and finite creation, which we have found constitutive of the earlier Reformed theology, and on the related conception of *historica series*. After completing his analysis of the law, Polanus proceeds to a discussion of the Gospel, "that whole sum of doctrine concerning Christ, already shewn and manifested."[21] The Law-Gospel contrast here, like the law-covenant contrast in Musculus' system, manifests a concern for the historical dispensation of salvation while the discussion of Gospel and Christ together manifests the inseparability of the incarnate Word from his historical work as fulfilled in the Gospel Word. Indeed, Polanus argues a threefold meaning of *evangelium*: it indicates first the *historia Christi* or the historical books of the disciples concerning Christ, as stated by Mark (1:1), "The beginning of the Gospel of Jesus Christ, the Son of God." Second, *evangelium*, Gospel, indicates *generaliter* the doctrine of Christ and his Apostles, and third, it indicates *specialiter ac stricte* the "most blessed . . . work of redemption of the human race through Christ."[22] Polanus' definition of Christ's person properly considered (*in se*) reflects this historical and economical concern:

> Christ, properly considered, is the only-begotten, and eternal Son of God, made man for the sake of our salvation, anointed by God to be our final and eternal prophet, priest, and king, according to a mode of ordination which was before the foundation of the world.[23]

The designation *Christos* itself indicates this salvific purpose, as both the Greek *Christos* and Hebrew *Maschiach* indicate "the unction, according to which he is anointed to his work and his dignity by God the Father."[24]

Having defined the person of Christ, Polanus can now proceed to define the structure of his Christology:

> The faith or doctrine concerning Christ has two parts: first, concerning the person of Christ: second, concerning his work (*officium*).

> Consideration of the person of Christ is twofold: one, according to his essence, *tou logou*: the other according the economy of grace and salvation.[25]

In essential terms, then, the person of Christ is "*asunthetos* hypostasis in divina essentia a Patre ab aeterno genita," while in economic terms, "hypostasis *sunthetos*, id est, persona secunda Deitatis incarnata, ac proinde ac duabus naturis composita, personae unitate manente."[26] The incarnate Christ, Polanus emphasizes, is "one and singular: he is one Christ, not two, the same Son of Man who is Son of God: not one person Christ and another the Son of God, not one person divine, another human."[27] By "person," comments Polanus, adopting the language of late scholasticism, is meant a *suppositum*, and in Christ there is but one *suppositum*, one independent existent.[28]

The Ramist tendency to delineate exhaustive and inclusive categories and then to proceed to discussion of particulars by a process of bifurcation here manifests an important aspect of the Reformed Christology, an aspect, moreover, which it shares with the doctrine of predestination: it is a doctrine which grounds and clarifies the ecclesiology. Polanus, in fact, manifests parallels in his primary definitions: Christology refers first to the person of Christ *in se* and in terms of the relationship into which Christ comes by way of the work of salvation to the *totus Christus*, the church as body of Christ, and similarly, the doctrine of predestination refers both to Christ and to the *unitorum Christo*, those united to Christ as his body, the church.[29] Here again, it is not a matter of a single central dogma controlling all the rest but of several centers that together create the theological context in which other doctrines must be understood.

As we have learned to expect from the developing Reformed Christology, concentration upon the person of the mediator in the historical line of the covenant leads to a statement of the Anselmic argument for the God-man as a crucial component of the analysis of Christ's person. Polanus' Christology is no exception: indeed, Polanus presents one of the more elaborate amplifications of Anselm's argument. Christ's divine-human person is the very substance and import of the promises of redemption: "Causa cur Christum opportuerat esse simul hominem & Deum in una persona sunt gravissima."[30] Polanus delineates four distinct causes of or reasons for the humanity of Christ: the *iustitia Dei* demands that a man satisfy for the sins of mankind; the *modus satisfactionis*, moreover, requires that the law of God be fulfilled and the penalty for transgression be meted out. Again, a man must perform the work. The third cause is the pattern of our adoption as sons and liberation from the devil, and the fourth reason is our certitude of resurrection from the dead. But Christ also must be God, and this for two reasons: the magnitude of the evil to be overcome and magnitude of the good to be bestowed. Only God can bear the weight of sin and abolish the tyranny of the devil; only God can effect the highest good and restore the fallen creature according to his image.[31]

In the last of Polanus' "reasons" for the divine-human person of Christ, we encounter the issue of the end of man as the highest goal of the creature, the conferral and conservation of the *imago Dei*. As the highest good of the creature, the *imago Dei* cannot be grounded on the power of creatures whose present condition falls short of that end, but only on the God who is himself the *summum Bonum*. Tangentially, this argument for the divine-human person reflects the minute, but nonetheless influential, positive dimension of the argument with Osiander: if not apart from, then also prior to and following the problem of sin, the Son confers and conserves the image in us. Not merely the restoration but the positive constitution of human nature reflects the christocentric perspective of Polanus' system to the end that the functional, historical and economical perspective of the Christology does not reduce the person of Christ to a mere means in the work of salvation.

This concern for the centrality of the historical revelation of Christ to the Christian message carries over into the next series of determinations on the person of Christ and most clearly in the structural *partitiones* at the heart of the system. The first of these divisions we have seen already as the prologue to a discussion of the divine and human natures, but it is the sequence, above all, that is crucial:

> The faith concerning the person of Christ has two parts: first, concerning the natures in the person of Christ: second, concerning his state.
>
> The natures in the person of Christ are two: divine and human.
>
> The twofold state of the person of Christ is either of humiliation or of exaltation.
>
> Of the humiliation of Christ there are two parts: incarnation and fulfillment of the law.
>
> The parts of the incarnation of Christ are, the conception of Christ and the assumption of human nature, and the personal union of the two natures, lastly, the nativity.[32]

After his initial statement of the unity of the two natures in Christ, represented here by the first two propositions, Polanus shifts his focus to the doctrine of the "states" of Christ's person. The traditional christological problem of the hypostatic union now belongs, not to an independent *locus* of the person of Christ, but to the exposition of the states experienced by Christ: the problem of two natures in one person now appears not as an a-historical issue with ontological overtones, but as the underlying presupposition of the economy of the Son in his humiliation and exaltation. The result of this structuring is the development of the Christology in terms first of the states of Christ's person and second in terms of Christ's office or work as prophet, priest, and king, both of which categories stand in relation to the *historica series* of the covenant dispensation and to Polanus' sense of Christology as an issue belonging to the economy of salvation.

The Person of Christ as Self-determined in Humiliation

In the chapter immediately following his discussion of Christ's person, Polanus comes to the incarnation considered as the first part of the *status humiliationis*. Against the Lutheran position that would begin the humiliation subsequent to the incarnation Polanus argues that the *status humiliationis Christi* consists in the self-emptying (*exinanitio*) of the one who was in the form of God, his descent from heaven for our sake, his submission under and obedience to the law and his satisfaction to God for our disobedience. This self-emptying does not occur *kat ousian*, for Christ is essentially one with the Father and Spirit, but *kat oikonomian*, which is to say "according to the gracious dispensation" by which he assumes human nature.[33] Christ's humiliation, therefore, does not refer strictly to his divine nature which can neither be diminished nor subjected to death, but to his person and to the self-determined dispensation or economy by which the divine Son assumes flesh. In this sense, then, incarnation needs be viewed as *pars humiliationis Filii Dei*: it is the point at which the transcendent, infinite God enters the human sphere for the sake of our salvation.[34]

The doctrine of Christ's humiliation and exaltation which achieves such formal prominence in Polanus' system was not a concept which we found elaborated in Calvin's *Institutes*. Its appearance in Ursinus' *Doctrinae christianae compendium* is brief and hardly a major doctrinal determination. As Berkouwer notes, this is primarily a Lutheran and not a Reformed doctrine in its origin.[35] From its earliest formulations, the Lutheran doctrine of the two states reflected a concern for the relationship of incarnation and the doctrine of divine immutability:[36] it functioned as an explanation of the weakness, ignorance, and local presence of Christ incarnate despite the communication of divine attributes to the human nature.[37] In Reformed theology, however, the concept of the two states represents an emphasis on the soteriological message of the biblical account of the incarnation, life, sufferings, the death, resurrection, and ascension of Christ,[38] an essentially historical emphasis. Both natures undergo humiliation. The human nature suffers earthly humiliation, manifested by the contrast between the passion of Christ and his later exaltation to glory. Humiliation relates to the divine nature in terms of the self-emptying of the Son in his incarnation, the voluntary concealment of divine attributes, and the binding of his divinity to the infirmities of our flesh for the accomplishment of salvation, thus the Lutheran characterization of this doctrine as a mere *krupsis* or concealment.[39] When the *kenosis* or self-emptying is thus conceived as humiliation and concealment, it parallels the voluntary subordination of the Son to the office of the mediator and the execution of the decree.

Polanus now comes to the typically Augustinian question, springing from the strong determination of the unity of God and the essential equality of the persons, the *aseity* of the Son considered as to essence and the denomination of all acts *ad extra* as the common work of the Trinity: "since the incarnation of Christ is the common work of the whole sacred Trinity, why isn't the entire sacred Trinity incarnate?"[40] Polanus begins with a positive statement of his doctrine:

> The principal efficient cause and author of the incarnation is the entire sacred Trinity, Father, Son, and Holy Spirit, in such a way that the human nature is created and suited for the person of the Son by the Father, Son, and Spirit acting together.[41]

This determination is necessary in Christology just as the similar trinitarian determination of the decree is necessary in the *locus de praedestinatione* not only if the Son is to be considered as essentially equal to the Father and if the Trinity is to be viewed as one God, but also if the Son is to be seen as more than a mere means to an end in the economy of salvation: here, as in the *locus de praedestinatione*, the trinitarian determination of doctrine stands in the way both of an improper separation and subordination of the Son's will to that of the Father and of the relegation of the Father to the role of *Deus nudus absconditus*. The entrance of the Son into the temporal economy here maintains the unity and consistency of the divine will and, in a sense, relates the Father (and the Spirit) by way of the Son to the manifestation of God among men.

This trinitarian argument leads to a distinction between incarnation as the common work (*opus commune*) of all persons in the Trinity which terminates in the person of the Son and the assumption of human nature, which, in a restrictive sense, is the personal work of the Son alone. *Inchoatively*, the incarnation is a common work of the divine persons but *terminatively* it is the work of the Son. In this latter sense, incarnation is the *opus proprium* of the Son, a personal rather than an essential work, not a common but an economical or dispensative work (*opus oeconomicum*). Similarly, if the one divine substance is incarnate, it is nevertheless true that it is not the divine nature *simpliciter* that is incarnate but the "natura divina determinata in Filio, id est, hypostasis seu persona Filii."[42] We have seen this issue broached by earlier writers, Musculus and Vermigli specifically, but not so precisely argued.

The high sense of the Son's divinity, as defined by the concept of *aseity*, not only pressed Polanus toward an examination of the relation of the Trinity to the work of incarnation but also led him to develop a detailed examination of the causality of incarnation: the *causa impellens* or mercy of God toward perishing humanity, the *causa proka traktike* or the fall of Adam and the hereditary misery brought by it upon mankind combined with the powerlessness of the law to bring about salvation, the *causas efficientes* or the will and power of God as relating to the Son, and the *causa administrativa* or the ordering of things according to the eternal decree so that the Virgin might be the mother of the Messiah.[43] The first two of these causal arguments are of interest insofar as they maintain the substance in scholastic form of Calvin's definitively functional approach to Christology. Despite Polanus' interest in the eternity, essence, attributes, and decretive will of God, incarnation cannot be conceived in his system apart from the fact of human sinfulness: "had Adam not fallen and we by his fall come into our great misery, the Son of God would not have been incarnate."[44] This infralapsarian tendency appears most plainly from the promise of the *protevangelium* as a remedy for existent misery.[45] The anti-speculative thrust of Calvin's polemic against Osiander is maintained in Polanus' description of the causality of incarnation. What is more, the highly speculative possibility of integrating incarnation and fall into an eternal and necessary divine design, generated by attention to the eternal decrees as essential acts of God, fails to be actualized in his system. For all that God is eternal, the impelling cause of incarnation remains the "amor & misericordia Dei erga genus humanum quod per peccatum perierat."[46]

Polanus' analysis of the efficient causes is also significant since he here again enters upon the question of the Son's divinity and, thus, of the trinitarian ground of theology. The solution of the problem points us again toward the issue of intratrinitarian relations at the ground of the economy of salvation. Polanus speaks of the Son's willing to be incarnate and uses language which adumbrates the federalist terminology for the *pactum salutis* and which relates to the orthodox explanation of the exinanition and humiliation of the Son:

> The Son, indeed, is incarnate because he wills voluntarily to be made our sponsor, voluntarily subjecting himself to the Father not according to nature, but according to the voluntary arrangement (*oeconomia*) or dispensation: a natural subjection is, surely, distinct from an economic or dispensational subjection: he is made freely obedient to the Father, not according to the divine nature in itself (*in se*), but according to will: obedience, indeed, is not the natural act of a nature (*actus naturalis naturae*), but of the will or free accord of the person of Christ (*voluntarius personae Christi*).[47]

Without dwelling too long upon forms, we note the highly technical language, the scholastic method of careful division of topic as they contribute to the clearer formulation of this basic christological point in the Reformed system; the point itself we have seen in Calvin—scholastic method merely elaborates, distinguishes, clarifies and finds technical formulae.

In focusing this section of his Christology around the problem of the *exinanition* of the Son as the key to understanding Christ's person and the relation of the entire Trinity to the incarnation as the perspective for viewing the working-out of divine purpose in Christ, Polanus has emphasized those aspects of the christological problem that most pointedly raise the issue of the relation of the infinite to the finite in Christ and that most emphatically manifest the utter incapability, the ontological *non capax*, of the finite to receive the infinite, to comprehend it, to contain it and the gracious capability of the divine in its assumption of the flesh. The entire Christology, then, both in its organization and its substance, is oriented toward the saving work of the triune God and, to that end, is concentrated upon the person of the mediator as incarnate. Following the chapters dealing with the person of Christ and the incarnation and two states where this perspective on the doctrine is determined, Polanus sets forth his doctrine in a series of chapters: the conception of Christ by the Holy Spirit (cap. xiv), the *assumptio carnis* (cap. xv), the personal union (cap. xvi), and the birth from the Virgin (cap. xvii). The doctrine of Christ's person is now seen in a new light, receiving its exposition under and determined by the concept of the two states and belonging to the larger problem of the trinitarian economy and the historical dispensation of salvation.

On the basis of this and similar structuring of Christology by the orthodox Reformed writers, E. F. K. Müller argued that the assimilation of the doctrine of the two states into Calvinist dogmatics tended to have a disruptive effect on the doctrine of the person of Christ.[48] Although Polanus does in fact state this doctrine twice, his main exposition belongs to the *status humiliationis*. Polanus represents the concept of personal union not in terms of the eternal Son of God as something to be effected, but in terms of Christ and the Gospel as something made manifest in time. What apears to be a disruptive force acting upon a Chalcedonian Christology is a unitive force in the Reformed structure where the person of Christ becomes known only through his voluntary self-emptying and his work as mediator and where a historical or economical pattern in Christology conforms to the overall historical pattern of sin, fall, covenant, law, and gospel.[49]

Polanus defines the conception of Christ by the Holy Spirit as the formation of Christ's human nature "of the flesh and blood of the Virgin Mary" by the Spirit in such a way that the divine and human natures might be united in one person. The natures remain distinct in the union without a confusion of essence, properties, or operations.[50] This distinction must be maintained in Christian doctrine since a confusion of properties implies a confusion of natures, even as an absence of properties, implies an absence of natures. At this point Polanus inserts a reference to Luther showing that the polemic of the day was never far from his mind. Essential properties are not communicated between the natures.[51] Nevertheless, by reason of the grace of union, the humanity of Christ is raised to a dignity and nobility not possible for men conceived according to the natural order.[52]

Polanus' discussion of the obedience of Christ concludes his analysis of the *status humiliationis*. This obedience, also termed "the righteousness of Christ," represents "the other part of his humiliation, whilst he was in all things obedient to the Father." It consists in his fulfillment of the law and his payment for man's sin, the former an active obedience of Christ's entire life, the latter the passive obedience of the passion, death, burial, and descent into hell.[53] The passive obedience is to be understood as the part of Christ's obedience in which he "sustained the wrath of God against sin" in both body and soul. Polanus interprets this suffering as descriptive of the entire life of Christ and therefore disavows any soteriological distinction between the active obedience of Christ's life and the passive obedience to death.[54] The unity of Christ's work according to Polanus stems from an overarching theme of exinanition and humiliation, which begins with the incarnation and Christ's birth into a world of ills and infirmities and is brought to an end in his descent into hell.[55] Again we note in passing the historical structuring of doctrine.

In his *status exaltationis*[56] Christ overcomes the power of death "by his own divine power" to the end that man might be able to partake of the righteousness purchased by his death and live in the hope of the resurrection. Christ's ascension into heaven seals his promise of a future life for believers. It also reveals Christ as intercessor and as the one who sends the Holy Spirit.[57] The ascension is distinct from the sitting at the right hand of the Father. The ascent occurred once in the life of Christ, but insofar as Christ possesses power over heaven and earth in his divine nature, the *sessio* is perpetual.[58] This distinction is a reflection on both the *extra calvinisticum* and the Reformed interpretation of *exinanitio*. The Son of God, in his eternity and omnipotence, is always at the right hand of the Father, always one with the Father and the Spirit in the Godhead, even when he is given to man in the incarnation. Exaltation refers to the divine nature only in terms of the subordination of the Son in the office of the mediator and the economy of salvation.[59]

The Threefold Office in Polanus' Theology

In the second division of his Christology, Polanus defines the office of Christ as a work instituted "to bestow on the elect all things which are required to eternal salvation."[60] Christ's work and its application are intimately related to the doctrine of predestination in this formulation. Nevertheless, this is not a speculative or theoretical element artificially introduced into Polanus' Christology, nor is it a formal principle that guides the presentation of doctrine. Rather, it is a description of the fulness of God's grace manifest in the entirety of Christ's work, a description of the working-out of God's invincible intention to save. All those aspects of God's promise mediated incompletely and imperfectly under the Old Covenant are herein fulfilled.[61] Since the doctrine of Christ's office represents the work of his entire life, it is concurrent with the doctrine of the two states. The threefold office is understood of both natures, and the work of the office is attributed to Christ according to both natures so that the doctrine of the threefold office like that of the two states unites the concepts of Christ's person and work, though with less emphasis on historical order and more on the manner in which the eternal relates to the temporal in the economy and revelation of salvation.[62]

The establishment of the office itself stands as an example of this distinction between and reconciliation of the eternal and the temporal. Polanus sees the subordination of the mediator to the work of salvation as analogous to the pattern of *kenosis* and *humiliatio*: it refers to Christ's divinity not according to the person but according to the office. Ultimately, Reformed theologians would describe this suprapersonal conferring of office as the common work of the three divine persons: Christ's own will, the voluntary self-subordination, belongs to the bestowing of the office as much as the will of the Father and Spirit.[63] Indeed, writes Polanus, Christ was constituted as mediator before the foundation of the world, given to us as mediator by God according to the eternal decree, not because of any merit in us but because of the grace and love of God toward us under the covenant of grace. Thus, for the sake of our salvation the Son, equal by nature to the Father, has become mediator according to an entirely voluntary dispensation, less than God, indeed, less than himself.[64]

The underlying assumption throughout this christological development has been that the doctrine of the two natures, inherited as such from the patristic and medieval theologies, must now be interpreted *via* the description of the official work of the mediator in his two states. Rather than the categories of person and work *per se*, we encounter the structures of *status duplex* and *munus triplex*. The interpretive burden of the Christology becomes the relation of the two natures in the person of the mediator to the various aspects of humiliation, exaltation, and the office of prophet, priest, and king and, ultimately, the way in which the ongoing categories of Christ's official work, prophetic, priestly, and kingly, relate to the dynamic of *exinanitio, humiliatio, exaltatio*.[65]

In his prophetic office Christ perfects the work of prophecy by delivering to man "the whole word of God" both concerning the future of mankind and concerning true doctrine.[66] The priestly office represents Christ's expiation of sin and payment for the sins of the elect. Like Calvin, and against the Thomist conception of Vermigli and Zanchi, Polanus views Christ's merit both as the perfect satisfaction of the law and also as resting upon the decree. Thus the merit of Christ cannot be the foundation of our salvation in and of itself; rather the foundation of salvation is the will and ordination of God according to which the mediator was constituted. The dignity and power of Christ's merit, however, rest upon the divinity of Christ's person. This merit, therefore, stands as sufficient for all mankind.[67] Polanus makes a distinction between expiation and intercession, satisfaction and redemption. The former terms define the merit of Christ's passion and death, which is "sufficient for all the men of the world, if all did receive the same by faith." The latter represent the "powerful working of Christ" by which he bestows upon the elect the benefits of his death and endues them with perseverance "that they may not fall from grace."[68] Again, the concept of a limited atonement appears not as an unwarranted or overly rationalistic intrusion of the doctrine of the decree into the *locus* of Christ's priestly work, but rather a statement of the bounds of Christ's effective work as author of salvation. The concept stands as a corollary rather than as a result of the doctrine of election and as a sign of the profound interrelationship of Christology with predestination.

The priestly office also represents the continuing memory of Christ's sacrifice and under the category of Christ's exaltation, the intercession made to the Father for our sake. Even so, Christ's kingly office manifests his power over the church as its head and his defense of the church against its enemies.[69] Christ's office represents his post-resurrection work as well as the work of his earthly ministry, death, and resurrection: the threefold office demonstrates the unity of Christ's work with its application both in intention and act.[70] In the *munus triplex* the historical line of the promise is projected from the Old into the New Covenant, and the place of Christ in the divine economy is described. His own historical work, the historicity of his prophecy, priesthood, and kingship, provides the fulfillment of the old dispensation and the form of salvation offered under the new. But also, in view of the twofold anointing or divine appointment, the *munus triplex* indicates preeminently the vertical line of the divine will as it intersects and guides the line of the temporal economy. Again, the person of the mediator appears as the point in which the great tension of the Calvinist system, the timeless eternity of God meeting the historical finitude of man, *infinitum capax finiti*, is resolved.

Perkins' Doctrine of the Person of the Mediator and his Work

Perkins' Christology, like Polanus', represents a dogmatic realization of the christological motifs of earlier Reformed theology. Upon the credal articles which determine the outline of his exposition, Perkins builds a doctrinal structure that stresses the order and plan of redemption as revealed and accomplished in Christ. Even more than Polanus, Perkins expands upon the necessity of mediation. Given these initial emphases, we are not surprised to find that Perkins' Christology relates all concepts of Christ's person and work to the doctrines of the threefold office and the two states. Discussion of Christ's person as well as his work belongs to the analysis of the mediator's obedience in humiliation and his exaltation. At the very beginning of his system, in the definition of faith, Perkins writes of Christ:

> His Godhead is apprehended, not in respect of his efficacie or nature, but in respect of his efficacie manifested in the manhood, whereby the obedience thereof is made meritorious before God.[71]

This approach to Christology mirrors Calvin's stress on Christ as *Deus manifestatus in carne* and bears witness to the Reformed development of a Christology neither "from above" nor "from below" but in the historical line of the covenant-promise, as the nexus of the temporal causality of salvation and the eternal will of God to save. We see this perspective in Perkins' opening statement:

> The foundation and ground worke of the Covenant is Christ Iesus the Mediatour, in whome all the promises of God are yea and amen, and therefore he is called the *angel of the covenant*, & the *covenant of the people* to be made with all nations in the last age. Now then that we may proceed at large to open the substance of the covenant, wee are in the next place to come to that part of the Creede, which concernes the second person in Trinitie, set down in these words: *And Iesus Christ his onely Sonne*, & c. from which words to the very ende of the Creede, such points onely are laid downe, as do notably unfolde the benefits and the matter of the covenant. Now the second person is described to us by three things: first his titles: secondly, his incarnation: thirdly, his twofold estate.[72]

What is significant about Perkins' division of the topic—titles, incarnation, two states—is that it follows precisely the pattern (rather than the initially-stated organizational model) of Ursinus' *Doctrinae christianae compendium* and witnesses to the impact of the Heidelberg theology on English Reformed thought.

The first title of the savior considered by Perkins is "Jesus," the Savior's proper name. This name signifies for Perkins the "perfect and absolute" accomplishment of salvation considered according to both merit and efficacy.[73] Christ makes perfect satisfaction to God for sin in order that human nature might be mortified and die to sin.[74] Division here of Christ's work into categories of merit and efficacy points toward Perkins' later adaptation of the Lombardian formula of limited atonement to a specifically christological conception of limited intercession.

The title "Christ" is not a name properly so-called, but an "appellation" equivalent to the Hebrew "Messiah" and meaning "annointed." Even so, in the Old Testament there was a "legall annointing" of kings, priests, and prophets that was "a type and figure of the annointing of Christ." Perkins now completes the development we have seen, beginning with Calvin, toward an explicit concept of twofold anointing. The anointing of Christ

> was not with bodily oyle, but by the spirit, and it was more excellent than al other annointings were. . . . Christs annointing is according to both natures; for in what nature hee is a Mediator, in the same he is anointed: but according to both his natures ioyntly he is a mediatour: the godhead is no mediatour without the manhood, nor the manhood without the godhead: and therefore his annointing extends itselfe both to his godhead & to his manhood.[74]

This anointing provides the antitype and the fulfillment of the "legall annointing" of the Old Testament:

> his consecration whereby he was set apart to doe the office of a Mediatour betweene God and man: and therefore to be a King, a Priest, and a Prophet: a King to gather & withall to governe his Church and people: a Priest, to make satisfaction & intercession for the sinnes of the elect: a Prophet to reveale & teach his people the will of God his father.[75]

This, as argued earlier, was the implication of the doctrine of Christ's mediation as developed by Calvin and his contemporaries. It was also the basis in their theology for the underlying relationship postulated between Christ and the decree: the doctrine of the threefold office not only presses reconsideration of the christological problem but also presses theological meditation upon the work of Christ as, in a causal sense, the nexus of the temporal execution and the eternal intentionality of salvation. As Bavinck reasoned, "To conceive of the work of Christ as the exercise of an office is to relate that work to the eternal counsel."[76] Even so, in Perkins' exposition we now encounter the crucial issue of the designation or election of the second person of the Trinity, the concept of a God, "both electing and elected." Here also, the suprapersonal character of Christ's office implied by Calvin has become part of a formal determination of doctrine.[77]

> . . . though it be true that Christ is set apart to the worke of mediation, as he is Mediatour, or as he is man, yet as he is God he doth design & set himselfe apart to the same work. For to design the Mediator is a common action of the three persons, the Father, the Sonne, and the Holy Ghost; and yet considering the Father is first in order, and therefore hath the beginning of the action: for this cause he is said especially to designe, as when Saint John saith, *Him the Father hath sealed.*[78]

The mediator is also called the Son of God. This title Perkins refers to the eternal generation of the second person of the Trinity from God the Father. Immediately Perkins adds to his definition the qualifier of Christ's aseity: insofar as he is the Son, he does not exist from himself, but is begotten from the Father; yet insofar as he is God, the second person of the Trinity exists of himself and participates in the full essence of the Godhead. The begetting, as eternal, represents a priority of the Father only in order, not in time. Christ, as he is God, is fully divine and has all the properties or attributes of God. Here Perkins makes the crucial distinction between the second person of the Trinity considered as "Son" and the same second person of the Trinity considered as God: considered in terms of his sonship he is begotten and second in order; considered in terms of his essence he is God *a se ipso*—he has the attribute of aseity. He is "*non autohuios* tamen *autotheos*":

> For the thing itselfe, it is Christ; who must be considered two waies, as he is a Sonne, and as hee is God. As he is a sonne, he is not of himselfe, but the sonne of the father begotten of him: nevertheless as he is God, he is of himselfe, neither begotten, nor proceeding; for the essence or godhead of the Father is of itselfe without all beginning, but the godhead of the sonne is one and the same with the godhead of the Father: because by what godhead the Father is God, by the same and no other the sonne is God: therefore the sonne, as he is God, he is God of himselfe without beginning even as the Father. Whereupon it followes, that the Sonne is begotten of the Father as he is a sonne, but not as he is God.[79]

The generation of the Son is neither a "fluxe" or outflowing nor a "decision as when a thing is cut in peeces" nor a "propagation"; rather it is an eternal communication without "beginning, middle, or end" whereby "the father begetting and the sonne begotten are coeternall, and therefore equall in time." Thus the Son is not only essentially equal, but from our perspective equal even as generated, and the works of God must be ascribed equally to Father, Son, and Holy Spirit.[80]

Perkins' doctrine of the incarnation, much like Calvin's, partakes of the Anselmic structure, which conceives of the divine-human nature of Christ as necessary in some sense. It is clear, however, to Perkins that God cannot be constrained either by man's need or by a particular type of theological reasoning. The incarnation was necessary in order that man might again know God and that the proper satisfaction might be made for man's sin, yet necessary only "in respect of God's will, and not in respect of his absolute power." God, argues Perkins in genuinely Scotist fashion, might have saved mankind by other means, but he chose to appoint salvation through the incarnation of his Son. A similar pattern occurs in Perkins' *A Golden Chaine* where the doctrine of the incarnation appears as the "foundation" of "the execution of the decree."[81]

Nevertheless, once it is recognized that no external necessity can be placed upon God, there remains a necessity, under the divine will, that is met by the person of the mediator as God and man. Perkins, in other words, addresses the issue of the necessity of the God-man in terms of the soteriological problem, and, like Calvin, does so prior to his doctrine of incarnation and of the two natures in Christ: the structure of atonement as satisfaction provides the christological model, the person being defined in and through his historical work. Perkins can therefore argue, "it was necessarie that Christ should be God." In the first place, only God can save both body and soul. Second, in true Anselmic style, Perkins writes,

> There must bee a proportion betweene the sinne of man and the punishment of sinne: now the sinne of man in respect of the offence of the maiestie of God is infinite, in that he is infinitely displeased with man for the breach of his law: therefore the punishment of sinne must be infinite: and hence it followeth, that he which suffereth the punishment beeing man, must withall be God, that the manhood by the power of the Godhead may be supported, that in suffering it may vanquish death, & make a sufficient satisfaction.[82]

Equally so, the mediator must be a man: the very same nature in and through which God was offended must make amends.

> Adam sinned first, and in him all his posteritie: therefore it was necessarie that in man's nature there should bee a satisfaction made to God's iustice, and for this cause the Sonne of God must needs abase himself and become man for our sakes.[83]

Similarly, all men are required to fulfill the "very rigour & extremitie of the morall law" in order to be saved, in becoming man the Son of God, as man, fulfilled all righteousness. Third, it was necessary—and here we see a definite addition to the Anselmic argument to accommodate the Reformed emphasis on Christ's sacrificial death—that the redeemer suffer and die, and by his blood pay the price for sin: God cannot die; he thus needed to assume human nature for the completion of the work of salvation in self-sacrifice. Finally,

> he that must make reconciliation betweene God and man, must be such an one as may make request or speake both to God and man. For a Mediatour is as it were a middle person making intercession betweene two other persons.[84]

Even in *A Golden Chaine*, where the causal disposition of the treatise would lead quite naturally to a Chalcedonian Christology "from above," the emphasis falls on the doctrine of the person of the mediator as manifest in time for the execution of the decree, as the only possible answer to the problem posed by the Son's infinite and eternal divinity miraculously and graciously encountering the task of redeeming humanity in time and under the exigencies of finitude. "How," Perkins inquires, "can Christ bee subordinate unto Gods election seeing hee together with the Father decreed all things?" The mediator, he answers, is not subordinate to the decree as such but to its execution: he is the "foundation" of the execution of the divine decree, "called of his Father from all eternitie to performe the office of the mediatour, that in him all those which should bee saved might be chosen."[85] This ordained necessity of mediation, which even in Perkins' most causally rigid structure proceeds out of the problem of sin,[86] leads immediately to a discussion of the mediator as God-man, and as the link between divinity and humanity, to an analysis of the fittingness of the Son for incarnation: "for it is the office of the Sonne to have the administration of every outward action of the Trinitie, from the Father, by the Holy Ghost."[87]

Perkins' attention to the economic paradigm of Reformed Christology appears not only in his *An Exposition of the Symbole* but also and perhaps with more emphasis in *A Golden Chaine*. Perkins moves from the problem of sin to election and from thence to "Christ Jesus" as mediator of the saving will of God. The doctrine of the two natures appears first as the two requisite terms of the doctrine of reconciliation, God and man conjoined:

> Christs first nature is the Godhead, in as much as it belongeth to the Sonne, whereby hee is God. Phil. 2.6 . . Iohn 1.1. . . . It was requisite for the Mediatour to be God; 1. That he might the better sustaine that great miserie wherewith mankinde was overwhelmed. . . . 3. That hee might instille into all the elect eternall life and holinesse. Esa.43.12. . . . Christs other nature is his humanity whereby hee, the Mediatour, is very man. I Tim. 2.5. . . . It was necessarie that Christ should bee man. First, that God might be pacified in that nature, wherein he was offended. Secondly, that he might undergoe punishment due to sinne, the which the Godhead could not, being void and free from all passion.[88]

Not only do these structures produce a powerful sense of the interrelationships of the eternal will of God to save and the temporal economy, they also produce, for Perkins, a strong connection between doctrine and the practice of Christian piety: "Christ's incarnation must be a pattern to us of a most wonderfull and strange humility."[89] Christ's self-humiliation in the very act of being made man provides a model of humility for the believer which is effective from the moment God grants that grace by which the heart is altered and inward pride abolished.[90] We see in Christ the image of all our infirmities but as willingly suffered by one who deserved no such trials: he knew temptation, fear, anger and even "forgetfulness of his office imposed on him by reason of the agony astonishing his senses"—thirst, weariness, subjection to death. But as these trials all devolve upon mankind not by nature but as a result of the fall, he was subject to them

> not by necessity of his humane nature, but by his free-will and pleasure, pitying mankind. Therefore, in him such infirmities were not the punishment of his owne sinne as they are in us; but rather part of that his humiliation which he did willingly undergoe for our sakes.[91]

Historical and economic issues so define Perkins' approach to the christological problem that, like Calvin and Musculus, he presents not the expected Christology "from above" but that distinctive mixture of elements "from above" and "from below" that we have denominated a Christology in the historical line of the covenants. This historical approach to the person of the mediator as divine and human within the economy of salvation provides Perkins with the horizontal background for describing the vertical intrusion of the divine into the temporal and the created order. Despite all the elements of Christology "from above," his doctrine of the person of Christ, the assumption of the flesh and the two natures now stands as determined not by the ontological problem of the divine Son uniting with a human nature but by the soteriological issue of the identity of the mediator in the economy of salvation.

Thus, the discussion of the person of the mediator and his fitness for the work of redemption provides Perkins both in his *An Exposition of the Symbole* and *A Golden Chaine* with the point of departure for discussing the traditional first issue of the christological *locus*, the doctrine of the two natures. We may fairly say that this pattern, instituted by Calvin and Musculus, has become normative for early orthodoxy. Indeed, for Perkins, the union of natures stands as a clarification of mediation, the great soteriological issue: in *A Golden Chaine* his chapter on the union of natures begins:

> Now followeth the Union of the two natures in Christ, which especially concerneth his Mediation, for by this union it cometh to passe that his humanity did suffer death upon the crosse in such sort, as he could neither be overcome, nor perpetually overwhelmed by it.[92]

To this end, the "uniting of natures" that there might be a mediator between God and man, "three things" are requisite: conception "by the wonderful power and operation of God" of the Virgin Mary, sanctification of the human nature following its conception for the sake of its office, and assumption of that nature by the word, the second person of the Trinity.[93]

The effect of Perkins' organization of the christological *locus* has been to draw attention away from the speculative nature of Alexandrian Christology and of the Chalcedonian statement while nevertheless making Chalcedonian orthodoxy the foundation of the understanding of Christ's person: the union of Christ's person

> consists in this, that the second person the Sonne of God doth assume unto it manhood in such order, that it being void of all personall beeing in it selfe, doth wholly and onely subsist in the same person.[94]

Therefore, "the Godhead of the Sonne and the manhood concurring together, made but one person."[95] The human nature is whole, a body and soul, but it is a nature only and not of itself a person. It does not subsist apart from the "person of the word."[96] The union does not destroy or confuse either the divine or the human nature, both of which retain their properties and distinct operations.[97] The result of the hypostatic union is the perfection and enrichment of the human nature to the end that it might be the means by which the Godhead works man's redemption.[98]

As in the thought of Polanus, Keckermann, and Bucanus,[99] here in the Christology of Perkins, even as the terms of the Chalcedonian and post-Chalcedonian determinations of the Greek Fathers are applied to the Reformed Christology, the paramount concern is for the historical person of the mediator who is both God and man. The eternality of the person, though prior to and pertaining to the foundation of incarnation, cannot be discussed apart from the incarnate one: the a-historical paradigm of Chalcedonian Christology is drawn into the realm of God's saving work, the eternal being manifest in the temporal. And the eternality of the Son's person, together with the understanding of incarnation as an act *ad extra* of the entire Godhead, functions not so much as a structural determinant of Christology as a statement of the trinitarian ground.

Following his rather lengthy discussion of the time, place, and manner of Christ's birth,[100] Perkins turns to "the estate of Christ after his birth, which is twofold, the estate of humiliation and the estate of exaltation."[101] The first of these states, humiliation, "is the condition of Christ the Mediatour, in which he abased himself even to the death of the crosse" for the sake of his priestly office and the satisfaction for man's sin.[102] The humiliation is to be considered of both natures. Not only was the manhood of Christ "abased and humbled," but also the Godhead

> was abased; not as it is considered in it selfe: for so it admits of no alteration or change: but in respect of the flesh or manhood assumed; under the which, as under a vaile, the godhead lay hid from the first moment of the incarnation to the time of his resurrection, without any great manifestation of his power and majestie therein.[103]

Perkins describes the *humiliatio* as "Christs execution, his Buriall and Descending into Hell." These three successive degrees of humiliation reflect the three degrees of exaltation.[104] The passion and therefore the humiliation of Christ consist in the "whole malediction or curse of the Law, containing in it all manner of adversities and miseries both of body and minde."[105] The Passion

> . . . may be reduced to three heads; the temptation of Christ, his ignominies and slaunders, his manifold sorrowes and griefs, especially those which stand in the apprehension of the unsupportable wrath of God.[106]

Perkins insists that the unity of the work arises in the unity of the person:

> by reason of the union, the godhead workes all things in the matter of our redemption, in and by the manhood. And hereupon the flesh of Christ, though it profit nothing of itselfe, yet by the vertue which it receiveth from the person to which it is joyned, it is *quickening flesh*, & the *bread of life*.[107]

He includes the incarnation in the *status humiliationis* by stating that "the time of the Passion was from the very birth of Christ to his resurrection.[108] Perkins also denominates two causes of the passion: the "efficient" or "principall" cause is "the determinate counsell & foreknowledge of God" and the "impulsive cause that mooved God to worke our salvation was nothing in man (for all mankind was shut up under unbeleefe . . .) but the will and good pleasure of God within himselfe."[109] This argument accords with Perkins' previous unwillingness to place any necessity upon God.

The state of exaltation is described in the Creed by the three stages of resurrection, ascension, and the seating of Christ on the right hand of the Father.

Christ's resurrection represents victory over death for the sake of all men, accomplished by the power of the divinity of Christ.[110] His ascension is a removal of his body from earth to fellowship with the Father, to a position of honor, glory, power, designated by the words "and sitteth on the right hand of God the Father."[111] Christ rules from heavenly places according to both natures. Exaltation refers specifically to Christ, the designated mediator, who is in some sense subordinated to the Father; it does not apply to the person of the Son who is coequal with the Father and therefore eternal, omnipotent, and omnipresent.[112]

In this description of the *status exaltationis*, the *extra calvinisticum* functions to allow the subordination of the mediator to the will of the Father and while maintaining an orthodox trinitarian doctrine and a coherent christological structure. Whereas Calvin's statement of the *extra calvinisticum* referred specifically to the paradox of God given but not contained in the flesh, taking the moment of incarnation as its basis, Perkins' statement of the doctrine, like that of Polanus, now also relates to the distinction between the Son of God as God and the Son of God as anointed mediator, taking the *exinanitio* as its point of departure and reflecting the paradox of an official subordination of the Son, which implies no ontological subordination. This systematic refinement enables Perkins to explain not only the *exinanitio* or *kenosis* but also the exaltation of Christ and the election of mediator without subordinating the Son to the Father.

For Calvin it had been sufficient to show that the saving will of God through the Son was prior to the sending of his Son. In the increasingly sophisticated systems of developing orthodoxy, a stricter, clearer formulation was needed if the possible subordinationist implications of Calvin's fluid use of the name Christ and of his conception of the election of the mediator were to be overcome. The presence of careful trinitarian arguments at several points in Perkins' Christology represents the working-out of a primary implication and a resolution of a major tension in Calvin's systematic thought.

3. PREDESTINATION AND ITS CHRISTOLOGICAL REFERENT IN THE THEOLOGY OF POLANUS AND PERKINS

The Decree as Essential and Free Act of God

One of the major changes brought about in the structure of Polanus' system by the publication of the *Syntagma* was the consolidation of the doctrine of predestination under one *locus*. The effect of this change was to separate the doctrines of predestination and providence while retaining the typically scholastic *species genus* relationship between the concepts: in the general definition of the divine decree, Polanus distinguishes the *decretum Dei generale* or *providentia* from the *decretum Dei speciale*, which, by synecdoche, is called *praedestinatio* or more accurately, *specialis praedestinatio*. This special predestination refers not to all created things as does providence but only to rational creatures.[113]

Discussion of providence is reserved for a subsequent *locus* (below creation) and, at that point, election and reprobation do not appear: Polanus will instead discuss a "special providence" which refers to the church and the elect.[114] The discussion of the execution of the decree, which had previously appeared together with providence in the *Partitiones*, now appears as part of the doctrine of *specialis praedestinatio*, specifically as its "effects" and "adjuncts." The entire discussion of predestination—and here we see the beginnings of the high orthodox and fully rationalized scholastic pattern—has been subsumed under the topic *de operibus Dei internis*.[115]

The *opus Dei*, Polanus declares, is that which God does for his own glory. This definition, however, stands in need of clarification: in John 6:28 Jesus declared, "This is the work of God, that you believe on him whom he has sent" or, again in John 4:34, "My portion is to do the will of him who sent me, and to complete his work." The work of God, therefore, more closely defined, is the establishment of God's kingdom, the restoration of life to lost souls, and the spreading of the light of the Gospel for the salvation of the world: the *opus Dei*, thus, is "that which God has enjoined upon his servants." Or, it is that which God himself does, "quod Deus ipse operatur."[116] At this point in the system, Polanus restricts himself to the specific issue of what God himself does: he distinguishes between internal or external acts of God and those things or works produced by them. The efficient cause of all these works is God himself, and their final cause is the glory of God.[117]

This series of distinctions allows Polanus to focus on the *opera Dei interna* without losing sight either of the ultimate end, the *gloria Dei*, or the proximate ends, particularly the soteriological work announced by Jesus. The *opera Dei interna* are distinguished into *personalia* and *essentialia*.[118] The personal works of God are those works or acts proper to the persons of the Trinity considered individually according to their personal agency and according to the persons considered as formal principles (*pro ratione personae suae tanquam formali principio*). The fathers therefore speak of "opera Dei oeconomica seu actiones oeconomica" with reference to the *modus operationis* or *dispositio* of the divine persons. These personal operations are of two sorts: the *opera Dei simpliciter personalia*, according to which the persons subsist in relation to one another, the Father generating the Son, the Son being begotten of the Father, the Father and the Son "spirating" the Spirit, and the Spirit proceeding from the Father and the Son, and the *opera certo modo personalia*, which, as works terminating upon created things, involve the whole Godhead and have as their principle and cause the common power of the divine persons but have as the terminus of operation (*terminus operationis*) one of the divine persons by reason of the internal economy of the Godhead. These latter are acts such as the voice of the Father at the baptism of Jesus or the incarnation, mediation and atoning work of the Son, or the sanctifying work of the Spirit: considered *inchoative*, these are the common work of God; considered *terminative*, they are the work of individual persons.[119]

Polanus next discusses the *opera Dei essentialia*, which are the undivided work of the entire Trinity considered *simpliciter* and which terminate upon the divine essence:

> The essential works of God are those performed by the divine essence, the Father, Son, and Holy Spirit in common, and completed in creatures; which is to say the common work of the Father, Son, and Holy Spirit, willed *communiter* by the Father, Son, and Holy Spirit according to the unity of divine essence and directed *communiter* toward creatures. The point of distinction between the essential and personal works of God is that the former have as their principle the divine essence absolutely considered, operating by the divine power possessed in common by the persons. . . .[120]

These works, however, in their enactment, manifest the economy or order of the persons: the Father works *immediate per Filium* and the Father and the Son work through the Spirit. The Father, indeed, is effective in his working (*efficax*) but by the Son and Spirit. Nor does the Son work without the Father and Spirit.[121] The Father may be called the "efficient cause" as he is the *principium* of the divine economy, but the *opera essentialia* nevertheless refer to the one divine essence and not to individual persons: there is one essential *principium*, one act, one effect.[122] The essential work of God may, therefore, be defined primarily as *opera Dei interna communiter*[123] or more specifically as "the wise and free internal act of divine will, which is to say the eternal counsel and decree of God."[124] The counsel and the decree, moreover, are but one and the same *propter simplicissimam essentiam Dei*.[125]

Although Polanus brings to bear upon his doctrine of God the philosophical language of being and essence, the entrance of philosophical categories here, specifically in the definition of the decree as the act of the divine essence, does not of itself bring about a greater degree of determinism. For Calvin's experiential emphasis did not preclude a metaphysical implication, and Calvin, as much as any of the early orthodox, insisted on the sovereign causality of God in all things. As for the ultimate understanding of the decrees as the essential acts of God, this emerges more as the result of a theological meditation in the Augustinian tradition on the problem of time and eternity in relation to the being of man and of God and as an extension of the distinction between the decree and its execution, rather than as an attempt to make more rigid an already deterministic soteriology. Since the decree is not in time but in eternity and since the mind and will of God cannot be partitioned or divided in any way from the essence or between the persons, the decree must belong to the divine essence. As Polanus notes, the distinction of persons does not point to a distinction of acts but only to a personal distinction *quoad modum agendi in operationibus essentialibus*.[126] Thus, Polanus can argue that the decree remains "hidden and dark" to man and can be known only insofar as it is revealed *ad extra* in the Word of God, in the mediation of Christ, and in its effects in the order of salvation.[127]

For this definition of the decree as an essential act of God to be the beginning point of a philosophical determinism, it would need to be developed or elaborated so as to involve the assumption that God's acts, as determined by his essence, are not free and that God works under limitation and by necessity in decreeing what he decrees. Quite to the contrary, definition of the decree as essential act of divine will in no way refers to a limitation of the divine activity or ultimately to any necessity whatsoever: instead this definition grounds the decree upon the utter freedom of the divine will.[128]

Consideration of the divine essence touches not only on the question of necessary being as the ground of contingent being but also on the question of the essential equality of the persons of the Trinity and their common operation in all essential acts *ad intra* and in every act *ad extra*. Definition of the decree as an essential as distinct from a personal act within the Godhead stands as a corollary to the doctrine of Christ's aseity, the teaching that the divinity of Christ considered as to essence is *autotheos*,[129] and identifies the decree as the work of the entire Godhead apart from the issue of personal relation. The decree is therefore not the act of God the Father apart from God the Son or God the Spirit: it is not the *proprium* of one divine *modus existendi* as apart from the others and thus is not an act in the recesses of the Godhead somehow abstracted from the work of the Son and the Spirit in the economy of salvation. Stress on essence and the definition of the works of God *ad extra* as originating in the essence as *opera essentialia* serves only to emphasize the trinitarian ground of the system.[130]

Polanus now digresses momentarily from his strict division of topics to distinguish between the eternal decree considered as providence and the various conceptions of fate or necessity so frequently compared to it. There is first, the *fatum physicum* of the Aristotelian world view according to which causes in the order of nature produce uniform effects—which is to say a natural necessity or necessity of nature resting upon the principles of the natural world. There is, in contrast both to this theory of natural necessity and to the Christian concept of an eternal counsel, the *fatum Stoicum*. Stoic fate is a natural necessity according to which all things occur in an ordained series of events which no power, not even the divine, can stay. *Fatum Christianum* or *theologicum & verum fatum* rests on no natural necessity but on the free and eternal decree of God. The argument is clearly between the latter two.[131] Polanus clearly views the decree as belonging to another order of being than created things and, therefore, can follow Calvin and other early Reformed theologians in avoiding a doctrine of philosophical necessity: not only do Polanus' definitions point away from a necessitarian metaphysic—as we have seen immediately above—but his subsequent argument militates specifically against such doctrine.

Having manifest the freedom of the decree both as an eternal work of God and as distinct from the toils of philosophical necessity, Polanus proceeds to an analysis of the "definitions and the nomenclature" of categories within the decree. His basic distinction is between the *decretum beneplaciti* and the *decretum signi Dei*.[132] The *decretum beneplaciti* directs and ordains all things to their ends, though not in such a way as to make God the author of sin. In respect to sin it is the *decretum energetikon* insofar as God ordains the circumstances and directs the ends, but not in the sense that God actually commits sin. God, indeed, permits sin according to the wisdom and power of his universal governance and not as the result of failure to govern or as part of a vague permissiveness.[133] This declaration concerning the divine permission brings Polanus to the will of God as God makes it known in signs, the revealed or designated will, the *decretum signi* that rests on the *voluntas signi*. Here a distinction needs also to be made between the *decretum praecipiens* and the *decretum permittens*: by the former God imposes and requires those things of which he approves or prohibits those things of which he disapproves; by the latter he decrees to permit.[134] Thus he is not the author of sin, for sin does not belong to the decree either efficiently, or preceptively, or even as positive permission; rather sin exists "according to the permitting decree." For, as Polanus argues, "it is one thing to be *of* the decree and another to be according to the decree: the former represents a causal relation; the latter antecedently knows but is not a cause but merely a collateral circumstance which precedes the thing."[135]

The decree is absolute: it is prior to all means and all secondary causes, an unconditioned efficient cause. By no stretch of the imagination can temporal things or conditions be placed prior to something which belongs to the eternal counsel of God.[136] Yet, argues Polanus, this eternal *decretum absolutum* ought not to be viewed as something so hidden in the recesses of Godhead that it is not revealed in the Word of God; nor ought it to be imagined as a decree disconnected from subordinate causes that works without means, an arbitrary, blind decree opposed to the *decretum ordinatum*; all such definitions are denied. "Indeed, we confess (by way of an example graciously given)," concludes Polanus, "that God has from eternity decreed to love and to save us: and thus to love and to bless us in Christ, to call us to Christ, to justify and to save through the apprehension of Christ in faith."[137] Essential work of God, absolute and eternal without respect of temporal conditions: the decree is all this, but it is also, of its very essence, focused upon Christ and the work of salvation because these too belong to the nature of God. If absolute, the decree is also most just, most righteous. On this point Polanus again manifests a Scotist rather than a Thomist tendency: "Decretum Dei est iustissimum: qua eius causa est voluntas divina, quae est suprema regula omnis justitiae & rectitudinis: a nulla igitur creatura jure accusatur."[138] The divine will, the *voluntas Dei*, then is distinguishable from and prior to the decree—"decretum est effectus voluntatis." Clearly, for Polanus, *voluntas* is the determinative category in God:

> God, indeed, first and foremost, wills himself, that is, his essence, wisdom, goodness, justice, power, glory, and his other essential properties and, although most free from all coaction, he is not able not to will this, because of a necessity of nature: even so he wills all his internal and external works, those internal and personal works by necessity of that same nature, while his internal, essential works

and all external works, according to a will most free of all things, according to which he is able either to will or not to will. God therefore wills himself; but he does not decree himself; he does not decree his essence and persons, for that is his nature; nor is he able not to be Jehovah, one in essence and three in person and to be such he wills necessarily.[139]

From the very beginning of the exposition, therefore, Polanus' view of the decree as essential act of God relates directly to the identification of God as trinity and to the saving work of God in Christ: *what* God essentially wills to decree must be predicated upon *who* God is!

Special Predestination as Election and Reprobation
        On the question of whether or not predestination should be taught or whether the church should omit it, Polanus produces a set of *sententiae Pelagiani*: the doctrine is hidden and above human comprehension; it renders salvation doubtful "quum praedestinationis arcanum vere absconditum sit in Dei aeterna consilio," the problem of the *deus nudus absconditus*; it stands in the way of calling and worship; it leads to despair for those who number themselves among the reprobate; it undermines piety.[140] The doctrine, comments Polanus, ought not to be omitted but taught "in Scholis & templis." In response to the first objection, he notes that no doctrine wisely and clearly taught by Christ and the Apostles ought to be ignored, and predestination is one such doctrine. As for the difficulty we have in understanding the doctrine, that is no valid impediment; for God is ever beyond comprehension, as well illustrated by other crucial doctrines—trinity, creation of the world *ex nihilo*, the two natures of Christ. The remaining objections Polanus simply declares false: the doctrine has been given by God and therefore is for our edification and correction.[141] Definition follows:

> Predestination, specially so-called, is the decree of God by which all rational creatures are destined from eternity to certain ends, beyond this temporal and natural life, and are drawn toward them by certain means preordained from eternity. I say, beyond this temporal or natural life—for predestination pertains to the spiritual and heavenly life; since all men, according to their animal life are equal, as Paul teaches (I Cor. 15:45ff). I add *concerning means*, since predestination is both of ends and of means. God has indeed predestinated individual rational creatures to certain ends; and indeed the same God has preordained the means by which they shall be drawn to their ends.[142]

        This definition Polanus clarifies with a series of axioms relating to the causes, effects, and parts of predestination. The cause of predestination is simply God himself, who ordains the ends of all things and then brings about those ends through his most free will (*liberrima voluntas Dei*). The decree, then, is "absolute" since it rests on no cause outside of God, and no end but the glory of God and the salvation of the elect, the former being the highest end and the latter the subordinate end.[143] The effects of the decree include the creation of rational creatures and the permission to sin (*peccati permissio*) so that the basic pattern of Polanus' formulation is supralapsarian, though not in the sense that the objects of divine predestination are mere possibilities, *creabilis et labilis*: "For predestination is in God: not, therefore, as undertaken at length after mankind had fallen away or sinned; rather it precedes the creation and fall of rational creatures."[144] Polanus' intention is simply to establish the priority of the decree over all temporal events. As for the parts of predestination, there are two: election and reprobation.[145]

The final axiom, the division of predestination into its parts, election and reprobation, brings Polanus to the subject of his next discussion: "In quo de Electione Christi & beatorum Angelorum" and "In quo de Aeterna electione nostra ad vitam aeternam."[146] "Eternal election is the predestination, in the divine mind, of rational creatures to a gracious and blessed end. And moreover it is first *of Christ*, and then (of) *those united to Christ*."[147] "The eternal election of Christ," continues Polanus, "is that predestination by which God designated from eternity his only begotten Son, so that also in his human nature he might be Son of God and head of angels and of men, and mediator between God and angels and men."[148] Christ's work, therefore, rests on the profound *sola gratia* of God's electing will, and it stands not as a mere means to the end of the decree but as the first and foremost statement of the meaning of election. We saw an adumbration of this idea in the theology of Calvin and Musculus; we saw it develop toward definition in the work of Beza, Ursinus, and Zanchius. Polanus sets it forth as an axiom of Reformed doctrine.

Not only does Polanus present the election of Christ as the primary issue to be addressed in understanding the divine work of salvation, he also proceeds to develop a mediation-christology in miniature within his *locus* on the election of Christ. For only in the union of the divine and human in Christ, in the person and the purpose of the mediator, can the election of Christ be understood, and only in the way that the one God works in and through Christ can his saving purpose be comprehended. Incarnation and the election of Christ become, for Polanus, corollaries in the explication of the divine mode of entry into the temporal economy:

> Christ is, according to both natures, divine and human, one Son of God, not two: according to the divine, by natural generation from the Father, so that, thus, according to it he is Son of God, not elected, but generated; according to the human (he is Son of God) truly first by eternal election, in the second place by creation in the image of God, and in the third place by the grace of personal union with the divine nature.[149]

In terms of Christ as the God-man, his humanity eternally designated to his work, Polanus can move to address the various titles and descriptions of Christ: *caput, mediator, medius, redemptor, liberator, reconciliator.*

These arguments lead Polanus to his concluding "axiomata" concerning the doctrine of Christ's election: "The election of Christ is the foundation and main support of the election of angels and men"—"Electio Christi est fundamentum et firmamentum electionis Angelorum & hominum."[150] There can be no subordination of Christ as God, but the subordination of Christ as mediator and as elect man stands as the foundation of the work of salvation; the implication of Polanus' statement here accords well with Perkins' declaration, cited earlier, "The foundation and ground work of the covenant is Christ Jesus the Mediatour, in whome all the promises of God are yea and amen."[151] Yet Polanus refrains from calling Christ himself the *fundamentum electionis*. Rather, the *fundamentum electionis* is the *electio Christi*, which, as a work of God, represents the primary act in the execution of the decree. A similar distinction would be made by Antonius Walaeus, one of the Leyden professors who sat at Dort,[152] and by Ames, despite slight differences in terminology.[153] The concept of Christ as *fundamentum electionis* becomes problematic when the name Christ is no longer loosely applied after the fashion of Calvin but applied strictly as the title of the elected mediator. Christ, in this restrictive sense, cannot be prior to the decree of God.

The eternal election of those united to Christ is the election or separation of those angels and men who are, according to the divine good pleasure, given Christ to be their head and who shall therefore subsist in his virtue and perfection.[154] More restrictedly, then, the term predestination means the "predestination of the saints" the *specialis hominum electio* according to which God has "ordained to eternal life those to whom, according to his gracious benevolence, he wills to give a celestial inheritance": Adam, Even, Abel, Enoch, Noah, Abraham—indeed, all who have been his servants since the beginning of the world.[155]

> The election of men to eternal salvation is that predestination by which God from eternity has given to Christ those men upon whom he has willed to have mercy so as to give them life eternal, that is, by which he has decreed in himself from eternity which men he would take to himself out of the rest and make exempt from the common destruction, adopt as sons in Christ, effectively call to communion in Christ, justify in Christ, and glorify; so that they might contemplate the glory of Christ in eternity and in him participate in the inheritance of heaven and in life eternal.[156]

In Polanus' definition we observe two primary issues: first, as with Ursinus, the definition of election itself contains in brief a survey of the *ordo salutis*; and second, this powerful causal focus affirms the christocentric character of the system. Every element of the *ordo* is understood *in Christo*.

Christ and the Decree: Trinitarian Ground and Christological Focus

At this point Polanus inserts the crucial christological issue, the relation of Christ, as Son and God, to the decree and its execution. The determination of "Christ" as the title of the mediator who is subordinate to the decree and the designation of the efficient cause of election as God does not have the effect of making the Father a *deus nudus absconditus*, a hidden God somehow divorced from the work of redemption. The meaning of election itself is christological and, as christological, rests on the identification of the mediator as one person, fully God and fully man, in his humanity one with us, in his divinity equal to the Father and the Spirit. This crucial focusing of election on and in Christ cannot and must not be lost in the exegesis of passages like I Thessalonians 5:9 and Ephesians 1:3-5 where the Father is presented as the first and efficient cause of election and Christ Jesus as the material cause within the complex of secondary causality. Therein lay a problem for Reformed theology, as defined by Calvin's causal exegesis of these passages. We saw Beza work past the exegetical problem and press home the trinitarian-christological issue in his exegesis of Ephesians 1:5. Zanchius provided a similar formulation in his analysis of predestination. Now Polanus addresses the problem: "Constituit nos Deus ad salutem obtinendam per Dominum nostrum Iesum Christum"—"Deus" indicating here "that one essence in three persons, Father, Son, and Holy Spirit."[157]

By way of argument in support of this concept of a trinitarian election in Christ, Polanus cites texts referring to the elective activity of the persons individually: the activity of the Father is most clearly stated in John 3:37; 17:2, 6, 11, 24. "When the Father gives to Christ those to whom he will give eternal life, this is nothing other than that the Father elects in Christ those whom he will draw to life eternal."[158] Indeed, Paul speaks specifically of the Father in Ephesians 1:3-5 who elects us in Christ before the foundation of the world. Yet, argues Polanus, this cannot refer to the Father restrictively: election belongs to the essential, to the trinitarian work performed by the whole Godhead, not to the work of generation and spiration, which is the *proprium* of the persons considered individually:

> The Father indeed elects us, not as Father, since election is not the proper work of the person of the Father; but as God, for as much as election is the common work of the whole sacred Trinity, of which the principle is the Father.[159]

Even as election must be viewed as the common work of the three persons, assurance also will rest, for Polanus, on the work of God as the work of the Father by the Son through the Spirit.[160] Here we do not have the case of a systematic principle, predestination, firming other doctrine but, instead, other doctrinal *foci* serving as boundary-concepts around which the doctrine of predestination crystallizes.

This doctrinal construct of Polanus is the formula cited by Barth as the "way past the dilemma" of the *deus nudus absconditus* posed so radically in Barth's analysis of Calvin and of Dort. Barth knew of no other example of the formula. J. K. S. Reid noted it in Bucanus' *Institutions* but failed to make the connection between Bucanus and Polanus. But this is precisely the formula argued by Beza in his analysis of Ephesians 1:5-6 and by Zanchi in his exhaustive treatments of trinity and predestination, and it is a formula utilized not only by Polanus and Bucanus but, as we shall see, by Perkins, Scharpius, and Keckermann.[161] We may safely say that the positive doctrinal development of early orthodoxy prior to Dort—as distinct though never separate from its polemics—was not the development of a speculative doctrine of election and reprobation *per se* but of the elaboration of the double decree in the light of more encompassing theological, in this case, trinitarian and christological concerns.

This trinitarian definition of election, which involves the Son and the Spirit explicitly, in no way predicates election upon the temporal activity of Son and Spirit: the cause of election is in God alone and is in him from eternity. No temporal thing can be the cause of election, for election rests entirely upon the grace of God; thus neither the foreknowledge of faith or of good works is the cause of our election to life eternal. God first decrees the end and then the means so that faith and works, as means, depend on the decree.[162] The efficient or impulsive cause of election, then, is in God alone. Even so the *materia* or *materialis causa* is also the divine decree and the *forma* is ordination of some to life eternal through the use of the means set forth by God.[163] Only when he discusses the means of election does Polanus descend to the order of temporal causality, and here again he is strictly christocentric:

> The means of salvation are: the mediation of Christ given to us by the Father and sent into this world at the end of time, comprehending which Christ did and suffered for us and in our place; and also therefore the gift, according to which God the Father has given Christ to us, is the effect of our eternal election. This mediation of Christ is a meritorious and proximate efficient cause of all subsequent means, which are the effects of our eternal election and which pertain to the way we ought to walk in this world; and they are these: effectual calling, saving faith, our justification before God and glorification or sanctification in this life, the good works brought about in us, the cross or affliction, and the gift of perseverance.[164]

Again the entire *ordo salutis* appears in the definition of election but now in relation to the mediation of Christ. Even when Christ's work is considered as a means, a *medium*, of the execution of the decree, it is not to be regarded as one means among others. It is the primary means upon which all others depend; indeed, in the execution of the decree, viewed restrictively or proximately, it is the efficient cause of the other means. Polanus affirms the priority of Christ's mediation over the other elements of the temporal *ordo*:

> the subject of election *en ho*, in which we are elect, is Christ, not as he is God, neither as he is merely man, but as he is *theanthropos* and our mediator. For in Ephesians 1:4 the Apostle clearly teaches that God the Father elected us IN CHRIST. The work was accomplished, indeed, by this means in which we are elect: since without that means union between electing God and elect men would not have been possible. Therefore Christ is the bond by which God and the elect shall be conjoined. Truly the means could be none other than Christ, the Son of God, as he is *theanthropos*: since he has predestinated us in order that he might adopt us as sons, as further in Eph. 1:5.[165]

The crucial issue for Polanus, as for Calvin and Beza, is the language of mediation and the identification of the *mediatoris persona*. Christ can be *medium*, means to an end, because he is *medius*, situated between the extremes, the reconciler between unreconcilables. In short, the early orthodox doctrine of predestination as stated by Polanus stands or falls on the basis of its christological referent: the language of *medius* and *mediator* so carefully developed by his predecessors provides the key to understanding the relation of Christ to the execution of the decree, even as the trinitarian formula and the concept of Christ's aseity provide the key to understanding the relation of Christ, as God, to the decree itself.

The object of this election, Polanus concludes, is not each and every human being (*non sunt universi & singuli homines*) but only those whom God has chosen to draw beyond nature (*supra naturam evehere*) and to give the gift of eternal life. There are, in other words, nonelect who are left in their sins unto damnation. This election is free, immutable and most just. It is confirmed by the Spirit, declared in temporal symbols, confirmed by innumerable spiritual and corporeal gifts, and restored for the eager performance of good works (*Firma quoad nos redditur studio bonorum operum*).[166] Thus election is known in and by its objects as an undeserved and gracious gift. Polanus notes two external and two internal testimonies to election: the Gospel and the Sacraments testify to electing grace externally and generally; our spirit and the Holy Spirit testify inwardly and individually. Our own spirit or conscience witnesses to our justification by faith before God while the Holy Spirit reveals our election by an infusion of grace. Our assurance, therefore, is not carnal, but spiritual, not belonging to sense or to experience, but to faith.[167] For Polanus, as for many other of the orthodox, the question of personal assurance could not be resolved into an empirical *syllogismus practicus*.[168]

The Problem of the Nonelect

Polanus comes finally to the problem of reprobation: it is, he says, an issue not so much difficult to explain as odious to those ungraced children of the world (*ingratae filiis huius mundi*), yet it is a doctrine both necessary and useful to the elect in understanding the glory of God. Reprobation simply means the nonelection of God, the preterition of those not chosen for salvation.[169]

> Eternal reprobation, is the divine predestination, according to which it pleased God to pass over certain rational creatures in the election to eternal life, to destine them to eternal destruction, to leave them in their sins, and to condemn them on account of his most just judgment. . . . The parts or acts of reprobation are two: First, the destination of the reprobate to eternal death; second, the ordination of the means of execution of the decree of reprobation, to which belongs their condemnation on account of sin by a most just judgment.[170]

This definition places God as the efficient cause of reprobation, but it neither makes sin the effect of reprobation nor God the author of sin. We do not see here an instance of predestination as a prior principle from which system is deduced. Instead it is a doctrine of predestination formulated in terms of the needs of system as a whole: condemnation to eternal death results only as payment for sin.

> Reprobation indeed precedes damnation, but not as its cause, truly only as an antecedent collateral circumstance. Certainly every cause is an antecedent, but not all antecedents are causes. Thus damnation follows reprobation not as an effect but only as a consequent. Surely all effects are consequent, but not all consequents are effects.[171]

The fact that reprobation is the coordinate of election does not lead to an elaborate development of that doctrine. Even in the early orthodox systems reprobation appears not as the parallel to election in doctrinal importance but as an appendix or clarification at the end of the chapters on the decree and predestination. This approach to the doctrine of reprobation appears not only in Polanus but also in Walaeus and in the *Canones Synodi Dordrechtanae*. Following Calvin, Polanus seems to have recognized in the doctrine of predestination an epistemological problem. The decree cannot be known in itself but only in its execution, only through the mediation of the Word.[172] Theology studies the connection between the decree and its execution, and the emphasis of doctrinal exposition, whatever the placement of predestination within the system, is upon the mediation of God's saving will in Christ. Reprobation, the dark shadow upon this most hopeful and soteriologically oriented doctrine of the decrees, stands less than coordinate with election precisely because it is not positively or actively mediated by God, a point made most clearly by Polanus' contemporary, Bartholomaus Keckermann.[173] Elaboration of the doctrine of predestination in early orthodoxy occurs, therefore, in a christological pattern and on the side of election. In the work of Polanus the dark "labyrinth" of the eternal decrees is suffused with light not by means of purely metaphysical speculation or rationalistic philosophy but by the development, within the doctrine of predestination itself, of a christological structure drawn out of the trinitarian ground of theology and directed toward the historical dispensation of the mediator's work.

Perkins' Doctrine of the Decree

A similar soteriological interest defined in terms of the relation of Christ to the decree appears in William Perkins' several analyses of the doctrine of predestination. We look to his *A Golden Chaine*, where we have already detected a juxtaposition of Christology with election, to his *An Exposition of the Symbole*, and in particular to his *A Treatise of the Manner and Order of Predestination*, where the decree has been explicated as a series of "acts" of God.[174] Of course, Perkins recognizes that this ordering represents only his own sense of logical priorities in the work of salvation:

The nature of God, is his most lively and most perfect essence. The perfection of the nature of God, is the absolute constitution thereof, whereby it is wholy complete within itselfe, Exod. 3.31. . . . Act. 17.14. . . . The Simplenesse of his nature, is that by which he is void of all logicall relation in arguments. He hath not in him subject or adjunct. Ioh. 5.26. . . . Ioh. 14.6. . . . I. Ioh. 1.7. . . . Neither is God subject to generalitie, or specialty: whole, or parts. . . . Therefore, whatsoever is in God, in his essence, and all that he is, he is by essence.[175]

Like Polanus, Perkins defines the decree as an essential act of God. As such, it stands in direct relation to the doctrine of the Trinity. Indeed, in Perkins' *A Golden Chaine*, where the synthetic causal order is the principle of organization, the doctrine of the decrees follows not upon the divine attributes but upon the exposition of God as trinity.[176] Perkins' definition of the decree, moreover, stands in very close proximity to his declaration of the aseity of Christ's divine nature:

Although the Sonne bee begotten of his Father, yet neverthelesse he is of and by himselfe very God: for hee must bee considered either according to his essence or according to his filiation or Sonneship. In regard of his essence he is *autotheos* that is, of and by himselfe very God: for the Deitie which is common to all the persons is not begotten. But as he is a person and the Sonne of the Father hee is not of himselfe, but from another: for hee is the eternal Sonne of his Father. And thus he is truely said to be *very God of very God.* For this cause he is said to be sent from the Father. Iohn 8.42. . . . This sending taketh not away the equality of essence and power, but declareth the order of persons. Iohn 5.18. . . . His proper manner of working is to execute actions from the Father by the Holy Ghost. I Cor. 8.6 . . . Ioh. 5.19.[177]

This analysis stands in direct relation to the opening argument of the following chapter:

Thus far concerning the first part of Theologie: the second followeth, of the workes of God. The workes of God are all those which he doth out of himselfe, that is, out of his divine essence. These are common to the Trinitie, the peculiar manner of working alwaies reserved to every person. . . . The worke or action of God is either his decree, or the execution of his decree.[178]

Any discussion of an essential action of God must relate not only to the Father but also to the Son and, of course, to the Spirit. The decree, as essential act, belongs equally to the persons of the Trinity, but its execution must be described according to the order of the persons: the Father "is the beginning of actions, because he beginneth every action of himselfe, effecting it by the Sonne and the holie Ghost."[179] Both in eternity and in temporal execution the decree functions not as the work of a *deus nudus absconditus* but as the work of the triune God.

Perkins defines the decree as "that by which God in himselfe hath necessarily, and yet freely, from all eternity determined al things."[180] All things and all actions that occur belong to the divine decree, even the actions of the wicked;

this must be so, for if God had "nilled" the actions of the wicked, they would never have existed at all. Yet, like Calvin and Beza, Perkins refuses to make God the author of sin or the cause of evil. Perkins states his case against absolute evil and against a final causality of evil: the acts of the wicked

> of their own nature are and remain wicked; yet in respect of God's decree they are some waies good, for there is not anything absolutely evill. I Pet. 3.17. . . . The thing which in its owne nature is evil, in God's eternall counsell is respectively good, in that it is some occasion & way to manifest the glories of God in his iustice, and his mercie.[181]

Perkins here draws on the scholastic differentiation between the *voluntas* or *opus proprium* and the *voluntas* or *opus alienum* of God.

Perkins' basic definition, "The decree of God is that by which God in himselfe hath necessarily, and yet freely, from eternity determined al things,"[182] so emphasizes the divine freedom as to avoid the imposition of necessity on God or the implication of a necessity in God. God acts "according to his good pleasure" and effects in and through his decree exactly what he wills.[183] Perkins can thus point to a *concursus* between the willing permission of God and evil acts contrary to the positive will of God: God is no "bare permissive agent."[184] Yet a distinction must be made between "operation" and "operative permission."[185] The decree may be necessary but it "doth not take away freedom of will in election, or the nature and property of second causes."[186]

> Gods operation, is his effectuall producing of all good things, which either have beeing or mooving, or which are done. Gods operative permission, is that by which he onely permitteth one and the same worke to be done of others, as it is evill, but as it is good he effectually worketh the same. Gen. 50.20 . . . Gen. 45.7 . . . Esa. 10.5, 6, 7. . . . God permitteth evill by a certaine voluntary permission, in that hee forsaketh the second cause in working evill. . . . he neither instilleth an abberation in the action, nor yet supporteth, or intendeth the same, but that he most freely suffereth evill and best disposeth of it to his owne glory.[187]

Within this causal framework, Perkins can define predestination, election and reprobation in such a way as to incorporate elements of the supra and infralapsarian positions, the former appearing in his insistence on the utter priority of the divine willing, in his arguments concerning first and final causes, and the latter being evidenced in his analysis of the divine permission "forsaking," or "passing over" in the arguments concerning secondary and instrumental causes. The decree can, therefore, appear both as archetypal design and as remedy for sin: it is the one eternal act of the divine will which creates, maintains, and resolves all things.

In his *An Exposition of the Symbole*, Perkins comes to his doctrine of predestination by way of the definition of church as "a peculiar company of men predestinated to life everlasting, and made one in Christ."[188] The "principall cause of the Church, is the good pleasure of God whereby he hath before all worlds purposed to advance his Elect to eternall salvation," but in addition to this eternal will or determination there must be a bond to join the members of the company together temporally, that is, in union with Christ. "This union," adds Perkins, "maketh the Church to bee the Church."[189] Immediately, then, Christology and predestination draw together—in *A Golden Chaine* because of the issues of the trinitarian willing of God and the remedy from sin; here because of need for a temporal means by which the eternal purpose is carried out. In no case can the decree be conceived *extra Christum.* Here too, Perkins sees Christ and the decree of election as constituting the historical community, "the Family of God" from Abraham onward.[190]

Analysis of the doctrine divides into four sections: definition, the "order" of the doctrine, the "parts," and the "use" of the doctrine.[191]

> *Predestination* may thus be defined: *It is a part of the counsell of God, whereby hee hath before all times purposed in himselfe to shew mercie on some men, and to passe by others, shewing his justice on them for the manifestation of the glory of his own name.* First, I say, it is a part of his counsell, because the counsell or decree of God, universally extends it selfe to all things that are: and Predestination is Gods decree so far forth as it concernes the reasonable creatures, especially men. Now in every purpose or decree of God, three things must be considered; the beginning, the matter, the end. The *beginning,* is the will of God whereby he willeth and appointeth the estate of his creatures: and it is the most absolute, supreame, and soveraigne cause of all things that are, so far forth as they have beeing: having nothing either above itselfe or out of itselfe, to be an impulsive cause to moove or incline it, and to say otherwise, is to make the will of God to be no will. . . . Gods will is not ruled by another rule of reason or iustice, but itselfe is an absolute rule both of iustice and reason. . . . The *matter* of his purpose, is a decreed manifestation of two of the most principale attributes of the Godhead, *mercie* and *iustice.* . . . The *end* of the counsell of God, is the manifestation of his owne glorie, partly in his mercy, and partly in his iustice.[192]

Having thus defined predestination, Perkins proceeds to an analysis of the doctrine based upon Romans 9. The argument of the chapter, states Perkins, concerns Paul's "griefe . . . for his brethren the Iewes" and his mode of working out a basic theological objection to the doctrine of the rejection of Israel. This makes Perkins' formal analysis of predestination one of the most exegetically oriented analyses of the early orthodox period. The basic issue can be presented as a syllogism:

> If the Iewes be reiected, then *the word of God is of none effect*: that is, then the covenant made with the forefathers is void: but the covenant cannot be voide: therefore the Iewes are not reiected. The assumption he takes for graunted, and denies the consequence of the proposition. And the grounde of his deniale is, because there is a distinction betweene man & man, even among the Iewes, whereby some are indeed in the covenant, some not.[193]

Thus, not all the children of Jacob are truly Israel (v. 6), or as next argued, (v. 7) there is a distinction to be made even among the children of Abraham, the one in whom all nations are blessed, for Isaac alone and not Ishmael "is a sonne of promise"; Paul manifests "a double seede," one fleshly, the other spiritual and, thus, "two kind of sons," one of the flesh and the other "the sonne of the promise, or the sonne of God."[194] Furthermore,

> the distinction betweene Isaac and Ismael, whereby one is in the covenant of grace, the other not; stands not in their foreseene faith and unbeleefe, and the fruites of them: but in the purpose and will of God itselfe. For Isaac is called *the child of promise*, because by vertue of it he was borne and beleeved, and was adopted the childe of God and made heire of the covenant given to Abraham: and therefore consequently the right of adoption befell him by the meere good pleasure of God, which is the first cause of our salvation without respect of anything in the person of Isaac. For what God by his promise brings to passe in time, that he most freely decreed before all times.[195]

This character of the divine choice is made clear in verses 11-13 where Paul declares that the distinction already existed before the children were born.

> Hence it is manifest, that there is an unchangable decree of election of some men (for he that takes al, and excepts none, can not be said to choose) to salvation, depending upon the alone will of God; and therefore necessarily by the law of contraries, there is an opposite decree of reprobation: for in that God ordaineth some to eternall salvation, he testifies thereby, that his purpose is to passe by some without shewing of mercy.[196]

The text itself demands a doctrine of double predestination though, here, as elsewhere, Perkins does not establish reprobation as the exact coordinate of election.

Perkins on the Ordering of the Decree: Trinitarian Ground and Christological Focus

Having thus laid the exegetical ground of the doctrine, Perkins' *An Exposition of the Symbole* passes on to the formal argumentation and the division of the subject. The pattern of argument now parallels closely *A Treatise of the Manner and Order of Predestination.* In both treatises, Perkins holds to his basic assumption of the simplicity of God and the absence of logical distinctions from the divine mind, but he sees a necessity for developing the doctrine "for our understanding sake" as a series of "acts" or "degrees." The scholastic mode of argument clarifies and defines by distinction and division of the subject. Predestination itself here appears as "the counsell of God touching the last end or estate of man out of this our naturall life" since by nature all men are alike but only some are prepared by God for "the spirituall and heavenly life."[197] The means by which God accomplishes this counsel are two: creation and fall. The former is the positive act of God to make a finite and mutable creature, man, in his own image; the latter occurs by divine permission: "the will of God is not the cause of the fall, but the will of man left unto itselfe by God."[198] The pattern, here, creation and fall as means, indicates a supralapsarian tendency, but the emphasis on divine permission manifests a tendency in the opposite direction, away from rigid causal patterning, in this case away even from Calvin's strict definition. Perkins can distinguish two acts or degrees in the counsel itself—the eternal purpose and the decree to execute the purpose; these are not separate in God but are "distinctly considered" as referring to ends and to means. In the first, God decrees some to honor and some to dishonor; in the second, ordaining means to this end. This latter decree also has two parts—the decree concerning creation, fall and "the shutting up of all men under damnation" and the "application" of means to individual persons. Nevertheless, in this treatise, Perkins' main interest is with the divine purpose to elect and rejectindeed, primarily with election.[199] Not only does Perkins formally divide predestination into the two coordinate halves of election and reprobation, but conceives the decree of election as a double act even as he previously divided the divine counsel: a distinction must be made between the end and "the meanes tending to the end," between God's "eternall purpose and election" or "betweene the decree and the execution thereof."[200] There is, thus, an eternal election but also an "actuall election made in time" when God selects individuals out of the mass of mankind and brings them "to the kingdome of his owne Son."[201]

The distinction derives from St. Paul's epistle to the Romans 8:29-30, where the apostle

> . . . distinguisheth the decree into two acts, foreknowledge, whereby he doth acknowledge some men for his owne before the rest, and predestination, whereby he hath determined from eternitie to make them like unto Christ.[202]

This foreknowledge Perkins defines as a fore-choice of certain individuals and not a foreknowledge of faith. The central Pauline point, according to Perkins, is the act of predestining on which salvation and the causes of salvation rest. It would be absurd to conceive of God as reacting to foreknown faith since that faith, as a means to salvation, must itself rest on God's predestination if it is to be certain.[203] It is also improper to separate foreknowledge and predestination so as to make the former the cause of the latter: "the prescience & purpose of God are by the Holy Ghost put for the same thing."[204] This particular point of Pauline exegesis reflects Calvin down to the finest detail.[205] The definition of predestination given by Perkins looks directly to the christological focus of Calvin's theology: predestination is in Christ and is a will to make man "like unto Christ." "Now if men are elected that they might beleeve, they are not elected because they would beleeve"; the same thing, i.e., belief, cannot be both cause and effect.[206]

Perkins defines the first act of election as a "part & beginning of the divine purpose" but includes in his definition an infralapsarian element. According to the first act of election,

> God doth take certaine men which are to be created, unto his everlasting love and favour, passing by the rest, and by taking maketh them vessels of mercy and honour.[207]

God's second act of predestination "is the purpose of saving or conferring glory, whereby he doth ordaine or set apart the very same men which were to fall in Adam, unto salvation and celestial glory."[208] This act has five divisions or "degrees," the first of which is "the ordaining of a Mediatour."[209] Perkins draws an explicit connection between his Christology and the doctrine of predestination:

> The ordaining of a Mediatour is that, whereby the second person beeing the Sonne of God, is appointed from all eternitie to bee a Mediatour betweene God himselfe & men. And hence it is, that Peter saith, that 'Christ was foreknowne before the foundation of the world.' And well saith Augustine, that 'Christ was predestinated to bee our head.' For howsoever as hee is (*logos*) the substantiall word of the Father, or the Sonne, he doth predestinate with the Father, and the Holy Ghost; yet as hee is the Mediatour, he is predestinated himselfe.[210]

The divinity of Christ, the fully-developed determination of the intratrinitarian activity relating to the work of salvation and a sense of what can only be called the 'official subordination' of the Son as mediator, structurally parallel in the distinctions between the eternity of God and the economy of salvation to the *kenosis* or *exinanitio*, here become the foundation of Perkins' understanding of the decree. The designation of the mediator, a concept only hinted at by Calvin, has become in Perkins' theology a fully realized structure.

Similar determinations of doctrine occur in Perkins' system, *An Exposition of the Symbole*. He refers to

> the actuall or reall foundation of Gods election, & that is Christ: and therefore we are said to be chosen *in Christ*. He must be considered two waies: as he is God, we are predestinate *of him*, even as we are predestinate of the Father and the Holy Ghost. As he is our Mediator, we are predestinate *in him*.[211]

This structure, like the one cited immediately above, parallels the determination concerning the ordaining of the mediator, supports the concept of Christ as *fundamentum electionis* against subordinationist error,[212] and provides the ground for Perkins' description of Christ as the foundation of the mediated work of God:

> For when God with himselfe had decreed to manifest his glory in saving some men by his mercy, he ordained further the creation of man in his own image, yet so by his own fal he should infold himselfe & all his posterity under damnation: this done, he also decreed that the Word should be incarnate actually, to redeem those out of the former misery, whom he had ordained to salvation. Christ therefore himselfe was first of all predestinate as he was to be our head, & as Peter saith, *ordained before all worlds*; and we secondly predestinate in him, because God ordained that the execution of man's election should be in him. Here if any demand, how we should be assured that Christ in his passion stood in our roome and stead, the resolution will be easie, if we consider that he was ordained in the eternal counsel of God, to be in our surety and pledge & to be a publike person to represent all the Elect in his obedient sufferings: and therefore it is that Peter saith, that he *was delivered by the foreknowledge and determinate counsell of God*. And Paul, that *grace was given unto us through Christ Jesus before the world was*.[213]

This delineation of the common trinitarian ground of predestination and Christology appears as the speculative culmination of the early orthodox inquiry into the problem of the decrees. It stands in clear relationship to the federalist doctrine of the *pactum salutis*, the covenant of redemption made between the Father and the Son as the foundation of the divine covenanting with man.[214] Yet precisely here Matthias Schneckenburger criticized the scholastics and particularly the federalists for postulating a form of determinism in which the logic of the *ordo salutis* and the decree impinged on the inherent freedom of the intratrinitarian relationships.[215] What was the motive of Perkins and Polanus in proposing this structure? The answer appears, I believe, in analysis of the remainder of Perkins' exposition.

Like Polanus, Perkins attempted to avoid a rigid determinism by excluding the fall from the decree: "No man," he stated, "is absolutely ordained to hell."[216] In Adam, the federal head of humanity, all had the power to refrain from sinning. Adam's sin resulted from the free response of his will to the devil's temptation. Following Vermigli and Ursinus rather than Calvin, Perkins argued that Adam's act was "contingent and not necessary," made possible by God's "permission and desertion."[217] Perkins also denies causal imputation of Adam's sin to posterity for the sake of the decree; Beza provides no model here. Adam lost the gift of grace and the wholeness of his faculties and with these losses the ability to transmit the image of God in which he had been created to his posterity. Perkins clearly hopes to maintain the freedom of secondary causes while asserting the complete sovereignty of God in the work of salvation; and this sovereignty will appear *a priori*, beginning with the intra-trinitarian determination of the pattern of salvation and proceeding to the execution of the decree rather than as an *a posteriori* rationalization.

Following his description of the designation of Christ as mediator, Perkins passes on to the second of the "five degrees" within the second great act of predestination: "the promising of him being ordained," the revelation of Christ as the one who will obtain the grace necessary to the end of man's salvation.[218] God conjoins this revelation with the command to believe but not in such a way as to conflict with his electing purpose:

> . . . the promise is made onely to beleevers; but the commaundement is given to beleevers & unbeleevers also. For the elect are mingled with the wicked in the same assemblies. . . . God by exhortations to repentance, meaneth to leave those without excuse, whome he doth see will never repent.[219]

The next degree of Perkins' schema reflects this distinction between the universality of the command and the particularity of the promise. For we now come to the "exhibiting of the Mediatour" in "the fulnesse of time" or, in other words, the actual payment for sin promised in the previous degree. Here a distinction must be made between the "potentiall" and "actuall efficacie" of Christ's work.[220] Potentially "in respect of merit and operation" the efficacy of Christ's work is infinite, but in actuality "the price is payd in the counsell of God, and as touching

tionship established between the divine will or intention to save and the temporal enactment of salvation manifests the consistency of God's will and the certainty of his promises founded on and revealed in the person of Christ.[235]

In locating this analysis of the systematic relationship of predestination and Christology in systems so different in their orderings of doctrine, we most probably have denominated one of the underlying concerns of Reformed doctrine in the early orthodox period. On the one hand we have seen a variety of placements of the doctrine of the decrees indicating a variety of systematic and of specifically soteriological concerns, but on the other we have seen, in most of these systems, and despite the varying placement of the doctrine, an underlying emphasis on the priority of Christ as God to any and all essential acts of God, on the christological ground of the work of salvation. In other words, the trinitarian-christological concern stands prior in a systematic sense both to the desire of some theologians to ground the *ordo salutis* or the life of the church on the divine causality and to the desire of other writers to place the discussion of divine causality in an *a priori* position. If we cannot argue a predestinarian metaphysic on the basis of systematic placement, neither can we argue it in terms of the relation of Christ to the decree, which is, of course, the prior issue in a system organized around several doctrinal centers. For though the statement of the doctrine of predestination has become more elaborate in a scholastic sense and, indeed, more speculative in terms of its statement of logical priorities, it has not become more deterministic than that of Calvin, nor has it become any less christologically oriented. Indeed, the relationship of Christ to the decree has been clarified and elaborated, and full determinism has been avoided in favor of categories of divine permissive willing and free or contingent activity of secondary causes. There can be no *deus nudus absconditus* because the divine persons who together set forth the decree also enter into the economy of salvation according to their mode of existence, their relation to the other persons. There can be no *deus nudus absconditus* because the Christ who redeems is, according to his divinity, the God who decrees.

When Perkins finally comes to argue the doctrine of reprobation he maintains his supralapsarian logic but refrains from making reprobation fully coordinate with election:

> The decree of reprobation is a worke of Gods providence, whereby he hath decreed to passe by certaine men . . . for the manifestation of his iustice and wrath in their due destruction: or, it is his will, whereby he suffereth some men to fall into sinne. . . .
>
> It hath . . . two acts. The first is the purpose to forsake some men, and to make known his iustice in them. This act hath a finall cause, but no impulsive cause out of God. . . . The second act is the ordaining of them to punishment or due destruction. . . . And the ordination is of the most iust will of God, yet not without respect of originall and actuall sinnes. For as men are actually damned for sinne: so God hath decreed to damn them for the same sinne. Yet notwithstanding sinne is not the cause of the decree of reprobation. . . .[236]

In his *An Exposition of the Symbole*, he points out that the eternal decree to love some in Christ and to hate other men for the manifestation of justice must be interpreted according to the fact that God actually neither loves nor hates non-existent creatures: the elect he loves as actual beings in Christ; the reprobate he hates as actual beings in Adam.[237] The foundation of the execution of the decree of reprobation, therefore, is the fall of Adam and the "generall corruption of man's nature" so that, again, none are condemned but for sin.[238]

EPILOGUE: THE EARLY ORTHODOX CODIFICATION

In the theologians of the turn of the century, the productive period running from approximately 1590 to 1610, we have encountered a fourth generation of Reformed thinkers, men whose theology was grounded not only on the *Institutes* of Calvin or the *Loci communes* of Musculus or Vermigli but also on the established confessional theology of the Reformed churches and its elaboration and defense in the works of Beza, Ursinus, and Zanchius. This is a theology conscious of its own tradition and development, aware of its roots in patristic and medieval theology, but aware also of the distinctive contribution of the Reformation and its first codifiers. We have seen, therefore, in our examination of the early orthodox doctrines of Christ and predestination not only change but also continuity. On the one hand, the scholastic method has been brought to a high degree of sophistication, not without attention to the great medieval synthesis provided in the writings of Aquinas and Scotus. Great attention has been given, moreover, to the tradition of christological and trinitarian orthodoxy reaching back into the early centuries of the church. On the other hand, these early orthodox thinkers have also been deeply concerned to develop the structures, motifs, and doctrinal interrelationships emphasized by their predecessors in the Reformed tradition. In particular, great attention has been given to the way in which the seeming unreconcilables of the eternal infinite and the temporal finite are reconciled savingly in Christ: Christology and the doctrine of the decree still function coordinately to describe the gracious divine involvement in history, the causal and redemptive nexus of the temporal and the eternal. And insofar as the decree defines Christ as the one source of salvation, the system remains christocentric.

The doctrine of predestination has, in this stage of the development of orthodoxy, become the subject of speculative elaboration. Polanus and Perkins both drew out in greater detail the essential acts of God and the relationship of the decree, as essential act, to the Godhead. Perkins in particular pressed the issue of logical ordering of "acts" or "degrees" in the decree itself while Polanus emphasized the decree as the product of the *voluntas Dei*. Nevertheless, the doctrine of predestination has hardly become, in these thinkers, a principle from which system is deduced; instead it has been defined in terms of certain other boundary concepts—Trinity, the consistency of the divine willing, salvation by the event, onely for those which are elected and predestinated."[221] The unity and oneness of purpose in God is shown forth in the unity of Christ's work. "For the Sonne doth not sacrifice for those, for whom he doth not pray: because to make an intercession and sacrifice are conjoyned: but hee prayeth only for the elect and for beleevers."[222]

The atonement is limited in the sense that sacrifice is conjoined to sanctification. Perkins thus conjoins the eternal decree with a temporal work: "the price is appointed and limited to the elect alone by the Fathers decree and the Sonnes intercession and oblation."[223] Christ not only merits salvation but also effectively works salvation in those to whom it has been promised and for whom it has been performed.[224]

> Christ bare their person, and stood in their roome upon the crosse, for whome hee is a Mediatour: and consequently, whatsoever Christ did as a Redeemer, the same did all those in him, and with him which are redeemed: Christ dying, rising againe, ascending, & sitting at the right hand of the Father, they also die with him, rise againe, ascend, and sit at the right hand of God. Now that all of these things can truly be said of the elect only, and of such as beleeve, I proove it thus. To say that any one of the wicked, which are to perish forever, is raised up in Christ rising againe, is flat against the truth; because the raising up of Christ is . . . his actuall absolution from their sins for whome he died; for even as the Father by delivering Christ to death, did in very deede condemne their sinnes imputed unto Christ, for whome he died; so by raising him up from death, even *ipso facto* hee did absolve Christ from their sinnes, and did withall absolve them in Christ.[225]

Perkins demonstrates his awareness of the traditional language of limited atonement in his use of the scholastic formula of sufficiency and efficiency, but the weight of his exposition rests on the issue of the efficacy of the atonement and specifically on the relationship of God's redeeming act in Christ to man's condition and need. The saving work of Christ cannot be intended for all, but only for those engrafted into Christ.[226] Even so God's justice is not cancelled by his mercy but is borne by Christ for the sake of his mercy. Perkins thus makes clear the identity of the saving intention of God and the intention of Christ in the application of his benefits.[227] Perkins cannot accept the possibility that the infinite merit of Christ's death was intended by God to effect without qualification the salvation of all men and subsequently hindered by the very iniquity it strove to abolish. Christ received the full wrath of God against sin for the sake of those adopted in him.[228] This christological limitation of the extent of atonement here, as in Ursinus' system, insures the unlimited efficacy of Christ's work.[229]

The central issue of Perkins' soteriology is God's grace as it is mediated in Christ. Grace is irresistible and is given only in one way: man receives and experiences the gracious will of God mediately, rather than immediately, insofar as Christ the mediator supplies the middle term between the gracious will of the transcendent God and the sinful will of finite man, the recipient of God's grace. The efficacy of atonement is limited by the extent of actual, effective mediation;

damnation occurs where God's saving will is not mediated.[230] The two final degrees of salvation, "the applying of him being exhibited . . . and the accomplishment of the application," describe the work of "saving or conferring glory."[231] In this work Christ is given to believers in Word and Sacrament, by means of the "instrument of a true faith," for the sake of their final glorification "whereby God shall be all in all by Christ in all the elect."[232] These various degrees of God's acts of predestination as elaborated by Perkins have provided us entrance into a speculative discussion of the decree quite unlike the formulations we encountered in the work of Calvin or even Beza, Ursinus, and Zanchius. Yet, as in the other aspects of Perkins' system that we have examined, the governing factor is not a purely metaphysical problem but the relationship of Christology and soteriology to the decrees.

The "order" of the decrees set forth by Perkins bears comparison with the similarly speculative but theologically distinct "order" argued by Jacob Arminius. Writing several years later and attempting to provide an alternative to both the supra- and infralapsarian conceptions of predestination, Arminius postulated four separate decrees of God according to which God first wills to save and only subsequently chooses the elect out of those who accept the grace offered in Christ.[233] Whereas Perkins maintained a single, consistent will and intention in God and postulated the degrees or *gradus* within the one decree only for the sake of explication, Arminius described, by means of several decrees, an antecedent and a consequent will of God. Antecedently God wills that all mankind be saved on condition of belief, but in his consequent will he responds to the foreknown acts of men, thereby resting salvation on human choice.[234] Much in contrast to this defection from the Reformed *sola gratia*, the "order" that Perkins describes in the decree buttresses at every turn the Reformed conception of the *ordo salutis*. Indeed, the degrees or *gradus* within the decree seem to be a speculation designed solely for the sake of asserting an eternal and of course metaphysical ground for the entire temporal dispensation of divine grace in each of its stages.

The *a priori* character of this speculation obviates the danger noted by Schneckenburger: Perkins' ordering of the decree and, in particular, his statement of the intra-trinitarian ground of the decree and its execution, allow nothing to impinge on the freedom of the Godhead. The entire doctrinal structure points to a divine self-determination made in the freedom of the infinite, triune life of the Godhead. The purpose of such a structure much like the underlying concern of Tertullian's attack on the modalism of Praxeas, is the correlation of the eternal truth of God's existence and will with the manner in which God has revealed himself in the economy of salvation. In this speculation, the person of the mediator in the two states of his life and work is shown to be the point of contact in and through whom the vertical axis in theology representing God's sovereign will conjoins with the horizontal axis representing the historicity of human life as it receives the divine promises of salvation. The direct and necessary rela-

grace alone, God as good and therefore not the author of sin, the gift of salvation in Christ. If the definition, by way of speculative elaboration, has become more precise, the causal structure has hardly become more rigid than that described by Calvin, Vermigli and Musculus. Indeed, the two supralapsarians, Polanus and Perkins, have both insisted on the freedom of secondary causality, have argued (with Vermigli and against Calvin) that God does in fact permit some things such as sin, have placed the fall in a less positive relation to the decree than had Calvin, and have consistently refused to define reprobation as the exact coordinate of election (this in agreement with Calvin). Polanus' placement of the decree in relation to the doctrine of God has stated pointedly a relationship between God and his eternal counsel that was always resident in Reformed theology, but placement itself, as we have seen, does not amount to a redefinition of the doctrine or of its function. Finally, both Perkins and Polanus have stressed the christological implications of the divine willing and, in so doing, have manifested the decree as the eternal divine willing which becomes effective in time, only in and through Christ.

This interest in Christ as the nexus of temporal and eternal, finite and infinite, has been manifested in two crucial places in the system—first, in the statement of the eternal ground of the decree and of the saving work of the mediator as an intra-trinitarian determination involving the three persons of the Godhead. The doctrine of the essential work of God includes a stress on the Son as voluntarily elect, as self-designated to his work and, by way of this formula, a stress on incarnation and mediation as the center of the system, as the focal point of the execution of the divine will. Second, the christological *locus* itself has undergone considerable development. Whereas in the theology of Beza, Ursinus, and Zanchius, the chief christological interest seems to have been the development of Reformed doctrine in the context of traditional definition and the careful delineation of the elements of the Reformed position, the emphasis in the systematic works of Perkins and Polanus is far broader: indeed, with the threefold office concept drawn from Calvin and the doctrine of the two states adapted to the need of Reformed theology from Lutheranism, the early orthodox Christology presents a new structure, modeled in its essential emphasis preeminently upon the Christology of Calvin's *Institutes*. What was not as apparent in the work of Beza, Ursinus and Zanchius now reappears, in more complex formulation, as the dominant motif: Christology as itself structured in terms of the economy of the divine will as it enters history; a Christology not so much from above as in the historical line of the covenant-promise; a Christology which, as the nexus of divine and human, eternal and temporal, clearly occupies the central place in the structure and working of the system as a whole.

As far as the issue of "central dogmas" is concerned, we may fairly say that this theology, like the theology of the first codifiers, crystallizes around multiple foci. There is not one single controlling dogma, and the establishment of one doctrine as central, in the sense of a single point according to which the whole system is designed and from which the whole system is deduced, appears to have been an enterprise quite far from the mind of the thinkers examined. Instead, we have seen a tendency toward the methodical elaboration of all doctrines according to the techniques of division of topic and definition of terms known to us as "scholasticism." The doctrine of Christ and his work has received considerable attention: indeed, if we were to select one doctrine in which crucial structural modifications were made and to which the attention of theologians had been consistently drawn as a focal point for positive development and elaboration, we would necessarily select the Christology over the doctrine of predestination. At very least, these two doctrines received equal attention, and predestination, whatever its placement, retained its functional character as a description of the consistency of the divine will both essentially and in its temporal manifestation. Throughout this development, moreover, we have seen consistent attention paid to the relationship of these doctrines and to the fact that Christ stands somehow prior to the decree even when mediation belongs to the execution of the eternal purpose. In Beza and Zanchi and, then, more clearly in Perkins and Polanus, the trinitarian referent of the Christology has manifest the priority of Christ. In short, the concept of "Jesus Christ electing and elected" which overcomes the threat of a "predestinarian metaphysic" and of a *deus nudus absconditus* appears not as a theme barely hinted at but as a fundamental interest, indeed, as a norm for early orthodoxy. The person of Christ cannot be reduced to the status of mere means to an end; rather, at the very heart of God, the underlying will to save is defined by the willingness of the Son, himself the God who decrees, to assume the form of a servant and become the means of salvation.

VII

CHRIST AND THE DECREE
IN THE DEVELOPMENT OF EARLY ORTHODOXY:
RETROSPECT AND PROSPECT

A century of development and change lies between the posting of the *Ninety-five Theses* and the promulgation of the *Canons* of Dort. What began as a movement of protest and reform rapidly became a fully-developed exposition of theological principles. Luther and his contemporaries in the early reform were the fathers both of Lutheranism and of Reformed theology. The Augustinian piety and scriptural preaching so powerfully represented by the early reformers was soon given systematic form by Melanchthon (1521) and by Zwingli (1525). Melanchthon's *Loci communes* and Zwingli's *Commentarius de vera et falsa religione* were but the beginning of the vast work of preparing an intellectual structure for the defense of Reformed piety and doctrine.

By mid-century an astonishing array of catechisms, confessions, systems of piety, and systematic expositions of the creed had appeared. Melanchthon's *Loci communes* had taken more and more the form of a complete system of doctrine. Bucer had produced a brief but systematic statement of belief for Strassburg. Several more treatises had appeared from the pen of Zwingli. Bullinger, Zwingli's successor, had written his own theological compendium. In Geneva, Calvin had prepared several editions of his *Institutes*, a catechism, and the *Instruction de la foy*; Pierre Viret had written his exposition of the creed. In Bern, Musculus' exegetical program had produced much of the material that would form his *Loci communes*. Peter Martyr Vermigli was completing his stay at Oxford. In all of these writers of the second generation of Reform, we encounter a tendency toward doctrinal definition, toward the development of theological system and strictly determined dogmatic *loci*. Particularly in Musculus and Vermigli we saw a reliance, albeit at times critical and polemical but frequently constructive, upon the categories and distinctions of medieval scholasticism. Calvin's statements concerning the scholastics are mostly polemical, but even in his theology we have detected a reliance on old and established, specifically Scotist, patterns of thought.

When we add to this systematic development the several full systems to appear on the Lutheran side in addition to Melanchthon's *Loci communes*, namely Urbanus Rhegius' *Formulae . . . loquendi de praecipuis christianae doctrinae locis* (1535), Erasmus Sarcerius' *Loci aliquot communes et theologici* (1538),

Johann Spangenberg's *Margarita theologica* (1540), David Chytraeus' *Catechesis* (1555)—modeled on Melanchthon's *Loci*—and his *De studio theologiae recte incohando* (1562), and Nicholas Hemmingius' *Enchiridion theologicum* (1557), we have a portrait of a reform movement little averse to theological system—and good reason to doubt the frequent impression given by histories of the period and even by scholarly monographs that, with Luther, an iron curtain came down across the theological world severing the domain of scholasticism from the domain of reform. Indeed, Luther's strident declamation in his disputation at Heidelberg and in his disputation against scholastic theology that theology cease to be done in the mode in which he had learned it, seems to have been interpreted by subsequent Reformers not as an attack on theological discipline—certainly not on the *locus* method!—but as a demand that system be rewritten.

Once the dates of the major confessions and early systems have been set before us, we are able to see the consistent development of Protestant system toward a Protestant orthodoxy beginning in 1521, the year Melanchthon published his *Loci*, barely four years after the posting of the *Ninety-five Theses*. Once, moreover, that the gradual character of the change has been recognized and once we realize that there was never a generation of Protestant Reformers unaware of or unable to cope with the complexity of scholastic argument (Luther, Bucer, Calvin, Musculus, and Vermigli were trained in scholastic theology; Ursinus, Zanchius, Beza and the rest wrote scholastic theology), there remains no possibility of representing Protestant orthodoxy as a strange distortion. Instead it is a product of the historical growth of Protestantism standing in some methodological discontinuity but in general doctrinal continuity with the Reformation.

We began our study at a midpoint in this process of development. Lutheran and Reformed positions are clearly defined and bitter polemic had begun between these two major branches of the Reformation. Reformed theology appears not as a monolithic structure—not, in short, as "Calvinism"—but as a form of Augustinian theology and piety capable of considerable variation in its form of presentation, and capable also of clarification and augmentation on fine points of doctrine. Calvin, Musculus, Bullinger, and Vermigli, far from being a terminal point in the movement of Protestant doctrine, provided the basis of later soteriological structures. Shortly before the death of Calvin, the Heidelberg theologians began to draw together several of the central themes of Calvin's thought with the covenantal doctrines of Bullinger and Musculus. We see no distinct break but a continuous process of theological and systematic development. The great systems of the latter part of the sixteenth century carry forward this pattern. If they are more speculative than the earlier Reformed theologies, they are nevertheless respectful of the priority of revelation, and they direct their speculation toward the establishment of an eternal ground for the temporal *ordo salutis*. Polanus, Perkins, and their contemporaries sought to ground both the doctrine of the decrees and the doctrines concerning the economy of salvation

in Christ. Their systems therefore present a clearer determination of the relationship of Christ to the divine decrees than that set forth by earlier Reformed
theologians.

As a central doctrine of the developing soteriological structure, the doctrine
of Christ was transformed in terms of two doctrinal emphases. Early Reformed
orthodoxy was drawn to a closer examination of the Chalcedonian formula and
of later implications of Greek patristic thought. Although this accommodation
took place largely in polemical works, it had also an impact on system. Whereas
Calvin had been able to affirm that the two natures were united in the one person
of Christ or that the person of the mediator assumed flesh, later Reformed
theologians affirmed with more precision the union of human nature with the
divine in the person of the only-begotten Son of God. This utilization of Greek
patristic thought including the late concept of an enhypostatic union with its
corollary, the anhypostasis of the human nature, although characteristic of the
sophisticated analyses of the early orthodox systems, never became the central
interest of Reformed Christology.

The systems of late sixteenth century Reformed theology move consistently
to present an impeccably orthodox statement of the doctrine of Christ's person
within a structure of mediation. On the one hand, they guard themselves against
the charge of christological heresy by incorporating a traditional standard of
orthodoxy into their exposition while on the other, they move freely to adapt
the structure of their Christology to the needs of the system. The doctrinal
structures of the *status duplex* and the *munus triplex* receive their mature formulation providing Reformed Christology with its basic outlines and providing,
also, a Christology suited to the needs of an Augustinian *ordo salutis*. In brief,
the fully developed early orthodox Christology was grounded in the conception
of the Son's aseity, in the continuation and fulfillment of the covenantal *historica
series* in the successive states of Christ's work and person, and in the epistemological and causal distinctions resolved in the office of the mediator according
to which the eternity of God and his will are related to the economy of salvation.
Precisely here, in these christological structures, the doctrine of Christ moves
ineluctably into relation with the entire *ordo salutis*, at last making clear that
relation adumbrated between it and the doctrine of predestination in the thought
of Calvin and his contemporaries. Rather than develop a predestinarian system—
rather than expending the greater portion of effort in system-building upon developing the doctrine of predestination—the early orthodox developed a broad
spectrum of doctrines, sketched out their interrelationships and established Christology as a central doctrinal issue and, equally importantly, concentrated upon
the elaboration of a historical and economical pattern drawn out but not completed
in the thought of their predecessors. Predestination, of course, was the focal
point for exposition of the divine causality, but it depended itself on the *loci* of
God and the Trinity and was so developed in the light of its relation to other
doctrines that, far from being a principle from which other doctrines derive, it

stands as a sign of salvation by grace alone and as a causal guarantor of the theocentric causality and christocentric soteriology pressed by the system as a whole.

The early orthodox writers, in achieving this balance of ontic and economic motifs—the causal chain and the *historica series*, both resolved in Christ—produced a system that, in its extreme moments, might disrupt the balance in one direction or the other, leaning on one side to the overly metaphysical and causally controlled systems of Maccovius and Voetius and on the other to the primarily historical, economical patterns of Cocceius and Witsius, but which could also generate the elaborate interplay of causal and covenantal structures in the works of thinkers like Burmann, Heidegger, and van Mastricht. In these latter systems, the resolution of distinctions concerning human finitude and divine transcendence in terms of the saving work of the triune God would continue to represent the underlying positive thrust of system.

Over against the previous scholarship, I would make two points. First, the thesis of the "predestinarian system," Schweizer's central-dogma theory, applies no better to the orthodox system than it does to Calvin's thought. Second, the notion that Calvin's christocentrism and his placement of the doctrine of predestination in the 1559 *Institutes* imply a deemphasis or diminution of the impact of the causal focus of his theology must also be rejected. As we have learned from Barth, the various placements of the doctrine of predestination point to multiple implications of that doctrine, not the least of which is its relation to the Christology and its soteriological importance. What we encounter in all of the Reformed systems from Calvin to Polanus and, indeed, in the orthodox system as far as Turretin and Heidegger, is a theology with multiple *foci* in which the definitively theocentric causal pattern guarantees the thoroughly christocentric soteriological structure. What we have seen, then, in the course of this essay is the inapplicability of the central-dogma theory as such to the study of Reformed orthodoxy: that theory, as a representative of a particular method in theology, belongs to the nineteenth century and stands as a mode of theological thinking foreign to the dynamic of late sixteenth and of seventeenth century thought.[1] There are, indeed, crucial *loci*, organizational patterns and principles—Trinity, Christ, the divine causality, covenant, but the idea of a central dogma and a single organizing principle for scholastic orthodoxy is an anachronism.

Anachronistic also is the claim that the development of Reformed orthodoxy brought about the formulation of a deterministic system: the orthodox are no more and no less deterministic than Calvin himself. This issue for all the theologians noted in this essay is the establishment of the divine will in Christ as the ground and foundation of our salvation—what might be called a soteriological determinism. But this is no philosophical determinism: as J. K. S. Reid remarked of Calvin's doctrine, predestination belongs to a different order of being from our willing and therefore does not interfere with human responsibility.[2] Rather than philosophical determinism, we encounter in these thinkers, on the side of

providence and the overarching divine causality, a Scotist conception of pa-
nergism or a standard scholastic conception of the concurrence of divine and
human willing, without any sense of a determinism or necessity inherent in the
will itself or in the order of being of which man is a part. Predestination stands,
simply, as the guarantee of divine sovereignty in the work of salvation; indeed,
as the guarantee of the efficacy of Christ's work. In this doctrinal assumption
there is continuity from Calvin's time onward into the early orthodox codification.

While it is true that late sixteenth century thinkers developed doctrine in a
more speculative, logical pattern than either Calvin or Bullinger, there were
certain elements in the work of both these thinkers that pointed toward the later
developments. Bullinger did contribute to the development of prolegomena and
to the federalist emphasis on *historica series*. Calvin provided a clear model for
later causal exegesis of Pauline passages dealing with the doctrine of predestination, he formulated much of his theology around distinctions between the temporal and the eternal, and he provided basic christological structures for later
development. In addition, the speculative, logical tendencies of the later thinkers
found positive precedent in the theological treatises of Musculus and Vermigli.
We must overcome the tendency of scholarship to minimize the impact of earlier
scholastic thought and of Aristotelian categories upon the first period of the
systematization of Reformed thought. In Musculus and Vermigli, at least, these
patterns of thought were present and well defined. Moreover, the later Reformed
thinkers did not deviate from the practical interests of their predecessors. Ursinus'
scholasticism had as its point of departure the practical purpose of catechesis,
and Zanchius, even in his most speculative moments, would pause to describe
the use of his doctrine to faith. This interest in the usefulness of doctrine as a
support of faith, that is, as an aid to the *apprehensio fiducialis* of saving doctrine,
was also characteristic of Perkins' and Ames' approach to theology.

The emphasis of early orthodox thinkers on detailed, often speculative, and
invariably rationally argued doctrinal determinations relates also to the positive
development of doctrine that we have traced over a half century from Calvin
and Bullinger to Polanus and Perkins. It was important, and indeed necessary,
for the perpetuation of the Reformed churches and their faith that doctrine achieve
precision and consistency comparable to that of the Lutheran and Roman alter-
natives. Fundamental principles such as the trinitarian ground of theology moved
toward more complete formulation. This trinitarian motif in particular represents
the positive doctrinal achievement of early orthodoxy, appearing both in the
Christology and the doctrine of predestination in Perkins' system, in the doctrine
of predestination in Polanus' *Syntagma* and Bucanus' *Institutions*, and at the
heart of DuMoulin's epistemology.[3] Similar formulations occur in the systematic
works of Trelcatius, Wollebius, Amesius, Ussher, and Downame.

In other words, even as Reformed theology in the period of early orthodoxy,
chose not to commit itself to a primarily epistemological ordering of doctrine
but adopted patterns which tended to manifest the ontic, causal issues of theology,

it retained as basic to theology the fundamental distinctions and resolutions resting on an apprehension of the mediated character of saving knowledge and of God's saving will, distinctions and resolutions characteristic of the insight of Calvin and his contemporaries. Thus, in Polanus' *Syntagma*, and even in a high orthodox system like Turretin's *Institutio theologicae elencticae*, where a fully developed doctrine of God and his attributes with all the scholastic and philosophical language of essence and being appears prior to treatment of predestination, the determining factor in the system is not a speculative interest in the metaphysics of causal determinism but a soteriological interest in the manner in which God relates to his world in Christ.[4] This is indeed a deterministic system, but as with Calvin, the stress is upon hope in Christ and the utterly free grace of the transcendent God in making possible the salvation of believers; and the divine determination, lodged in another order of being, does not infringe upon the freedom or contingency of events in this, the order of finite being.

    Another issue intimately related to the problem of anachronism characteristic of the central-dogma theory is the issue of development in doctrine and movement in history. The assumption of the study has been the neutrality of movement and change: neither the term "orthodoxy" nor the word "scholasticism" has been used pejoratively or in laudatory fashion; they are purely descriptive. Much of the scholarship has described changes in Reformed theology after Calvin as distortions, a description which involves both a theological value judgment (which is not at all based on historical evidence or historical methodology) and the assumption that a development in the history of thought can be frozen at some arbitrarily designated optimum moment. There is an essential absurdity in criticizing theologians in 1570 or 1590 or 1610 or 1650 for not remaining true to Calvin. Calvin was not their only predecessor and the context of thought in their day demanded different formulation. We do not criticize Ritschl for not being true to Schleiermacher or Barth for not being true to Ritschl. So also should we cease to ask Polanus or Ames or the Synod of Dort or the Westminster Assembly to be true to Calvin. The historical analysis of Protestant orthodoxy must describe development and change, continuity and discontinuity; it ought not to postulate golden ages or optimum moments from which all else is decline.

    What I believe this study has consistently shown is that the early orthodox writers were not simply unthinking epigoni who fastened upon one aspect of early Reformed doctrine and because of a penetration into theological issues unequal to that of the Reformers, created a whole theology around the one motif. We have seen a true development and adaptation of theological system on a large scale—an effort to draw toward completion doctrinal structures not fully elaborated at an earlier stage of the Reformation. Particularly in the thinkers who adopted Ramist logic—Perkins, Polanus, Scharpius, Ames—there is attention to the architecture of system, the interrelationship of doctrines within a perspicuously defined pattern for the whole. The interest in architectonic issues parallels and supplements an interest in the full statement of issues within each doctrinal *locus*.

Perkins and Polanus, with other thinkers of their generation, provided Reformed theology with its second major synthesis and systematization of themes just prior to the internecine dispute with Arminius. They achieved a systematic balance between predestination and other soteriological motifs. In their thought we perceived at last the convergence of the parallel lines of christological and predestinarian doctrinal development, the convergence of which can only occur in the infinite depth of the Trinity. And when the lines do converge in the realization that the Son considered as God is the source, while considered as mediator in union with the human nature, the self-determined executor of the decree, then on this infinite scale we also perceive the ultimate doctrinal "arch" of which not predestination but the trinitarian ground of all theology is the keystone. This structure had developed from Calvin onwards, reaching its fruition at the end of the century in the codification of early orthodoxy.

It is, moreover, in this balance and interpenetration of christological with predestinarian motifs, as reconciled in the trinitarian formula, that we must find the systematic ground of Reformed theology. The entire thrust of the systematic development that we have traced is toward a soteriologically-oriented description of the way in which infinite God, utterly inaccessible to finite man in his aspirations toward an eternal hope, succeeds in Christ and through Christ in the historical dispensation or economy of salvation and in the individual causality of redemption in drawing the finite to Himself. This underlying issue of the reconciliation of opposites—the finite and the infinite, the temporal and the eternal, the human and the divine—is manifest both in the christological motifs (the *aseity* of Christ's divinity, the reality of his humanity, and the related *extra calvinisticum*) and in the *sola gratia* of the decree. It is manifest as well in the desire of the system to assert the consistency of the divine purpose with its temporal enactment and in the consequent pressure exerted on the system to reach from a description of the enactment of salvation in Christ and in the *ordo salutis* to a description of the trinitarian activity in which the persons of the Godhead freely determine the course of the economy of salvation. The systematic ground of Reformed theology must be sought, therefore, in this series of formulations of the underlying issue of God's reconciling purpose and in the interpenetration of several crucial doctrinal *loci* rather than in any single *locus*. We can speak of one ground of doctrine, however, because all aspects of the system relate to and derive from the saving intention, eternally conceived, by the three persons of the one God in the unity of their will and wisdom.

In all of the early orthodox systems we have examined, we have seen a certain formalism, a growing tendency to produce well defined, positive doctrine, and a considered use of logical argumentation (not to be confused with rationalism). We encounter, to be sure, a rigidly theocentric causality of salvation, but it is hardly more rigid than the predestinarianism of Calvin and far more open than Calvin to the consideration of problems of secondary causality involving the divine permission. Beside this causal rigidity and the increased systematization of doctrine, we do encounter a propositional rigidity uncharacteristic of earlier Reformed thought. But we must distinguish the form from the content: a propositional rigidity does not of itself indicate a priority of reason over revelation or a departure from the christocentric soteriology of the Reformation. Exposition of theology by means of logical propositions was characteristic of the Ramist as well as the more traditionally Aristotelian systems; and the Ramists, particularly Perkins and Ames, provided an impetus to the development of pietism. These final considerations taken together with the positive contribution of Reformed orthodoxy to the development of Christology in relation to predestination within a finely tuned soteriological structure are sufficient to refute the contention that early orthodoxy produced an unbalanced system which overemphasized the doctrine of predestination. In addition, we should be prepared to recognize a positive development of doctrine in early orthodoxy. For it was here that Reformed theology meditated profoundly on the underlying problems of the relationship of the timeless and transcendent God to the temporal order of salvation. The systems produced during this period provide discussion of the relationship of the persons of the Trinity *ad intra* and of the nature of God as a ground of the work of God *ad extra*. This is indeed a form of theological speculation, but it is a speculation guided by the needs of piety, for the sake of the soteriological emphasis of doctrine. As Karl Barth noted at the beginning of his *Church Dogmatics*,

> not merely the most important but also the most relevant and beautiful problems in dogmatics begin at the very point where the fable of 'unprofitable scholasticism' and the slogan about the 'Greek thinking of the Fathers' persuade us that we ought to stop.[5]

NOTES

I. INTRODUCTION

[1]For a survey of earlier analyses of the phenomenon of orthodoxy see Robert Scharlemann, *Aquinas and Gerhard: Theological Controversy and Construction in Medieval and Protestant Scholasticism* (New Haven, 1964), pp. 13-18.

2. *Die Glaubenslehre der evangelisch-reformierten Kirche*, 2 vols. (Zurich, 1847) and *Die protestantischen Centraldogmen in ihrer Entwicklung innerhalb der reformierten Kirche*, 2 vols. (Zurich, 1853).

3. Cf. *Centraldogmen*, I, pp. 152, 174.

4. Friedrich Schleiermacher, *The Christian Faith*, trs. Mackintosh and Stewart (N.Y., 1963), p. 200. On Schweizer's theology see: Brian A. Gerrish, *Tradition and the Modern World: Reformed Theology in the Nineteenth Century* (Chicago, 1978), pp. 119-136.

5. *The Christian Faith*, pp. 557-558; cf. Schweizer, *Glaubenslehre*, II, pp. 457-461 on the operation of the Holy Spirit as the source of the consciousness of absolute dependence.

6. Cf. *Glaubenslehre*, II, p. 200; cf. Gerrish, p. 128.

7. Cf. the comments of Walter Kickel, in his *Vernunft und Offenbarung bei Theodor Beza* (Neukirchen, 1967), pp. 7-8.

8. See the survey of scholarship in Emile Doumergue, *Jean Calvin, les hommes et les choses de son temps*, 7 vols. (Lausanne, 1899-1917), IV, pp. 407-408.

9. Ferdinand Christian Baur, *Vorlesungen über die christliche Dogmengeschichte* (Tübingen, 1865), I, part 7, p. 143. Also see Martin Werner, *The Formulation of Christian Dogma*, trs. Brandon (London, 1957), pp. 3-5.

10. F. C. Baur, *Lehrbuch der christlichen Dogmengeschichte*. (Tübingen, 1858), 314 et seq. and *Theologisches Jahrbuch* (1847), pp. 309-342. Baur nevertheless was able to argue elsewhere that the point at which the doctrine of predestination is perceived, for Calvin, is not metaphysical but rather "ethical-religious" and a matter of human consciousness of the problem of sin and grace: see his *Geschichte der christlichen Kirche* (Tübingen, 1863), IV, 407. This posthumous work seems to represent a later and more considered opinion than the *Lehrbuch*: it may well be that Baur assimilated the criticism of Schneckenburger and altered his opinion.

11. *Geschichte der protestantischen Dogmatik* (Berlin, 1854), I, 7-9.

12. Ibid., I, 185-189.

13. Ibid.,I, 120-122.

14. *Theodor Beza: Leben und ausgewählte Schriften* (Elberfeld, 1861), p. 320.

15. *Geschichte des deutschen Protestantismus* (Marburg, 1852); and *Die Dogmatik des Protestantismus im 16. Jahrhundert*, 3 vols. (Gotha, 1857).

16. *Geschichte des deutschen Protestantismus*, p. 13: "Das Princip seines Systems selbst ist der Glaube an das absolutum Dei decretum. Die Prädestinationslehre ist daher das Nervengewebe seiner ganzen Doctrin, indem die gesammte Menschheit bei ihm nur als Masse rechts und willenloser Subjecte erscheint."

17. *Prädestination und Verantwortlichkeit bei Calvin* (Neukirchen, 1937), p. 22.

18. *Theodor Beza*, pp. 347-348.

19. Heppe's *Dogmatik*, despite problems of organization and selection, remains a primary work of introduction to the orthodox theology; it is available in translation as *Reformed Dogmatics Set*

184   NOTES

Out and Illustrated from the Sources, revised and edited by Ernst Bizer, translated by G. T. Thomson (London, 1950; repr. Grand Rapids, 1978). Hereinafter abbreviated "RD."
20. RD, p. 154.
21. Amandus Polanus von Polansdorf, *Syntagma theologiae christianae* (Geneva, 1617); Lucas Trelcatius, *Scholastica et methodica locorum communium institutio* (London, 1604); Franciscus Gomarus, *Disputationes theologicae*, in *Opera theologica omnia* (Amsterdam, 1644); Joannes Maccovius, *Loci communes theologici* (Amsterdam, 1658); Hieronymus Zanchius, *Opera theologicorum*, 8 vols. (Geneva, 1617), cf. *De natura dei* in vol. 1.
22. John Calvin, *Institutio christianae religionis* (Geneva, 1559); Gulielmus Bucanus, *Institutiones theologicae seu locorum communium christianae religionis* (Lausanne, 1602).
23. Peter Martyr Vermigli, *Loci communes* (London, 1576); Wolfgang Musculus, *Loci communes* (Basel, 1560; 1564); William Ames, *Medulla S. S. theologiae* (Amsterdam, 1623; London, 1630).
24. Zacharias Ursinus, *Doctrinae christianae compendium sive commentarii catechetici* (Neustadt, Leiden, Geneva, 1584); Lambert Daneau, *Christianae isagoges ad christianorum theologorum loci communes* (Geneva, 1583); William Perkins, *An Exposition of the Symbole or Creed of the Apostles*, in *Works* (Cambridge, 1612-1619), vol. I.
25. Bartholomaus Keckermann, *Systema S. S. theologiae* (Heidelberg, 1602); Antonius Walaeus, *Loci communes S. theologiae*, in *Opera* (Leiden, 1643)—note that Walaeus' brief *Enchiridion religionis reformatae* (in ibid.) follows the pattern indicated above for Vermigli and Ames, at least with regard to the placement of predestination at the head of the *ordo salutis; Doctorum et professorum in academia Leidensi Joh. Polyandri, Andr. Riveti, Ant. Walaei et Ant. Thyssii, Synopsis purioris theologiae* (Leiden, 1618); John Downham, *The Summe of Sacred Divinitie* (London, 1630?).
26. *Geschichte des Pietismus und der Mystik in der reformierten Kirche, namentlich in der Niederlande* (Leiden, 1879), pp. 24, 207-211.
27. Matthias Schneckenburger, *Zur kirchlichen Christologie: Die orthodoxe Lehre vom doppelten Stand Christi nach lutherischer und reformierter Fassung* (Pforzheim, 1848), and *Vergleichende Darstellung des lutherischen und reformirten Lehrbegriffs*, herausgegeben durch Edw. Guder, 2 vols. (Stuttgart, 1855).
28. *Vergleichende Darstellung*, I, pp. 31-32.
29. In *Theologische Jahrbuch* (1848), pp. 73-77.
30. E.g., Z. Ursinus; cf. Althaus, pp. 155-163, 221-222.
31. *Vergleichende Darstellung*, I, p. 32.
32. Ibid., p. 33.
33. Ibid., p. 34; cf. Schneckenburger's argument in *Studien und Kritiken* (1847), pp. 972-977: the concept of predestination springs from the inner consciousness of the justified elect, even in the thought of the theologians of later orthodoxy. Cf. the analysis of Schneckenburger in William Hastie, *The Theology of the Reformed Church in its Fundamental Principles* (Edinburgh, 1904), pp. 151-155. Hastie's own view of Reformed theology leans toward the interpretations of Schweizer and Baur though rejecting the anthropological emphases of Schweizer's (and Schleiermacher's) theology (pp. 155-157).
34. Both Weber and Bizer view the development of Protestant orthodoxy with a jaundiced eye despite the fact that Weber traces the development and realization of an inner principle while Bizer argues for the reintroduction of scholastic philosophy. In Weber, therefore, the Schweizer-hypothesis has made a full turn, having become a negative rather than a positive analysis of the situation.
35. Weber, II, 1, 99.
36. Cf. ibid., 98, 100, 106.
37. Weber, II, pp. 98-99.
38. Cf. ibid., I/2, p. 312 with II, p. 99.
39. Ibid., II, p. 100-101.
40. Ibid., II, p. 102.
41. Cf. ibid., II, p. 107, 125-126.

42. Weber, I/1, p. 240. Reappraisal of Calvin's and of Zwingli's theology as christocentric has been the thrust of scholarship since Paul Jacobs, *Prädestination und Verantwortlichkeit bei Calvin*, (Neukirchen, 1937) and Gottfried W. Locher, *Die Theologie Huldrych Zwinglis im Lichte seiner Christologie*, I, *Die Gotteslehre* (Zurich, 1952).

43. Ibid., pp. 241-242.

44. Ibid., p. 245.

45. Weber, II, pp. 119-120.

46. Ibid., pp. 128-136, 157-166.

47. Cf. the extremely brief commentary on the Reformed Christology in ibid., I/2, pp. 131-150.

48. Ibid., II, p. 107.

49. Ibid., II, p. 106.

50. *Frühorthodoxie und Rationalismus*, (Zurich, 1963), p. 6.

51. Cf. Bernhard Pünjer, *History of the Christian Philosophy of Religion from the Reformation to Kant*, trs. W. Hastie (Edinburgh, 1887), pp. 168-178, with Ernst Lewalter, *Spanische-jesuitische und deutsch-lutherische Metaphysik in des 17 Jahrhunderts*, (Hamburg, 1935), pp. 31-36.

52. Cf. Karl Reuter, *William Ames: the Leading Theologian in the Awakening of Reformed Pietism*, trs. Douglas Horton (Harvard Divinity School Library, 1965), and E. F. K. Müller, "Bartholomäus Keckermann," in RPTK, X, 195-196.

53. Charles S. McCoy, "Johannes Cocceius: Federal Theologian," in *Scottish Journal of Theology*, XVI (1963), 354, 364-369. McCoy, who presents an energetic reappraisal of the work of Cocceius, nevertheless falls into the trap of assuming that, "starting with the Eternal Decree of predestination, the Reformed scholastics deduced their systems" (p. 366). This creates an artificial contrast between Cocceian theology and other forms of Protestant orthodoxy: if a Protestant scholastic is a theologian who began his system with a statement of the decree, then there were no Protestant scholastics.

54. Reuter, *William Ames*, pp. 171-180.

55. *An Exposition of the Symbole*, in *Workes*, vol. I.

56. *Frühorthodoxie*,pp. 6-15 (Beza); 16-32 (Ursinus); 32-50 (Daneau).

57. "Die reformierte Orthodoxie und der Cartesianismus" in *Zeitschrift für Theologie und Kirche* (1958), pp. 306-372.

58. Van Til's *Compendium theologiae* (Bern, 1703), and *Theologiae utriusque compendium* (Leiden, 1704), are examples of Cartesian-federalism. On Voetius' controversies, see Kurtz, *Church History*, (N.Y., 1889-90), III, 54-56; and Bizer, "Die reformierte Orthodoxie," pp. 308-326.

59. Bizer, "Die reformierte Orthodoxie," pp. 319-322. The argument here hinges on the continuity of Aristotelian method, useful perhaps in Beza's day but outmoded in Voetius'. But the use of Aristotelian categories did not indicate, in either the sixteenth or the seventeenth century, a tendency to place reason over revelation or a tendency to emphasize natural theology. The problem is more the increasing use of an Aristotelian hermeneutic in the interpretation of Scripture: cf. John Dillenberger, *Protestant Thought and Natural Science* (N.Y. and Nashville, 1960), pp. 56-57.

60. A. C. McGiffert, *Protestant Thought before Kant* (London, 1911), pp. 186-189; and Gerrit Jan Hoenderdaal, "The Life and Struggle of Arminius in the Dutch Republic," in *Man's Faith and Freedom: the Theological Influence of Jacob Arminius* (N.Y., 1973), p. 23.

61. *Die Prinzipien der deutschen reformierten Dogmatik im Zeitalter der aristotelischen Scholastik* (Leipzig, 1914), p. 193.

62. Ibid., pp. 172-174; on the problem of Maccovius' theology, cf. Berkouwer, *Divine Election* (Grand Rapids, 1960), pp. 17-19 and Abraham Kuyper, *Johannes Maccovius* (Leiden, 1899); cf. S. D. van Veen, "Johannes Maccovius," in RPTK, v. 12, pp. 36-38.

63. Cf. the introductory argument and bibliography in my "Perkins' *A Golden Chaine*: Predestinarian System or Schematized *Ordo Salutis*?" in *Sixteenth Century Journal*, vol. IX, no. 1 (April, 1978), pp. 69-81.

64. *Der evangelische Glaube nach den Hauptschriften der Reformatoren, II. Zwingli* (Tübingen, 1919), pp. 304-305.

65. *Der evangelischer Glaube nach den Hauptschriften der Reformatoren, III. Calvin* (Tübingen, 1919), p. 278.

66. Cf. the works of Jacobs and Locher cited above, and Wilhelm Niesel, *The Theology of Calvin*, trs. Knight (Philadelphia, 1956).

67. Basil Hall, "Calvin Against the Calvinists," in *John Calvin*, ed. G. E. Duffield (Appleford, 1966), p. 29.

68. Ibid., p. 28.

69. Ibid.,p. 27.

70. Cf. Otto Gründler, *Die Gotteslehre Girolami Zanchis und ihre Bedeutung für seine Lehre von der Prädestination* (Neukirchen, 1965).

71. Karl Barth, *Church Dogmatics*, 4 vols., edited by T.F. Torrance and G.W. Bromiley (Edinburgh, 1936-1969), II/2, p. 84; hereinafter cited as CD. I depart from Barth's final theological judgment on orthodoxy, as will become apparent in the course of this essay, insofar as I believe that these traditional Reformed models, with their strong doctrine of predestination, are christocentric, though obviously not in a Barthian sense. Analysis of Barth's own christocentrism lies beyond the scope of the present study.

72. Ibid., pp. 77-78.

73. In the preceding discussions of the development of Reformed orthodoxy and of scholarly treatment of that development, two main lines of argument may be noted: the methodological line which reacts to the formalization and codification of doctrine per se and to the increasing use of rationalistic argument, philosophical categories, and above all earlier (medieval) scholastic distinctions that characterize this process of formalization; and the doctrinal line that sees the key to Protestant orthodoxy as the quest for systematic unity around one particular central dogma, in the case of Lutheranism, justification, in the case of Calvinism, predestination. By singling out for analysis the second of these issues, I in no way minimize the importance of the first. I only reserve it for further study. The issues of hermeneutics, epistemology and the development of systematic prolegomena—the *principia theologiae*—are the subject of my present research, made possible in part by a grant from the Mellon Foundation. As an introduction to epistemological problems and to the scholarship in general, see Richard A. Muller, *"Duplex Cognitio Dei* in the Theology of Early Reformed Orthodoxy," in *The Sixteenth Century Journal*, pp. 51-61; on a specific problem treated in the *locus de scriptura*, see my "The Debate Over the 'Vowel Points' and the Crisis in Seventeenth Century Hermeneutics," in *Journal of Medieval and Renaissance Studies*, vol. X, no. 1 (Spring, 1980), pp. 53-72.

74. Cf. Jacobs, pp. 108-114; for a representative argument in Calvin's *Institutes*, see II.xii.3.

75. Wendel, pp. 229-232.

76. *Calvinism and the Amyraut Heresy: Protestant Scholasticism and Humanism in Seventeenth Century France*, (Madison, 1969), pp. 32, 131-139.

77. Cf. Lucus Trelcatius, *Scholastica et methodica locorum communium institutio* (London, 1604), p. 3; and Johann Poliander, thesis XII in *Propositions and Principles of Divinitie Propounded and Disputed in the University of Geneva . . . under M. Theod. Beza and M. Anthonie Faius*, trs. John Penry (Edinburgh?, 1595).

78. See below, epilogues to parts I and II.

79. *An Introduction to Scholastic Philosophy, Medieval and Modern*, trs. Coffey (repr. N.Y., 1956), pp. 3-142.

80. For further discussion of the problem of continuity and discontinuity with medieval scholasticism, see my *"Vera Philosophia cum sacra Theologia nusquam pugnat*: Keckermann on Philosophy, Theology and the Problem of Double Truth," in *Sixteenth Century Journal*, xv/3 (1984), pp. 341-365. Also see Robert Scharlemann, *Thomas Aquinas and John Gerhard* (New Haven: Yale, 1964).

81. Matthias Flacius Illyricus, *Catalogus testium veritatis*, cited by Preus, I, p. 36.

82. Cf. Julius Kaftan, *The Truth of the Christian Religion*, trs. George Ferries (Edinburgh, 1894), vol. I, pp. 262-264.

II. PREDESTINATION AND CHRISTOLOGY
IN THE THOUGHT OF CALVIN

[1]Jacobs, pp. 74-84.

2. Cf. Jacobs, p. 63.

3. *Inst.*, III.ii.7, where Calvin defines "faith" and compare *Inst.*, I.ii.1, where Calvin sets forth the architectonic theme of the *duplex cognitio Dei*.

4. Emmen, *Christologie van Calvijn* (Amsterdam, 1935), pp. 69-70.

5. *Inst.*, I.ii.1.

6. *Inst.*, III.ii.7. The definition appeared for the first time in the 1539 edition and is a noteworthy reflection of the trinitarian ground of Calvin's thought.

7. Commentary on John 17:3, CO, XLVII, 376. Calvin notes that, when in the Gospel, "the Father is placed in the prior *locus*, it does not refer to the order of faith, as if our minds descend from knowledge of God to Christ: but the sense is that God is known by the interposition of the mediator" (my translation). Note the technical connotation of the term *locus* in reference to the "prior" position of the Father and the contrast produced thereby with the phrase "order of faith": "Nam quod priore loco statuitur pater, non refertur ad ordinem fidei, quasi mens nostra Deo cognito ad Christum postea descendat: sed sensus est, Deum mediatore demum interpositio cognosci."

8. CO, I, 253-1151 collates the editions produced between 1539 and 1554 in Latin; also see the text of the 1541 French edition, *Institution de la Réligion Chrestienne*, ed. Pannier, 4 vols., (Paris, 1961); and cf. the collation of editions in OS, III, pp. vi-xlviii.

9. CD II/2, p. 85.

10. Commentary on John 16:12, CO, XLVII, 361: "admonet Christus se illam temperasse pro eorum modulo" and John 1:11, CO, XLVII, 10: "Ubi prius erat filius Dei, illuc eum evangelista dicit venisse. Significat ergo novum et extraordinarium praesentiae modum, quo se filius Dei manifestavit, ut illum homines propriore intuitu conspicerent." Also *Inst.*, I.xi.3; II.vii.2; ix.2. This distinction and those following draw on the late medieval distinction between God's *potentia absoluta* and *potentia ordinata*: cf. the discussion of these terms in Heiko Oberman, *The Harvest of Medieval Theology*, revised ed., (Grand Rapids, 1967), pp. 30-56.

11. Commentary on John 6:57, CO, XLVII, 156.

12. Commentary on John 14:6, CO, XLVII, 324. Translations follow, with occasional emendation, *Calvin's New Testament Commentaries: A New Translation*, ed. David and Thomas Torrance, 12 vols. (Grand Rapids, 1959-1972).

13. *Inst.*, II.xiii.4.

14. Cf. Willis, pp. 44-60 and Albert C. Outler, "The Person and Work of Christ," in *A Companion to the Study of St. Augustine*, ed. Battenhouse, (N.Y., 1955), pp. 349-352.

15. *Inst.*, II.xiii.4.

16. Hermann Bauke interpreted this twofold emphasis as a Nestorian tendency in Calvin's thought ("Christologie," in RGG[ii], I, 1628). I am inclined to agree with Schneckenburger that the *extra calvinisticum* is an effort to show that the human nature of Christ is *homoousios* with man just as the divine nature is *homoousios* with the Father. This latter interpretation is supported by *Conf. Gall.*, art. xv and *Conf. Belg.*, art. xix.

17. Cf. Heiko Oberman, "The 'Extra' Dimension in the Theology of Calvin," in *Journal of Ecclesiastical History*, XXI (1970), pp. 60-61.

NOTES

18. Ibid., pp. 61-62, and Willis, pp. 7, 74-75.
19. Willis, pp. 74-75.
20. "The 'Extra' Dimension," p. 62. I do not follow Oberman in denying that the negative, *finitum non capax infiniti* represents Calvin's thought. Calvin was himself involved in the anti-Lutheran polemic which eventually produced the phrase. The epistemological implications of the phrase are much like those of the nominalist *finiti et infiniti nulla proportio*: see Oberman, "Some Notes on the Theology of Nominalism," in *Harvard Theological Review* (1960), pp. 57-60.
21. Cf. *Inst.*, II.xii.2.
22. *Inst.*, I.iv-v; II.i.1-4; ii.12-25.
23. Commentary on John 14:7, CO, XLVII, 325.
24. Commentary on John 14:10, CO, XLVII, 326.
25. John S. Bray, *Theodore Beza's Doctrine of Redestination* (Nieuwkoop, 1975), pp. 90-93.
26. Commentary on Ephesians 3:11, CO, LI, 183.
27. Commentary on Romans 11:34, CO, XLIX, 231.
28. Commentary on John 10:16, CO, XLVII, 244.
29. Commentary on John 6:40, CO, XLVII, 147.
30. Cf. Bray, pp. 90-92.
31. *Inst.*,III.xxi.1.
32. Karl Reuter, *Das Grundverständnis der Theologie Calvins* (Neukirchen, 1963), pp. 132-138. Cf. the study by Thomas F. Torrance, "Knowledge of God and Speech about him according to John Calvin," in *Theology in Reconstruction* (London, 1965), pp. 76-88; also see below, this chapter, section 2, note 103. Both Reuter and Torrance trace motifs in Calvin's theology to the influence of John Major, the editor of Scotus' *Opus Parisiense*. Reuter argues the broad, late medieval, theological context of Calvin's thought—not only the dominant Scotist line of thought, but also the more fully Augustinian theology of Gregory of Rimini and the Ockhamist or nominalist thought both of Ockham and of Biel concerning the power and will of God (pp. 142-144). Note the sense of distinction between temporal and eternal and of the divine transcendence in Gabriel Biel, *Epitome et collectorium ex Occamo circa quatuor sententiarum Libros* (Tübingen, 1501; repr. Frankfurt am Main, 1965), I, d. xl, q. unica, art. 1: "Secundo patet: quod praedestinatio ex parte dei est eterna, patet: quia quicquid est deus vel in deo est eternum. Quantum tamen ad illud quod importat secundum vitam eternaliter vel collationem gratie: posset dici temporalis. Non tantum simpliciter: quia non supponit per creatura: sed pro deo: et connotat creaturam. . . ." The value of Reuter's work in tracing out theological themes in Calvin to medieval antecedents is unquestionable. His thesis is, however, weakened by the assumption that Calvin learned scholastic theology from John Major, an assumption that is undocumentable at best. See Alexandre Ganoczy, *Le Jeune Calvin: génèse et évolution de sa vocation réformatrice* (Wiesbaden, 1966), pp. 187-190.
33. Cf. Reuter, pp. 183-184.
34. Cf. A. M. Hunter, *The Teaching of Calvin* (London, 1950), pp. 96-99; also Luchesius Smits, *Saint Augustine dans l'oeuvre de Jean Calvin*, 2 vols. (Assen, 1957-58); vol. I, pp. 96-110; and J. B. Mozley, *A Treatise on the Augustinian Doctrine of Predestination*, 2nd edition (N.Y., 1878), pp. 267; 393-409. Wendel and Niesel should be consulted on this as on all problems concerning Calvin's theology. The fourth volume of Emile Doumergue, *Jean Calvin, les hommes et les choses de son temps*, is still a useful survey of Calvin's thought. The epoch-making work in the field is Paul Jacobs' *Prädestination und Verantwortlichkeit bei Calvin* which documented carefully the soteriological intention of Calvin's doctrine of predestination. Hans Otten, *Calvins theologische Anschauung von der Prädestination* (Munich, 1938) adopts a more traditional approach to the subject but, in its basic argument, tends to support Jacobs' thesis. Among the works available in English, Fred H. Klooster, *Calvin's Doctrine of Predestination* (Grand Rapids, 1961) presents a well-balanced account.
35. Doumergue, IV, 357.
36. Hermann Bauke, *Die Probleme der Theologie Calvins* (Leipzig, 1922), pp. 84-85. Bauke

views Calvin's theology as a *complexio oppositorum* which has no single dogmatic center (*ibid.*, pp. 16-19).

37. Cf. Wendel, p. 269.
38. *Inst.*,III.xxi.5.
39. *Inst.*, III.xxi.7.
40. CD, II/2, p. 85.
41. *Ibid.*, pp. 83-84.
42. Cf. Barth, CD II/2, p. 86. Note his categorical denial of the idea of a 'predestinarian system' not only for Calvin but also for Calvin's successors.
43. *Ibid.*, p. 86.
44. *Inst.*, I.xvi; III.xxi.7; cf. Wendel, p. 268.
45. *Inst.*, I.xvi.22; cf. I.xvi.6.
46. Wendel, p. 268.
47. Cf. Otten, p. 99 where he reflects on the priority of predestination over providence in the 1539 edition. Barth disagrees (II/2, p. 46).
48. Cf. *Inst.*, I.xvi.9: "Unde iterum videmus non temere in scholis inventas fuisse distinctiones de necessitate secundum quid, et absoluta: item consequentis et consequentiae: quando ossa Filii sui Deus, quae a fractura exemerat, fragilitati subiecit, atque ita restrinxit ad consilii sua necessitatem quod naturaliter contingere potuit." Calvin here clearly accepts and utilizes the language of necessity as found in, for example, Aquinas, *Summa theologiae*, I, q. 19, art. 3 and Duns Scotus, *In quatuor libros sententiarum*, ed. Gratianus Brixianus (Venice, 1490), I, dist. 39, q. 35. Cf. Mozley, pp. 399-401.
49. CO, LI, 148-150; cf. Barth, CD II/2, p. 88; note also Calvin's reference to Eph. 1:3 in *Inst.*, III.xxii.10: "Nam a serie causarum et effectuum facile colligitur, ubi dicit Paulus nos esse refertos omni benedictione spirituali, sicut nos elegerat Deus arte mundi creationem . . . quia elegit Deus tantum quos voluit." The fourfold Aristotelian structure of causality appears also in Inst., III.xiv.21.
50. Inst., I.xvi.8-9, on providence; II.xii.7 on the birth of Christ and cf. *De aeterna prae-destinatione dei*, CO VIII, 354-355, 360, also on providence.
51. Mozley, p. 396.
52. Reply to Bolsec, CO, VIII, 182. And compare the distinction made between predestinar-ianism and determinism by J.K.S. Reid in his introduction to *John Calvin, Concerning the Eternal Predestination of God* (London, 1961) pp. 25-27. Also see the discussion of the controversy in Henry, *The Life and Times of John Calvin* (N.Y., 1851-52), vol. II, pp. 130-137.
53. *Inst.*, III.xxii.10.
54. *Inst.*,III.xxiv.3: Calvin here argues that assurance begins with the Word and that believers must therefore seek assurance of salvation from the Gospel rather than from an attempt to penetrate the eternal ordination of God. On the other hand, God has revealed in the Gospel his eternal election as the cause of salvation: "Sed ubi eam nobis patefecit Deus, altius conscendere oportet, ne effectus causam obruat. Quid enim magis absurdum et indignem, quum Scriptura doceat nos esse illuminatos, sicuti nos Deus elegit, lucis huius fulgore oculos nostras perstringi, ut attendere ad electionem recusent?"
55. *Inst.*, II.xvii.1.
56. CO, XLIX, 158: "Certum est enim ideo notari ordinem, ut sciamus a gratuita Dei adoptione tanquam a prima causa pendere, quod sanctis omnia in salutem succedunt."
57. *Inst.*, III.xxi.5-7; xxii.6. If Augustine does not draw out a causal pattern of the decrees, he does provide Calvin with a model for the doctrine of *praedestinatio gemina*: see *De civ. Dei*, XV.1 (PL.41.437)—on the two cities: "Quas etiam mystice appellamus civitates duas, hoc est duas societates hominum: quarum est una quae praedestinata est in aeternum regnare cum Deo; altera, aeternum supplicium subire cum diabolo." Cf. XXI.xxiv (PL.41.736-741); *De perfectione justiciae hominis*, cap. xiii.31 (PL.44.308), ". . . in eo genere hominum, quod praedestinatum est ad inter-

itum"; and *De anima et eius origine*, IV.xi.16 (PL.44.533): ". . . quos praedestinavit ad aeternam vitam misericordissimus gratiae largitor: qui est et illis quos praedestinavit ad aeternam mortem, justissimus supplicii retributor. . . ." The causal argument most certainly derives from the medieval scholastic development of the doctrine of predestination.

58. *Inst.*, III.xxiii.8; cf. Otten, pp. 66-67. Otten argues that this concept of reprobation is a corollary of the doctrine of particular rather than general predestination. It is part of Calvin's particularistic soteriology and not an overly speculative concept.

59. Dowey, pp. 213-216; Jacobs, pp. 147-148.

60. *Inst.*, III.xxiii, 3-4, 8.

61. Jacobs, pp. 145-146.

62. Barth (CD, II/2, p. 111) has not fully discerned the relation of Christ to the decrees in Calvin's theology, but he does see more clearly than any historian of Reformed orthodoxy the scope of this doctrinal problem as it developed after Calvin (cf. ibid., pp. 111-115).

63. *Inst.*, III.xxii.7: "Christus electionis facit authorem." Also note II.xiii.3: "Christus author salutis" and the commentaries on John 13:18 and 17:8-10 in CO, XLVII, 310-312, 379-381. Cf. Klooster, p. 20.

64. *Inst.*, III.xxii.7: "Interea quanvis se medium Christus inserat, sibi tamen ius eligendi communiter vendicat cum Patre. Non de omnibus, inquit, loquor: scio quos elegerim Iohan. 13.6.18" This argument is overlooked by J. K. S. Reid, "The Office of Christ in Predestination," in *Scottish Journal of Theology*, I (1948), pp. 5-19; 166-183; cf. Wiley, p. 164.

65. Commentary on John 13:18, loc. cit. Note how the structure of this doctrine reflects the *extra calvinisticum*.

66. The chapter entitled "The Final Resurrection" (III, xxv) follows directly upon Calvin's discussion of the confirmation of election in calling (III, xxiv); cf. Klooster, p. 29.

67. Cf. Niesel, pp. 169-181 and Klooster, pp. 34-36. Niesel, against the arguments of Barth in CD, II, 2, pp. 335-336, denies that the *syllogismus practicus* occurs in Calvin's thought; Klooster follows Niesel to a limited extent, acknowledging that Calvin treads a fine line: "he does not urge men to look at their own good works. Rather, his repeated emphasis is upon the work of Christ, which is performed in them" (p. 34).

68. *Inst.*, III.xxiv.5.

69. Niesel, pp. 178-179.

70. *Inst.*, III.xxiv.1-6.

71. Barth, CD, II/2, pp. 333-340 and Berkouwer, *Divine Election*, pp. 279-306 where there is a detailed analysis of the Barth-Niesel debate over the *syllogismus practicus*.

72. *Inst.*, III.xxiv.1-5.

73. Inst., III.xxiv.1.

74. *Inst.*, III.xxiv.1.

75. *Inst.*, III.xxiv.3.

76. *Inst.*, III.xxiv.3.

77. *Inst.*, III.xxiv.3.

78. *Inst.*, III.xxiv.4.

79. *Inst.*, III.xxiv.5.

80. *Inst.*, III.xxiv.4. Cf. the commentary on II Peter 1:1-12 in CO, LXXXIII, 449-450 and the analysis in Berkouwer, *Divine Election*, pp. 302-303 and in Klooster, p. 34.

81. Niesel, pp. 180-181.

82. Doumergue, IV, 220. A similar view of Calvin's orthodoxy vis-a-vis Chalcedon is put forth by J. L. Witte, "Die Christologie Calvins," in *Das Konzil von Chalkedon*, ed. Aloys Grillmeier. Witte's study is accurate, but it suffers from its attempt to maintain the parallel between Calvin's Christology and that of Chalcedon. The only other full-scale treatment of Calvin's doctrine of Christ is Egbert Emmen, *De Christologie van Calvijn* (Amsterdam, 1935). The reader is advised to consult the surveys of Calvin's theology by Doumergue, Niesel, and Wendel and the relevant chapter in Alexandre Ganoczy, *Calvin, théologien de l'église et du ministere* (Paris, 1964).

83. Doumergue, IV, 220.

84. Cf. Robert S. Franks, *The Work of Christ*, (London and N.Y., 1962), pp. 339, 342, 344. The differing trinitarian perspectives of East and West naturally provide the ground of this christological distinction: cf. the delineation of the trinitarian issue in Walter Kasper, *Jesus the Christ* (London and N.Y., 1976), pp. 257-258.

85. Cf. Aloys Grillmeier, *Christ in Christian Tradition*, (N.Y., 1965), pp. 308, 310, 326-328, 467. J. N. D. Kelly, *Early Christian Doctrines* (N.Y., 1960), pp. 305-306 manifests the concern of the Antiochene Christology for the historicity and concreteness of the God-man.

86. Cf. Augustine, *Enchiridion*, cap. 33-35 (PL.40.248-250; also NPNF, 2nd ser., vol. III, pp. 248-249) with the *Libri duo cur Deus homo*, lib. I, cap. xix-xxv, in *S. Anselmi ex Beccensi abbate Cantuariensis archepiscopi opera omnia* (PL.158).

87. See *Breviloquium*, IV.i-ii, in *Opera Omnia*, vol. 5 (Quaracchi, 1891).

88. Cf. Wendel, pp. 216-220; Pannenberg, *Jesus—God and Man*, pp. 124, 221-223.

89. Cf. Witte, pp. 494-495; Emmen, pp. 69-70.

90. *Inst.*, II.xii.1. Cf. Berkhof, *Systematic Theology*, p. 369.

91. Cf. Seeberg's analysis of Scotus' argumentation, *Textbook of the History of Doctrines*, II, pp. 156-157. It would be impossible to trace the entire history of the problem of a necessary mediation—but it is clear that the Scotist assault upon Anselm's logic belongs not only to the critical perspective of Scotus over against previous attempts to draw revelation and reason together but also to the more positive theological direction given Scotus thought by earlier Franciscan teaching. Bonaventure also had denied the absolute necessity of satisfaction and had described the pattern of Christ's work as resting on the will of God: cf. Zachary Hayes, *The Hidden Center: Spirituality and Speculative Christology in St. Bonaventure* (N.Y., 1981), pp. 173-175. In Hayes' analysis, the originality of Bonaventure's Christology lies in the unity of soteriology with Christology and the manner in which this unified exposition of Christ and his work relates to "the entire cosmos both in terms of its fundamental structures and in terms of its history" (p. 157). We see here a certain continuity between the Franciscan (Bonaventuran and Scotist) concerns in Christology and soteriology and the basic patterns in Calvin's thought—the virtual merger of *loci* on Christ's person and work and the combination of a strong historical interest with a creative pressure upon the Anselmic theory of mediation. As we shall see below in the examination of Musculus' Christology (chapter 3, section 2) the first codification of Reformed theology stands in strong continuity with some elements of medieval theology—in particular, with the positive advances relating to the actual working-out of salvation—while at the same time stripping away some of the more speculative elements, such as questions like, why does God not unite with the whole universe or with angels or with the human race as a whole (on these issues in Bonaventure, cf. Hayes, pp. 64-66).

92. *Inst.*, II.xiii-xiv. Calvin gravitates—especially in the commentaries and when encountering the mystery of incarnation—toward this phrase, "God manifest in flesh": cf. comment on Luke 1:35 in CO, XLV, 31: "Quamvis enim manifestatus sit filius Dei in carne" and "apparuit etiam in humana carne Dei filius." And again in the comment on John 1:1, CO, XLV, 1: "*In principio erat Sermo. Hoc exordio aeternam Christi divinitatem praedicat: ut sciamus aeternam esse Deum, qui manifestatus est in carne.*" Perhaps most notable is the comment on I Tim. 3:16—"It is impossible to speak more appropriately of Christ's person than with these words: God manifest in the flesh"—"Non potuit magis proprie de Christi persona loqui, quam his verbis: Deus manifestatus in carne" (CO, LII, 289-290).

93. *Inst.*, II.xiii.3-4; cf. the discussion of the anointing of Christ, II.xv.2.

94. *Inst.*, I.xiii.7-13.

95. Inst., II.xiii.4.

96. *Inst.*, II.xiv.1.

97. Commentary on John 17:5 in CO, XLVII, 378. Cf. Luke 1:35, in CO, XLV, 31.

98. Cf. *Inst.*, II.xiv.7: "aeternum Dei Sermonem, et Christum, unitis in unam personam duabus naturis. . . ." with II.xiv.6: "extendimus ad totam Mediatoris personam, ut vere et proprie sit Filius Dei, qui et natus ex est Virgine, et se victimam Patri in cruce obtulit."

99. Commentary on John 20:28, in CO, XLVII, 444. Note Harnack's statement that the Antiochene theologians "held before the Church the picture of the historical Christ at a time when the Church in its doctrinal formulae was going further away from Him" (*History of Dogma*, IV, p. 170). Jill Raitt, "The Person of the Mediator: Calvin's Christology and Beza's Fidelity," *Occasional Papers of the Society of Reformation Research*, I (Dec. 1977), pp. 53-80 stresses the polemical and external rather than the positive internal development of Reformed Christology and therefore quite naturally settles upon the problem of heresy and orthodoxy vis-a-vis Chalcedon; cf. the comments in my "Christ in the Eschaton—Calvin and Moltmann on the Duration of the *Munus Regium*," p. 4, note 13. Pannenberg admirably states this distinction between Calvin's christological paradigm and the more traditional forms: "in distinction from Scholasticism, Calvin understood Jesus' divine-human person, not his human nature, as the bearer of his office as mediator, and in this way he interpreted the doctrine of the two natures itself through the mediator concept" (*Jesus—God and Man*, p. 124).

100. *Inst.*, I.xiv.9.

101. *Inst.*, I.xiii.10; II.xii.5.

102. Warfield, "Calvin's Doctrine of the Trinity," in *Calvin and Calvinism*, pp. 247-252.

103. *Inst.*, I.xiii.19, 25; cf. Warfield, pp. 233-243. The terms employed here by Calvin are *autotheos* and *a se ipso*, from which aseity is derived. Similarly these terms are the basis of debate with the anti-trinitarians: Cf. Calvin's *Expositio impietatis Valentini Gentilis*, in CO, IX, 368: "Atque haec una furendi causa quod Athanasius filium facit *autotheon*. Unde perspicuum fit hunc esse causae statum, quod contendit Valentinus Christum aliunde esse Deum, qui ab alio mutuatus sit id quod est. Valde enim logodaedalum, qui eius personam sumpsit, delectant iste voces: unum esse Deum patrem, qui et sit *autotheos*, et solus *autousian* in se habeat." Whereas Greek trinitarian formulations tend to emphasize the relations of the persons and can subordinate the Son in terms of his begottenness, viewing the Father as the source of divinity, the Western formulations—even those of the scholarly Ambrose, well versed in Greek trinitarian theory—tend to deny the form of sub-ordination. Cf. Ambrose, *De Fide*, II.viii.65 (NPNF, 1 ser., vol. X, p. 231; PL.16.596), where he sets down as a principle, "Greater and less are distinctions proper to corporeal existences; one who is greater is so in respect of rank or qualities, or at any rate of age. These terms lose their meaning when we come to treat of the things of God." Both Ambrose (cf. further, II.x.69-70, PL.16.597-598) and Augustine, *De Trinitate*, I.vi-vii, (PL.42.825-829); xiii (PL.42.840-844); II.i-v (PL.42.845-851); *Enchiridion*, xxxv (PL.40.249-250), refer all subordinationist passages to the *kenosis*, the taking of the form of a servant, or to Christ's human nature. In particular, the subordinationism of John 14:28, "My Father is greater than I" is explained in terms of Phil. 2:6-7, in contrast to the tendency among the Greek fathers to refer John 14:28 to the Son's generation: cf. Athanasius, *Four Discourses Against the Arians*, I.xiii (PG.26.37-40); Gregory of Nazianzus, *Theological Orations* IV.7 (PG.36.111-114); John of Damascus, *Exposition of the Orthodox Faith*, IV.xviii (PG.94.1182). Augustine in particular argues to the effect that the generation of the Son, as relational and not essential, implies no subordination: *De Trinitate*, II.i.2-3; XV.xxvi.47 (PL.42.1094-1095).

104. *Inst.*, I.xiii.17-18.

105. Ibid.; cf. Niesel, p. 59.

106. Warfield, p. 237.

107. CO, XI, 560.

108. CO, XI, 560. Cf. Warfield, p. 238.

109. Cf.Shedd, *A History of Christian Doctrine* (New York, 1902), I, 339-345.

110. Cited by Gaberel, II, 227. A survey of these controversies is available in Antonio Rotondo, *Calvin and the Italian Anti-Trinitarians*, trs. John and Anne Tedeschi, *Reformation Essays and Studies*, vol. 2 (St. Louis, Center for Reformation Research, 1968).

111. *Expositio impietatis Valen. Gentilis* (1561), in CO, IX, 368.

112. Wendel, pp. 167, 169.

113. *De trinitate*, V-VII, in PL.42 and NPNF, 1st ser., vol. III; cf. J. N. D. Kelly, *Early Christian Doctrine* (New York, 1960), pp. 271-276.

114. The influence of Calvin's conception of a *munus triplex* is seen in nearly all the systems of later Protestant orthodoxy, Lutheran as well as Reformed; on this see E. F. K. Müller, "Jesu Christi dreifaches Amt," in RPTK, VIII, 733-741 and John Frederick Jansen, *Calvin's Doctrine of the Work of Christ* (London, 1956), pp. 26-32. For treatment of this doctrine by later dogmaticians see Heppe, *Reformed Dogmatics*, chap. 18, pp. 448-487 and Heinrich Schmid, *Doctrinal Theology of the Evangelical Lutheran Church* (repr., Minneapolis, 1961), part III, chap. 2, pp. 337-376. Also see Klauspeter Blaser, *Calvins Lehre von den drei Ämtern Christi* (Zurich, 1970). There is, of course, a single office which is threefold in character: *Inst.*, II.xv.1—"tribus partibus constare quod ei iniunctum a Patre munus fuit."

115. *Inst.*, II.xv.2; cf. Berkouwer, *The Work of Christ*, p. 65.

116. *Inst.*, II.xiv.3, 4.

117. Ibid., II.xii.1; cf. Emmen, pp. 71-72.

118. Commentary on Hebrews 1:9, CO, LV, 18.

119. Commentary on John 6:38, CO, XLVII, 146. Cf. *Catechisme*, CO, VI, 19; and the comment on John 20:28, CO, XLVII, 444. Humiliation and exaltation are similarly affirmed of both natures: commentary on Phil. 2:10, CO, LII, 29.

120. Contra Jansen, p. 102.

121. Cf. Berkouwer, *The Work of Christ*, p. 63, where the term "superpersonal" is used. The super- or suprapersonal character of Christ's office appears, negatively, in Calvin's comment on Matt. 26:39, "O my Father, if it be possible, let this cup pass away from me"—Calvin comments, "He declines and refuses to perform, *as far as He may*, the office of Mediator" (*Harm. Ev.* in CO, XLV, col. 723, my italics): "quia mediatoris officio defungi, quantum in se est, renuit ac detrectat." Further on Calvin notes, "Iam vero si Christum oportuit captivam tenere suam voluntatem, ut eam subiiceret Dei imperio, quamvis recte moderata esset quam sollicite nobis reprimanda est affectuum nostrorum licentia. . . ."

122. *Inst.*, II.xv.2.

123. *Inst.*, II.xv.2, 5, 6; cf. my "Christ in the Eschaton."

124. Berkouwer, *The Work of Christ*, p. 58.

125. *Inst.*, II.xvi.4.

126. Thomas Aquinas, S.T. III, q. 26, a.2.

127. Cf. Lombard, *Sententiarum* III, d. 19, a. 5, 7; with Duns Scotus, *In quatuor libros Sententiarum*, III, d. 19, a. 5.

128. *Inst.*, II.xiv.3, 6. Cf. Aquinas, S.T., III, q. 26, a. 2: "Ad tertium dicendum quod, licit auctoritative peccatum auferre conveniat Christo secundum quod est Deus, tamen satisfacere pro peccato humani generis convenit ei secundum quod homo. Et secundum hoc dicitur Dei et hominum mediator" with *Inst.*, II.xii. Stancarus appears to have followed the Thomistic pattern of definition and to have affirmed Christ as *mediator* according to his human nature only. This affirmation makes a crucial distinction between the terms *medius* and *mediator*: the former describes Christ's middle position between God and man while the latter manifests the work of satisfaction as a reconciling work accomplished not by God in and of himself but by God in and through the human nature of Christ. Thus *mediator* referred specifically to the human nature while *medius* referred to the status of the person in whom two natures thus conjoined. On the earlier development of this point, see A. M. Landgraf, *Dogmengeschichte der Frühscholastik*, 8 vols. (Regensburg, 1952-56), vol. II, pt. 2, pp. 288-328; pp. 310-311 and 324-327 dealing specifically with the *medius/mediator* distinction. A movement away from such strict separation of the ideas of Christ as *medius* and Christ as *mediator* toward a more historically-oriented and more integrally-formulated Christology appears already in the time of Aquinas: Bonaventure could declare, "verumtamen *mediator* esse non posset, nisi est *medius*" (III *Sent.* d. 19, a. 2, q. 1, ad. 1). According to Hayes, Bonaventure's concept of Christ as *mediator* "presupposes the existence of the *medium* as one who shares in the being of God and of man" and points toward a powerful historical motif in Bonaventure's thought (p. 87). Similar statements appear in Scotus (III *Sent.* d. 19, q. unica) "unde tandem concludit quod Christus dicitur mediator non secundum divinam sed secundum humanam in qua illa suscepit quibus nos toti trinitati

194   NOTES

reconciliat ut passionem mortemque. . . ." but "quod mediatoris officio congruit cum medium sapiat proprietatem utriusque extremorum." See Joseph Tylenda, "Christ the Mediator: Calvin versus Stancaro," in *Calvin Theological Journal*, VIII (1973), pp. 5-16, 131-157.

129. Commentary on Philippians 2:10, in CO, LII, 29.

130. Armstrong, pp. 138, 166, 189, 266. Cf. the similar arguments of R. T. Kendall, *Calvin and English Calvinism to 1649* (Oxford, 1979), pp. 13-18. While it is true that Calvin does not utilize the precise language of the later controversy, it cannot be convincingly argued (as Kendall endeavors to do) that Calvin's thought is substantially different from later Reformed orthodoxy: Christ's death is, according to Calvin, full payment for our sins (Inst. III.xvi.5-7; xvii.1-6) but particular in its application (Inst. III.iii.1). Kendall entirely misreads Calvin's successors on this point—Beza in particular is even more explicit concerning the infinite sufficiency of Christ's death (see below, chapter four, section 2). Also see, W. Robert Godfrey, "Reformed Thought on the Extent of the Atonement to 1618," in *The Westminster Theological Journal*, vol. 37, no. 2 (Winter, 1975), pp. 133-171. Calvin clearly denies any hypothetical extension of Christ's work to the sins of the reprobate: cf. Commentary on I John 2:2, in CO, LV, 310.

131. CO, LV, 309.

132. Commentary on I John 2:2, in CO, LV, 310: "Qui hanc absurditatem volebant effugere, dixerunt, sufficienter pro toto mundo passum esse Christum: sed pro electis tantum efficaciter. Vulgo haec solutio in scholis obtinuit. Ego quamquam verum esse illud dictum fateor: nego tamen praesenti loco quadrare." Also note *Inst.*, II.xvi.16 and III.xxii.1.

133. *Inst.*, III.iii.1; xxiv.3.

134. Contra Armstrong, pp. 137-138; *Inst.*, III.xxii.7; II.xvii.5; II.ii.35; xxii, i, 7, 10; *De aeterna praedestinatione dei*, CO, VIII, col. 336.

135. *Inst.*, II.vi.1; cf. III.xxiv.1, 5, 6.

136. *Inst.*, II.xv.6.

137. Commentary on I Timothy 2:5, in CO, LII, 269-271; note particularly the connection between mediation and intercession, and Calvin's interpretation of the apostle's "all" as "all classes of men." If this constitutes a distortion of the text to fit the concept of a predestinating will of God, the distortion is not Calvin's but belongs to the traditional Augustinian exegesis of this and like passages: cf. Augustine, *Enchiridion*, cap. 103 (PL.40.280-281); *De correptione et gratia*, sec. 44 (PL.44.913). Also see Calvin's comments on John 17:9 in CO, XLVII, 380. The phrase "all classes" of men is crucial in later Reformed discussions of limited or "definite atonement." This phrase was particularly important in the debates at Dort: see William Robert Godfrey, "Tensions within International Calvinism: the Debate on the Atonement at the Synod of Dort, 1618-1619," unpublished Ph.D. dissertation (Stanford, 1974) for discussions of the problem of the universal implications of I Tim. 2:3-4, I John 2:2, and John 3:16. On the matter of limited intercession Calvin's commentary on John 17:9, "I pray not for the whole world, but for those whom thou hast given me" is definitive. A good discussion of "definite atonement" in Calvin's theology which recognizes Calvin's hesitance to develop a strict formula is Archibald A. Hodge, *The Atonement* (1907; repr., Grand Rapids, 1975), pp. 387-391.

138. Jurgen Moltmann, *The Crucified God* (N.Y., 1974), pp. 257, 259.

139. *Prädestination und Verantwortlichkeit*, p. 74.

140. Ibid., p. 77: Jacobs here cites Calvin's 1537 catechism, Christ is "le gaige de nostre election."

141. Cf. Reid, "The Office of Christ," pp. 9-10, 11-12.

142. *Inst.*, II.xii.1.

143. Ibid., and cf. the commentary on John 17:1, in CO, XLVII, 374-375. Wendel (pp. 227-232) shows the relation of Christology and, specifically, the sufficiency of Christ's work to the decree to have a twofold purpose: first it rests on a denial of the *communicatio idiomatum in abstracto* (according to which the value of Christ's sacrifice could derive from the infinitude of the Son's person) and on the underlying Scotist pattern of Calvin's thought which identifies the decretive will of God as the sole ground of the merit of Christ.

144. Cf. *Inst.*, II.xvii.1.
145. Ibid.
146. *Inst.*, II.xvii.6.
147. *De aeterna praedestinatione dei*, in CO, VIII, 267.
148. Romans 1:4 in the Latin of the Vulgate reads as follows: ". . . qui praedestinatus est Filius Dei in virtute, secundum spiritum sanctificationis. . . ." Augustine (*Confessions*, X.xliii.68, in PL.32.808 and NPNF, 1st ser., I) states that Christ is the mediator in his human nature only; yet he also affirms a designation of the Son by the entire Godhead to the work of redemption: cf. *De peccato originali*, cap. 33, in PL.44.404 and NPNF, 1st ser., V. 249. On the predestination of the human nature see *De praedestinatione sanctorum*, xiv.31, in PL.44.982-983, also NPNF, 1st ser., V, 512-513. Seeberg, *Textbook*, p. 200, note 1, comments that this conception of the predestination of Christ's human nature in Augustine's thought and the general tenor of Augustine's Christology implies "variance with Greek conceptions, which became significant in the theology of the West." Further, "The West had, therefore—in independence of the East—its own christological Theory" (p. 261). This is strongly supported by Harnack's argumentation, *History of Dogma*, V, pp. 127-133, 277-281.
149. Lombard, *Sent.* III, d. vii, q. 3; Thomas Aquinas, *Summa theologica*, III, q. 24. Scotus, *In Sent.* III, d. 7, a. 3, argues a foreordination of Christ's human nature to union with the divine and to glory—and in the second "dubium" raises the issue of a predestination of the Son of God as God: the predestination of Christ to be the Son of God cannot, he answers, be abstracted and referred to the natures separately.
150. Billot, *De Verbo Incarnato* (1912), p. 355, as cited in *Dictionnaire de Théologie Catholique* (Paris, 1903-1950) tome VIII, 1 partie, col. 344.
151. Calvin recognizes this passage as dealing with the designation or declaration of Christ as the Son of God by means of the power of God in the resurrection: he does not always connect it with the doctrine of predestination; CO, XLIX, 10; cf. II.xiv.6.
152. *Inst.*, II.xvii.2, citing I John 4:10: "Non quod priores dilexerimus eum; sed ipse nos prior delixit, ae Filium suum misit *hilasmon* pro peccatis nostris I Iohan.4.10. Clare his verbis demonstratur, Deum, nequid suo erga nos amori obstaret, reconciliandi modum statuisse in Christo." This is much like the formulation of the election of Christ set forth by Augustine in *De dono perseverantiae* (cap. 67, in PL.45.1033-1034, cf. NPNF, 1st ser., V. 552): "Therefore he predestinated Him and us, because both in Him that He might be our head, and in us that we should be His body, He foreknew that our merits would not precede, but that His doings should." Augustine's references in this chapter are, like Calvin's, Johannine (John 10:30; 14:28).
153. *Inst.*, III.xxii.6, citing I Peter 1:19-20.
154. Cf. Hayes, *The Hidden Center*, pp. 190-191, esp. note 129 citing Bonaventure, *Sent.*, III, d. 11, a. 1, q. 2, fund. 4 and I, d. 7, dub. 2.
155. *Inst.*, II.xiv.3, 6; and compare Calvin's description of the kingly office (II.xv.3-5) where the divinity and humanity of Christ together fulfill the office of the mediator.
156. Commentary on Philippians 2:10, in CO, LII, 29. Significantly, Augustine uses the Philippian hymn in order to explicate the subordination of Christ to the Father in connection with his statement, "He is Mediator, then, in that he is man" (cf. *De peccato originali*, cap. 33) indicating in this late work (A.D. 418) not that the name of the mediator belongs to the human nature only but that the Son of God becomes mediator only when he subordinates himself in the form of a servant and thereby becomes, officially, "inferior to the Father." This type of formulation—moving away from the declaration that Christ is mediator according to his human nature only—appears also in the letter to Volusianus (Ep. 137, sec. 9, 12, dated A.D. 412): "now he has appeared as the Mediator between God and men, that, uniting the two natures in one person, He both exalted what was ordinary by what was extraordinary, and tempered what was extraordinary by what was ordinary in himself"; and again, pressing not only the idea of the person of the mediator but also the aseity of the Son as contrasted with his voluntary *humiliatio*, "this Word of God, I say, took to Himself . . . the soul and body of a man, and made, by union of Himself therewith, the one person Jesus

Christ, Mediator between God and men, in His Deity equal with the Father, in his flesh, i.e. in His Human nature, inferior to the Father—unchangeably immortal in respect of the divine nature, in which He is equal with the Father, and yet changeable and mortal in respect of the infirmity which He has through participation with our nature" (PL.33.519, 520-521; NPNF, 1st ser., vol. I, p. 477-478). Cf. *Enchiridion*, cap. 108 (PL.40.282-283). Also note Calvin's own use of Augustine, Ambrose and other fathers (Cyril and Chrysostom) against Stancarus, CO, IX, 357-358; cf. Smits, vol. I, pp. 102-103.

157. Commentary on John 6:38, in CO, XLVII, 146; cf. 6:40, col. 147. Also see the commentary on I Peter 1:20, in CO, LV, 225.

158. Commentary on John 17:6-8, in CO, XLVII, 378-380. It should be noted that this is also one of the implications of the *extra calvinisticum*: even during the incarnation, the Son dwells in heaven and himself wills to be born and to suffer (*Inst.*, II.xiii.4).

159. Commentary on John 6:38, in CO, XLVII, 146. Cf. Augustine, *De fide rerum quae non videntur*, sec. 5: "For thus it behoved that He should be born as Man, albeit He was ever God, by which birth He might become a God unto us. Hence again the Prophet says concerning Him, 'Thy Throne, O God, is for ever and ever . . . therefore God, Thy God, hath anointed Thee with the oil of gladness above Thy fellows' (Ps. 45:6-7). This anointing is spiritual, wherewith God anointed God, the Father, that is, the Son: whence called from the 'Chrism,' that is, from the anointing, we know Him as Christ" (PL.40.175, NPNF 1st Ser., vol. III, p. 339). Also Ambrose, *De Fide*, I.iii.24: "This God who anoints, and God Who in the flesh is anointed is the Son of God. . . . You see, then, that God is by God anointed, but being anointed in taking upon Him the nature of mankind, He is proclaimed the Son of God" (PL.16.556). Also see Augustine's comment on the Psalm, PL.36.505-506: "Unctus est ergo Deus a Deo: quo oleo nisi spirituali? . . . Unctus est nobis Deus, et missus est nobis. . . . Deus ergo homo, et ideo unctus Deus, quia homo Deus, et factus est Christus." In Augustine's (and the Vulgate's) numeration, it is Psalm 44; the relevant text is *Enarratio in Psalmum* xliv.19: see NPNF 1st Ser., vol. VIII, p. 151, and compare, for a Greek view, Gregory of Nazianzus' comment on the same text, "he was anointed with Godhead, for this anointing is of the manhood" (*Theological Oration*, IV.ii, PG.36.105-106). As noted above, Calvin himself does not follow Augustine's interpretation of the text, but the patristic and specifically Latin view does return in the work of later Reformed writers: cf. below, on Ursinus, Polanus, and Perkins.

160. Similar statements occur in the debate with Stancarus, in CO, IX, 337-342, 349-358.

III. THE SYSTEMS OF CALVIN'S CONTEMPORARIES

1. *Sermonum decades duae. De potissimus verae religionis capitibus. . . .* (Zurich, 1549) followed by *Sermonum decas tertia* and *Sermonum decas quarta* in 1550 and the final volume, *Sermonum decas quinta* in 1551. A translation into German appeared (the *Hausbuch*) in 1553, into Dutch in 1563, French in 1564, and into English in 1577. I have followed the translation of *The Decades* published by the Parker Society, 4 vols. (Cambridge, 1851).

2. *Compendium christianae religionis decem libris comprehensum* (Zurich, 1556). The work appeared also in German as *Summa christenlicher Religion* (Zurich, 1556) and in French, *Resolution des tous les points de la réligion chrestienne* (Geneva, 1556). It was also translated into English as *Commonplaces of Christian Religion* (London, 1575).

3. *Confessio et expositio simplex orthodoxae fidei, & dogmatum Catholicorum syncerae religionis Christianae, concorditer ab Ecclesiae Christi ministris, qui sunt in Helvetia, Tiguri, Bernae . . .* (etc.) (Zurich, 1566). I follow the text of Schaff, CC, vol. 3, pp. 233-306.

4. Following the text of the first Latin edition: *Compendium christianae religionis decem libris comprehensum* (Zurich, C. Froschauer, 1556), hereinafter, *Compendium*.

5. *Compendium*, Lib. I; cf. *Confessio*, cap.i. In this pattern Bullinger is at one with Hyperius'

De theologo, seu de ratione studii theologici (Basel, 1556), Lib. III (on this see Preus, I, pp. 86-87). Similarly, Viret's *Exposition familiére sur le symbol des apostres* begins with a prolegomenon to theology dealing with the sources of theology and the problem of the knowledge of God. So also the *Confessio fidei Gallicana* (1559) and the *Confessio Belgica* (1561). The first articles of these confessions treat of general and special revelation, the latter being contained in the Scriptures: in Schaff, CC, vol. 3, pp. 359-362, 383-389. From this period, the *Scots Confession* (1560) and the *Articuli XXXIX Ecclesiae Anglicanae* (1562) also treat of the sufficiency of Scripture (*Conf. Scot.*, art. xix; *Art. Ang.*, art. vi) and the latter of the canon, the relation of Old and New Testaments and of ancient creeds (art. vi-viii). Neither, however, adopts the rationalized order of the Swiss, French, and Belgic documents (in Schaff, CC, vol. 3, pp. 463-464, 489-492).

6. Cf. David C. Steinmetz, *Reformers in the Wings* (Philadelphia, 1971), p. 140. Both Peter Walser in his *Die Prädestination bei Heinrich Bullinger im Zusammenhang mit seiner Gotteslehre* (Zurich, 1957), p. 83 and Ernst Koch, *Die Theologie der Confessio Helvetica Posterior* (Neukirchen, 1968), p. 19 state that Bullinger did not produce what from our present point of view would be considered a systematic theology. It is nevertheless true that the *Compendium* satisfied the needs of Reformed systematics in its own day and provided an influential model for later Reformed systems. It was also considered as a system by Heinrich Heppe in the compilation of his *Dogmatik*. Koch's study, it should be noted, is a systematic analysis of Bullinger's theology which uses the *Confessio* as the key to Bullinger's thought and as its organizing principle.

7. Compendium, II.i.

8. Ibid., II.ii.

9. Ibid., II.ii.

10. Ibid., II.iii.

11. Ibid., II.iv.

12. Ibid., III, argument.

13. Ibid., II.vii.

14. Ibid., II.vii. Cf. V.vi.

15. Ibid., II.viii: "Atque hoc est illud foedus quod in sacris literis Deus cum humano genere percussisse dicitur, quod cum Noe primo initum est, inde vero reparatum cum Abrahamo, in libros relatum a Mose, & demum a Christo sancitum & confirmatum. Hoc vero foedus cum hominibus Deus his legibus iunxit, ut Deus humani generis Deus sit, cuncta illi suppeditet, ac per Christum perficiat & coelestia bona communicet: vicissim vero homines, hunc Deum solum & praeter eum nullos alios agnoscant, huic uni fidant, hunc invocent, venerentur, hunc adorent, huic fidi esse perseverent, illiusque leges in omni vita sua observent." Cf. Koch, pp. 388-393. See Joachim Staedke, *Die Theologie des jungen Bullinger* (Zurich, 1962), pp. 62-68 for a magisterial presentation of Bullinger's federal theology in contrast with the rather less profound covenant theory of Zwingli; also Jack Warren Cottrell, "Is Bullinger the Source for Zwingli's Doctrine of the Covenant?" in *Heinrich Bullinger 1504-1575: Gesammelte Aufsätze zum 400.Todestag*, 2 vols. (Zürich, 1975), vol. I, pp. 75-83.

16. Cf. the foundational study by Leonard Trinterud, "The Origins of Puritanism," in *Church History*, vol. 20 (1951), pp. 37-57; also Jens Moeller, "The Beginnings of Puritan Covenant Theology," in *The Journal of Ecclesiastical History*, vol. 14, no. 1 (1963), pp. 46-67 and Richard L. Greaves, "The Origins and Development of English Covenant Thought," in *The Historian*, vol. XXI (1968), pp. 21-35. An important alternative was proposed by John von Rohr, "Covenant and Assurance in Early English Puritanism," in *Church History*, vol. 34 (1965), pp. 195-203. The monergistic underpinning of Bullinger's doctrine is well discussed in Lyle D. Bierma, "The Covenant Theology of Caspar Olevian," (Ph.D. dissertation, Duke University, 1980), pp. 41-54. An alternative view which seeks unsuccessfully to pose Bullinger's duopleuric definition against the predestinarian theology of Geneva is J. Wayne Baker, *Heinrich Bullinger and the Covenant: The Other Reformed Tradition* (Athens, Ohio, 1980).

17. See Richard A. Muller, "Covenant and Conscience in English Reformed Theology: Three

Variations on a Seventeenth Century Theme," in *Westminster Theological Journal*, vol. XLII, no. 2 (1980), pp. 308-334.

18. *Compendium*, Liber V, *De Gratia Dei mundo in Christo exhibita, ac de iustificatione*. Also, Liber VI, *De Fide, Evangelio et Poenitentia*. The soteriology of the *Compendium* is hardly at odds with that of Bullinger's *Confessio*, albeit that the structural differences between the two documents are great. On the latter work see Walter E. Meyer, "Soteriologie, Eschatologie und Christologie in der Confessio Helvetica Posterior," in *Zwingliana*, XII, (1964-68), pp. 391-409.

19. *Compendium*, V.i.

20. Ibid.

21. Ibid., V.ii, citing I John 4:9-10 and Titus 3:4-7.

22. Ibid., V.iii: *"Deum ab aeterno destinasse gratiam suam, quod eam mundo per Christum exhibere velit."*

23. Ibid., V.iii.

24. Ibid., V.iv. I am not certain how widespread the description of Christ in his work as *medicina* was in the later Middle Ages, but the phrase does appear in Scotus: cf. *In Sent.* III, d. 19, a. 2: ". omnes electi prius previdebant & predestinabant ad gratiam & gloriam quam previderent passio christi: ut medicina contra lapsum: sicut medicus prius vult sanitatem hominis quod ordinet de medicina ad sanandum." Similarly, Gabriel Biel, *Collectorium super IV libros Sententiarum* (Tübingen, ca. 1500), III, d. 19, questio unica, art. 2, con. 4.

25. Ibid., V.iv.

26. Ibid., V.v-vii: cap. v is entitled, "Christum Iesum pro peccatis nostris mortuum esse & satisfecisse, atque peccata nobis plene remittere"; cap. vi, "Qua ratione satisfactio Christi nobis propria fiat, quomodo item a peccatis liberemur & iustificemur"; and cap. vii, "Iustitiam Christi & redemptionem non operibus sed fide a nobis percipi nostramque fieri." Bullinger nowhere addresses the problem of limited atonement or limited redemption—in the flow of his system, however, the limit is imposed insofar as the faith which necessarily receives Christ is itself divine gift.

27. Ibid., V.vii.

28. Ibid., VI.i (cited above, note 11).

29. Ibid., VI.i.

30. Ibid., VI.ii.

31. Ibid.,VI.iv: "Post creationem in articulis fidei nostrae redemptionem confitemur. Nam cum initio homo a Deo iustus bonusque creatus esset, sua culpa peccato morti & damnationi obnoxus factus est, ut iam (quemadmodum & nos qui in peccatis nascimur et concipimur) liberatore opus haberet: quem Deus aeterno suo consilio destinavit, atque Iesum Christum universo orbi liberatorem constituit. Hunc per Patriarchas & Prophetas veteribus promisit, ac nobis exhibuit."

32. Cf. Ibid., VI.v and vi.

33. Ibid., VI.v: "Quoniam vero Christus Dominus inseparabilis ac totus, non ex dimidio, salvator & redemptor noster est, per communicatio nem idiomatum. . . ."

34. Walser, pp. 76, 143, 280, and passim.

35. Cf. Walser, pp. 79-80.

36. Cf. *Compendium*, VI.xiv.

37. *Compendium*, II.viii.

38. Ibid.

39. Walser, p. 248. Walser argues that God's covenant, the Son's mediation, and the Spirit's continuing work form the trinitarian ground of Bullinger's theology.

40. Cf. Koch, p. 88.

41. CD II/2, p. 84.

42Ibid., p. 84.

43. Conf. Helv., x.1, 2.

44. Cf. Koch, pp. 93-95.

45. Conf. Helv., xiv.3.

46. Ibid., xvi.2.

47. Koch (p. 93) documents Bullinger's resistance to speculative consideration of election *extra Christum* in correspondence with Beza (in 1566) relating to the *Confession*.

48. *Conf. Helv.*, x.4.

49. Ibid., x.5-7.

50. Ibid., x.9.

51. Ibid., x.7-9.

52. Ibid.,xi.1.

53. Cf. Koch, pp. 415-417 and especially (p. 417): "Der Bundesgedanke ist insofern der Zentralbegriff der Confessio, als sich in ihm die durchlaufenden theologischen Aspekte und Motive schneiden und er der beste Ausdruck für das die Theologie der Confessio bestimmende theologische Denkschema ist. . . . ." In this context also Koch can argue the interrelationship of the protoeuangelion and the eternal predestination of Christ (p. 420) and the relation of these and other explicit topics of the Confession to the overarching historical schema (p. 424).

54. *Conf. Helv.*, xi.8.

55. Koch, pp. 112-117 and in particular the crucial citation of Bullinger's attack on Brenz (p. 113, note 33): "in qua tamen corporis veritatem vel naturam & circumscriptionem, nunquam deposuerit, sed hominem quem semel assumpsit, retineat indissolubili nexu sibi copulatum in sempiternum."

56. Ibid., xiii-xiv.

57. *Loci communes sacrae theologiae* (Basel, 1560, 1568, 1573) citations follow the 1573 edition, hereinafter referred to as *Loci communes*. I have also consulted the 16th-century English translation, *Commonplaces of Christian Religion* (London, 1563, 1578). The best biography of Musculus is still Ludwig Grote, *Wolfgang Musculus, ein biographischer Versuch* (Hamburg, 1855). Also W. Hadorn, "Wolfgang Musculus," in RPTK, XIII, 581-585; Paul Musculus, "Wolfgang Musculus en Lorraine et Alsace," in *Société de l'Histoire du Protestantisme Français* (Oct.-Dec., 1931), pp. 487-501; Paul J. Schwab, *The Attitude of Wolfgang Musculus toward Religious Tolerance* (Yale, 1933). The latter work contains a useful bibliography.

58. *Loci communes* (1573), particularly cap.42-45 wherein Musculus deals with God's nature, sufficiency, omnipotence, and will (pp. 394-421).

59. Ibid., cap.45 (p. 409).

60. Ibid., Occam is frequently cited: e.g., cap.44-45, pp. 407, 408, 414; Lombard, pp. 409, 414; Scotus, e.g., cap.18, p. 144; Biel, e.g., cap.35, p. 355. Lombard very often provides Musculus with basic definitions.

61. *In Esaiam Prophetam commentarii locupletissimi ac recens editi . . .* (Basel, 1570) and *In Evang. Matthaeum commentarii. Tribus tomis digesti, quibus non solum singula quaeque exponuntur, sed & quid singulis Marci & Lucae differentibus locis notandum sit, diligenter expenditur* (Basel, 1544).

62. *Loci communes*, cap. 14-18 (pp. 130-151).

63. Ibid., cap. 14 (p. 130). Musculus comments that the Latin words *foedus, pactum*, and *testamentum* are used "indiscriminatim" to render *berith* and *diatheke*. *Testamentum* alone of the three points toward a death confirming and conferring its benefits and is referred by Christians specifically to Christ as *mediator* and *testator*.

64. Ibid. (pp. 130-131).

65. Ibid., cap.14 (132).

66. *Loci communes*, cap.14 (p. 132).

67. Ibid., cap.14 (p. 133B): "Sunt quidem tria tempora principalia, quibus totus mundus comprehenditur: utpote, promum quod fuit ante legem, secundum sub lege, tertium post legem. Deinde sunt tres insignes personae, veluti singulorum temporum duces, Abraham, Moses, Christus. Et habet unumquodque tempus singularem suam religionis dispensationem, quae etiam in Scripturis *berith*, id est, pactum vel foedus vocatur. Inde tamen non consequitur, esse tria foedera substantialia, salutem generis humani concernentia. Unus est Deus & pater omnium, qui super omnes est, & per omnia, & in omnibus. Unus est Dominus servator & redemptor omnium Christus Iesus, unus est

Spiritus sanctus, unus est regnum electis ae benedictis inde ab origine mundi paratum, una est vocationis coelestis gratia, una est fides, una spes vitae aeternae, unum est corpus, unus populus, & una ecclesia electorum catholica propterea dicta, quod ab initio mundi ad finem usque universos comprehendat electos & fideles: & unicum est ac perpetuum foedus Dei cum electis omnibus sancitum & firmatum, & una est & perpetua pietas & iustificatio credentium. Verum dispensatio unius foederis, gratie, fidei, ecclesiae, religionis ac pietatis non est unica & perpetua, sed secundum qualitatem temporum pro consilio divinae sapientiae aliter atque aliter instituta."

68. *Loci communes*, cap.16 (p. 135). On Musculus' importance to the development of federalism, see Gass, *Geschichte der protestantischen Dogmatik*, vol. I. p. 132; Heinrich Heppe, *Geschichte des Pietismus und der Mystik*, pp. 208-209; and Gottlob Schrenck, *Gottesreich und Bund im Älteren Protestantismus* (Gütersloh, 1923), pp. 50-51, 212-214.

69. *Loci communes*, (pp. 137-138).

70. Ibid. (p. 138).

71. Ibid., cap.16 (pp. 136-137).

72. Cf. Heiko Oberman. *The Harvest of Medieval Theology*, pp. 30-56, 81, 203-210, 224, 245-256, 261; and David C. Steinmetz, *Misericordia Dei*, pp. 51-55.

73. *Loci communes*, cap.17 (p. 139).

74. Ibid., p. 140.

75. *In Mattheum*, p. 2, col. b.

76. Ibid., p. 3, col. a-b.

77. *Loci communes*, cap.17 (p. 141).

78. Ibid.

79. Ibid., p. 141.

80. *Loci communes*, cap.17-18. Cf. *Inst.*, II.xii; and the introductory section of Melanchthon's *Loci communes* (1521), CR, XXI, 84-85. Also see Brunner's analysis of Melanchthon's christological insight in *The Christian Doctrine of Creation and Redemption* (Philadelphia, 1952), p. 271. This early edition of Melanchthon's *Loci* is more overtly antagonistic to the older theology and its speulative tendencies than later editions. Melanchthon comments, in the passage in question, that extended discussion on the mysteries of trinity and incarnation is useless, "since this is to know Christ, to know his benefits." The impact of Melanchthon's argument on early Reformed theologians like Bullinger and Musculus who first encountered the Reform through the writings of Luther and Melanchthon must have been considerable.

81. *Loci communes*, cap.18 (p. 145): "Sic, inquiunt, tres sacrae Triadis personae operatae quidem sunt in opere incarnationis huius, verum una ex illis tantum carnem induit. Arbitror ista nihil habere incommodi, si curiositati non serviant. Meo tamen iudicio, incarnari oportuit, nec patrem, nec Spiritum sanctum, sed verbum, non solum ob id quod filius est in divinitate, perque ipsum conditus est mundus: sed & hac potissimum ratione, quod verbum consilium illud est Dei, patri coaeternum, de salvando genere humano propositum, in quo nostra redemptio praedestinata fuit ab aeterno, in quo etiam electi sumus in adoptionem filiorum Dei, sicut Ephesiorum primo videre licet. Quare non potuit opus redemptionis nostrae perfici, nisi per hoc verbum: quia nec debuit, nec potuit discrepare ab aeterna voluntatis Dei praedestinatione."

82. *In Evang. Matthaeum*, Matt. 12:18 (p. 340).

83. Ibid.

84. Ibid.

85. Ibid.: "Nam ut filius Dei est, non est electus, sed ut est servus, nunctus, & Apostolus Dei, in hunc mundum ad nostram redemptionem missus. Neque; insolens est, si pater dicatur filium eligere ad obeundum aliquod peculiare munus. Ideo scilicet prophetae vocarunt Christum electum Dei. . . . Et I Pet. 2. vocatur lapis a Deo electus."

86. Ibid., p. 609 (commenting on Matt. 27:63-64).

87. *Loci communes*, cap.24 (p. 227B).

88. Ibid. (p. 228).

89. Ibid.

90. Ibid., cap.24 (p. 228B).

91. Ibid.(p. 228): ". . . diserte expressit particulam hanc Apostolus dicens, Qui elegit nos antequam iacerentur fundamenta mundi. Ephes. 1. Atqui priusquam mundus fieret, nemo mortalium erat uspiam. Elegit igitur nondum existentes: tantum abest, ut qua maneat electis gloriandi occasio."

92. Ibid. (p. 228).

93. Ibid. (p. 229).

94. Cf. ibid., cap.8, 10 (pp. 15-20, 23-30); also Ritschl, III, pp. 249-250.

95. *Loci communes*, cap.24 (p. 229).

96. Ibid., cap.24 (p. 229B).

97. Ibid. (p. 229B).

98. Ibid., cap.24 (p. 230): "Consideranda igitur est electionis ac salutis nostrae firmitudo, in eo quod beneplacito, voluntate ac proposito constat eius, cui voluntas est liberrima, ius summum in omnia, veritas immutabilis, placitum in sempiternum stabile, propositum efficacissimum, & potentia nulli impedimento obnoxia. Huc accedit, quod ista cum natura divinae bonitatis conveniunt, cuius proprium est misereri ac benefacere mortalibus. . . . Quare impossibile est, ut electio nostri, secundum illius placitum, voluntatem ac propositum facta mutetur, & irrita reddatur."

99. Ibid., cap.24 (p. 230).

100. Ibid., (p. 230).

101. Ibid. (p. 230).

102. Ibid. (p. 230).

103. Ibid., cap.24 (p. 230): "Quare mysterium hoc electionis nostrae non debemus dimidatum ac divulsum, sed utrisque illius partibus coniunctis plenum & integrum sincera fide summaque cum religione, admiratione & gratitudine in Christo mediatore, capite ac servatore nostro, inspicere: & ad certitudinem salutis nostrae in cordibus nostris confirmandam considerare, quomodo eodem consilio Dei, eadem aeternitate, adeoque & firmitudine electio nostri cum mysterio Christi nitatur & subsistat."

104. Ibid., cap.24 (pp. 230-231).

105. Ibid.

106. Ibid.

107. Ibid. (p. 232).

108. Ibid. (p. 232).

109. Ibid.(p. 233).

110. Ibid., cap.24 (p. 233).

111. Ibid.: "Magister Sententiarum dicit lib. 1. dist. 40. Praedestinavit eos quos elegit, reliquos vero reprobavit. Item: Reprobavit quos voluit, non propter futura merita quae praevideret, veritate tamen rectissima, & a nostris sensibus remota. Reprobos hic non vocamus eos, qui propter innatam maliciam sunt reprobi, & diversi a sinceris & bonis . . . sed eos, quos Deus reiecit ac reprobavit, cum elegeret quos volebat." Cf. p. 234, again citing Lombard: "Primum, quoniam electio salvandorum ante mundi facta est constitutionem, consequens esse, tum damnatorum quoque factam esse reprobationem. Deinde reprobatos eos esse hoc ipso, quod non sunt electi & praeordinati ad vitam. Sic magister Sent. lib. 1. dist. 40. Deum ab aeterno quosdam non eligendo reprobasse dicit."

112. Ibid. (p. 233).

113. Ibid. (p. 234).

114. Ibid., cap.9 (pp. 20-23).

115. *Loci communes*, cap.9 (p. 22B).

116. Ibid., cap.9 (pp. 22B-23A).

117. Ibid., cap.9 (p. 23A); cf. Gass, I, 135-138. Musculus does not here provide a basis for the so-called *syllogismus practicus*, but rests the certainty of salvation on faith and the personal consciousness of faith, of adoption, and of election. But cf. the comment on Matthew 5 (*In Evang. Matthaeum*, p. 79): "quod bonis operibus fides nostra velut alitur, provebitur, & corroboratur. . . .

Electionis ac reprobationis divinae inscrutabilia sunt iudicia, qua propter opus est externis testimoniis quibus declarentur, & ad mortalium usque cognitionem pertingant. Deo alioqui non est opus, ut per facta externa ad cordium nostrorum cognitionem perveniat, cum sit cordium, & cognitionum nostrarum scrutator & cognitor." Good works stands as the fruit of faith and as its corroboration— indeed as an external testimony of God's election.

118. *Loci communes*, cap.9 (p. 23A): "Ad hunc modum arbitror posse sobrie et utiliter arbitri causam, quantumuis contentiosam a pijs hominibus iuxta fidei analogiam, & sacrarum Scripturarum simplicitatem considerari, cui multa ab hominibus ad disputandum paratis, non sine obscuratione veritatis & turbatione conscientiarum immiscentur: qualia sunt quae de praescientiae ac providentiae Dei necessitate, de fato, de contingentia disputantur: quorum labyrinthum qui sapit, studiose in hoc causa fugiat. Fideles homines non disceptant de secretis consilijs Dei, quibus omnia omnium gubernantur, nec inquirunt causas, vim & operationem illorum, neque disputant de contingentibus, sec unicum hunc scoptum in hac causa spectant, ut humani generis corruptione in Adam, & restaurationem quae per Christum est, utiliter & ad gloriam gratiae Dei cognoscant."

119. *In Evang. Matthaeum* (p. 226), on Matt. 11:26.

120. Ibid.

121. Ibid.

122. *Indivi Pauli Epistolas* . . ., I Tim. 2:5-6, in loc.: "est sufficiens pro omnibus facta redemptio: verum inde non consequitur, sic esse sublatam captivitatem satanae, ac servitutem peccati, ut nemo mortalium in illa periturus detineatur amplius."

123. *Loci communes D. Petri Martyri Vermigli* (London, 1576; revised, 1583); trs. as *The Commonplaces of D. Peter Martyr Vermigli* (London, 1583). A survey of Vermigli's life and thought is found in Steinmetz, pp. 151-161; a life and bibliography is in DNB.

124. Cf. Klaus Sturm, *Die Theologie Peter Martyr Vermiglis wahrend seines Aufenthalts in Strassburg* (Neukirchen, 1971), pp. 37, 271.

125. *Loci communes*, fol. a2, recto. On Vermigli's theology see: John Patrick Donnelly, "Calvinist Thomism," loc. cit. and the same author's *Calvinism and Scholasticism in Vermigli's Doctrine of Man and Grace* (Leiden, 1975). The problem of knowledge is discussed by Vermigli in *Loci communes* (1583), I.vi and II.xviii. Detailed discussion of the individual works which are represented in the *Loci communes* and *Another collection of certaine Divine matters and Doctrines* (London, 1583) as well as writings published during Vermigli's lifetime both in England and on the continent is available in Marvin W. Anderson, *Peter Martyr, A Reformer in Exile (1542-1562): A Chronology of Biblical Writings in England and Europe* (Nieuwkoop, 1975).

126. *Loci communes*, fol. a5, recto; cf. II.i-ii.

127. Ibid., fol. a5, recto; cf. II.i-ii.

128. CD II/2, p. 84.

129. J. C. McClelland, "The Reformed Doctrine of Predestination according to Peter Martyr," in *Scottish Journal of Theology*, vol. 8 (1955), p. 255.

130. Donnelly, *Calvinism and Scholasticism*, p. 131.

131. *Loci communes*, II.xvii.1 (p. 411): "Vere quidem Deus ad nos venire dicitur, multis modis. Proprie tamen & singulariter venit filius Dei, qui ipse est vere Deus, in natura humana ad servandum humanum genus. Etsi enim Deus sit ubique, tamen eum venisse dicimus, quoniam induit naturam humanam: atque ita dicimus venisse ad nos, & sese nobis, repraesentasse & Patrem & Filium, & Spiritum sanctum. Etsi enim opera Trinitatis, quod ad interna attinet, sint singularia, qualia sunt generare, spirare, procedere, ista enim fiunt a vi divina, quae tribus personis est communis, tamen ea, quod ad externa attinet, sunt indivisa. Cur ergo, inquies, solus Filius dicitur incarnatus?"

132. Ibid.,"Durum quidem illud videri potest, idem esse & efficientem causam, & effectum."

133. Ibid.

134. Cf. Augustine's epistle to Nebridius, Letter xi.2, 4 (PL.33.75-76; cf. NPNF, 1st ser., vol. I, pp. 229-230) with *De fide et symbolo*, ix.18 (PL.40.190-191) and *Enchiridion*, cap. xxxv (PL.40.249-250). These texts are also found in NPNF 1st ser., vol. III, pp. 328-329, 249. Also see

the analysis of Augustine's Christology by Albert Outler in *A Companion to the Study of Augustine*, ed. Battenhouse (N.Y., 1955), pp. 346-351.

135. K. R. Hagenbach, *A History of Christian Doctrines*, trs. E. H. Plumptre (Edinburgh, 1880-81), vol. I, p. 376, citing *De Trinitate*, II.xviii (PL.42.863-866) and *Contra Sermonem Arianorum*, III.iv (PL.42.685-686).

136. *Loci communes*, II.xvii.2 (p. 411).

137. Ibid., II.xviii.5 (p. 422).

138. Ibid.

139. Ibid., p. 617, col. 1-2.

140. Sturm, p. 128.

141. *Loci communes* (appendix), pp. 1113-1114.

142. *Loci communes*, II.xvii.11 (p. 415).

143. Ibid., p. 416.

144. Ibid., II.xviii.7 (p. 423).

145. Cf. Ibid., II.xvii.15-21 with II.xviii.13-26.

146. Ibid., II.xvii.15 (p. 417): "Neque mihi quispiam dixerit, potuisse Deum alia ratione mundum redimere, neque fuisse omnino necessarium ad hominem salutem, ut filius Dei cruci affigeretur. Quia semel constituerimus, Deum sapientissimum, iustumque rerum aestimatorem, agnoscemus illum, quando hoc medium nostrae salutis elegit, naturam peccati vehementissime detestatum esse, cum decreverit Filium suum dare in mortem, & quidem ignominiosam, ut a suis electis peccatum depelleret."

147. Ibid., II.xvii.16.

148. Ibid., II.xvii.19.

149. Ibid., II.xvii.19 (p. 419).

150. Ibid., (p. 419): "Nam si quaesiveris, utrum necessarium fuerit, ut filius Dei sic moretur: respondeo, necessitatem coactionis nullam hic esse statuendam: nihil enim est in Dei violentum. Neque etiam naturae necessitas ulla fuit. Quamuis etiam in natura divina multa sint necessaria, quale est, ut sit unus, trinus, Filium genuerit, & caetera id genus: tamen nefas est existimare, ullum effectum externum ab eo necessitate naturali proficisci: cum quicquid facit, libere atque ultro facit, & illi, quod nolit, liberum sit non facere. Neque hic statuimus necessitatem ex hypothesi finis: Nam salus humana, multis aliis rationibus & vijs, modo ille voluisset, parari poterat. Sed necessarium fuit, Christum mori ex hypothesi divinae providentiae, atque consilij: quod Deus ita fore decrevisset. Id autem fecit potissimum ad suam infinitam dilectionem declarandam."

151. *In duos libros Samuelis prophetae . . . commentarii* (Zurich, 1567) p. 332 recto, as cited in Donnelly, *Calvinism and Scholasticism*, p. 65. Of course, the Samuel commentary appeared posthumously sixteen years after the commentary on I Corinthians, from which the latter argument is taken—and Vermigli might well have modified his opinion. We must not place too much weight of interpretation on either passage.

152. *Loci communes*, II.xviii.15 (p. 426).

153. Ibid., II.xviii.17 (p. 426).

154. Ibid.

155. *In epistolam s. Pauli apostoli ad Romanos . . . commentarii* (Basel, 1558).

156. Donnelly, *Calvinism and Scholasticism*, pp. 125-129.

157. *Loci communes*, III.i.1. (p. 443). In the following section I will follow the tractate on predestination as printed in the 1583 edition of the *Loci*, III.i.1-58. On the division of the treatise, cf. McClelland, "Predestination," p. 261. Another treatise on predestination appears in the appended material (pp. 992-994) at the end of the 1583 *Loci communes*—its authenticity has been questioned by McClelland, *Visible Words of God* (Edinburgh and London, 1957), p. 264, and I have not, therefore, utilized it in the above analysis.

158. *Loci communes*, III.i.1 (p. 443); cf. III.i.2 and 6 (pp. 443, 446).

159. Ibid., III.i.3 (p. 445).

160. Ibid., III.i.4 (p. 445).
161. Ibid.
162. Ibid., III.i.5 (p. 445).
163. Ibid. (p. 446).
164. Ibid. (p. 446): "Neque hac praedestinatione mutantur naturae rerum, quod attinet ad necessitatem, & contingentiam. . . ."
165. Ibid., III.i.9 (p. 447).
166. Ibid. (p. 448).
167. Ibid. (p. 448).
168. Ibid. (p. 448).
169. Ibid. (p. 448): "Imo si ita accipiatur praedestinatio, erit rebus omnibus communis. Neque aliud ista vox significabit, quam Dei de creaturis suis aeternam dispositionem ad usum aliquem suum. Caeterim Sacrae literae hanc vocem non facile usurpant, nisi de electis: quamuis in 4. cap. Actorum legatur, Convenerunt ad faciendum, quodcunque manus tua, & consilium praedestinaverat, ut fieret: quae tamen verba si ad mortem Christi, & humani generis redemptionem referantur, extra salutarem electionem non egrediuntur. Sed si ad illos quoque spectent, qui adversus Dominum convenerunt, reprobos etiam comprehendunt. Nunc autem nos iudicabimus de Scripturis, quemadmodum illae plerunque loqui solent. Itaque theologi etiam Scholastici, electos tantum reprobos aiunt praedestinari. Eam sententiam nos quoque in praesentia sequemur, non sane propter rationem, quam adducunt: illa enim valde infirma est, ut postea docebimus suo loco, sed quoniam video Scripturas plerunque ita loqui. Quare in hac tractatione sanctos tantum sub nomine praedestinationis comprehendimus. Atque de hac causa puto Augustinum librum suum inscripsisse, de Praedestinatione sanctorum, quae significat decretum Dei, quo sancti instituti sunt ad communionem salutis: praedestinationi vero, per antithesin reprobationem opponemus."
170. Ibid., III.i.10 (p. 448).
171. Ibid. (p. 448).
172. Ibid., III.i.11 (p. 449): "Dico igitur praedestinationem esse sapientissimum propositum Dei, quo ante omnem aeternitatem decrevit constanter, eos, quos dilexit in Christo, vocare ad adoptionem filiorum, ad iustificationem ex fide; & tandem ad gloriam per opera bona, quo conformes fiant imagini filii Dei, utque in illis declaretur gloria & misericordia Creatoris."
173. Ibid., III.i.11 (p. 449).
174. Ibid., III.i.10 (p. 449): "Meminisse etiam debemus, amorem, electionem & praedestinationem Dei ita inter se ordinari, ut sese certa ratione consequantur. Primum notitiae Dei offeruntur omnes homines non felices, imo egeni & miseri, quos Deus pura simplicique misericordia diligit, eis bene vult, illosque discernit ab aliis, quos praeterit, & sua benevolentia non complectitur, atque illi hac discretione dicuntur eligi: electi autem ad finem destinantur."
175. Ibid., III.i.15 (p. 451).
176. Ibid., III.i.58 (p. 474). Cf. III.i.50.
177. Ibid.,III.i.58.
178. Ibid., III.i.11 (p. 449).
179. *Institutes*, II.xvii.2; III.xiv.17; xxiv.5.
180. Cf. *Summa theologica*, Part I, Qq. 22, 23; all citations and quotations of the *Summa* will refer to the Leonine text as published by Biblioteca de Autores Christianos, Madrid, 1951).
181. *Loci communes*, III.i.15 (p. 451). Ritschl, III, p. 269 notes a similarity between this doctrine and the thought of Bullinger and Aretius. Yet, unlike Bullinger who very nearly equates predestination and election, Vermigli subordinates predestination to election. Bullinger does not follow the Thomist pattern.
182. McClelland, pp. 259-260, 271.
183. Cf. McClelland, pp. 262, 268-269. On this point I am in disagreement with Donnelly ("Calvinist Thomism," pp. 445, 448) who feels that Vermigli and Zanchi propose "a stricter doctrine of predestination than Calvin." Stress on the freedom of secondary causality is typical of later

orthodoxy (e.g., Turretin, *Inst. theol.*, Locus IV, quaes. iv, sec. v-viii) and even appears in its confessional documents: cf. *Conf. West.*, chap. iii, art. 1.
184. McClelland, p. 259.
185. *Loci communes*, III.i.15 (p. 451). Cf. Donnelly, *Calvinism and Scholasticism*, p. 132.
186. Ibid., III.i.25, 38-39 (pp. 457, 462-463).
187. Ibid., III.i.25 (p. 457).
188. The concept of "*historica series*" as a formal principle uniting the ancient messianic promises, the conception, birth, crucifixion and resurrection of Christ; uniting also the explication of law and gospel, of sin and the reconciling grace by which mankind is brought to life eternal (CR, XXI, 605-606) exerted a powerful influence on the development of the orthodox systems: see Althaus, *Die Prinzipien*, pp. 45-54 passim, and the discussion in Karl Dieterich Pfisterer, *The Prism of Scripture: Studies on history and historicity in the work of Jonathan Edwards* (Bern and Frankfurt, 1975), pp. 230-233. The magisterial study of this concept in Melanchthon's thought is surely in Peter Fraenkel, *Testimonia Patrum: the Function of the Patristic Argument in the Theology of Philip Melanchthon* (Geneva, 1961), pp. 52-109.
189. Anthony Hoekema, "The Covenant of Grace in Calvin's Teaching," in *Calvin Theological Journal*, vol. 2 (1967), pp. 133-161.
190. For a discussion of the issue between Calvin and Bullinger, see Berkouwer, *Divine Election*, pp. 191-194, 201.
191. I use the term "covenanted" in tandem with the concept of the regenerate life advisedly and with reference to Calvin's discussion of Hebrews 8:6-13, 9:16-23 and to *Inst.*, II.ix.1.
192. Cf. Thomas Aquinas, *Summa theologiae*, III, q. 61, art. 1, ad 3.

IV.   PREDESTINATION AND CHRISTOLOGY
IN THE THOUGHT OF THEODORE BEZA

1. The best modern biographical study of Beza is Paul F. Geizendorf, *Théodore de Bèze* (Geneva, 1949); also see Henri Clavier, *Theodore Beza; un aperçu de sa vie aventureuse, de ses travaux, de sa personalité* (Cahors, 1960). A brief biographical and theological study is available in Steinmetz, *Reformers in the Wings*, pp. 162-171. Older biographical studies include Heinrich Heppe, *Theodore Beza, Leben und ausgewählte Schriften* (Elberfeld, 1861); and Henry M. Baird, *Theodore Beza; the Counsellor of the French Reformation* (N.Y., 1899). Beza's contribution to the development of the orthodox doctrine of predestination is treated in Bizer's *Frühorthodoxie und Rationalismus*; also Walter Kickel, *Vernunft und Offenbarung bei Theodor Beza* (Neukirchen, 1967) and John S. Bray, *Theodore Beza's Doctrine of Predestination* (Nieuwkoop, 1975).
2. *Geschichte der protestantischen Dogmatik*, v. I, pp. 120-122; Augustus Neander, *Lectures on the History of Christian Dogmas*, trs. Ryland, 2 vols. (London, 1858), v. II, pp. 666-681; Reinhold Seeberg, *Text-book of the History of Doctrines*, trs. Hay (Grand Rapids, 1952), v. II, p. 451; Friedrich Loofs, *Leitfaden zum Studien der Dogmengeschichte* (Halle, 1906), pp. 906, 935; and Ritschl, *Dogmengeschichte des Protestantismus*, v. III, pp. 294-295.
3. *Frühorthodoxie*, p. 6. Bizer here acknowledges his debt to the work of Hans Emil Weber.
4. *Ibid.*
5. Bizer, *Frühorthodoxie*, pp. 7-8; Kickel, *Vernunft und Offenbarung*; Johannes Dantine, "Les Tabelles sur la doctrine de la prédestination par Théodore de Bèze," in *Revue de Théologie et Philosophie*, XVI (1966), pp. 365-377; Basil Hall, "Calvin Against the Calvinists," in *John Calvin: A Collection of Distinguished Essays*, ed. G. Duffield (Grand Rapids, 1966), pp. 19-37; Steinmetz, pp. 168-169.
6. Hall, p. 27 and Steinmetz, pp. 168-169. But note that when Beza wrote the *Tabula* (1555),

Calvin had not yet established his view that predestination should be developed out of soteriology (1559).

7. *Tabula praedestinationis*, in *Tractationes theologicae*, 3 vols. (Geneva, 1570-1582), vol. I, pp. 170-205. (The *Tabula's* text is divided into chapters and the chapters into brief aphorisms: citations in the notes following will give chapter and aphorism.) The *Tabula* is also frequently referred to by the heading affixed to Beza's diagram of the decrees (*Tractationes*, I, 170): "Summa totius christianismi, sive descriptio & distributio causarum salutis electorum, & exitii reproborum, ex sacris literis collecta." This heading has been understood by some scholars to indicate that the *Tabula*, despite its contents, was intended as a system of theology: cf. Kickel, p. 99 and Hall, p. 27ff. But the heading refers to Christianity—not to the system of Christian theology. The *Tabula* was written during a time of controversy over the doctrine of predestination between Calvin and Bolsec and following a promulgation by the town council of Bern prohibiting sermons on predestination (November 17, 1554). This may have something to do with Beza's stress on the homiletical use of the doctrine in his aphorisms. As debate over predestination continued Beza also produced his *Ad sycophantarum quorumdam calumnias, quibus unicum salutis nostrae fundamentum, id est aeternam Dei predestinationem evertere nituntur, responsio Theodori Bezae Vezelii* (Geneva, 1558) against Sebastian Castellio. This latter work is a point by point refutation of Castellio's argument and adds little to the positive formulation of doctrine (cf. Bray, p. 73). Both of these works of Beza were translated into English in the sixteenth century.

8. *Tabula*, cap.viii.4, margin: "Ex reprobationis consideratione discintur humilitas."

9. *Ibid.*, cap.viii.2.

10. *Ibid.*, cap.iii.6.

11. Cf. Ibid., cap.ii.4; iv.2, 3; vi.1, 3; vii-viii.

12. Ritschl, *Dogmengeschichte*, vol. III, p. 296.

13. *Tabula*, cap.ii.3.

14. *Tabula*, cap.ii.4.

15. Karl Barth, CD, II/2, pp. 127-130.

16. *Tabula*, cap.iii-iv; yet Beza can anticipate later formulations, as is seen by his letter to Calvin of 29 July 1555, in *Correspondance*, I, 169-172.

17. *Tabula*, cap.ii and cap.iii. Cf. Kickel, p. 101. Kickel comments that Beza's mention of the effects of the decree at this point evinces an empirical and inductive method. The text does not bear this interpretation, however, since Beza does not reason from the effects to the decree, but rather bars such speculation.

18. *Tabula*, cap.iv-v. Dantine ("Les Tabelles," pp. 371-372) and Bray, pp. 91-93, 140 argue that the distinction between the decree and its execution separates Beza from Calvin and may even mirror distinctions in Aquinas' *Summa*. Not only does this distinction belong to Calvin's theology as a basic epistemological issue—it is also a theological truism like the distinction between *potentia absoluta* and *potentia ordinata*. Cf. Johann van Staupitz, *Eternal Predestination and its Execution in Time*, trs. Nyhus in Heiko Oberman, *Forerunners of the Reformation* (N.Y., 1966), pp. 175-200.

19. *Tabula*, ii.2, 3, 6.

20. Ibid., cap.iii.1, 3.

21. Cf.Steinmetz, p. 167.

22. *Tabula*, cap.iii.4, 5.

23. *Dogmengeschichte*, III, 295.

24. Ibid., cap.iv.1-4.

25. Ibid., cap.iv.2: "Deus igitur clementissimus electorum pater, iustitiam illam suam infinita misericordia temperans, Filium unicum suum, eiusdem secum substantia, Deumque aeternum designavit, qui tempore constituto verus homo fieret." Also cap.iv.3-4: "Primum ut, coniunctus in unum Iesum Christum naturis duabus, tota illa hominus corruptio in uno homine prorsus emendaretur. Deinde qui omnem iustitiam impleret, quique & satis potens ad iudicum Dei sustinendum, & satis dignus sacerdos placando coelesti Patri existeret, iustus pro iniustus moriens. . . ."

26. Kickel, pp. 167-168.

27. *Tabula*, cap.iv.5, 6. Cf. below, section 2 on Beza's *Confessio* and note the careful description of the limited extent or application of Christ's work in Beza's response to Andreae at Montbéliard: *Ad Acta Colloqui Montisbelgardensis Tubingae edita Theodori Bezae responsionis, pars altera* (Geneva, 1588), p. 215-217; and cf. the able analysis in W. Robert Godfrey, "Reformed Thought on the Extent of the Atonement to 1618," in *The Westminster Theological Journal*, vol. XXXVII, no. 2 (Winter, 1975), pp. 141-143.

28. *Ad Acta Colloqui Montisbelgardensis*, p. 200: "Aliter igitur Christus considerandus est ut causa praedestinationis officiens cum Patre et Spirito Sancto: aliter ut primum ipsius Praedestinationis, de servandis per misericordiam in ipso electis effectum."

29. *Tabula*, cap.vi.1.

30. Ibid., cap.vi.3.

31. Ibid., cap.vi.2.

32. Archibald A. Hodge, *The Atonement* (1907; repr., Grand Rapids, 1974), p. 403. Hodge's interpretation of traditional Reformed theology presents the limitation of atonement more as this question of the relationship of the divine intention to save to the limited effect of the Gospel among men. William Robert Godfrey (op. cit.) also stresses the problem of the divine intentionality. Moreover, the terms at issue in the debate over limited atonement, including the relationship of the efficacy of atonement to the decree of election, were not invented or deduced by Protestant orthodoxy but were inherited from the older scholastic theology of Lombard, Aquinas, Aureolus, Durandus, Duns Scotus and Gabriel Biel (see Seeberg, II, 198-199). The doctrine of developing Reformed orthodoxy represents simply the adjustment of the system on this point to the *sola gratia* of Reformation theology.

33. *Tabula*, cap.vii.

34. Ibid.,cap.viii.1.

35. The confession was first published in French in 1558 and 1559. It appeared in Latin in 1560 translated by Beza himself. The *Confessio* was widely received: an edition appeared in London (1575) and there are English translations dating from 1565 and 1572. A contemporary French version with notes by Michel Reveillaud is available in *La Revue Reformée*, VI, nos. 3-4 (1955). Hereinafter Beza's confession will be abbreviated as *Conf. chr.* The outline of the theology of Beza's *Confessio* found in the following section should be compared with Jill Raitt, *The Eucharistic Theology of Theodore Beza: Development of the Reformed Doctrine* (Chambersburg, Pa.; 1972), pp. 10-18.

36. *Confessio christianae fidei, et eiusdem collatio cum Papisticis Haeresibus . . . adjecta est altera brevis eiusdem Bezae fidei Confessio* (London, 1575), i.3.

37. *Conf. chr.* iii.5.

38. Ibid., ii.2.

39. Ibid., ii.3.

40. Ibid., ii.4.

41. *Conf. Gall.*, i-vii; *Conf. Belg.*, i-ix (in CC, vol. III, pp. 359-364, 383-393.) Beza's *Altera brevis fidei confessio* (1559) follows a more synthetic order than his larger *Conf. chr.*, but the exposition is extremely brief and permits no major systematic conclusion. The late *Theses theologicae* (1586) cannot rightly be called a system by Beza. They do, via the students of Beza and Faius, reflect the early orthodox codification of doctrine, though not in as elaborate development as the systems of Ursinus and Zanchius and hardly at the level of detailed systematization accomplished by writers like Polanus, Perkins, Bucanus, Keckermann.

42. *Quaestionum et responsionum christianarum libellus, in quo praecipua christianae religionis capita kat epitome proponunter* (Geneva, 1584), pp. 95-125, on providence, predestination and the divine will.

43. *Quaestionum et responsionum*, pp. 95-125.

44. Bray, p. 76; cf. Kickel, p. 141 and Dantine, "Les Tabelles," p. 374.

45. Beza's catechism appeared in Geneva in 1575 and in translation as *A Little Catechisme* (London, 1578). The *syllogismus practicus* appears in section v, quest. 1 and sec. vi, quest. 6.

46. *Tractationes*, I, pp. 200-201; cf. *Quaestionum*, pp. 133-134.

47. *Tractationes*,I, pp. 186-188.

48. *Ecclesiastes* (Geneva, 1588), p. 36 as cited by Bray, and see the discussion of the *syllogismus practicus* in Bray, pp. 108-110.

49. Bray, p. 110.

50. *De praedestinationis doctrina et vero usu tractatio absolutissima. Ex Th. Bezae praelectionibus in nonum Epistolae ad Romanos caput a Raphaele Eglino Tigurino theologiae studioso in schola Genevensi recens excepta* (Geneva, 1582); Kickel, pp. 136-146.

51. In his commentary on the same passage Calvin notes that Paul first states the outward facts of man's situation manifested in the election of Jacob and the rejection of Esau and then moves logically upward to the cause, the eternal election of God (CO, XLIX, 179-180). Kickel's own comment concerning "the wonderful word of promise" is less related to Paul's "vessels of wrath made for destruction" and "vessels of mercy, which he has prepared beforehand for glory" than the concept of an individual election and reprobation. The problem of corporate election is precisely that not all the children of the elect nation are elect as individuals. Cf. John Murray, *The Epistle to the Romans* (Grand Rapids, 1959-1965), II, 15-24. Bray, pp. 129-130 far more effectively describes the problematic points of Beza's exegesis.

52. *Jesu Christi Domini Nostri Novum Testamentum, sive Novum Foedus, cuius Graeco contextui respondent interpretationes duae: una, vetus; altera, Theodori Bezae. Eiusdem Theod. Bezae Annotationes, in quibus ratione interpretationis vocum reddita . . .* (Cambridge, 1642), Romans 9:18, *in loc.* (col. 431): "Atqui otiosus Deus, Deus non est: nec item Deus omipotens qui invitus aliquid finat. Restat ergo ut quod permittit, volens permittat. . . ." (Hereinafter cited as *Annotationes*.)

53. Ibid., citing *Enchiridion*, cap. 100.

54. Ibid., Rom. 8:28, *in loc.* (1642, col. 425).

55. Ibid., Rom. 9:21, *in loc.* (1642, cols. 432-433): "Qui *Massae* nomine humanum genus corruptum intelligunt, mihi non satisfaciunt in huius loci explicatione. . . ."

56. *Annotationes, in loc.* (1642, col. 568-569).

57. Ibid., *in loc.* (1642, col. 570): "*Quos adoptaret in filios per Christum Jesum.* . . . Explicat Apostolus quomodo accipiendum sit quod ante dixerat, nos in Christo electos ab aeterno, ita nempe ut Christus substernatur Dei aeterno consilio; quatenus per eum unum constituit omnes electos ad suum finem adducere. Nec enim Christum hic considerat nude & seorsim ut Deum Patri *homoousion*, & per omnia aequalem, (qua ratione non in ipso, sed ab ipso, sicut & a Patre & a Spiritu, electi sumus, cum Dei *ousia* dividi nec possit nec debeat) sed ut mediatorem & Deum manifestatum in carne: in quo uno gratis adoptati & reconciliati servantur omnes saluti destinati, quem propterea vocat Augustinus *praedestinatorum caput.* cuius verba vide (lector) lib. De praedest. sanctorum, 1. cap.19 & 2. cap.24 & tractatu in Joan. 17." A similar formulation appears subsequently (col. 571) as Beza elaborates v. 5: "In sese . . . quibus verbis excludit Apostolus quaecunque usquam sunt extra ipsum Deum, ut significet Deum in suis eligendis nihil neque praesens, (solus enim est aeternus) neque futurum in coelo aut in terra, sed seipsum unum spectasse, in quo uno sapientissimi & justissimi sui consilii causas invenerit: qua ratione minime excluditur a Patre, sed cum illo Filius & Spiritus, cum hi tres sint unus Deus."

58. *Conf. chr.*, iii.1-2. In addition to the *Confessio* and the *Quaestionum et responsionum* Beza's *Adversus sacramentariorum errorem pro vera Christi praesentia in coena Domini, homiliae duae* (Geneva, 1574) and *De hypostatica duarum in Christo naturarum unione* (Geneva, 1579), the latter written in response to Chemnitz' *De duabus naturis in Christo* (1570) are also important for an understanding of his Christology, as are the published *Acta* of the Montbeliard Colloquy.

59. *Conf. chr.*, iii.3-4.   60. Ibid., iii.5.

61. Ibid., iii.6.

62. Ibid., iii.7.

63. Ibid., iii.8. Cf. Kickel, pp. 107-108.

64. Ibid., iii.8. Matthias Schneckenburger in his excellent *Vergleichende Darstellung des lutherischen und reformirten Lehrbegriffs* (Stuttgart, 1855) saw this necessitarian impulse as driving

Beza further from the spirit of Calvin's theology than any other Reformed thinker of the sixteenth century (vol. II, p. 154).

65. *Confessio*, iii.8, as cited above; cf. *Inst.*, III.xxiii.3 and Kickel, pp. 108, 124-126.
66. *Quaestionum et responsionum*, p. 107-108.
67. Ibid., p. 110-111.
68. Ibid., p. 111.
69. Ibid., pp. 114-115.
70. Ibid., p. 117.
71. Ibid., pp. 85-99. Beza clearly affirms the Scotist priority of will in his gloss on Romans 9:20 ("O man, who art thou that repliest against God"): "Cum enim Deum ita velle & facere constet ex manifestis testimoniis, quae haec audacia est, hominem (id est cinerem) Deo responsare, atque adeo in jus vocare? Quod si quis neget ita expeditum esse nodum, respondeo nullam esse ullis in rebus firmiorem demonstrationem, ut quae nitatur certissimo isto principio, Dei voluntatem esse justitiae regulam" (*Annotationes, in loc.*, p. 431).
72. Ibid., pp. 85-88.
73. Ibid., p. 92, cf. 88.
74. Ibid., pp. 96-97.
75. *Conf. chr.*, iii.9-11.
76. Cf. Heppe, RD, pp. 341-349.
77. *Conf. chr.*, iii.16.
78. Ibid., iii.17.
79. Ibid., iii.18.
80. Ibid., iii.19.
81. Ibid.
82. Ibid., iii.20.
83. Ibid.
84. Ibid., iii.21.
85. Note that the Lutheran Christology, for all its disagreement with the Reformed over the *communicatio idiomatum*, was ultimately as convinced in its acceptance of the doctrine of Christ as mediator according to both natures: cf. DTEL, pp. 338-339.
86. Cf. *Quaestionum et responsionum*, pp. 20-24 with the *Epistolarum theologicarum Theodori Bezae Vezelii, liber unus*, 2nd edition (Geneva, 1575), epistle xxviii, pp. 159-168. The epistle does not give the name of the person to whom it was originally addressed, but it is dated from Geneva, the calends of September, 1568.
87. *Quaestionum et responsionum*, pp. 20-21. Cf. Raitt, "The Person of the Mediator," p. 65.
88. Ibid., p. 24.
89. Cf. ibid., p. 25.
90. Ibid., pp. 21-22.
91. Ibid., pp. 22-23.
92. Ibid., pp. 23-24.
93. *Epistolarum theologicarum Theodori Bezae Vezelii*, pp. 159-160.
94. Ibid., p. 160: "& quanuis recte dicant Patres neutram naturam separatim consideratam esse mediatricem, tamen hoc non est ita accipiendum ut iste vult, quasi videlicet sic describatur persona & non officium. Mediatoris enim nomen nihil aliud quam reconciliationis munus & officium declarat, quod tamen obire non potuerit, nisi qui Deus simul & homo sit. Nam si homo tantum esset, maneret semper divisa a Divinitate natura humana: & si vicissim Deus tantum esset, nulla esset Dei cum homine coniuncto: ideoque Christus non esset mediator, id est, non reconciliasset Deum & homines, quod significavit Augustinus his verbis, Divinitas sine humanitate non est mediatrix, & humanitas sine divinitate non est mediatrix: sed inter divinitatem solam humanitatem solam mediatrix humana divinitas & divina humanitas Christi: id est Christus non est mediator sive reconciliator, quatenus Deus tantum, vel quatenus homo tantum, sed quatenus homo Deus & Deus homo, in una eademque persona."

95. Ibid., p. 160.

96. Ibid., p. 160.

97. Ibid., pp. 160-161: "Respondeo non esse hic nobis considerandam naturam divinam absolute, sed cum relatione, id est, in ipsa hypostasi verbi, quod solum (non autem Pater & Spiritus sanctus) humanam naturam assumpsit. Iam vero nihil impedit, quominus Verbum, etsi, quod ad essentiam attinet, coaequale est Patri (in qua nimirum unica & tota, perinde ut Pater, subsistit, sua ab illo proprietate distinctum) tamen Patri quod ad officium reconciliandi humani generis subordinetur, non secundum naturam, inquam, sive secundum essentiam, quae unica est, sed propter officium mediationis sive reconciliationis. Itaque Verbum sic est causa eminens adeoque author mediationis, respectu humanae naturae assumptae (a qua separandum quidem non est, sed tamen distinguendum) ut nihilominus respectu Patris, ex cuius voluntate has mediationis partes in se recepit, mediae etiam causae rationem sustineat. Neque inde colligere potest Stancarus, nos esse Arrianos: Primum, quod totam hanc subordinationem, quae ordinis est non gradus, in officio duntaxat ponimus, non in essentia neque in ipsa hypostasi. . . ."

98. *Conf. chr.*, iii.22.

99. Cf. *Response de M. Th. de Bèze aux Actes de la conference de Montbéliard imprimées a Tubingue* (Geneva, 1587).

100. *Conf. Chr.*, iii.24.

101. Cf. Godfrey, "Reformed Thought on the Extent of the Atonement to 1618," pp. 141-143. The *Quaestionum et responsionum* does not offer much clarification on this point since it contains no extended analysis of the *satisfactio Christi* and its application. Beza does comment (p. 56) we apprehend Christ in the moment we have faith and thereby we find realized in ourselves the election which was obtained before the foundation of the world.

102. Cf.Raitt, *Eucharistic Theology*, pp. 10-30. Tadataka Maruyama, *The Ecclesiology of Theodore Beza: The Reform of the True Church* (Geneva, 1978), pp. 22, 139-148, 198-199. Johannes Dantine has argued that the rationalistic element in Beza's theology coupled with Beza's predestinarianism leads to the postulation of an "impersonal" Christ who is little more than a means to the end of God's decree ("Das christologische Problem im Rahmen der Prädestinationslehre von Theodor de Beze," in *Zeitschrift für Kirchengeschichte*, 78 (1966), pp. 81-96). The doctrinal structures we have examined above serve to refute this contention. Beza did affirm the impersonality of Christ's human nature, but this was the result of his polemical encounter with Lutheran Christology and the ensuing recourse to patristic and medieval christological distinctions, and in no way the result of predestinarian speculation.

103. Bray, p. 74.

104. *The Summe of Sacred Divinitie briefly and methodically propounded . . . more largely and clearly handled* (London, 1630?), Booke II, chapters i-iv. Keckermann's *Systema sacrosanctae theologiae* (Heidelberg, 1602) may reflect and rationalize both this order and the order of Vermigli's *Loci communes* in its placement of predestination immediately prior to the Christology.

105. The christocentric piety of Beza's homilies, particularly of the late *Homiliae Theodori Bezae Vezelii, in historiam Domini resurrectionis* (Geneva, 1593), has been emphasized by Armand Duckert in his *Théodore de Bèze: Prédicateur* (Geneva, 1891), pp. 24-28, 36-38.

V.   REFORMED THEOLOGY IN HEIDELBERG;
ZACHARIAS URSINUS AND JEROME ZANCHI

1. See: Derk Visser, *Zacharias Ursinus: The Reluctant Reformer, His Life and Times* (New York, 1983), Sudhoff, C. *Olevian und Z. Ursinus; Leben und ausgewählte Schriften* (Elberfeld, 1857), and the articles by Theodor Ney in RPTK, XIV, 358-362 and XX, 348-353 are also useful. Bard Thompson, H. Berkhof, et al., *Essays on the Heidelberg Catechism* (Philadelphia, 1963) contains a wealth of historical, biographical and theological material.

2. On the sources of the catechism see A. Lang, *Der Heidelberger Katechismus und vier verwandete Katechismen* (Leipzig, 1907) and the two volumes by Walter Hollweg, *Neue Untersuchung zur Geschichte und Lehre des Heidelberger Katechismus* (Neukirchen, 1961); Zweiter Folge (Neukirchen, 1966). Hollweg argues for a Bezan influence on the Catechism while H. Berkhof, "The Catechism in its Historical Context," in *Essays*, p. 82 argues the contrary. *Doctrinae Christianae compendium sive commentarii catechetici* (Neustadt, Leyden, Geneva, 1584; Cambridge, 1585); also *Explicationes catecheseos* in *D. Zachariae Ursini theologi celeberrimi . . . opera theologica quibus orthodoxae religionis capita perspicue & breviter explicantur*, 3 vols., ed. Quirinius Reuter (Heidelberg, 1612), vol. I, col. 48. Although throughout the present chapter I refer to Ursinus' catechetical lectures by their earliest title, *Doctrinae christianae compendium*, references will be made to the version of the lectures found in Ursinus' collected works, entitled *Explicationes catecheseos*. The earlier edition will be abbreviated *Doct. chr. comp.* and the latter *Expl. cat.* In the main, the *Expl. cat.* presents a smoother, more flowing style than the *Doct. chr. comp.* but textual differences appear to be minor in the *loci* pertaining to the doctrines of Christ and predestination. I have followed the translation of G. W. Williard (Columbus, 1851) but have made corrections from *Expl. cat.* where necessary. The early development of Ursinus' theology up to but not including preparation of the *Heidelberg Catechism* is discussed by Erdmann Sturm in his *Der Junge Zacharias Ursin: Sein Weg vom Philippismus zum Calvinismus* (Neukirchen, 1972). Influences on Ursinus included Melanchthon, his first teacher, Calvin and Vemigli.

3. Cf. Wulf Metz, *Necessitas Satisfactionis? Eine systematische Studie zu den Fragen 12-18 des Heidelberger Katechismus* (Zurich and Stuttgart, 1970), 125-126. Also see O. Ritschl, *Dogmengeschichte*, III, 257-267.

4. Ibid., col. 92. Cf. Bizer, *Frühorthodoxie und Rationalismus*, 24. Bizer feels that this structure follows Beza into the realm of rationalism and rationalistic argument; and it is true that Beza does employ the Anselmic structure in the christological exposition of his *Confessio christianae fidei* in connection with the concept of Christ as the "one covenant of salvation" under both the Old and the New dispensations. There is an affinity here, not only between Beza and Ursinus, but between both of these thinkers and the rest of the Reformed tradition. For it is a fact that Calvin also accepts these very arguments and juxtaposes the problem of the Old and New Testaments with the Anselmic conception of the necessity of mediation in the final edition of the *Institutes* (cf. *Inst.*, II, xi, xii). In addition the Anselmic argument was such a commonplace in the sixteenth century that its presence in Ursinus' work demonstrates no particular influence, either Lutheran or Reformed. Jacobs sees this very Anselmic structure, employed as a means by which to focus the whole of theology on the mediator, as the guarantee of christocentric emphasis in the Heidelberg Catechism. See his *Theologie reformierter Bekenntnisschriften* (Neukirchen, 1959), 64-65, 101. Neither is this structure to be described as overly rationalistic, based as it is on the scriptural *a priori*; cf. H. Berkhof, "The Catechism as an Expression of Faith," in *Essays on the Heidelberg Catechism*, 98-99.

5. *Expl. cat.*, col. 92; this exposition bears a strong resemblance to that of Ursinus' earlier catechisms; cf. Sturm, 259-260.

6. *Expl. cat.*, col. 105.

7. Ibid., col. 95.

8. Ibid., col. 96; "fundamentum & summa totius Christianae doctrina."

9. Ibid., col. 96.

10. *Expl. cat.*, col. 98.

11. Ibid., col. 99.

12. Ibid., cols. 99-100.

13. *Expl. cat.*, col. 138.

14. Ibid., col. 141.

15. Ibid., col. 142.

16. Cf. Lyle Bierma, "The Covenant Theology of Caspar Olevian," (Ph.D. dissertation, Duke University, 1980), pp. 112-119.

17. *Expl. cat.*, col. 142.

18. Ibid., col. 142-146; cf. col. 152-153.

19. Ibid., col. 144-146.

20. *Expl. cat.*, col. 147.

21. Ibid., col. 147.

22. Ibid., col. 150.

23. Ibid., col. 154.

24. *Loci theologici*, in *Opera*, I, col. 534: "Mediator apud Deum est inferior Deo. Deus Isrealis non est inferior seipso. Ergo non est Mediator. Respondemus: Maiorem concedi de officio, sed non de natura. Nihil enim obstat, quominus aequalis, apud aequalem fiat pro aliis intercessor & Mediator, etiam inter homines. Sic Filius, & Deus est unus cum Patre, & se ad officium Mediatoris demittit sine diminutione naturae, potentiae, Maiestatis, & Divinitatis suae. . . ."

25. Ibid., col. 543: "Filius autem, & spiritus sanctus huic Patris voluntati assentiantur, ac per seipsos fieri velint, quod Pater per seipsos vult fieri."

26. Ibid., col. 543.

27. *Expl. cat.*, col. 159: ". . . est vera de officio: de natura negatur, ex eadem regula quarta generali: inequalitas officii non tollit aequalitatem naturarum vel personarum."

28. *Loci theologici*, col. 540-541.

29. Ibid., col. 540.

30. Ibid., col. 468: "Deus sit essentia spiritualis, intelligens, aeterna, alia a creaturis omnibus, incomprehensibilis, in seipsa perfectissima, immutabilis, immensae potentiae, sapientiae & bonitatis, justa, verax, casta, misericors, beneficia, liberrima, irascens peccatis: quae est Pater aeternus, qui Filium imaginem suam ab aeterno genuit, & Filius imago Patris coaeterna, & Spiritus sanctus procedens a Patre & Filio: sicut patefacta est divinitas certo verbo, tradito per Prophetas & Apostolos, & testimoniis divinis, quod Pater aeternus, cum Filio & Spiritu sancto coelum & terram, & omnes creaturas in eis creaverit, & adsit omnibus creaturis, ut eas conservet ac regat sua providentia, & bona omnia in omnibus operetur: & quod in genere humano, condito ad imaginem suam, elegerit ac colligat sibi aeternam Ecclesiam propter Filium, & per eum, ut ab ea, haec una & vera Divinitas, juxta verbum divinitus traditum, agnoscatur, & colatur, & in vita aeterna celebretur, & sit judex justorum & injustorum."

31. *Expl. cat.*, cols. 163-165.

32. Ibid., col. 163.

33. Ibid., col. 164: "*Officium mediatoris* requirebat in Christo naturam vere humanam sumtam ex nostra natura, quae peccaverat, & quae erat per ipsum redimenda, & c. ut supra. Oportebat eandem naturam pati, quae peccaverat. At nostra natura peccavit. Ergo eandem oportebat Christum assumere, non autem ex nihilo creatam, aut de coelo demissam, & c. nec tantum assumere, sed etiam retinere, & carnem nostram manere in aeternum: quia ea conditione pater nos recipit in gratiam, si filio suo maneamus insiti. Haec consolatio in aeternum nobis est necessaria, quod Christus sit frater noster, gestet carnem nostram. *Sumus caro de carne eius & os de ossibus eius* (marg. Eph. 5.30). Hanc consolationem amitteremus, si Christus non vere assumsisset & retineret naturam nostram: quoniam sine ea non esset frater noster."

34. Ibid.,col. 165.

35. Ibid., col. 165: "Sic *logos* non est tota persona Mediatoris, etsi sit per se tota & integra persona secunda divinitatis."

36. Ibid., col. 165.

37. Ibid., col. 166.

38. *Systematic Theology*, p. 331.

39. *Expl. cat.*, col. 166.

40. Ibid., cols. 166-168.

41. *Loci theologici*, col. 500.

42. Cf. Ibid., cols. 500, 505, 534, 544.

43. Ibid., col. 175.

44. Ibid., cols. 175-176.

45. Ibid., col. 176.

46. Ibid., col. 177.
47. Ibid., col. 168.
48. Ibid., col. 167.
49. Ibid., col. 168.
50. Ibid., col. 168.
51. Ibid., col. 168.
52. Ibid., cols. 107-108, 215-216.
53. Ibid., col. 173.
54. Ibid., cols. 174-175.
55. Ibid., cols. 215-216.
56. Ibid., col. 178.
57. Ibid., col. 187.
58. Ibid., cols. 189-192; cf. Calvin's commentary on I Cor. 15:27-28 in CO, XLIX, col. 229-230. On Christ's aseity see Ursinus' *Loci theologici* in *Opera*, I, p. 542.
59. Ibid.,col. 192 (question 51 in the catechism).
60. *Epistola D. Zachariae Ursini ad amicum de praedestinatione: totam de ea disputationem erudite & breviter explicans: & consilium, quoad infirmi hic sequantur, ostendens in Miscellanea catechetica, seu collectio eorum quae catecheticis explicationibus prius sparsa in texta fuerunt . . . opera extrema Davidis Parei* (Heidelberg, 1612), appended to vol. III of the *Opera*, separate pagination.
61. Ibid., col. 28E.
62. Ibid., col. 28.
63. Cf. *Summa contra gentiles*, III.clxiii.2; *Summa theologica*, I, q. 23, art. 1 and 3.
64. *Misc. cat.*, col. 29B-C; cf. Ritschl, *Dogmengeschichte*, III, 262; also Vermigli, *Loci communes*, III.1; Musculus, *Commonplaces*, cap.xxvii (p. 515, col. 1). The distinction is denied by Calvin, *Inst.*, III.xxiii.8.
65. *Misc. cat.*, col. 29.
66. Ibid., col. 29.
67. Cf. Melanchthon, *Loci communes*, in CR, XXI, 85; also Vermigli, *Loci communes*, III.i, and cf. above, chapter III, section 3.
68. *Misc. cat.*, col. 29.
69. Ibid., cols. 29-30.
70. Ibid., col. 30.
71. Ibid., col. 30.
72. Ibid., col. 30.
73. Ibid., col. 30.
74. Ibid., col. 30.
75. Ibid., col. 30. Bizer's view of Ursinus as a rigid necessitarian has no basis here: cf. *Frühorthodoxie*, p. 24.
76. *Expl. cat.*, col. 214.
77. Ibid., col. 214.
78. Ibid., col. 214.
79. Ibid., col. 215.
80. Ibid.,col. 215.
81. Ibid., cols. 215-216.
82. Ibid., col. 215.
83. Ibid., col. 216.
84. Ibid., col. 216.
85. Hermann Bavinck, *The Doctrine of God*, trs. William Hendriksen (Grand Rapids, 1951), 358.
86. Ibid.
87. *Expl. cat.*, col. 61; cf. Ritschl, III, 261.
88. Ibid., col. 217.

89. Ibid., col. 217.

90. See: Christopher Burchill, "Girolamo Zanchi: Portrait of a Reformed Theologian and His Work," in *Sixteenth Century Journal*, xv/2 (Summer, 1984), pp. 185-207, Charles Schmidt and Johann Ficker, "Zanchi" in RPTK, v. XXIV and O. Clemen, "Zanchius" in RGG^{ii}, V, 2071. The only recent study of Zanchi's theology known to me is Otto Gründler, *Die Gotteslehre Girolami Zanchis und ihre Bedeutung für seine Lehre von der prädestination* (Neukirchen, 1965), a careful study of Thomistic and Calvinistic influences on Zanchi's thought in terms of the doctrine of God and his attributes. Gründler's analysis of predestination is unfortunately limited to an examination of Zanchi's *De natura Dei*. Gründler does not employ either the *De praedestinatione sanctorum* or Zanchi's summation of Christian doctrine, the *De religione christiana fides*. He also omits mention of *De ecclesia* in which Zanchi manifests another systematic function of the doctrine of predestination.

91. *De praedestinatione*, in *Opera*, VIII, col. 279ff. and *De natura Dei*, in *Opera*, II, col. 476ff.

92. Cf. Donnelly, "Calvinist Thomism," p. 444.

93. *De natura Dei*, III.iv, "Voluntas Dei, & semper iusta est: & regula omnis iustitiae."

94. Calvin's influence is difficult to document, though one of Zanchi's earliest works, written while he was still in Italy, the *Compendium praecipuorum capitum doctrinae christianae* (in *Opera*, VIII) is a fragmentary compend of Calvin's *Institutes* based upon either the 1543 or 1545 edition. The *Compendium* follows the order of this third major rescension of the *Institutes*, adding *De confessione peccatorum* as a tenth *locus*, following *De poenitentia*; and *De scandalo* as a fourteenth *locus* following *De libertate christiana*. The fifteenth *locus* (xiii in the *Institutes*) is *De traditionibus humanis*: after this, as a conclusion to his *Compendium*, Zanchi makes as a separate chapter *De traditionibus ecclesiasticis*. Chapters xiv-xxi of the *Institutes* are omitted, and with them the topics predestination, providence, sacraments, prayer, political government, and Christian life. See Joseph Tylenda, "Girolamo Zanchi and John Calvin," in *Calvin Theological Journal*, X (1975), 101-141 for an examination of the relationship of the two men as evidenced in their letters.

95. Cf. *De praedestinatione*, col. 308-309, 311, etc. I have found no citation of Beza in this treatise, nor any of Calvin.

96. Cf. Donnelly, "Calvinist Thomism," pp. 444-445, 454-455. Donnelly's conclusion, that the Reformation cannot ultimately be described according to Lortz' thesis of a theology grounded on a defective nominalistic philosophy but must be seen as a theological movement which used a variety of medieval insights, including the Thomist, is essentially correct. We need to emphasize, however, in addition to the Thomist, a Scotist influence which may appear even in Zanchi and certainly is clear in Musculus, Calvin, and among the writers of the late 16th century, Polanus and Junius.

97. Cf. *De praedestinatione*, col. 280 where Zanchi speaks of the "voluntas absoluta seu arcana" emphasizing the immutability of God's will and also, perhaps, manifesting a Scotist tendency.

98. Ibid., cols. 281, 286, 305.

99. Ibid., col. 305.

100. Ibid., cols. 305-306; *De natura Dei*, col. 481.

101. Cf. Gründler, p. 112, who maintains that Zanchi was a supralapsarian.

102. *De praedestinatione*, col. 307.

103. Cf. *De civitate Dei*, XV, cap. 1; and *Summa theologica*, I, q. 22.

104. *De natura Dei*, col. 485: "Quo melius mysterium hoc intelligatur, res a posteriori, hoc est, ab effectis, provigesta sunt, ante oculos nobis proponenda est. Videmus in primis creatum a Deo fuisse hominem, ad imaginem & similitudinem suam. Deinde cernimus, creatum hominem a Deo volente & sciente, permissum fuisse in peccatum labi, mortieque obnoxium fieri, & in eo totum quoque humanum genus. Tertio animadvertimus, a peccato & morte non omnes eripi, neque etiam in eis relinqui. Sed quosdam a peccato ad iustitiam, & a morte ad aeternam vitam, per Christum misericorditer liberari. Reliquos vero in peccatis suis, & in morte, in cuius fauces propter peccatum incurrerunt, iusto Dei iudicio, relinqui."

105. Ibid.

106. *De praedestinatione*, col. 387.

107. Ibid.,cols. 317-318.

108. *Opera*, I, cols. 4-7, 42-82.

109. Ibid., I, cols. 35, 37, 41, 44, 46, 47, 59, 60, 97, 110, etc.

110. Ibid., I, cols. 25-32, 229-294 passim, 423-437.

111. *De tribus Elohim*, col. 540: "His autem diversis nominibus distinguuntur tantum officia & persona: non autem essentia. Quare, quod etiam Mediator contendit, post tot allata testimonia: Patrem solum esse *autotheon*, hoc sensu: quia ipse solus a seipso est, & nihil habet ab alio: Filius autem quicquid est & habet, totum habet a Patre, & est Deus de Deo: qua de causa omnia semper accepta fert Patri: totum hoc facile damus. Sed vicissim ipse quoque fateatur, Christum etiam *autotheon* alio esse sensu: nempe quod sit Deus per essentiam (sic enim loqui liceat explicandi causa) quae essentia tametsi communicata est, omnis tamen principii expers sit: & tam sit soipsa in Filio, quam est in Patre."

112. Ibid., col. 540: "Sic de vita. Filius enim quod habeat vitam, habet a Patre.Io.5.29. Sed illa vita quia est eandem cum vita Patris, non est ab alio, sed a seipsa. Atque ita Christus est *autozon*, & *autozoe*, sicut & Pater. Idem de essentia dico. Est itaque ipse quoque Filius hoc, quem explicavi, sensu *autotheos* & ex consequenti, ratione huius essentiae, quae eadem est prorsus in Patre, & in Filio, Pater & Filius unus tantum sunt Deus."

113. Ibid., col. 169.

114. Ibid., cols. 169-170.

115. *De natura Dei*, col. 517.

116. Ibid., "Nam quod praemiserit, per Iesum Christum, quasi distinguens Patrem qui nos praedestinavit, a Christo per quem praedestinavit: discriminat Christum a Patre in hoc negotio, tanquam Mediatorem ab eo, apud quam Mediatorem pro nobis agit. . . . in quonam firmata sit nostri electio: eoque quanam in re nostri praedestinationem inquirere, contemplari, & spectare debeamus, nempe in Christo. Quare qui se iam vident in Christo per fidem, eos certos esse debere de sui electione, quia facta est in solo Christo Domino nostro."

117. Ibid., col. 535: "Itaque cum ait Apostolus, nos electos fuisse in Christo: Christus proponitur considerandus, non ut purus Deus, neq: ut simplex homo: sed ut Deus & homo simul, cum officio Mediatoris aeterna." When Gründler (pp. 115-116) cites from the same section (col. 535) "Christum esse primum praedestinationis effectum" as evidence that Christ is the effect of the decree rather than, in Barth's language, electing God, he misses the point of Zanchi's distinctions according to which Christ both promulgates the decree and, as mediator, stands subordinate to it. Gründler emphasizes the latter part of the distinction to the exclusion of the former.

118. *Opera*, VIII, col. 453 se seq.

119. *De religione christiana fides*, cap. I, art. i-ii in *Opera*, VIII.

120. Donnelly well says that "Zanchi should not be seen as an incipient rationalist, for his loyalty to the principle of *sola scriptura* cannot be questioned" and then follows the point with careful documentation: see his "Italian Influences on the Development of Calvinist Scholasticism," in *Sixteenth Century Journal*, vol. VII, no. 1, p. 92. The scriptural principle of theology together with the relation of scripture as Word to Christ as Word appears powerfully in Zanchi's *Praefatiuncula in locos communes: cur priore loco de sacris Scripturis agendum sit: & quae methodus servanda* (in *Opera*, VIII, cols. 297-452): "Sed nec Deus ipse, vere & salutariter cognosci a nobis potest sine Scripturis, quae sunt ipsius sermo, Ioh. 1. *Deum nemo vidit unquam: Filius qui est in sinu Patris, ille nobis enarravit*" (col. 319).

121. Ibid., I.xii-xiii.

122. Ibid., I.xiv.

123. Ibid., II.i-iii.

124. Ibid., III.i-ii.

125. *De ecclesia*, in *Opera*, VII, part II, col. 51 et seq.

126. Ibid., col. 65: "Quod cum omnes essemus ex eadem terra ac massa, perditi in Adamo, obnoxii morti: tamen hac massa, elegerit sibi nos atque exaltarit in hunc excelsum dignitatis gradum,

nempe, ut essemus sponsa Christi, filii Dei, haeredes aeternae vitae, & totius mundi: item, ut essemus sancti, immaculati, ut fieremus una caro cum Christo, & corpus eius, ut cum illo in aeternam regnemus in coelis, & omnes creaturae nobis inservirent, omniaque beneficia, quae per Christum nobis parta sunt, assequeremur, idque gratis, pro sua misericordia & beneplacito."

127. *De religione christiana fides*, III.iii.

128. Cf., ibid., III.iv.

129. Ibid., III.v.

130. Ibid., III.vi-vii.

131. Ibid., III.viii.

132. Ibid.

133. Ibid.

134. Ibid., IV-VI.

135. Ibid., IV.i.

136. Cf.ibid., V.i.

137. Ibid., VI.v.

138. Ibid., VII.i.

139. Ibid., VII.iv.

140. Ibid., VII.iv. Cf. VII.vi. Cf. Aquinas, *Summa theologica*, II, q. 81, a. 4. We note the similarity between Zanchi's doctrine and that of Aquinas with the qualification that this is also the generally accepted doctrine of German Reformed theology, including the Heidelberg Catechism: see Hodge, *The Atonement*, p. 116.

141. Ibid., IX.ii.

142. Ibid., IX.iv.

143. Ibid., X.i.

144. Ibid., XI.i.

145. Ibid., XI.i.

146. Ibid., XI.ii.

147. Ibid., XI.v, viii.

148. Cf. Gründler, pp. 124-126.

149. *De incarnatione filii Dei*, in *Opera*, VIII, col. 30. "Primum, ante Mundi constitutionem, Filium fuisse a Patre destinatum ad sumendam formam servi, seu humanam naturam . . . propter salutem nostram."

150. Ibid., col. 31.

151. *De religione christiana fides*, XI.iv; cf. *De incarnatione*, col. 16.

152. *De religione christiana fides*, XI.ix.

153. Ibid., XI.x.

154. Ibid., XI.xii.

155. Cf. ibid., XI.xv; XII.vi. Zanchi is remembered as having stressed the *unio mystica* as the ground of the imputation of Christ's benefits to us: indeed he strongly presses (XII.iii) a theme of union or communion with Christ as the form of salvation—"Ad veram salutis participationem, quam necessaria sit vera unio seu *koinonia* cum Christo."

156. Ibid.,XII.i.

157. Cf. Olivier Fatio, *Méthode et théologie: Lambert Daneau et les débuts de la scholastique reformée* (Geneva, 1976).

158. *Propositions and principles of divinitie propounded . . . in the University of Geneva . . . under M. Theod. Beza and M. Anthonie Faius* (Edinburgh?, 1595): note the general order and in particular see thesis XII in which J. J. Poliander distinguishes between analytic and synthetic, preferring the synthetic method.

159. *Quaestionum et responsionum*, pp. 85-99.

VI. CALVINISM AT THE CLOSE OF THE SIXTEENTH CENTURY:
POLANUS AND PERKINS

1. On Ramus see Walter Ong, *Ramus, Method, and the Decay of Dialogue* (Cambridge, Mass., 1958) and Perry Miller, *The New England Mind: the Seventeenth Century* (N.Y., 1939), chapters 5 and 6. Moltmann's distinction between the *heilsgeschichtlicher Aposteriorismus* of the Ramists and the *dogmatischer Apriorismus* of "Bezan" orthodoxy, cannot be maintained. Polanus, Perkins, and Ames all utilize Ramist patterns of argument and also formulate doctrine in an *a priori* manner. In addition, the covenantal theology developed in Heidelberg by Olevian, Ursinus, and Zanchius was non-Ramist and fully Aristotelian. If aware of the value of *a posteriori*, salvation-historical motifs, this theology was also quite certain of the value of the dogmatic *a priori* and in no way hostile to the less-developed systematic forms produced by Beza. Cf. Jürgen Moltmann, "Zur Bedeutung des Petrus Ramus fur Philosophie und Theologie im Calvinismus," *Zeitschrift für Kirchengeschichte*, LXVIII (1956-57), pp. 295-318; and for a cogent argument against Moltmann in the context of Olevian's theology, see Bierma, "The Covenant Theology of Caspar Olevian," pp. 229-238.

2. *Partitiones theologicae*, trs. as *The Substance of the Christian Religion* (London, 1596), p. 1; hereinafter cited as *Substance*. The Polanus bibliography is quite small: Ernst Staehelin, *Amandus Polanus von Polansdorf* (Basel, 1955) and Heiner Faulenbach, *Die Struktur der Theologie des Amandus Polanus von Polansdorf* (Zurich, 1967) are the only items known to this author. The reader should also consult Ritschl's *Dogmengeschichte*, III, pp. 291-293, Gass' *Geschichte*, I, pp. 396-404 and the brief article in RGG[iii]. Staehelin reproduces Polanus' teaching syllabus but gives little analysis of his thought—although he notes (p. 76) Polanus' hesitance to speculate about the decrees, particularly the decree of reprobation. Faulenbach gives an exhaustive analysis of Polanus' prolegomena, but deals with the rest of the system selectively, viewing predestination as the central focus (cf. pp. 173-174, 314-319). References to the *Syntagma* follow the Geneva edition (1617), one volume, folio. I have also checked citations of *The Substance of the Christian Religion* against Polanus' reduced version of the *Partitiones*, printed in the *Syntagma* as *Synopsis totius Syntagmatis*, unpaginated, immediately following the title page.

3. Cf. William Ames, *Medulla s.s. theologiae* (Amsterdam, 1623) and the introduction by John Eusden to his translation, *The Marrow of Theology* (Durham, N.C., 1983) pp. 15-16. Alexander Schweizer in his "Die Entwickelung des Moralsystems in der reformierten Kirche," in *Theologische Studien und Kritiken* (1850), p. 53, comments that Ramist logic is an essential part of the thought of both Polanus and Ames. Hugo Visscher, *William Ames: His Life and Work*, trs. Horton (Harvard Divinity School Library, 1965), p. 80 disagrees, denying Polanus' Ramism. Faulenbach settles the issue in favor of a critical use of Ramist principles by Polanus (pp. 25-27) together with more traditional Aristotelian structures.

4. *Syntagma*, IV.i-iii; *Substance*, pp. 13-14; cf. Gass, I, p. 399.

5. Even so Thomas Watson in his *A Body of Practical Divinity* (1696) relates the decrees to the immutability of God, but in the course of his system emphasizes covenantal theology and personal appropriation of Christ through faith. Watson's system, a commentary on the Westminster *Shorter Catechism*, emphasizes the practical uses of doctrine under each *locus*. It also perpetuates in English federalism the tradition reaching back to Ursinus, Olevian and Bastingius of credal or catechetical lectures as the basis of systematic theology.

6. Faulenbach tends to view the order of the system as a sign of increased determinism, but offers little actual proof of effect on other doctrines. He does not deal with Polanus' soteriology as a whole. As with Calvin, Ursinus, and Zanchius, the principle of election enters Polanus' ecclesiology, but this is more the continuance of the Augustinian tradition and the polemic against the Roman hierarchy than an intrusion of metaphysical categories for their own sake.

7. CD, II/2, p. 78. This is clear in Polanus' argument on the problem of original sin and the imputation of guilt. He speaks of the former as that sin arising from the wrongful exercise of free

will by the first parents, which descends by "carnal generation" to all mankind. Original guilt in Adam brought death to man while original corruption caused a corruption of human nature, a darkness of mind, a disorder of the affections. Polanus does not derive the fall or the imputation of guilt from the decrees—thus refusing to follow the more deterministic line of Beza on these points: see *Substance*, pp. 9, 13, 23-24, 31-32; *Syntagma*, VI.iii. The conception of human sin found in Bucanus' *Institutions* is similar, and in view of its more covenantal scheme is still further from Beza: Adam's sin was voluntary and is imputed to all men because Adam is the foundation of all mankind (pp. 159-61, 436).

    8. Ritschl in *Dogmengeschichte*, III, pp. 291-92, notes that Polanus speaks of God's love, showing a Zwinglian influence, much in the way that Calvin employs the term *gloria dei* to describe the eternal purpose. Cf. James Orr, *The Progress of Dogma* (Grand Rapids, 1962), pp. 295-96. Orr feels this to be a departure from Calvin's position, but he states his case with restraint, without accusing the later Calvinists of devising a metaphysical principle of organization.

    9. Barth, CD, II/2, p. 78.

    10. CD, II/2, p. 79.

    11. Gisbert Voetius, *Disputationes* (1648-49) in RDB, pp. 269, 289, 290. Cf. Marshall Knappen, *Tudor Puritanism* (Chicago, 1965), p. 219. On Perkins' life see the article "William Perkins" by Sidney Lee in DNB, and for a more critical appraisal, Ian Breward, "The Significance of William Perkins," in *The Journal of Religious History*, vol. IV (1966-67), pp. 113-28.

    12. *Geschichte des Pietismus und der Mystik in der reformirten Kirche* (Leiden, 1879), pp. 24-26. August Lang, *Puritanismus und Pietismus* (Neukirchen, 1941), pp. 109-119; Christopher Hill, *Puritanism and Revolution* (New York, 1964), p. 217.

    13. F.Ernest Stoeffler, *The Rise of Evangelical Pietism* (Leiden, 1965), p. 55; the second volume is entitled *German Pietism During the Eighteenth Century* (Leiden, 1973). In this latter study Stoeffler notes that Perkins' and Ames' views of theology and its purpose "wedded now to the Cocceian methodology" was instrumental in the formulation of Lampe's theology (p. 233).

    14. "Calvin Against the Calvinists," loc. cit., pp. 29-30.

    15. Ian Breward (ed.), *The Work of William Perkins* (Appleford, 1970), p. 83.

    16. Ibid., p. 85.

    17. R. T. Kendall, *Calvinism and English Calvinism to 1649* (New York, 1979), pp. 29-33, 54-56.

    18. Lang, p. 115.

    19. Cf. Richard A. Muller, "Perkins' *A Golden Chaine*: Predestinarian System or Schematized *Ordo Salutis*?" in *Sixteenth Century Journal*, vol. IX, no. 1 (April, 1978), pp. 69-81. *A Golden Chaine* is found in Perkins' *Workes*, vol. I, pp. 11-117.

    20. Cf. Herman Rennecherus, *Aurea salutis catena* (Herborn, 1589), trs. *The Golden Chayne of Salvation* (London, 1604), an extended theological analysis of the Pauline passage.

    21. *Substance*, p. 63; cf. *Synopsis totius syntagmatis*, Lib. VI.

    22. *Syntagma*, VI.xi (p. 360, col. 1).

    23. Ibid., VI.xii (p. 362, col. 1); cf. Muller, "Christ in the Eschaton," pp. 53-55.

    24. Ibid., VI.xii (p. 362, col. 1).

    25. Ibid.

    26. Ibid.

    27. Ibid.

    28. Ibid.

    29. Ibid., VI.xii (p. 362, col. 1).

    30. Ibid., (p. 362, col. 2).

    31. Ibid., (pp. 362-363).

    32. From *Synopsis totius syntagmatis*; Lib. VI.

    33. *Syntagma*,VI.xiii (p. 363, col. 2).

    34. Ibid.

    35. G. C. Berkouwer, *The Work of Christ*, pp. 35-36; also E. F. K. Müller, "Doppelter Stand

Christi," in RPTK, vol. XVIII. The most important study of this doctrine is still Schneckenburger's *Zur kirchlichen Christologie*, which unfortunately does not refer directly to Polanus.

36. Müller, "Doppelter Stand Christi," p. 757, lines 5-20; cf. Bruce, *The Humiliation of Christ*, pp. 115-116.

37. Hoogland, p. 45.

38. Müller, "Doppelter Stand Christi," p. 757.

39. *Syntagma*, VI.xxii; cf. Wollebius, *Compendium*, I.xviii.1. The concealment is often called by the Reformed "occultatio" as in Zanchius' *De incarnatione*, Lib. I, in *Opera*, VIII, col. 34; cf. Bruce, pp. 126-129; Hoogland, p. 49. This is not at all to be confused with the Lutheran sense of *krupsis* associated with Brenz and the Tubingen theologians, according to which the human nature of Christ receives the divine attributes in the *genus majestaticum* of the *communicatio idiomatum* but hides them in the course of the *humiliatio* (see Schmid, DTEL, pp. 389-391).

40. *Syntagma*, VI.xiii (p. 364, col. 1).

41. Ibid.

42. *Syntagma*, VI.xiii (p. 364, col. 1).

43. Ibid. VI.xiii (p. 364, col. 1-2).

44. Ibid.

45. Ibid.

46. Ibid.

47. Ibid., (col. 2).

48. Müller, "Doppelter Stand Christi," p. 758.

49. Schneckenburger, *Zur kirchlichen Christologie*, pp. 6, 17-18.

50. *Substance*, p. 65; *Syntagma*, VI.xvi. It is here, of course, that the Chalcedonian boundary of Polanus' exposition comes to the fore and the hypostatic union is discussed at length.

51. *Substance*, pp. 65-66; *Syntagma*, VI.xvi (p. 379, col. 2C), and cf. Bucanus, *Institutions*, II.xv.

52. *Syntagma*, VI.xvi (p. 378, col. 1); *Substance*, p. 66; cf. Hoogland, pp. 76-77.

53. *Substance*, p. 70; *Syntagma*, VI.xii.xviii (p. 385ff.).

54. *Substance*, pp. 69-79; Staehelin (pp. 50-51) states that Polanus was the author of the official answer to Piscator's insistence on the soteriological value of only the passive obedience set forth in November 1603 by the national synod of French Protestants at Gap.

55. *Syntagma*, VI.xviii (p. 387, col. 1) and VI.xix (p. 408, col. 1); cf. *Substance*, pp. 70-71; Inst., II.xvi.5.

56. *Substance*, pp. 75-78; *Syntagma*, VI.xxii.

57. *Substance*, pp. 76-77.

58. Ibid., p. 78; *Syntagma*, VI.xxvi; cf. Bucanus, *Institutions*, cap. xxxviii, sec. 13.

59. *Syntagma*, VI.xxii; cf. Hoogland, p. 52.

60. *Substance*, p. 78; cf. *Syntagma*, VI.xxvii (p. 428, col. 1): "Officium Christi, est quod ipse solus inde ab initio mundi est Mediator inter Deum & electos ad vitam aeternam, a Deo impetrans & efficaciter conferans electis omnia quae ad aeternam ipsorum salutem requiruntur, atque adeo ipsam vitam aeternam."

61. Calvin, *Institutes*, II.xv.1; also, Keckermann, *Systema sacrosanctae theologiae* (Geneva, 1611) as cited by Heppe in RD, p. 410 and Brunner, *The Doctrine of Creation and Redemption*, pp. 273-274.

62. *Substance*, p. 79; *Syntagma*, VI.xxvii. (p. 430, col. 1). Cf. *Syntagma*, VI.xxix (p. 441, col. 2) and note Ames, *Marrow*, I.xix.11-13 where Ames shows prophet, priest, and king to be the "order" of Christ's office according to human need, historical effecting, and personal application; also Berkouwer, *The Work of Christ*, p. 60.

63. *Syntagma*, VI.xxvii (p. 434, col. 1): "Persona Christi a Persona Dei Patris distinguitur secundum hypostaseos naturam realiter: secundum officium vero distinguitur a Deo non per naturam, sed per voluntariam oeconomiam seu dispensatione gratiae. Itaque eadem persona quae secundum naturam Deus est aequalis Patri, secundum voluntariam dispensationem & Deo & seipsa minor

est. . . ." Cf. *Syntagma*, VI.xxiii (p. 364, col. 1): "Incarnationis aeterni Filii Dei *causa efficiens princeps* atque autor est tota Sacrosancta Trinitas, Pater, Filius, & Spiritu Sancto. . . ." Cf. Scharpius, *Cursus theologicus*, I, col. 819: "Hinc Pater maior Christo dicitur, non tamen excluditur voluntas Christi, aut Sp. Sancti: servatur enim in Christi ordinatione ad officium idem agendi modus, qui aliis Dei actionibus: ideo Deo essentialiter sumpto tribuitur, I. Cor. 1.36. Materia seu subiectum officii est persona Mediatoris, quia propter officium facta est incarnato, & duarum naturarum unio personalis."

64. *Syntagma*, VI.xxvii (p. 428, col. 2 - 429, col. 2): ". . . dicitur de aeterno Dei Filio, Christo Domino, qui inde ab initio mundi fuit atque est inter Deum & filios Dei seu creaturas rationales ad imaginem Dei conditas Mediator, per quem solum illae statim initio habuerunt, & habent beatitudinem, hoc est communionem & fruitionem Dei tanquam summi boni. . . . Mediatorem autem apud Deum nacti sumus non ex nostro merito, sed ex gratia & amore Dei erga nos, quia eum nobis suscitavit Iehova Deus Noster, id est, ratione federis gratuiti, sed quatenus nobiscum gratuitum fedus iniit. . . . Datus est nobis Mediator apud Deum juxta aeternum decretum Dei. . . ." Cf. Ibid. VI.xxvii (p. 434, col. 1) as cited above, note 123.

65. Cf. Pannenberg, *Jesus—God and Man*, p. 124 (as cited above, chapter II, note 207). Note how Ames in 1623 still follows as the central christological interest of his system this historical pattern: "the Person of the Mediator," considered according to the union of the two natures is encountered first as the divine answer in the temporal economy to the problem of sin (see *Marrow*, I.xvii.8-14) so that the identification of the "person" as eternal occurs from the vantage point of his historical manifestation and must be defined in terms of his office (I.xix, particularly 16, 20, 28 where the divine-human person of the mediator appears from the various aspects of the office) and in his states (I.xx-xxiii). The weight of Ames' exposition falls upon the exposition of the *status duplex* as considered of the mediator as God-man (I.xx.3).

66. *Substance*, p. 80; *Syntagma*, VI.xxix; cf. Faulenbach, pp. 52-53.

67. *Syntagma*, VI.xxvii (p. 437, col. 2).

68. *Substance*, pp. 80-81; Cf. *Syntagma*, VI.xxix (p. 442, cols. 1, 2): "Expiatio nostrorum peccatorum est prima Sacerdotalis officii Christi pars, dum Christus offerens Deo Patri unicum sacrificium suiipsius, poenam pro peccatis electorum persolvit, ac reconciliandum electos Deo, & ad redimendum illos ad omni potestate Diaboli. . . . Intercessio apud Deum pro nobis, est altera Sacerdotalis officii Christi pars, dum satisfactione sua efficit, ut Pater nos in gratiam recipiat & aeternum servet." Polanus does not conceive of a single, separate *locus* of atonement, but deals with this problem under three heads—the death of Christ, the priestly office, and the covenant of grace.

69. *Substance*, pp. 81-82; cf. *Syntagma*, VI.xxix (p. 442, col. 2 - p. 443, col. 1). The kingly office is therefore sometimes referred specifically to the *status exaltationis* as an aspect of Christ's office not clearly witnessed during the *humiliatio*; yet the *munus regium* is eternal since it belongs to the *munus triplex*. On the eternity of the *munus regium*, see the "Excursus: the duration of the *munus regium* in the theology of Calvin's successors," appended to Muller, "Christ in the Eschaton." Also, cf. Berkhof, *Systematic Theology*, pp. 409-410 and Pannenberg, *Jesus—God and Man*, pp. 218, 223. Pannenberg's critique of the doctrine of the kingly office in Reformed theology does not sufficiently take into account the differences between Reformed and Lutheran theology on the interpretation of *kenosis* and wrongly cites Keckermann as simply assigning the kingly office to the *status exaltationis*. What Keckermann says is, "Sicut propheticum & sacerdotale munus praecipue ad statam humiliationis pertinet, ita regium officium statum exaltationis potissimum complectitur: etsi in statu humiliationis aliquot Regiae suae dignititu & potestatu specimina ediderit" (*Systema ss. theologiae*, III.v).

70. Cf. Ames, *Medulla*, I.xix.11-13.

71. *An Exposition of the Symbole*, p. 125, col. 1A; cf. Schneckenburger, *Vergleichende Darstellung*, II, 228. Cf. the similar structure in Viret's *A verie familiare exposition of the Apostles Crede*, fol.Dv, recto-verso; so also Ames, *Medulla*, I.xviii; and Watson, *A Body of Practical Divinity*, IV.2; also Downame, *The Summe of Sacred Divinitie*, II.i-iv.

72. *An Exposition of the Symbole*, p. 165, col. 2. Perkins' Christology stands as the longest

single doctrinal segment of *An Exposition of the Symbole* and it contains not only the dogmatic material to be discussed above, but an abundance of Christ-centered meditation or Christ-piety in which Perkins examines the "uses" of the doctrine.

73. Ibid., cols. 1D-2A.

74. *An Exposition of the Symbole*, p. 168, col. 2-169, col. 1.

75. Ibid., p. 169, col. 1. Perkins stands at one with the other early orthodox on the issue of the eternity of the kingly office and the eschatological subordination of Christ to the Father: as he is God, Christ has an eternal kingdom; as he is mediator "his kingdome shall cease, not simply, but in respect of the outward manner of administration"—the subordination refers not to the person of the mediator as God-man but to his human nature and to his mystical body, the church: cf. ibid., p. 172, col. 2.

76. Herman Bavinck, *Our Reasonable Faith: A Survey of Christian Doctrine*, trs. H. Zylstra (Grand Rapids, 1956), p. 333.

77. Cf. Ames, *Marrow*, I.xviii.12: "the office imposed upon his person."

78. An Exposition of the Symbole, p. 169, col. 1A-B; also, see Wollebius, *Compendium*, I.xvii, props. 3, 4, 6, 8; Ames, *Marrow*, I.xix.4-6 (where the *pactum salutis* enters the formulation); *Conf. West*, VIII.i and iii; Watson, *A Body of Practical Divinity*, IV.6 (p. 192); and John Owen, *Salus Electorum, Sanguinis Jesu; or, The Death of Death in the Death of Christ* (1647), Book I, chapter 3, in *The Works of John Owen*, edited by William H. Goold (London, 1850-53), vol. X, pp. 163-174. Cf. Keckermann, *Systema*, III.iii.13: "Christus ab aeterno Patre ad officium omne suum unctus est ab aeterno, in tempore vero ad idem missus. . . . Christus unctus est, non quidem oleo aliquo corporali sed aeterno Patris decreto & ordinatione, per communionem Spiritus S."

79. Ibid., p. 171, col. 1-2, and margin.

80. Ibid., p. 171, col. 2 - p. 172, col. 1.

81. *An Exposition of the Symbole*, pp. 177-178; cf. *A Golden Chaine*, ch. XV (p. 24); also see Schneckenburger, *Zur kirchlichen Christologie*, pp. 45-46.

82. *An Exposition of the Symbole*, p. 173, col. 2.

83. Ibid., p. 177, col. 2.

84. Ibid., p. 177, col. 2.

85. *A Golden Chaine*, ch. XV (p. 24, col. 1-2).

86. Cf. ibid., ch. XIV with XV.

87. Ibid., ch. XV (p. 24).

88. Ibid., ch. XV (pp. 24, col. 2-25, col. 1).

89. *An Exposition of the Symbole*, p. 178, col. 1B.

90. Ibid., p. 178, cols. 1C-2A.

91. *A Golden Chaine*, ch. XV (p. 25).

92. Ibid., ch. XVI (p. 25, col. 1-2).

93. Ibid.

94. *An Exposition of the Symbole*, p. 181, col. 1A. The concept of the impersonality of the human nature, not stated by Calvin, actually represents a step beyond Chalcedon.

95. Ibid., p. 180, col. 2C.

96. Ibid., p. 181, col. 1C.

97. Ibid., col. 2A-C; cf. Schneckenburger, *Vergleichende Darstellung*, II, 194-195.

98. *An Exposition of the Symbole*, p. 181, col. 2D.

99. Keckermann, *Systema ss. theologiae*, III.ii: "Persona Christi est substantia Mediatoris, divina & humana natura constans." And Bucanus, *Institutions of Christian Religion*, cap. II (pp. 13-14) begins by defining the word "Christ" as the "anointed Saviour," the promised "King . . . Priest, and Prophet" and then asks, "Doth this name Christ signify his nature or his person?" Bucanus answers, "His person subsisting in both his natures, and not this or that nature alone: for it is a name concrete, as the Grammarians speak, not abstract." Only after addressing the true divinity and true humanity of the person of Christ (pp. 14-18) does Bucanus broach the issue of the eternal personhood of the Son (p. 18).

100. Ibid., p. 182, col. 1 - p. 185, col. 2.
101. Ibid., p. 185, col. 2A; cf. Schneckenburger, *Zur kirchlichen Christologie*, p. 44.
102. *An Exposition of the Symbole*, p. 185, col. 2B.
103. Ibid.
104. Ibid., p. 205, col. 1C.
105. Ibid., p. 186, col. 1D.
106. *An Exposition of the Symbole*, p. 181, col. 2D. Following Calvin, and like Polanus, Perkins includes the active obedience in the work of the salvation of mankind. Again the emphasis is on the historical Christ who is apprehended in his manhood but who mysteriously works our salvation not by his merits but by reason of his person, which is divine. Cf. Schneckenburger, *Zur kirchlichen Christologie*, pp. 52-53.
107. *An Exposition of the Symbole*, p. 186, col. 2D.
108. *A Golden Chaine*, p. 28, col. 2C-D.
109. *An Exposition of the Symbole*, p. 186, col. 1.
110. Ibid., p. 235, col. 1A.
111. Ibid., p. 246, col. 2A-B, and p. 251, col. 2D—p. 252, col. 1A.
112. Ibid., p. 252, cols. 1D-2C.
113. *Syntagma*, IV.vii (p. 243, col. 1).
114. Cf. ibid., VI.i, vii, viii; *Substance*, p. 44.
115. This is the subject of the entirety of *Syntagma*, Liber IV.
116. *Syntagma*, IV.i.
117. Ibid.
118. Ibid., IV.ii.
119. Ibid., IV.ii.
120. Ibid., IV.iii (p. 437, col. 1).
121. Ibid.
122. Ibid.
123. Ibid.,IV.v.
124. Ibid., IV.vi.
125. Ibid.
126. Cf. *Synopsis totius syntagmatis*, Lib. IV.
127. *Syntagma*, IV.vi (p. 242, col. 2).
128. Ibid., IV.vi (p. 238, col. 2 and p. 240, col. 1). Cf. RD, pp. 137-138.
129. *Syntagma*, III.v (col. 205).
130. Cf. Berkhof, *Introduction*, p. 73.
131. *Syntagma*, IV.vi (p. 239, col. 2).
132. Ibid., IV.vi (pp. 239-240).
133. Ibid. (p. 240, col. 1).
134. Ibid.
135. Ibid.
136. Ibid. (p. 240, col. 1-2).
137. Ibid. (p. 240, col. 2).
138. Ibid., IV.vi (p. 241, col. 1).
139. Ibid. (p. 242, col. 2). Cf. the discussion of God's willing *ex necessitate naturae*, *Syntagma* II.xix (p. 161, col. 2) where Polanus explicitly cites Aquinas from the *Summa contra Gentiles*. Also see Minges, vol. II, pp. 133-134, 158-161, 167-168.
140. Ibid., IV.vii (p. 243, col. 2).
141. Ibid., p. 243, col. 2 - p. 244, col. 1.
142. Ibid., IV.vii (p. 244, col. 1).
143. Ibid., IV.vii (p. 244, col. 1).
144. Ibid.
145. Ibid.

146. Ibid.,IV.viii, ix.

147. Polanus' italics; ibid., p. 244, col. 2A: "Aeterna electio, est praedestinatio creaturarum rationalium in mente divina ad gratiosum beatumque finem. Estque tum *Christi*, tum *unitorum Christo*." Similarly, Johannes Scharpius, *Cursus theologicus in quo controversia omnes de fide dogmatibus hoc seculo exagitatae*. In duos tomos divisis (Geneva, 1620), tome I, col. 243: "Electio pro ratione subiecti duplex est. 1. Christi. 2. Unitorum Christo."

148. *Syntagma*, IV.viii (p. 244, col. 2A-B): "*Aeterna electio Christi*, est praedestinatio qua deus Filium suum ungenitum designavit ab aeterno, ut etiam quo ad suam humanam naturam esset Filius Dei & caput Angelorum & hominum, & Mediator inter Deum & Angelos hominesque." Cf. Scharpius, *Cursus theologicus*, I, col. 243: "Electio Christi est praedestinatio qua Deus ab aeterno filium suum fore caput hominem & Angelorum & Mediatorem inter se & electos decrevit. Isa.42.1. Matt.12.18. I Pet.1.20. Electio unitorum Christi est vel Angelorum vel hominum."

149. Ibid., IV.viii (p. 244, col. 2): "Christus est secundum ambas naturas, divinam & humanam unus Filius Dei, non duo: secundum divinam quidem, naturali ex Patri generatione, sic ut secundum illam sit Filius Dei non electus, sed generatus, secundum human verotum electione eterna, tum creatione ad imaginem Dei, tum gratia unionis personalis cum divina natura."

150. Ibid., IV.viii (p. 244, col. 2).

151. *An Exposition of the Symbole*, p. 165, col. 2C.

152. Walaeus, *Opera* (Leyden, 1643), I, p. 329, col. 1 and II, pp. 247-249.

153. Cf. Ames, *Medulla*, I.xxv.29.

154. *Syntagma*, IV.viii (p. 244, col. 2).

155. Ibid., IV.ix (p. 245, col. 1).

156. Ibid. (p. 245, col. 1).

157. Ibid. (p. 245, col. 1).

158. Ibid.

159. Ibid.: "Caeterum *dari Christo a Patre* ambiguum est: nam quosdam dedit Pater Christo quos Apostolos designaret, quosdam Pater dedit Christo quos aeternam servaret. . . ." Cf. Scharpius, *Cursus theologicus*, I, cols. 244-245: "Causa efficiens principalis electionis est Deus Pater, Filius, & Sp. S. . . . Subiectum *en ho* in quo electi sumus est Christus, non qua est Deus tantum quia ita est efficiens causa electionis. Ioh.13.18 non quia homo tantum quia merus homo non idoneus erat in quo eligeremur, sed qua *theanthropos* & Mediator noster, Eph.1.5. in illo autem electi sumus."

160. Ibid.,IV.ix (p. 249).

161. Cf. Barth, CD, II/2, p. 111 with Reid, "The Office of Christ in Predestination," p. 15: Reid notes the structure in Bucanus' *Institutions*, cap. xxxvi, but fails to realize its importance to Reformed theology in general. Cf. Scharpius, *Cursus theologicus* I, cols. 244-245; Bucanus, *Institutions*, cap. ii and xxxvi; Keckermann, *Systema*, I.vi; III.i-ii, and below on Perkins.

162. Ibid., IV.ix (p. 425, col. 2 - p. 426, col. 1).

163. Ibid. (p. 248, col. 1).

164. Ibid., IV.ix (p. 248, col. 2).

165. Ibid., IV.ix (p. 248, col. 2): "Electionis subiectum *en ho*, in quo electi sumus, est Christus, non quatenus Deus, nec quatenus nudus homo, sed quatenus *theanthropos* & Mediator noster. Nam Eph.1.v.4. Paulus Apostolus perspicue docet, quod Deus Pater nos elegerit IN CHRISTO. Medio enim, in quo eligeremur, opus erat: quia sine illo non poterat fieri unio inter Deum eligentem & homines electos. Ita Christus est vinculum, quo Deus & electi conjunguntur. Medium vero aliud esse non debuit quam Christus Filius Dei quatenus *theanthropos*: quia praedestinavit nos quos adoptaret in filios, ad Eph.1.v.5."

166. Ibid. (p. 249, col. 1).

167. Ibid. (p. 249, col. 2).

168. Ibid., p. 249; cf. Barth, CD, II/2, p. 337. Even Dort, which pointed with more certainty than either Polanus or Perkins to the "fructus electionis infallibiles," refused to follow the Bezan pattern of denominating external fruits but referred assurance to the "testimonio Spiritus Sancti" one evidence of which was the "desire to perform good works" rather than works themselves (in Schaff,

CC, vol. III, pp. 554, 573: *Canones Synodi Dordrechtanae*, cap. I, art. xii; cap. V, art. x). Similarly, Bucanus, *Institutions*, cap. xxxvi (pp. 445-446); Perkins, *A Golden Chaine*, p. 113, col. 1; Ames, *Medulla*, I.xxx.12-17; Hommius *LXX Disputationes*, cap. 64; Watson, *A Body of Practical Divinity*, v. 6. Heppe (RD, pp. 176-177) cites also and to the same effect Wollebius, Cocceius, Heidegger, and Keckermann.

169. *Syntagma*, IV.x (p. 250, col. 1).

170. Ibid. (p. 251, col. 1).

171. Ibid. (p. 252, col. 1).

172. *Syntagma*, IV.vi (p. 242).

173. *Systema ss. theologiae*, III.i (col. 173).

174. *Works*, vol. II, pp. 607-608; cf. the similar argumentation in Ames, *Marrow*, I.xxv.19-20.

175. *A Golden Chaine*, ch. I (p. 11, col. 1-2).

176. Cf. *A Golden Chaine*, chs. V and VI, pp. 14-16.

177. Ibid., p. 14, col. 2 - p. 15, col. 1 (my italics).

178. Ibid., ch. VI, p. 15, col. 1.

179. Ibid., p. 14, col. 2.

180. Ibid., p. 15, col. 1.

181. Ibid., p. 15, col. 2; cf. Ritschl, *Dogmengeschichte*, III, pp. 301-302.

182. *A Golden Chaine*, cap. VI (p. 15, col. 1).

183. Ibid., p. 15, col. 1.

184. Ibid., p. 16, col. 1.

185. Ibid., p. 15, col. 2 - p. 16, col. 1.

186. Ibid., p. 15, col. 2; cf. Ritschl, *Dogmengeschichte*, III, p. 303.

187. *A Golden Chaine*, p. 15, col. 2 - p. 16, col. 1.

188. *Workes*, I, p. 277, col. 2.

189. Ibid., p. 277, col. 2.

190. Ibid., p. 278, col. 1.

191. Ibid., p. 278, col. 1; cf. *A Golden Chaine*, chap. 15 (p. 24, col. 1) where Perkins speaks of "the foundation . . . the means . . . (and) the degrees" of election.

192. *Workes*, p. 278, cols. 1-2.

193. Ibid., I, p. 278, col. 2.

194. Ibid.

195. Ibid., p. 278, col. 2 - p. 279, col. 1.

196. Ibid., p. 279, col. 1.

197. *A Treatise*, *Workes*, II, p. 606, col. 1.

198. Ibid., p. 606, cols. 1-2; cf. *A Golden Chaine*, chap. 6 (p. 15, col. 1).

199. *An Exposition of the Symbole*, p. 281, col. 1-2; cf. *A Treatise*, p. 607, col. 1.

200. *A Treatise*, p. 607, col. 1C-D.

201. *An Exposition of the Symbole*, p. 282, col. 1.

202. Ibid., p. 281, col. 1D.

203. Ibid., col. 2A.

204. *A Treatise*, p. 607, col. 2C; Perkins cites II Tim. 2:19 and Rom. 11:1, 2, 5.

205. *Institutes*, III.xxii.1-2.

206. *An Exposition of the Symbole*, p. 281, col. 2.

207. *A Treatise*, p. 607, col. 2D - p. 608, col. 1A.

208. Ibid., p. 608, col. 1B.

209. Ibid., col. 1C.

210. Ibid., p. 608, cols. 1D-2A; cf. *A Golden Chaine*, p. 105, col. 2A.

211. *Workes*, p. 282, col. 2A; cf. Polanus, *Syntagma*, IV.ix; Bucanus, *Institutions*, cap. xxxvi (p. 430); Downham, *The Summe*, II.ii-iv; Johannes Cocceius, *Summa theologiae* (Leiden, 1662),

cap. xxxiv.22 and xxxvii.31; and Trelcatius, *Scholastica et methodica locorum communium*, II.ii, v, vi; Ames, *Medulla*, I.v.19.

212. Compare Arminius, *Works*, I, 247; II, 99-100.

213. *An Exposition of the Symbole*, p. 282, col. 2A-B.

214. Cf. Caspar Olevian, *De substantia foederis gratuiti inter Deum et electos* (Genevva, 1585), a work which was known to Perkins and may have influenced his thought; for later formulations see Turretin, *Institutio theologiae*, XII.ii.12 and Witsius, *De oeconomia foederum Dei cum hominibus* (Utrecht, 1694), II.ii.1; and on the English scene, Edward Fisher, *The Marrow of Modern Divinity* (London, 1645-48), part I, p. 37; also the moderate, Richard Baxter, *Catholike Theologie* (London, 1675), I.ii.38.

215. *Vergleichende Darstellung*, II, pp. 150-151. If Schneckenburger's criticism does not apply to the early orthodox position, it nevertheless represents an insight into the seed of determinism in the *pactum salutis* doctrine: see Richard A. Muller, "The Spirit and the Covenant: John Gill's Critique of the *Pactum Salutis*," in *Foundations: A Baptist Journal of History and Theology*, vol. 24, no. 1 (Jan. 1981), pp. 4-14.

216. *An Exposition of the Symbole*, p. 159, col. 2A-B.

217. *A Treatise*, p. 612, col. 1D.

218. Ibid., p. 608, col. 2A.

219. Ibid., p. 608, col. 2B-C.

220. Ibid., p. 609, col. 1C-D. Cf. Ames, *Marrow*, I.xxiv.9 where we also see a hint of Lombard's formula and where the emphasis, as with Calvin and Ursinus, falls on limited intercession. Also, Polanus, *Substance*, pp. 80-81; *Syntagma*, VI.xxvii.

221. *A Treatise*, p. 609, col. 1.

222. Ibid.

223. Ibid.

224. Ibid., col. 2.

225. Ibid., p. 609, col. 2A-B; cf. Heppe, *Geschichte*, pp. 25-26.

226. *A Treatise*, pp. 607-608; clearly reflecting Calvin on John 17:26, in CO, XLVII, col. 391.

227. *A Treatise*, p. 609, col. 2A-B; *An Exposition of the Symbole*, pp. 186-187.

228. *A Treatise*, p. 609, col. 1C-D; *An Exposition of the Symbole*, p. 186, col. 1C-D.

229. Cf. Murray, *Redemption*, pp. 64-65.

230. *A Treatise*, pp. 607-608; *A Golden Chaine*, p. 105, cols. 1C-2A.

231. *A Treatise*, p. 608, col. 1C.

232. Ibid., p. 610, col. 1D.

233. *Declaratio sententiae* (1608), in *Iacobi Arminii . . . Opera theologica* (Leiden, 1629), p. 119; see further, below, chapter 7.

234. *Disputationes privitae*, XIX.v-vi, in *Opera*, p. 357, col. 2; cf. Pierre DuMoulin, *The Anatomy of Arminianisme* (London, 1620), pp. 28-32.

235. See Ames, *Marrow*, I.xxiv.7; also Keckermann, *Systema sacrosanctae theolgiae*, as cited in RD, p. 410: "This is the nucleus of the whole of theology and this is the supreme cause and the direct beginning of our deliverance from sin: I mean, the execution of the election administered through Christ's merit and efficacy, which the ancient, especially the Greek theologians call the *oikonomia*, i.e., dispensation, of the means leading to salvation."

236. *A Treatise*, p. 610, col. 2 - p. 611, col. 1.

237. *An Exposition of the Symbole*, p. 287, col. 2.

238. Ibid., p. 288, col. 1.

VII. CHRIST AND THE DECREE IN THE DEVELOPMENT
OF EARLY ORTHODOXY: RETROSPECT AND PROSPECT

1. Cf. Bauke, *Die Probleme*, pp. 22, 30-31. Bauke argues that the impact of post-Kantian philosophy upon German theology consisted, in part, in the introduction of a "systematic monism" that culminated in the central-dogma theories of the nineteenth century and the systems constructed around them: the similar movement in philosophy culminated in Hegelian idealism. Thus, the attempt to find such central dogmas in Calvin and, we add, his successors in the seventeenth century, has no historical merit.

2. Cf. Reid's introduction to Calvin's *Concerning the Eternal Predestination of God*, p. 26.

3. *A Treatise of the Knowledge of God* (London, 1634), pp. 56-57; and cf. my *"Duplex cognitio dei* in the Theology of Early Reformed Orthodoxy."

4. Cf. Turretin, *Institutio*, I.v.4: "Sed quando Deus proponitur ut objectum theologiae, non spectandus est simpliciter ut Deus in se . . . sed quatenus *revelatus*, et ut se in Verbo nobi patefacere dignatus est. . . . Nec praecise considerandus est sub *ratione Deitatis*, ut vult Thomas et post eum plerique Scholastici . . . sed ut *Deus noster* id est foederatus in Christo, quomodo se nobis in Verbo patefecit. . . ."

5. CD, I/1, second edition, p. xiv.

Index

Abelard, Peter/Abelardian theology: 27
Althaus, Paul: 7, *183, 203*
Ambrose: 26, *190, 194*
Ames, William: 4, 6, 57, 70, 129, 154, 177, 178, 180, *182, 215, 216, 217, 218, 219, 221, 222, 223*
Amyraut, Moise: 11
Anderson, Marvin W.: *200*
Andreae, Johann: 92
Anselm/Anselmic argumentation: 26, 27, 41, 50, 67, 71, 73, 80, 88, 89, 95, 100, 118, 121, 132, 142, 143, *189, 209*
Apollinaris of Laodicaea: 45
Aretius, Benedictus: 38, *202*
Aristotle/Aristotelian: 6, 7, 11, 23, 39, 46, 102, 104, 105, 106, 119, 127, 150, 177, 180, *183, 215*
Arius: 45
Arminius, Jacob/Arminianism: 7, 108, 129, 167, 179, *223*
Armstrong, Brian: 11, 32-33, *184, 192*
Athanasius: *190*
Augustine, Aurelius/Augustinianism: 13, 19, 20, 21, 23, 26, 27, 29, 35, 44, 54, 55, 58, 61, 63, 65, 69, 70, 72, 73, 78, 84, 86, 96, 97, 105, 106, 109, 110, 111, 113, 114, 134, 149, 174, 175, *186, 189, 190, 192, 193, 194, 200, 201, 215*
Aureole, Peter: *205*

Baird, Henry M.: *203*
Baker, J. Wayne: *195*
Barth, Karl: 9, 18, 22, 43, 56-57, 73, 128-129, 155, 176, 178, 180, *184, 187, 188, 204, 215, 216, 221, 224*
Bastingius, Jeremias: *215*
Bauke, Hermann: 77, *185, 186, 224*

Baur, Ferdinand Christian: 2, 4, *181*
Baxter, Richard: *223*
Bavinck, Herman: 108, 141, *211, 219*
Berkhof, Hendrikus: *208, 209*
Berkhof, Louis: 101, *189, 210, 218, 220*
Berkouwer, Gerrit C.: 134, *183, 188, 190, 203, 216, 217*
Beza, Theodore: 3, 6, 8, 9, 13, 20, 57, 70, 77-93, 104, 106, 107, 110, 114, 115, 119, 120, 121, 122, 127, 129, 130, 153, 155, 157, 160, 165, 167, 169, 170, 171, 174, *183, 203-208, 209, 214, 215, 216, 221*
Biel, Gabriel: 46, *186, 196, 197, 205*
Bierma, Lyle D.: *195, 209, 215*
Bizer, Ernst: 5, 6, 7, 77, 83, 94, *182, 183, 203, 209, 211*
Blandrata, Giorgio: 29-30
Blaser, Klauspeter: *191*
Bolsec, Jerome: 23
Bonaventure: 27, 36, 109, *189, 191*
Bray, John S.: 20, 83, 94, *186, 203, 204, 205, 206, 208*
Brenz, Johannes: 45, *217*
Breward, Ian: 130, *216*
Bruce, A. B.: *217*
Brunner, Emil: *198, 217*
Bucanus, Gulielmus: 5, 46, 70, 145, 155, 177, *182, 205, 216, 217, 219, 221, 222*
Bucer, Martin: 46, 61, 109, 122, 123, 173, 174
Bullinger, Heinrich: 12, 38-46, 47, 48, 56, 60, 66, 67, 68, 70, 71, 72, 74, 88, 93, 95, 96, 106, 116, 119, 121, 122, 173, 174, 177, *194-197, 198, 201, 203*

Burchill, Christopher: *212*
Burmann, Franz: 128, 176

Calvin, John: 1, 3, 4, 5, 6, 7, 8, 9, 10, 11, 12, 13, 16-37, 38, 40, 41, 42, 43, 44, 45, 46, 47, 48, 49, 51, 54, 55, 56, 58, 60, 61, 65, 66, 67, 68, 69, 70, 71, 72, 73, 74, 77, 78, 79, 80, 81, 82, 83, 84, 85, 86, 87, 88, 90, 91, 92, 93, 94, 95, 97, 98, 99, 100, 101, 102, 104, 106, 107, 109, 116, 118, 119, 121, 122, 123, 127, 128, 129, 130, 134, 135, 136, 139, 140, 141, 142, 144, 145, 147, 149, 150, 153, 155, 157, 158, 160, 163, 164, 165, 167, 168, 169, 170, 173, 174, 175, 176, 177, 178, 179, *181, 182, 183, 185-194, 203, 209, 211, 212, 215, 217, 219, 220, 223*
Caroli, Pierre: 29-30
Castellio, Sebastian: *204*
Chapponeau, Jean: 29-30
Chemnitz, Martin: *206*
Chytraeus, David: 174
Clavier, Henri: *203*
Clemen, Otto: *212*
Cocceius, Johannes: 6, 7, 176, *183, 216, 222*
Confessio Belgica: 82, *185, 195, 205*
Confessio Gallicana: 82, *185, 195, 205*
Confessio Helvetica Posterior: 43-46
Confessio Hungarica: 93
Cottrell, Jack *195*
Council of Toledo: 35
Courtois, Jean: 29-30

Daneau, Lambert: 4, 7, 22, 70, 129, *182, 183*
Dantine, Johannes: 94, *203, 204, 205, 208*

DATE DUE

HIGHSMITH   #LO-45220